Intern

Travels of a ᴛ-ꜱʜɪʀᴛ, Second Edition

"This charming, intelligent narrative debunks myths on both sides of the globalization debate. Mixing historical perspective with current events, the book highlights that it's not market forces but avoiding them that creates winners in world trade ... a rich tapestry of globalization past and present that focuses on real people to rip fabrications on all sides of the debate ... a great read."

—*Asia Times*

"Don't miss this unusual book on economics."

—*The Hindu*

" ... thought-provoking. ... Regardless of your stance on global economics, you will find a lot to agree with and a lot to think about in *Travels of a T-Shirt*."

—*The China Daily*

THE TRAVELS OF A T-SHIRT IN THE GLOBAL ECONOMY

SECOND EDITION

An Economist Examines
the Markets, Power, and
Politics of World Trade

Pietra Rivoli

WILEY

For general information about our other products and services, please contact our Customer Care
Department within the United States at (800) 762-2974, outside the United States at (317)
572-3993 or fax (317) 572-4002.

Wiley publishes in a variety of print and electronic formats and by print-on-demand. Some material
included with standard print versions of this book may not be included in e-books or in
print-on-demand. If this book refers to media such as a CD or DVD that is not included in the
version you purchased, you may download this material at http://booksupport.wiley.com. For more
information about Wiley products, visit www.wiley.com.

ISBN 978-1-118-95014-2 (pbk); ISBN 978-1-118-95015-9 (ebk); ISBN 978-1-118-95016-6 (ebk)

Printed in the United States of America

10 9 8 7 6 5

In memory of my parents, Betty and Peter Rivoli.

CONTENTS

PREFACE

How Student Protests Sent a Business Professor Around the World

On a cold day in February 1999, I watched a crowd of about 100 students gather on the steps of Healy Hall, the gothic centerpiece of the Georgetown University campus. The students were raucous and passionate, and campus police milled about on the edge of the crowd, just in case. As speaker after speaker took the microphone, the crowd cheered almost every sentence. The crowd had a moral certitude, a unity of purpose, and while looking at a maze of astonishing complexity, saw with perfect clarity only the black and white, the good and evil. Corporations, globalization, the International Monetary Fund (IMF), and the World Trade Organization (WTO) were the bad guys, ruthlessly crushing the dignity and livelihood of workers around the world. A short time later, more than 50,000 like-minded activists had joined the students at the annual meeting of the WTO in Seattle, and by the 2002 IMF–World Bank meetings, the crowd had swelled to 100,000. Anti-globalization activists stymied meetings of the bad guys in Quebec, Canada, and Genoa, Italy, as well. At the 2003 WTO meeting in Cancun, the activists were joined by representatives from a newly energized group of developing countries, and world trade talks broke down across a bitter rich–poor divide. Anti-globalization activists came from college campuses and labor unions, religious organizations and shuttered textile mills, human rights groups and African cotton farms. Lumped together, the activists were named the globalization "backlash."

At first, the backlash took the establishment by surprise. Even the left-leaning *Washington Post*, surveying the carnage in Seattle, seemed bewildered. "What Was *That* About?" they asked on the editorial page the next day. From the offices on the high floors of the IMF building, the crowd below was a ragtag bunch of well-intentioned but ill-informed obstructionists, squarely blocking the only path to prosperity. According to conventional economic wisdom, globalization and free trade offered salvation rather than destruction to the world's poor and oppressed. How could the backlash be so confused?

B ack at Georgetown in 1999, I watched a young woman seize the microphone. "Who made your T-shirt?" she asked the crowd. "Was it a child in Vietnam, chained to a sewing machine without food or water? Or a young girl from India earning 18 cents per hour and allowed to visit the bathroom only twice per day? Did you know that she lives 12 to a room? That she shares her bed and has only gruel to eat? That she is forced to work 90 hours each week, without overtime pay? Did you know that she has no right to speak out, no right to unionize? That she lives not only in poverty, but also in filth and sickness, all in the name of Nike's profits?"

I did not know all this. And I wondered about the young woman at the microphone. How did she know?

I decided to investigate. During the following 6 years, I traveled the world to investigate the story of the people, politics, and markets that created my cotton T-shirt. I not only found out who made my T-shirt, but I also followed its life over thousands of miles and across three continents. The first and second editions of this book were published in 2005 and 2009, respectively, and I continue to speak with academic colleagues, factory owners, policymakers, activists, and students about the complex and important issues illuminated by the life story of this simple product. As I write this in June 2014, I am both amazed and humbled by the continued interest in this story.

W hat can the biography of a simple product contribute to current debates over global trade? When I began this project in 1999, I was pulled in one direction by my wish to tell this story but in another direction by my concern that the story was a lesser mode of inquiry, a methodology that was somehow not up to the task of illuminating the complex issue of global trade. In general, stories are out of style today in business and economic research. Little of consequence can be learned from stories, the argument goes, because they offer us only "anecdotal" data. According to accepted methodological wisdom in academic research, what really happened at a place and time—the story, the anecdote—might be entertaining but it is intellectually empty: Stories do not allow us to formulate a theory, to test a theory, or to generalize. As a result, researchers today have more data, faster computers, and better statistical methods, but fewer and fewer personal observations. Yet I now believe that while impersonal engagement with data and statistical models is a critical component of knowledge creation, critical as well is personal engagement and observation. The continued interest in *Travels of a T-Shirt*, and especially its adoption for a variety of university courses, has validated my early hope that biographies and stories can illuminate questions in economics and politics that data and statistical analyses cannot.

I remain inspired by the esteemed role of stories and biographies in scholarship in many disciplines outside of business and economics. Richard Rhodes, in his Pulitzer Prize–winning book, *The Making of the Atomic Bomb*, peels back, layer by layer, the invention of the atomic bomb. In the process, he illuminates the process of intellectual progress of a community of geniuses at work. Laurel Ulrich, in *A Midwife's Tale*, uses the diary of a seemingly unremarkable woman to construct a story of a life in the woods of Maine 200 years ago, revealing the economy, social structure, and physical life of a place in a manner not otherwise possible. And in *Enterprising Elites*, historian Robert Dalzell gives us the stories of America's first industrialists and the world they built in nineteenth-century New England, thereby revealing the process of industrialization. So, the story, whether of a person or a thing, might not merely reveal a life but illuminate the bigger world that formed the life. This remains my objective for the story of my T-shirt. And while economic and political lessons emerge from my T-shirt's story, the lessons are not the starting point. In other words, the point of my T-shirt's story is not to convey morals but to discover them, and simply to see where the story leads.

Of course there is no such thing as an objective storyteller, and I brought to *Travels of a T-Shirt* my own biases. Because I have spent my career teaching in a business school, and because of my academic background in finance and economics, I share with my colleagues the somewhat off-putting tendency to believe that if everyone understood what we understood—if they "got it"—they wouldn't argue so much. More than 200 years after Adam Smith advanced his case for free trade in *The Wealth of Nations*, we are still trying to make sure that our students, fellow citizens, and colleagues in the English department "get it" because we are sure that once they understand, everyone will agree with us. When I happened by the protests at Georgetown and listened to the T-shirt diatribe, my first thought was that the young woman, however well-intentioned and impassioned, just didn't get it. She needed a book—maybe this book—to explain things. But after following my T-shirt around the world, and after 15 years spent talking to farmers, politicians, factory owners, and labor activists, my biases aren't quite so biased anymore.

Trade and globalization debates have long been polarized on the virtues versus evils of market forces. Economists in general argue that international market competition creates a tide of wealth that (at least eventually) will lift all boats, while critics worry about the effects of unrelenting market forces, especially upon workers. Free trade in apparel, in particular, critics worry, leads only to a downward spiral of wages and working conditions that ends somewhere in the depths of a Charles Dickens novel. A primary lesson to emerge from my T-shirt's life story, however, is that the importance of markets is often overstated by both globalizers and critics. While my T-shirt's life story is certainly influenced by competitive economic markets, the key events in the T-shirt's life are less about competitive markets than they are about politics, history, and creative maneuvers to avoid market competition. Even those who laud the effects of competitive markets are loathe to experience them personally, so the winners in my T-shirt's life are adept not so much at competing in markets but in avoiding them. The effects of these avoidance maneuvers can have more damaging effects on the poor and powerless than market competition itself. In short, my T-shirt's story turned out to be less about markets than I would have predicted, and more about the historical and political webs in which the markets are embedded. In peeling the onion of my T-shirt's life—whether in 1999 or 2014—I kept being led away from traditional business topics and instead to history and politics.

Many once-poor countries (Taiwan or Japan, for example) have become richer due to globalization, and many still-poor countries (China or India) are nowhere near as poor as they once were. The poorest countries in the world, however, many in Africa, have yet to benefit from globalization in any sustained way. My T-shirt's life reveals the wealth-enhancing possibilities of globalization in some settings, but a "can't-win" trap for the world's poorest countries, a trap where both markets and politics seem to doom the economic future.

My T-shirt's story also reveals that the opposing sides of the globalization debate are co-conspirators, however unwitting, in improving the human condition. Economist Karl Polyani observed, in an earlier version of today's debate, his famed "double movement," in which market forces on the one hand were met by demands for social protection on the other.[1] Polyani was pessimistic about the prospects for reconciling the opposite sides. Later writers—perhaps most artfully Peter Dougherty—have argued instead that "Economics is part of a larger civilizing project," in which markets depend for their very survival on various forms of the backlash.[2] My T-shirt's story comes down on Dougherty's side: Neither the market nor the backlash alone presents much hope for the poor the world over who farm cotton or stitch T-shirts together, but in the unintentional conspiracy between the two sides there is promise. The trade skeptics need the corporations, the corporations need the skeptics, but most of all, the Asian sweatshop worker and African cotton farmer need them both.

In 2014, the echoes and effects of the anti-globalization protests of 1999–2005 are heard in many settings. Perhaps most importantly, the WTO-led "Doha Round" of global trade negotiations remains stalled more than a decade after the early talks were disrupted by protestors in Seattle. The Doha Round negotiations began with high hopes that developing countries and their concerns would finally be welcomed into the club of the Western countries that had historically written the rules governing world trade, and that the 159 member countries would agree to a broad new set of rules that would prioritize the concerns of poor countries. In 2014, however, I was not able to find anyone who was optimistic that the round would get back on track in the foreseeable future. "Doha is comatose," was the common judgment in 2014.

A second echo of the earlier globalization protests is the prominence of the inequality debate in today's moral and political discourse. This debate had a special parallel to the earlier globalization protests during the "Occupy" protests that took place in the United States during 2011–2012. Since the 1970s, both income and wealth inequality have increased sharply in the United States and in many countries, and the theme of economic justice permeated the Occupy movement as it had the anti-globalization protests. Whether the target was Wall Street bailouts and the financial system or the WTO and the trade regime, the common theme of the protests was that both power imbalances and market forces led to outcomes that rewarded the few—particularly the "1 percent"—at the expense of the many. A 2014 Pew Survey found that 62 percent of Americans—and an unlikely left–right alliance—believe that the U.S. economic system unfairly favors the powerful.[3] The root causes of growing wealth and income inequality have attracted large volumes of research in recent years, and there is some evidence that liberalizing trade and economic globalization have been contributing factors. While liberal trade boosts average incomes, it often has particularly deleterious effects for lower-skilled workers.[4] In 2014, the themes of economic security and justice that sparked the anti-globalization protests in 1999 were alive and well. A central conclusion of the T-shirt's story—that winners often avoid competition by "writing the rules" rather than competing in business— was steadily gaining currency in the political debates of 2014, and the ability of some interest groups to write the rules of the game is clearly one contributing cause of growing inequality.[5]

I could not have predicted when I began work on the first edition of this book that my T-shirt's story would be relevant for some of the most significant economic events of our time. The 45-year-old regime governing textile and apparel trade—first put in place following a John F. Kennedy election promise—expired in 2005 to leave a brave new world of many losers, a few big winners, and an uncertain future. At about the same time, in a stunning David–Goliath maneuver, the poorest countries of the world held global trade talks hostage over U.S. agricultural subsidies, particularly those on cotton, the main (or indeed the only) ingredient in my T-shirt. And in the days following September 11— below the public's radar screen—T-shirt sales and military support were bundled up in a bizarre negotiation between the Bush administration and Pakistan, a negotiation that revealed the surprising power still held by the U.S. textile industry. China, where my T-shirt spent much of its life, assumed center stage as the world's second largest economy. As I wrote the 2005 and 2009 editions of this book, China's strange capitalist police state swelled up like a balloon and flooded the United States with low-cost imports, forcing virtually every American company of any size to devise a "China strategy," meet the "China price," or manage the "China threat," while both Democrats and Republicans struggled to explain their position on the "China issue." By 2010, however, rising costs in China were dampening the "Made in China" phenomenon, and production of many goods began to gravitate to even lower-cost locations. Finally, in April 2013, the early student protestors at Georgetown proved to be tragically prescient. The collapse of Rana Plaza, a building housing dozens of garment factories outside the capital of Bangladesh, killed more than 1,100 garment workers. The Rana Plaza collapse was the single worst tragedy in the global history of the apparel industry. Virtually all of the production at Rana Plaza was destined for Western consumers. The Rana Plaza disaster reignited the "sweatshop" dialogue among activists, Western apparel companies, workers, and governments that had permeated the global textile and apparel industries from the Industrial Revolution in the 1800s to college campuses in the 1990s.

Shortly after I encountered the protests at Georgetown University in 1999, students peacefully occupied the university president's office and refused to budge until the university and its apparel suppliers agreed to address the alleged poor conditions under which Georgetown T-shirts and other licensed apparel were produced. Similar protests went on at dozens of universities across the country. During the next several years, the students and their compatriots around the globe made remarkable progress in changing the rules in the race to the bottom, in particular by engaging Western apparel companies to assume greater responsibility for working conditions in supplier factories. Following the Rana Plaza collapse in 2013, a new generation of students at Georgetown and a number of other schools quickly pressured their universities to require their suppliers to sign "The Accord," which obligated Western firms to assume responsibility for not only working conditions but also building structural integrity and fire safety.[6] In 2014, Polanyi's double movement is alive and well: As market forces push apparel production to lower and lower wage locations, forces of conscience and politics push back in the cause of safety, higher wages, and worker rights.

I thought, when I began this book, that I would in the end have a story that would help the students to see things my way, to appreciate the virtues of markets in improving the human condition. I do have such a story, I hope, but it is not the whole story. Economic and social progress is enabled not only by competitive markets but also by the forces of conscience that continue to rewrite the rules of global commerce.

In 2005, I spoke about the first edition of this book at the IMF in Washington. Hans Peter Lankes, one of the commentators, said that reading *Travels of a T-Shirt* was "sort of like circling a Buddhist stone garden. One slips into every conceivable perspective on this issue and there are no villains, only actors in what I call an epic struggle and a fantastically complex, forward-driving and culture transforming enterprise." If reading *Travels of a T-Shirt* is like "circling a stone garden," writing this book has involved circles, too. As I have continued to circle during recent years, I still have not met any villains. Every aspect of my T-shirt's life has become more and more complex, and each of the actors seem to be running a faster and more complicated race. Cotton farmers, lobbyists, seamstresses, textile mill owners, clothing recyclers, and politicians—each responds to competition in the global economy every day, and I hope to convey even a fraction of their experience and what it means for the rest of us.

Nearly a decade after the first edition of *Travels of a T-Shirt* was published, I still typically hear from a few readers each week. The most common question I have received during the past several years has been about my plans for a new edition. The second edition of the book covered events through 2008, and I am delighted by readers' interest in what has happened since that time. However, after much consideration, I decided against writing a 3rd edition. *Travels of a T-shirt* is a story that took place at a certain place and time about a particular T-shirt. I fear that a "new edition" of this narrative risks losing too much of the essence of the original story. At the same time, I did want to be responsive to the continued interest in what has happened in the world of my T-shirt since 2008. The compromise: An epilogue is now included at the end of the book. The epilogue provides updates through mid-2014 regarding many of the central themes, issues, and characters from the 2005 and 2009 editions of the book. I hope that readers will enjoy catching up with the places and people of *Travels of a T-Shirt* as much as I have. Updated ancillary materials, including data and graphs for the 2009–2014 period, are also now available at www.wiley.com/rivoli.

In 2013, the Planet Money team at NPR produced exceptional multimedia reporting inspired by this book. An extensive collection of videos, radio stories, and articles from the life of the Planet Money T-shirt is available at http://apps.npr.org/tshirt/#/title.

I now know who made my T-shirt: I am honored to know Nelson, Gary, Yuan Zhi, Geofrey, Yong Fang, Ed, Auggie, Julia, and so many others. I wish that everyone interested in international business and global trade could meet them, and see globalization through their eyes and experiences. This book is the next best thing.

PROLOGUE

Finding My T-Shirt's Likely Birthplace

Walgreen's Drugstore
Ft. Lauderdale, Florida
Spring 1999

The civic leaders of Fort Lauderdale have laid new paint over much of the city in recent years. The stoned surfers and rowdy college students are less visible now, pushed away from the beach with its new cafes and high-end hotels. The college students of the 1970s are parents now, and they have money to spend. The city bends toward the money like a palm tree, polishing, sweeping, painting. Yet, like tourist destinations everywhere, a scratch on the shiny paint reveals a bit of the tawdry underneath. Though the city fathers might prefer art galleries, it is T-shirt shops that line the beach because that is what people want to buy.

A large bin of T-shirts sat near the exit of a Walgreen's drugstore near the beach. The bin was positioned to catch shoppers on the way out, and it worked: Nearly everyone who walked by pawed through the bin, if only for a minute. The bin was full of hundreds of T-shirts, each priced at $5.99, or two for $10. All were printed with some Floridian theme, seashells, bright fish, or palm trees.

I reached in and pulled out a shirt. It was white and printed with a flamboyant red parrot, the word "Florida" scripted beneath. I went to the checkout line, and then stepped out into the sun and looked at the shirt through the wrapper.

"You're it," I thought.

Back in Washington, I took the T-shirt out of the poly bag and looked at the label. "Sherry Manufacturing," it said, and underneath, "Made in China." I typed "Sherry Manufacturing" into my search engine. A few minutes later, I had reached Gary Sandler, Sherry's president, on the telephone. "Sure," he said. "Come on down. We don't get many visitors from Washington."

Sherry Manufacturing Company is located in Miami's original industrial district, a bleak landscape of factories and warehouses not far from the airport. Gary Sandler is Florida-tanned and friendly, with a healthy skepticism about college professors. He is completely without pretension, but clearly proud of what he and his family have built. On the wall of his office are pictures of his children and his sales force.

Gary's father, Quentin, formed Sherry Fashions just after World War II, naming the company for his eldest daughter. Quentin started out as an independent wholesaler, going shop to shop along the beachfront, selling souvenir trinkets to the store owners. He would travel to New York to buy and return to Miami to peddle his wares during the tourist season. Then, as now, people liked to shop while on vacation, especially for souvenirs. Quentin found that trinkets with a tropical theme were especially popular with the visiting Northerners.

In the 1950s, options for "wearable" souvenirs were limited, and vacationers typically brought home trinkets rather than clothing. However, Quentin found that one of his most popular items was a souvenir scarf, a small cotton square printed with a Floridian motif. The scarf, like much of the tourist kitsch of the era, was made and printed in Japan. Before long, Sherry found itself in a classic wholesaler's predicament, with margins being squeezed between the suppliers and the retailers. In 1955, Quentin Sandler dispensed with his New York suppliers and opened his own cloth-printing shop in Miami. Sherry Fashions became Sherry Manufacturing Company.

In the mid-1970s, Gary Sandler quit college to join his father's company, and in 1986 became president. In mid-1999, the presidency passed to the third generation when Sandler's nephew (and Sherry's son) assumed responsibility for day-to-day operations.

Today, Sherry is one of the largest screen printers of T-shirts in the United States. It remains a business focused on the tourist trade. In Key West, Florida, and Mount Denali, Alaska, and many tourist spots in between, as well as in Europe, Sherry has T-shirts for sale. Sherry's artists design motifs for each tourist market, and the designs and locations are printed or embroidered on shirts in the Miami plant.

Sherry's inventory of blank T-shirts (as well as beach towels and baseball caps) fills a two-story warehouse. The blank goods go from the warehouse to the printing machine, which resembles a Ferris wheel lying on its side. Workers slide each shirt on the flat end of a wheel spoke, which then turns and stops briefly up to 14 times. Each time the wheel stops, a different color is shot through the tiny holes in the screen. When the shirt returns to the starting point on the wheel, a worker slides it off and passes it to another worker, who lays it flat on a drying conveyor belt. The next worker picks it up from the end of the drying belt and lays it flat on a second conveyor belt, which swallows it into a tunnel and shoots it out, neatly folded, from the other end. It's no longer underwear; it's a souvenir.

The shirts piled up in rolling carts tempt with scenes of beaches, mountains, skyscrapers, and glaciers. Each shirt will allow someone to take a bit of a place and wear it home. A walk through the warehouse adjoining the plant is a travelogue, too, but for the more adventurous. Where the shirts are headed you need sun lotion, but where they come from you need shots.

Gary Sandler buys T-shirts from Mexico, El Salvador, the Dominican Republic, Costa Rica, Bangladesh, Honduras, China, Pakistan, Botswana, India, Hong Kong, and South Korea. When I spoke with Gary again in 2008, the T-shirt business was tougher than it had been just a few years before: Competition—especially from abroad—was greater, the Miami labor market was more unpredictable, and overseas sourcing was more complicated. In addition, the economic downturn had severely affected the tourism industry, which had in turn affected Sherry's business.

My T-shirt is from China. It likely departed Shanghai in late 1998 and arrived in the port at Miami a few weeks later. All told, the shirt cost Sandler $1.42, including 24 cents in tariffs. The shirt was one of about 25 million cotton T-shirts allowed into the United States from China under the U.S. apparel import quota system in 1998. The shirt's journey, as we shall see, is a testimony to the power of economic forces to overcome obstacles. To arrive here, the shirt fought off the U.S. textile and apparel industries, Southern congressmen, and a system of tariffs and quotas so labyrinthine that it is hard to imagine why anyone would take the trouble. But Gary Sandler takes the trouble. Despite the best efforts of Congress, industry leaders, and lobbyists; despite the quotas, tariffs, and Chinese bureaucracy, China has the best shirts at the best price.

But China is a big place. Where, exactly, I asked Sandler, did the shirt come from? Sandler rif-ed through his Rolodex and pulled out a card. "Mr. Xu Zhao Min," the card read, "Shanghai Knitwear."

"Call him up," said Sandler. "He's a great guy. He'll tell you everything."

"Xu Zhao Min," I tried to read aloud.

"No, no," said Sandler. "Patrick. His American customers call him Patrick."

Patrick Xu and his wife accepted my invitation to visit Washington during their next trip to the United States.

Patrick Xu straddles East and West, rich and poor, communism and capitalism with almost cat-like balance. He travels to the United States two or more times each year, visiting old customers and scouring for new ones, watching the Western fashions and bringing ideas back to the factories. While Patrick is happy to sell white T-shirts to established customers like Gary Sandler, he does not see much of a future in white T-shirts for Shanghai Knitwear. There is too much competition from lower-wage countries and other parts of China, and soon, he believes, his hard-won customers will be sourcing T-shirts far from Shanghai. Patrick is trying to move up the value chain into fancier goods such as sweaters.

"Come to China," Patrick said during our first meeting in 1999. "I'll show you everything."

I wanted the whole story, I explained. Could he show me where the shirts were sewn? No problem. What about where the fabric is knit? Yes, of course. I pushed my luck: What about the yarn the fabric is made of? The spinning factory? Yes, he could arrange it. But this wasn't quite the beginning. What about the cotton? To tell the life story of my shirt, I had to start at its birthplace. I knew that China was one of the world's largest cotton producers. Could I go to the farm and see how the cotton is produced?

Patrick looked at the T-shirt. "Well, that might be difficult. I think the cotton is grown very far from Shanghai. Probably in Teksa."

"Teksa? Where is Teksa? How far away?" I asked. There was a globe on my desk and I spun it around to China. Could he show me Teksa on the globe?

Patrick laughed. He took the globe and spun it back around the other way. "Here, I think it is grown here." I followed his finger.

Patrick was pointing at Texas.

PART I

KING COTTON

Nelson and Ruth Reinsch at Their Farm in Smyer, Texas. (Photo Courtesy of Dwade Reinsch and Colleen Phillips.)

How America Has Dominated the Global Cotton Industry for 200 Years

REINSCH COTTON FARM
SMYER, TEXAS

U nlike French wine or Florida oranges, Texas cotton doesn't brag about where it was born and raised. Desolate, hardscrabble, and alternately baked to death, shredded by windstorms, or pummeled by rocky hail, west Texas will never have much of a tourist trade. Flying into the cotton country near Lubbock on a clear fall day, I had a view of almost lunar nothingness: no hills, no trees. No grass, no cars. No people, no houses. The huge and flat emptiness is jarring and intimidating at first, since one can't help but feel small and exposed in this landscape. Though I had traveled to dozens of countries and to almost every continent, during my first visit to Lubbock, Texas, I thought it was one of the most foreign places I had ever been. Somehow, since then, it has also become one of my favorite places. There is a very good chance that my T-shirt—and yours—was born near Lubbock, the self-proclaimed "cottonest city" in the world.

The people of this forbidding yet harshly beautiful place are well-suited to the landscape. Indeed, they are the product of it. The land has humbled them with its unpredictable temperament and its sheer scale, yet made them proud of each small success in taming and coaxing from it the fluffy white gold of the cotton plant. According to local legend, when God created west Texas, He made a mistake and forgot to fashion hills, valleys, rivers, and trees. Looking at His desolate and barren mistake, He considered starting over, but then had another idea. "I know what I'll do," He said. "I'll just create some people who like it this way."

And so He did.

Nelson Reinsch, cotton farmer, still stands tall and handsome at the age of 87. He laughs easily but speaks carefully. He calls his wife, Ruth, "Sugar," and every other woman "Ma'am." Nelson is a gentleman in the older sense of the word, well-mannered and considerate from the inside. We last met in 2008, and, remarkably, Nelson seemed not to have aged a bit since our first meeting in 2000.

In his 87 years, Nelson has missed four cotton harvests, all of them during his Navy service in World War II. Nelson and Ruth are happy enough (or perhaps just polite enough) to talk about the past if that is what their guests want to hear about. But they wallow not one bit in "the good old days," and their minds are opening rather than closing as they approach the ends of their lives. The world is still very interesting to Nelson and Ruth Reinsch. Of the many places and people I have visited during the research for this book, among my favorite times have been sitting in the Reinsch kitchen, eating (too much) of Ruth's cake and learning about cotton. In 2008, Nelson and Ruth remained on their farm in the middle of the west Texas emptiness. However, in that year Nelson scaled back his cotton operation and began to rent out much of his land.

Producing cotton is no longer the backbreaking physical process it once was, but every year Nelson and Ruth still battle both the whims of nature and the vagaries of markets. Each summer they take on the wind, sand, heat, and insects; and each fall, at harvest, they take on the world markets, in which they compete with cotton farmers from over 70 countries. The Reinsches' 1,000 acres can produce about 500,000 pounds of cotton lint if fully planted, enough for about 1.3 million T-shirts. That Nelson is ending his life in the same occupation in which he began tells us much about him. It also tells us much about the U.S. cotton industry.

History shows that almost all dominance in world markets is temporary and that even the most impressive stories of national industrial victories typically end with sobering postscripts of shifting comparative advantage. Within the baby boomers' lifetime, preeminence in consumer electronics has shifted from the United States to Japan to Hong Kong to Taiwan to China. Apparel production has moved from the American South to Southeast Asia to the Caribbean and back to Asia. Advantages in steel have moved from the U.S. Rust Belt to Japan to South Korea. But for over 200 years, the United States has been the undisputed leader in the global cotton industry in almost any way that can be measured, and other countries, particularly poor ones, have little chance of catching up. The United States has historically occupied first place in cotton production (though recently second to China), cotton exports (though occasionally second to Uzbekistan), farm size, and yields per acre.[1]

On the surface, cotton is an unlikely candidate for economic success in the United States. Typically, American industries compete with those in "like" countries. U.S. firms compete with Japanese automakers, German chemical companies, and Swiss pharmaceuticals. But for climatic reasons, few advanced industrial economies produce cotton. Instead, American cotton growers compete with producers in some of the world's poorest and least developed regions. If our labor costs—among the world's highest—have toppled or relocated industries as diverse as apparel, steel, and shipbuilding, how has U.S. cotton maintained its world dominance?

More broadly, how can an industry so basic and "downstream" as cotton production continue to thrive in an advanced, service-oriented economy? There would appear to be little sustainable advantage in an industry such as cotton. Models of business strategy would predict that dominance in such an industry can only be fleeting and stressful: The lack of product differentiation, the intense price competition, and the low barriers to entry make it scarcely worth the trouble. Business professor and strategist Michael Porter notes that:

> advantages [are] often exceedingly fleeting [in these industries].... Those industries in which labor costs or natural resources are important to competitive advantage also often have ... only low average returns on investment. Since such industries are accessible to many nations ... because of relatively low barriers to entry, they are prone to too many competitors.... Rapidly shifting factor advantage continually attracts new entrants who bid down

profits and hold down wages. ... Developing nations are frequently trapped in such industries. ... Nations in this situation will face a continual threat of losing competitive position. ...[2]

While this description of life on the economic precipice rings true for poor cotton farmers in South Asia and Africa, it does not describe the cotton industry around Lubbock. Year in and year out, American cotton farmers, as a group, are on top. What explains American cotton's success as an export commodity in a country that has experienced a merchandise trade deficit in each year since 1975? And what explains U.S. cotton producers' ability to export such a basic commodity to much poorer countries? Why here? Why was my Chinese T-shirt born in Texas?

Oxfam, the international development organization, believes it has the answer. According to a number of scathing Oxfam reports, the comparative advantage enjoyed by U.S. cotton farmers lies in their skill at collecting government subsidies.[3] In the fall of 2003, bolstered by Oxfam's research and resources, the poorest countries in the world cried foul against the richest at the opening of the World Trade Organization (WTO) trade talks in Cancun, Mexico. Tiny, desperately poor countries such as Benin and Burkina Faso stood firm and stared down U.S. negotiators: They charged that U.S. cotton subsidies were blocking their route out of poverty, and that it was impossible to compete with Uncle Sam's largesse to U.S. cotton farmers. In a soundbite that carried considerable punch, the poor countries pointed out that U.S. cotton subsidies exceeded the entire GDP of a number of poor cotton-producing countries in Africa. If the United States was going to champion the case for free trade, Americans needed to walk the walk as well as talk the talk. The stare-down continued for several tortured days until the talks collapsed and both rich and poor gave up and went home.[4] The point, however, had been made, and several months later the WTO ruled that U.S. cotton subsidies violated global trade rules and unfairly tilted the playing field toward American producers. In the summer of 2004, with the huge subsidies in the public spotlight, U.S. trade negotiators agreed not only to put cotton subsidies on the table, but to tackle the cotton issue "ambitiously, expeditiously, and specifically" during the Doha Round of trade negotiations.[5] As of the fall of 2008, however, the negotiations remained stalled, with most of the subsidies still in place.

There is no doubt that the subsidies are big and little doubt that they are unfair to poor countries. But anyone who believes that America's competitive power in the global cotton industry reduces to government subsidies should spend some time near Lubbock, Texas. While the subsidies are, of course, a boon to U.S. producers, the success of cotton growers such as Nelson Reinsch is a much more complex phenomenon.

First, the dominance of the U.S. industry predates by well over a century the implementation of national farm subsidies. As Chapter 2 describes, the U.S. cotton industry passed its competitors over 200 years ago. Therefore, while subsidies may account for some cost advantages today, they cannot be the longer-run explanation for the industry's dominance.

Second, the subsidy explanation for America's dominance gives short shrift to the astounding entrepreneurial creativity of the American growers. In many ways, the American cotton farmers are MBA case studies in adaptability and entrepreneurship. American cotton growers have adapted their production methods, their marketing, their technology, and their organizational forms to respond to shifts in supply and demand in the global marketplace. The shifts in demand and supply that reveal cotton's story as a business were sometimes gentle and predictable trends of ascendancy and decline, and the farmers could see what was ahead; but sometimes changes were sudden and cataclysmic, reshaping the world in front of them. In each case, the cotton farmers responded with a creative maneuver—a new idea, a new technology, a new policy. Whether it occurs by design or necessity, the open-mindedness and forward orientation that struck me within minutes of first meeting Nelson and Ruth Reinsch is a regional trait as well as a comparative advantage, because farmers in poor countries who are tradition bound—for whatever reason—rather than innovation bound, lose.

The American growers' remarkable adaptability and entrepreneurial resourcefulness have their roots in character but also in the institutions and governance mechanisms taken for granted in the United States, but which are lacking in many poor countries. In the United States, the farms work, the market works, the government works, the science works, and the universities work; and all of these elements work together in a type of virtuous circle that is decades away for the poorest countries in the world. In much of West Africa, with or without U.S. cotton subsidies, these institutional foundations for global competitiveness are weak. In addition, the institutions that are in place in many poor countries serve to funnel resources and power away from farmers rather than toward them.

While subsidies alone cannot explain U.S. dominance in this industry, the subsidies are but one example of a much broader phenomenon that has contributed to the U.S. farmers' seemingly immutable spot at the top. For 200 years, U.S. farmers have had in place an evolving set of public policies that allow them to mitigate the important competitive risks inherent in the business of growing and selling cotton. They have figured out how to compete in markets but also—and at least as important—how to avoid competing when the risks are too high. Put another way, U.S. cotton growers have since the beginning been embedded in a set of institutions that insulate them from the full strength of a variety of market forces.

When we consider the risks that a cotton boll faces on its way to becoming a T-shirt, it is a wonder we have clothes at all. The cotton can't be too hot, and it can't be too cold; it is susceptible to both too much water and too little; and it is too delicate to survive hail or even heavy wind and rain. Cotton plants are easily overtaken by weeds; there are dozens of varieties of pests that can take out a cotton crop; and crop prices are highly volatile. There is labor market risk as well, as workers must be available at a reasonable price when the cotton is ready to be weeded or picked. Every cotton farmer in the world faces these risks. And of course there are the normal business risks associated with falling prices and rising costs, foreign competition, and access to financing. As explained in Chapters 2–4, however, American cotton's story, and its success, have been about excellence in avoiding—or at least cushioning the impact of—these risks.

Today's proponents of markets and globalization can find much to like in the story of American cotton's victory, but the backlash can find support as well. For every noble victory in this industry, and for every case in which the Americans were smarter, faster, and better than the competition, there is a shameful victory as well. The most shameful of all was the cotton slave plantation, where the U.S. cotton industry was born, and where the Americans first trounced their foreign competition. Less shameful but still embarrassing are today's high subsidies. But to understand American cotton's long-run dominance, we should begin by agreeing to neither demonize nor romanticize American cotton farmers. During the 200 years in which the United States has dominated this industry, sometimes it was possible to win on the high road and sometimes it wasn't. My T-shirt's parentage in the fields of the American South has many things to be proud of, but some things to hide.

THE HISTORY OF AMERICAN COTTON

WINNING BY DUCKING THE LABOR MARKETS

Demand Pull: The Humble Class Gets a Taste for "Gaiety of Dress"

The world's first factories were cotton textile factories, and it was entrepreneurial developments in the production of cotton cloth and yarns that launched the Industrial Revolution in eighteenth-century Britain. A rapid-fire series of technical improvements in both the spinning and weaving of yarns made large-scale production possible and opened the way for the manufacture of textiles to move from the home and work-shop into the factory. The exploding productivity of the English cotton industry dramatically lowered prices, so that for the first time, the poor could dress attractively. A consumer class was born. Edward Baines, a nineteenth-century historian, described the consumer pull of cheap cotton clothing:

> It is impossible to estimate the advantage to the bulk of the people, from the wonderful cheapness of cotton goods ... the humble classes now have the means of as great neatness, and even gaiety of dress, as the middle and upper classes of the last age. A country-wake in the nineteenth century may display as much finery as a drawing room of the eighteenth.[1]

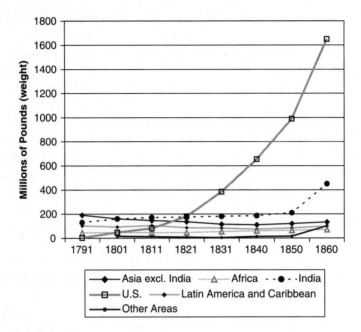

Source: Bruchey, 7.

Figure 2.1   Cotton Production (Millions of Pounds) by Region and Time

As technological innovation increased productivity, higher productivity in turn lowered prices. The lower prices spurred demand for textiles, which then left England starving for raw cotton. Once the British masses had a taste of "gaiety of dress," there was no turning back. The cheap cotton clothing available to the masses was the historical equivalent of today's $5.99 cotton T-shirt. Then, as now, consumer demand was behind the push and pull of world trade flows.

Of course, British demand for cotton does not fully explain American success in meeting that demand. Indeed, at the takeoff of the Industrial Revolution, the United States did not seem like a promising source of cotton at all. As Figure 2.1 shows, in 1791, the U.S. share of world cotton production was almost too small to be counted. The American South produced barely 2 million pounds of cotton in 1791, a minuscule amount compared to the output of producers elsewhere. It is doubtful that producers in Asia (primarily India), with production of nearly 400 million pounds, perceived much of a competitive threat from the American South.

The boom in U.S. cotton production that happened next was astounding. In 10 years, American production increased by 25 times. And by the outbreak of the Civil War, the South was producing more than a billion pounds per year, approximately two-thirds of the total world production. Cotton production was overwhelmingly export oriented. From 1815 to 1860, cotton constituted approximately half of the value of *all* U.S. exports, and more than 70 percent of all American cotton produced was exported, primarily to England.[2] In a relatively short period of time, American cotton farmers had trounced their foreign competition.

The victory did not come cheaply. First, the single-minded concentration of capital, labor, and entrepreneurial energies into cotton production left the American South far behind the North in broader industrial development, a gap that has narrowed decisively only during the past 25 years. Second, early American cotton production took place mostly, though not entirely, on slave plantations, and there is little doubt that this system of human captivity contributed significantly to the "productivity" of the American cotton grower. And while plantation slavery was undoubtedly the most horrible of the many labor systems in U.S. economic history, as we will see, slavery is not the only instance in which a horrific—or at least objectionable—labor system played a role in the production and trade of cotton clothing such as T-shirts. On this issue, today's trade skeptics have a point.

Slavery was the first significant American "public policy" that served to protect cotton growers from the perils of operating in a competitive market. For a number of reasons, relying on a competitive labor market— rather than on captive slaves—was a risk that growers were loath to assume, and it was also a risk that would have likely precluded the explosive growth in American cotton production.

Growing cotton in the antebellum South was mind-numbing, back-breaking physical labor. Beginning in mid-spring, the ground would be prepared for planting with hoes, and later, mule-drawn plows. Following planting, the battle of the weeds began. The tender cotton plant was not able to hold its own against the rapacious weeds, and so required the constant help of workers who guarded the young plants against their encroachment. Indeed, numerous journals and diaries reveal that keeping cotton "out of the grass" was perhaps the planters' biggest worry and the most physically demanding work.[3] Weeding and thinning continued, although at a slower pace, almost until the four-month harvest season began in late summer. On a large plantation, one worker could prepare, plant, weed, and harvest about 18 acres of cotton.

Critically, the timing and intensity of each of these tasks was dictated by the weather, so the growers were unable to predict their labor requirements beyond the weather forecast. During a very rainy spring, each field had to be weeded up to six times, which doubled the labor requirement during that season. The harvesting of cotton was perhaps the most unpredictable task. (Even today, Nelson and Ruth Reinsch cannot plan for Thanksgiving travel.) Cotton cannot be picked either in the rain or while still wet, and it typically takes three to four days to dry. A few days of rain, then, might leave pickers idle for a week. But once the cotton was open and dry, it needed to be picked as soon as possible, so that the tender fluffs did not blow away or fall to the ground. Cotton that had been rained on became spotted and weaker, so often planters tried hurriedly to get the cotton picked as rain clouds approached.

These exacting and unpredictable labor requirements were impossible to meet while relying on the market. As Gavin Wright has argued, farm labor markets in the American South barely functioned, if in fact they existed at all.[4] Farms were geographically dispersed, which made communication and transportation difficult. The very low population density, combined with uneven labor requirements throughout the year, as well as poor information flows, meant that a farmer who relied on the "market" to meet his labor needs might not be able to harvest his crop at any price. The problem of farm labor, then, was not limited to a shortage of workers or high wages. Rather, the problem was the absence of a well-functioning market where farm workers and growers could transact with any degree of effectiveness. Relying on the market to supply the right number of workers at the right time was a business gamble that cotton farmers preferred to avoid.

Even with a functioning labor market, however, it is doubtful that workers would have been attracted to opportunities as wage hands in cotton production. As a very early student of the cotton economy noted, "the difficulty or impossibility of inducing the whites to become wage earners while they were in contact with cheap land is undoubtedly the chief reason why the cotton industry in the country was developed by slave instead of by free labor."[5] Of course, the same could be said of blacks. In the absence of slavery, blacks as well as whites would prefer a farm of their own to work as wage hands. And, in the early years of the American South, land was available to all comers.

In summary, free labor—black or white—was unlikely to be attracted to wage work on Southern cotton farms, because of both the poor functioning of labor markets and the superior alternative available to these workers—the family farm. Slavery, then, allowed cotton farmers both a way to avoid the risks associated with transacting in the labor market and a way around the family labor constraint. Slavery also enabled the growers to cultivate greater acreage. The greater acreage in turn allowed cotton production to increase. The average farm size in the cotton South was nearly twice that of the free states of the North, and there was a strong positive relationship between farm size and relative cotton production, at least for farms below 600 acres.[6] Put simply, large farms were slave plantations, not family farms, and it was the slave plantations that produced most of the world's cotton by 1860.

Keep the Fiddler Well-Supplied with Catgut

Slave ownership alone did not guarantee successful large-scale cotton production. Effective systems of control, monitoring, and incentives were also required. These systems accounted for both the economic success of the slave plantation for the planters, and for the inhumanity of slavery. The profitability of the plantation depended not on slave ownership per se, but on the planter's ability to induce his slaves to perform repetitive and exhaustive physical labor at unpredictable times. Large volumes of cotton production required that the planter devise a "factory" system wherein a large number of workers performed repetitive tasks, and the factory "shift" could be activated at the whim of the weather. The planters were able to induce this repetitive labor on demand with a complex blend of positive incentives (e.g., prizes), negative incentives (e.g., whipping), and paternalism.[7] A common theme in slaveholder journals is that the planters had a moral duty to protect those "in dependent status," and that slaves who were well cared for and happy would be more productive. A large plantation owner in Georgia offered his own practices as exemplary:

> My first care has been to select a proper place for my "Quarter" well protected by the shade ... and to erect comfortable houses for my negroes. ... A large house is provided as a nursery for the children where all are taken at daylight, and placed under the care of a careful and experienced woman, whose sole occupation is to ... see that they are properly fed and attended to. ... I have a large and comfortable hospital provided for my negroes when they are sick ... [and] I must not omit to mention that I have a good fiddler, and keep him well-supplied with catgut, and I make it his duty to play for the negroes every Saturday night until twelve o'clock.[8]

Lest we be tempted to sign up, the writer later notes that his solicitous human resource policies reduced, but did not eliminate, the need for whipping. Whatever its motivation, paternalism clearly strengthened the control of the planter over his slaves and served as a governance mechanism. And when combined with constant monitoring, and the positive and negative incentives that ruled the workday, the planter's domination was complete.

To summarize, slavery was the first in a set of evolving public policies that served to insulate farmers from the perils of the market. American success in producing large volumes of cotton for world markets required a reliable supply of farm labor, but this labor was likely both unwilling and unavailable through a market mechanism in the pre–Civil War South. But slave ownership alone did not assure productivity. To induce slaves to perform the repetitive and exhausting tasks associated with cotton production, planters used a complex blend of governance mechanisms, including positive and negative incentives, paternalism, and monitoring. Many elements of the command-and-control factory system, of course, survive today in many industries. And complicated blends of incentive and monitoring mechanisms survive as well.

The lessons of the early American cotton industry are relevant for modern debates. America's early dominance of the cotton industry illustrates that commercial success can be achieved through moral failure, an observation especially relevant for T-shirts, which critics allege are produced under sweatshop conditions not far removed from slavery. But the early story of American cotton also reveals a critical lesson for the market-phobic: It was not the perils of the labor market but the suppression of the market that doomed the lives of the slaves. More generally, the tactic of suppressing and avoiding markets rather than competing in them continues today to be a viable business strategy, particularly in agriculture but also in other industries. This ability to suppress and avoid competition, as we will see, is often the result of a power imbalance between rich and poor, an imbalance that persists in world cotton agriculture today.

With the labor problem "solved" by slavery, unlimited land to the West, and unlimited demand from the East, the pieces were still not quite in place for American cotton's victory. In their westward expansion, cotton growers encountered perhaps the greatest production bottleneck in American economic history. Once they had pushed farther than 30 miles from the Atlantic coast, the cotton growers found that the lustrous and strong Sea Island cotton demanded by British mills would not bloom. Only Upland cotton, with a shorter fiber and stickier seed, would grow further west. However, while Sea Island cotton could be separated from the seeds with a simple roller gin modeled on an ancient device from India (the *Churkka* gin), this device was unable to separate the sticky seeds in Upland cotton from the lint.

The severity of this supply bottleneck is difficult to overestimate. A young and healthy slave could pick up to 300 pounds of cotton each day. Even children could typically pick 100 pounds per day. With the seeds, however, the cotton had no market. Since the roller gins would not remove the seed from Upland cotton, slaves were required to pick the seeds out by hand. So sticky and stubborn were the seeds, however, that a slave could clean no more than 1 pound per day. England's mills would die of cotton starvation at this pace.

So if it hadn't been Eli Whitney, it likely would have been some-one else, and soon. In the fall of 1792, the necessary ingredients for entrepreneurial success converged: a production bottleneck, an idea, a source of capital, and a way to make a profit. For developing countries today, the important part of the story is not Eli—poor countries have plenty of smart and inventive people—it is the convergence of all the ingredients necessary for forward leaps.

Eli Meets a Venture Capitalist

From his childhood in Massachusetts until his graduation from Yale, Eli Whitney was known to friends and family as a talented and inventive tinkerer. Following his graduation he traveled south to assume a position as a private tutor. What happened next is perhaps best related by Whitney himself, in a letter to his father dated September 11, 1793. Whitney's letter conveys his technical brilliance and entrepreneurial energy, but more touchingly, also the guilt and excitement of a young man who, in pursuing his entrepreneurial dream, has somewhat neglected his familial duties. He starts by admitting he should have written sooner to let his parents know what he was up to:[9]

> Dear Parent:
>   I received your letter of the 16th of August with peculiar satisfaction and delight. It gave me no small pleasure to hear of your health and was very happy to be informed that your health and that of the family has been so good since I saw you. . . . I expected to have been able to come [home to]

Westboro' sooner than I fear will be in my power. I presume, sir, you are desirous to hear how I have spent my time since I have left College. This I conceive you have a right to know and that it is my duty to inform you and should have done it before this time....

On the way to Savannah, Whitney had met the widow and family of Major General Greene of Revolutionary War fame. Mrs. Greene took a liking to the polite young man and invited him to spend a few days on the family's plantation before continuing his journey. When a group of Revolutionary War officers who had served under General Greene came to the plantation to pay their respects to his widow, the conversation soon turned to the pressing need for a mechanism to separate Upland cotton from its seeds so as to meet the British demand. The seeds, the planters were sure, were the only obstacle to their fortunes. "Gentlemen," Mrs. Greene remarked, "apply to my young friend, Mr. Whitney—he can make anything."

Whitney quickly protested that he had never seen either cotton or cottonseed. Yet he was immediately intrigued, as is evident from the next paragraph of his letter:

I went from N. York with the family of the late Major General Greene to Georgia. I went immediately with the family to their plantation... with an expectation of spending four or five days.... During this time I heard much said of the difficulty of ginning Cotton, that is, separating it from its seeds. There were a number of very respectable gentlemen at Mrs. Greene's who all agreed that if a machine could be invented which would clean the cotton with all expedition, it would be a great thing for both the Country and the inventor.

Critically, there was a venture capitalist at the Greene plantation, as Whitney explains later in his letter:

I involuntarily happened to be thinking on the subject and struck out a plan of a machine in my mind, which I communicated to Miller (who... resides in the family, a man of respectability and property). He was pleased with the Plan and said that if I would pursue it and try an experiment to see if it would answer, he would bear the whole expense, I should lose nothing but my time, and if I succeeded we would share the profits....

The machine worked, of course. Whitney's simple and elegant model was quickly duplicated throughout the South. The good news was that during the next eight years, cotton production rose 25-fold, and by 1820, more than 90-fold. The bad news was that more than any other single factor, Eli Whitney's cotton gin solidified the slave plantation in the cotton South. For the growers, it was good while it lasted. For the men and women who had been bought and sold and bred and whipped and captured and fiddled to, it was good when it ended.

Where Was the Competition?

Where, we have to ask, was the competition? What of India and China, especially? Why were these countries, world leaders in cotton production in the late 1700s, left in the dust by the Americans?

At the beginning, as Figure 2.1 shows, other countries continued to produce cotton in relatively stable quantities while American production soared. It was not a matter, then, of American producers squashing the competition with low-cost and efficient production. Instead, for the older cotton producers, it was business as usual. But business as usual was not good enough.

British demand for cotton had exploded with the new textile machinery and the burgeoning consumer class. It was not a matter of steady growth in demand, not a curve that the old cotton producers could ride profitably on into retirement. The British Industrial Revolution was a lightning bolt in cotton's story, like the cotton gin or the boll weevil or emancipation, which changed everything ahead. By 1860, Britain was consuming over a billion pounds of cotton per year, which was considerably more than the entire production of the world, excluding the United States.[10]

An explosion in demand required an explosion in supply. The question, then, becomes why the supply exploded in the United States rather than in the countries that had been the world's major producers since the beginning of the cotton trade. The question of American success becomes more intriguing when we note the remarkable lengths to which the British went—quite unsuccessfully—to reduce their risky dependence on American cotton.

Put simply, modern markets did not yet work in India or China, in cotton or in anything else. As economic historian David Landes advises, a useful way to understand why something in economic history did or did not happen at a certain place and time is to ask, Who would have benefited?[11] If cotton growers in India or China could have benefited by increasing their productivity, improving quality, and selling cotton to British mills, they would have done so. It appears, though, that they would not have benefited; the risks were too great, the rewards likely minimal. Capitalism of the type that rewards an idea, an improvement, or an initiative, had not yet taken hold in Asia. The foundations were lacking.

First, there were no property rights, or as Francois Bernier, a Frenchman who lived in India during the seventeenth century, wrote, no *mien et tien* (no mine and yours).[12] There were no incentives to improve age-old methods, to learn, to grow more, to do better. The agricultural workers were at the mercy of rulers who were often absent, and who changed and moved frequently. And even if wealth had been created, Bernier wrote, it had to be hidden lest it be extorted or seized.[13]

In China, too, cotton growers would not have benefited. Under the tyranny of the emperor, there was little reason to take a business risk in the modern sense of the term. As a Christian missionary remarked in the late 1700s, "Any man of genius is paralyzed immediately by the thought that his efforts will win him punishment rather than rewards."[14] As Landes notes, too directly for most tastes, China's "cultural triumphalism and petty downward tyranny made [the country] a reluctant improver and a bad learner."[15] Culturally, the Qing dynasty, which ruled China from the 1600s until the early 1900s, displayed an aversion to all things Western, and to change in general. A Jesuit passing through commented that the Chinese were "more fond of the most defective piece of antiquity than of the most perfect of the modern...."[16] In other words, all of the Eli Whitneys in China had no reason to try.

On the surface, of course, the American cotton victory over India and China appeared to be due to slavery. An 1853 observer confidently noted that American cotton growers' "superiority" was due to the "cheap, and reliable labor they derive from that patriarchal system of domestic servitude."[17] While certainly it was slavery that allowed the cotton factories on the plantations to produce such enormous volumes of cotton, India and China, too, had millions of people who were made to work for nothing by tyrannical rulers, millions of people who could not say no. Why these people were never organized to produce large volumes of cotton for export is another matter entirely.

Thus, while slavery allowed farmers to evade the risks of the labor market, it does not explain why other countries failed to seize the opportunities presented by the Industrial Revolution. The institutions necessary to support factory-style cotton production—property rights, incentive structures, what is today called "governance"—also had an important role to play. Governance still has an important role to play, which will remain the challenge for many poor cotton-producing countries. As we will see, all of the Eli Whitneys in Mali, Burkina Faso, and Benin often still have little reason to try.

All God's Dangers Ain't a White Man

Shortly before the beginning of the Civil War, James Henry Hammond of South Carolina—senator, former governor, plantation owner, cotton farmer—stood to address the U.S. Senate. In one of the most famous pieces of Southern political oratory of the era, Hammond thundered on about the destruction of the world that would surely accompany the demise of the slave cotton plantation. It was not just the Southern gentleman's way of life that Hammond sought to preserve, it was civilization itself:

> Would any sane nation make war on cotton? Without firing a gun, without drawing a sword, should they make war on us, we could bring the world to our feet.... What would happen if no cotton was furnished for three years?... this is certain: England would topple headlong and carry the whole civilized world with her, save the South.[18]

This dire prediction about the demise of civilization rested on the importance of cotton to the industrial centers of the Northern states and Europe. The giant textile mills that lined the rivers of the new industrial centers depended on the South to supply cotton. This bit of fluff, the boll as big as a fist yet lighter than a breath, reigned supremely, if not benevolently, over the world's new economic order. Southern cotton had a God-given monopoly. Because it could not be grown either in the Northern states or in England, Hammond reasoned, the industrial world would bow to cotton, and the South had nothing to fear:

> No, you dare not make war on cotton. No power on earth dares make war on cotton. Cotton is king.[19]

It is clear from his words that Hammond did not believe that the cotton kingdom could thrive under the rules of the North. To destroy the slave plantation was to destroy the cotton economy, or so he thought.

But while the Civil War eliminated slavery, the cotton economy of the South survived because public policy evolved to continue to protect the growers from the perils of the labor markets. Labor requirements in cotton production remained highly seasonal, and the challenge was still to have sufficient labor available at critical but unpredictable times in the cotton cycle. However, transacting in a labor market was fraught with risk, as the market still offered no guarantees about either the price or availability of labor at these critical times. Without the tight control of slavery, landowners needed an alternative system to bind labor to their land upon demand. The labor system that emerged—tenant farming, or "sharecropping"—fit the bill.

In exchange for their labor, the landowner provided the sharecroppers with housing and food (known as the *furnish*) as well as the right to hunt and to fish. By providing housing and food, rather than cash, the landowner bound the worker to the property and assured himself of labor at critical times. The worker was contractually bound as well, since he was indebted to the landlord through the harvesting of the crop.

A wide variety of public policies were instituted to bind the share-croppers to the land and insulate the cotton growers from the risks of transacting in the labor market.[20] Gradually, the legal definition of *share-cropper* shifted in favor of the landowners, especially through the passage of *crop lien laws*.[21] These laws changed the status of the sharecropper in the courts to a laborer who was paid wages in crops rather than a *tenant* with ownership of a share of the crop. The difference was critical. As a laborer, the sharecropper could not offer his crop for lien because it technically belonged to the landowner. The crop lien laws, then, shut the sharecrop-per out of the capital markets while widening access to capital for the landowners. Other laws, such as vagrancy laws and "alienation of labor" laws (which protected the landowner from having his labor hired away) also served to bind the sharecropper to the land. At the same time, planters opposed public schooling for blacks and poor whites, so illiteracy and lack of education kept the balance of power in the sharecropping arrangement heavily in favor of the planter, and limited the alternatives of the workers.

Moreover, the contractual arrangement between sharecropper and landowner left the sharecropper little hope of climbing out of subsistence. The sharecropper's dream—to own land—was thwarted by a cycle of perpetual debt whereby the sharecropper's share of each harvest was barely enough to settle the year's debts, and by exclusion from external capital markets. A remark reportedly made by Louis XIV of France is apt: "Credit supports agriculture as a cord supports the hanged."[22]

Ned Cobb, an Alabama cotton farmer, recalled the standstill that trapped him as a sharecropper. While he made six bales of cotton in 1908, a respectable crop:

It took all them six bales to pay Mr. Curtis. In the place of prosperin', I was on a standstill.... I had not a dollar left out of the cotton.... Mr. Curtis had Mr. Buck Thompson furnish me groceries... kept a book on me.... [Mr. Curtis] paid Mr. Thompson and I paid him—the deal worked that way—out of my crop. So he made somethin off my grocery bill besides gettin half my crop when the time came.[23]

Cobb's biography repeats this theme year after year. Some years, there was a little cotton left after paying the landlord; in other years, there was not enough to settle the debts and Cobb had to start the next year in the hole. Thanks to creative accounting, it was typical to come out even. In Macon County, Alabama, researchers uncovered a remarkable coincidence: 62 percent of black sharecroppers had come out even for the year in 1932.[24]

Ironically, the success that the planters had in devising public policies to keep the workforce docile and uneducated soon began to backfire. When the boll weevil began to ravage the southern cotton crop in the early 1900s, government extension programs were mobilized to spread advice to farmers on how to combat the weevil and save their crops. The news and advice reached the large farms and the educated farmers, but often passed by the poor and illiterate sharecroppers, black and white, who had to fend for themselves.[25] In 1921, approximately 30 percent of the cotton crop—predominantly that produced by small sharecroppers—was lost to the weevil.[26] Many were pushed off the land. Ned Cobb remembered the time well:

That was boll weevil time.... these white folks told the colored people if you don't pick them cotton squares off the ground and destroy them boll weevils we'll quit furnishin' you. Told em that—puttin the blame on the colored man for the boll weevil. Couldn't nobody pay his debts when the weevil et up his crop.[27]

"Yes," he added later, in reference to the weevil, "All God's dangers ain't a white man."[28]

For Deep South sharecroppers, not much changed from the end of the Civil War until the late 1920s: a few acres of tired soil, a few mules, a few bales at the end of the year, and a perpetual crushing debt.

But while this rhythm played on in the Deep South, a new type of cotton factory was rising in the West. By the early 1900s, Texas would be the country's largest cotton producer. By the 1920s, Texas would be selling cotton to China.

Cotton Factories Arrive in Texas

Texas and Oklahoma were the new cotton frontier, wide-open, blue-sky places with no crumbling plantation houses, no old ways of doing things, and plenty of room to build cotton factories. Between 1900 and 1920, the area around Corpus Christi was divvied up into huge landholdings on a scale never seen before, and rarely since, for the purpose of growing cotton. Henrietta King of Corpus Christi owned 1.4 million acres, Charles Taft owned over 150,000 acres, and C.W. Post—the man behind the cereal—owned 200,000 acres.[29]

The requirements for successful large-scale cotton farming had changed little from the pre–Civil War South. The landowners still required large numbers of workers to be available on demand to plant, weed, and harvest the crop at the whim of the weather. Relying on a labor market in the modern sense of the term was still fraught with risk and expense. How would the planter be assured that the market would provide for labor requirements when the weeds bloomed or the cotton opened? And what if the market wage went up or help was hired away by competitors?

Creative solutions abounded.[30] Planters imported monkeys from Brazil and tried to teach them to pick cotton, but the animals in the end were uncooperative. And geese, it turned out, will weed a cotton field when fenced in, and the farmers discovered that only two geese could weed an acre of cotton. They also discovered, however, that geese could not be trained not to trample cotton plants, and that insecticide is also goosicide. For a time, farmers also used flamethrowers to weed cotton fields, but taking fire down the rows of their livelihood proved too difficult for most. In the end, neither monkeys nor geese nor fire could accomplish the tasks as well as a captive labor force.

This time, to tie the labor to the land and to avoid the market, the cotton growers borrowed an idea from the North: the company town.

The Taft cotton ranch, near Corpus Christi, occupied 39 percent of the land of San Patricio County.[31] The ranch was organized as a corporation, but in reality it was a community in which people's lives—not just their work—were hierarchically managed for the purpose of cotton production. The ranch had company housing, schools, and churches segregated along ethnic lines for whites, Mexicans, and blacks. Like the "furnish" provided to old South sharecroppers, workers were paid partly in scrip, which could be redeemed only at company stores. Finally, like the plantation owner who kept his "fiddler well-supplied with catgut," the Taft Ranch provided holidays, music, and festivities as well, again designed for the three different ethnic groups. This entire system, of course, served to ensure that workers were around when the cotton needed to be planted, weeded, and harvested. The new cotton factories did not so much influence public policy; they *were* public policy over vast stretches of Texas.

These large and tightly controlled production systems were hailed as models of the farms of the future, models of productivity, efficiency, and profitability. Once again, successful large-scale cotton production depended on a factory system in which large numbers of workers were available on demand to complete the repetitive chores associated with weeding, planting, and picking. Once again, success depended on avoiding—not competing in—the labor market.

Of course, observers of the day also acknowledged that the economic success of these large Texas cotton "factories" also meant the demise of the smaller family cotton farms. It was sad but inevitable, the way of the future.

Well, maybe.

Perhaps someone forgot to tell Nelson and Ruth Reinsch.

BACK AT THE REINSCH FARM

Today, Lubbock, Texas, is indeed the "cottonest city in the world," and the surrounding farmland is the leading birthplace of the world's T-shirts. Lubbock has the world's largest cotton cooperative and the world's largest cottonseed oil mill, and the region produces nearly 30 percent of American cotton. Texas Tech University, on the west side of town, performs some of the most advanced cotton research in the world. And Lubbock is an international cotton center. A majority of the region's cotton is exported: loaded onto trucks and trains in Lubbock, and bound for ports on every U.S. coast. And at the bottom of this successful chain are neither plantations nor sharecroppers nor company towns nor even family farms, but people like Nelson and Ruth Reinsch.[1]

No single factor explains the success that cotton farmers in west Texas have had in competing in international markets. The growers are embedded in a web of institutions that help them to continue their tradition of shifting market risks away from themselves, and they continue to win as much by limiting competition as by competing. Texas cotton farmers have solved, once and for all, the age-old labor market risk problem associated with cotton production, creatively applying mechanization, scientific research, and public policy to the challenge. These producers were also leaders in the development of the modern agricultural cooperative, a brilliantly simple organizational form that allows cotton farmers such as Nelson and Ruth Reinsch to capture every shred of value from the cotton plant, backward into the oilseed and forward into blue denim. Texas cotton farmers are also masters of political influence, leading the U.S. government to assume the business risks—including price and nonpayment risks—that the farmers would rather not. Remarkably, the Reinsches and their west Texas neighbors have even taken control of the wild Texas climate. They can make it rain, they can stop the sand from blowing, and they can even freeze the cotton plant on a warm and sunny day.

Perhaps most significant, Lubbock is the center of the "Silicon Valley" of cotton production. The Lubbock area benefits from a highly symbiotic and virtuous-circle relationship between farmers, private companies, universities, and the U.S. government. The farmers, well-educated and entrepreneurial, both contribute to and benefit from the research that takes place in the universities and firms, while the U.S. Department of Agriculture (USDA) supports both the research and the farmers with funding, technical, and business assistance. Cotton growers in poor countries are challenged not so much by the prospect of competing with Nelson Reinsch, but by competing with the much larger and permanent advantages of this interlocking virtuous circle. Competing with Nelson is hard enough, but competing with Nelson as he is teamed up with Texas Tech, Monsanto, and the USDA is another matter entirely.

T o the untrained eye they might be hard to see, but a close look at the original seal of Texas Tech University shows 10 cotton bolls in the form of a *T*, each boll representing one of 10 cotton-producing counties that surround Lubbock (Figure 3.1). Indeed, Tech history buffs are quick to point out that the university was founded to support the cotton and textile industries. Today, though the University is widely acknowledged to be one of the most advanced centers for cotton research in the world, Tech is also a diversified national research university with distinguished programs in many academic fields.

In 2002, Dr. David R. Smith was appointed the new Chancellor of Texas Tech. Though Smith had spent a number of years in Texas, he was an Ohio native and a graduate of Cornell. According to marketing consultants hired by the new Chancellor, most people outside the region associated

Figure 3.1 Original Seal of Texas Tech University
(Photo Courtesy of *Texas Techsan* magazine.)

Texas Tech with sports. Smith believed that Tech needed to show the world a new image that reflected the University's diverse academic and research accomplishments. After all, the modern Texas Tech was about more than cotton farming and football.

The Chancellor proposed a new "visual identity system" for Tech, and in May 2005, he unveiled a new seal for the University. The seal had an academic emphasis, including an open book and a scholarly-looking key. In a nod to the University's agricultural heritage, a branch of vines decorated the bottom part of the seal. The cotton bolls were gone.[2]

An uproar followed. Generations of Tech alumni were bound to the cotton industry: cotton farmers, cotton traders, cotton ginners, cotton brokers, cotton scientists, cotton exporters. There were news conferences, town meetings, and angry blogs. Eddie Smith, chairman of the local cotton cooperative and a Tech alum, took umbrage not only at the removal of the cotton bolls but at the addition of the vines ("Vines are weeds in my cotton field," he complained to the local newspaper).[3] The alumni clung fast to their cotton tradition while the Chancellor argued that the time had come for Tech to move on.

John Johnson of the Plains Cooperative Cotton Association was telling me this story in late 2007:

> "So what happened?" I asked.
> "Oh, they're gone now," John told me.
> "The cotton bolls?"
> "No" John said, "the Chancellor and the marketing consultants."

Tech's new Chancellor, Dr. Kent Hance, was appointed in 2006. Hance is a Tech alum from Dimmitt, Texas, a tiny cotton community 90 miles and zero stoplights northwest of Lubbock. On the cover of the next issue of the *Techsan*—Tech's glossy alumni magazine—was a field of snow white cotton bolls in a Texas sunset.

In many years of thinking about international trade, I had never thought of tradition-bound and loyal university alumni as the basis for comparative advantage. But there it is: Tech looks after cotton, cotton looks after Tech, and Texas cotton is still winning in the global marketplace.

Today, it looks as though Nelson and Ruth Reinsch have arrived at something of a comfortable place. They are still here, bringing in the cotton each year, more than 50 years after they arrived. The virtuous circle works pretty well on the Reinsch farm: the machines, the chemicals, the genetically modified (GM) seed, the cooperatives, the university research, and the government programs. They can relax now, as Ruth kept telling me back in 2000. Only now, eight years later, is Nelson giving this a try.

C.F. and Hattie Move West (and Bring a Tractor)

As cotton continued its westward push in the 1920s and 1930s, the Reinsches moved, too. Although Texas had already become the nation's biggest cotton producer by 1890, at this time virtually all Texas cotton was produced in the eastern part of the state, bordering on the plantation South. By the 1930s, however, cotton began to take hold of the west Texas region surrounding Lubbock. It was during this period that C.F. and Hattie Reinsch arrived here with young Nelson, then a teenager.

The Reinsches come from a long line of early adopters and innovators. Cotton farmers near Lubbock were starting from scratch. There was no dismantling of the old ways to be accomplished, no old habits to break, no Old South traditions to hold back progress. This freedom to start from scratch undoubtedly explains why most innovations in cotton production spread from west to east rather than from east to west. They still do.

In 2007, I met with Wally Darneille, the new president of the Plains Cotton Cooperative Association in Lubbock. Wally had spent the previous 30 years in the cotton business in Alabama before moving to Lubbock in 2006 to assume his new role. Wally found a striking difference between the cultures of the cotton business in west Texas and Alabama: He told me that a change in practice that would have taken years in Mobile takes just months in Lubbock.

In the Old South, mule farming in cotton production persisted into the 1960s. In west Texas cotton country, it never started. When cotton farmers began to settle near Lubbock—the mid-1920s—the gasoline tractor arrived with them. Whereas the Old South cotton farmers gradually sold their mules and replaced them with tractors, cotton farming in west Texas used tractors from the beginning. This led to drastically different labor patterns in the two regions, differences that would have lasting implications.

Richard Day has divided the mechanization of cotton production to 1960 into four stages (see Figure 3.2).[4] In Stage 1, all land preparation and planting is mule-powered, and weeding is done by hoe. Cotton is handpicked. In Stage 2, some cultivation and weeding is also mule-powered, but land preparation is done by tractor. Cotton is handpicked. In Stage 3, the use of fertilizer increases cotton yields, and more cultivation and weeding is done by tractor implements, but cotton is still handpicked. Finally, in Stage 4, cotton is mechanically harvested and only a small amount of hand weeding remains in the spring and summer seasons.

Early tractor technology was capable only of the brute-strength chore of breaking the land in winter and so did little to solve the ancient labor problem of cotton production. There was little reason to buy a tractor for land breaking, since this chore required the least labor. Therefore, there was little incentive for Deep South cotton farmers to move from Stage 1 to Stage 2, since the labor force was still needed on demand for the rest of the year for weeding, cultivating, and harvesting, and the mules would be needed as well. Gradually, tractor implements became capable of the finer tasks of weeding between rows, though weeds close to the cotton plant still had to be pulled by hoe. On the other hand, growers at Stage 3 who had started with tractors had every incentive to mechanize the harvest or move to Stage 4, because of the highly uneven labor requirements associated with harvesting.

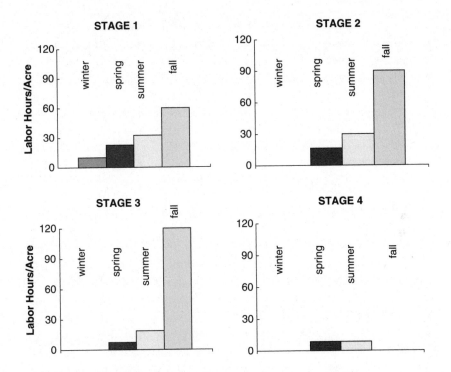

STAGE 1: Mule-powered land breaking and cultivation. Extensive hand weeding and hand picking.

STAGE 2: Tractor land preparation in winter. Mule-powered cultivation. Some hand weeding. Hand picking.

STAGE 3: Tractor-powered land preparation and cultivation. Some hand weeding. Hand picking.

STAGE 4: Complete mechanization with a small amount of hand weeding.

COTTON LABOR CYCLE:

Winter: land breaking
Spring: planting, cultivation, weeding
Summer: weeding
Fall: harvest

Source: Adapted from Day, p. 440.

Figure 3.2 Manual Labor Requirements in Cotton Production

Percentage of Work Done with Tractors

| | LAND BREAKING | | PLANTING | | CULTIVATING | |
STATE	1939	1946	1939	1946	1939	1946
ALABAMA	10	33	3	15	5	14
TEXAS	49	85	45	80	43	83

Source: Adapted from Street, p. 164.

Figure 3.3 Use of Tractor Power in Cotton Production, 1939 and 1946

The remarkable mechanical leapfrogging of the Reinsches and their west Texas neighbors is shown in Figure 3.3. By 1946, over 80 percent of Texas cotton production—including that on the Reinsch farm—had reached Stage 3, while in the Deep South, this stage had been reached by only 14 percent of cotton farmers. In 1946, more than 20 years after the widespread introduction of the tractor into west Texas cotton country, 67 percent of Deep South cotton farms were still exclusively mule-powered.

The reluctance of Deep South cotton farmers to trade in their mules for tractors in the move to Stage 3 was due largely to a faithful attachment to tradition and reluctance to change, as well as to the economics of small holdings. It was even due to an attachment to the animals themselves. In speaking to his biographer, Ned Cobb seemed to remember each of his mules—their colors, their names, their personalities, their quirks. To give up mule farming was to relinquish a way of life, and many were loath to do so, even as they clearly saw the future in front of them. Here is Ned Cobb, speaking in the early 1970s:

> I was a mule farmin' man to the last; never did make a crop with a tractor. I've owned some of the prettiest mules that ever walked the roads. Now there ain't none of my children, nary one by name, got a mule.[5]

Something was lost, of course, in the move from mules to tractors: You couldn't pet a tractor, or name it, and the machine had no personality at all. Into the mishmash of obsolete Southern traditions went the art of talking to a mule.[6]

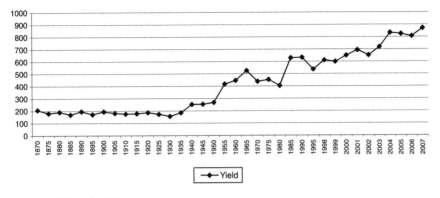

Source: USDA/NASS.

Figure 3.4   Cotton Yields (Pounds of Lint per Acre)

But while the Reinsches had nary a mule, either, there still was not a satisfactory mechanical way to pull the fluffy white lint from the cotton plant. From the settling of west Texas cotton country, this was done as it always had been, by men, women, and children pulling heavy sacks between the rows. And there was more to pick. Thanks to the introduction of advanced fertilizers, cotton yields were increasing (see Figure 3.4). While a traditional Deep South plantation might hope for 120 pounds per acre, by the 1950s, the Reinsches were coaxing nearly a bale (480 pounds) out of each acre planted in cotton. As Day's estimates show then, the labor necessary to harvest the crop from an acre of cotton had approximately doubled from the pre–Civil War South. At the same time, labor requirements during the rest of the year were dropping dramatically. Rather than solving the labor problem, the mechanization made the labor problem at harvest even worse.

White Guys Get All Draggy-Like

Though public policies had ameliorated growers' labor market risks since the beginning, on the eve of World War II the federal government entered the labor market directly to assume these risks on behalf of farmers. With the December attack on Pearl Harbor and the resulting drain of agricultural labor to the military, Congress charged the USDA with mobilizing women and children to bring in the crop. Farmers across the country insisted, however, that additional workers were needed, not just to harvest the crop, but even to win the war. Once again, it seemed, civilization teetered on the ability to get the cotton picked. Governor Olson of California wrote to Washington in 1942:

> Without a substantial number of Mexicans the situation is certain to be disastrous to the entire victory program, despite our united efforts in the mobilization of youth and city dwellers for emergency farm work.[7]

Congress responded in 1942 by authorizing the *Bracero* program, which allowed Mexican labor to enter the United States for short periods to work in agriculture. And Mexican farm labor, according to the growers, was much better than white labor, which was "lazy and draggy-like," or black labor, which exhibited "too much independence."[8] So, as Nelson went off to war at the age of 20, Mexicans flowed across the border to pick the Reinsches' cotton. Though the Bracero program was authorized as an emergency wartime measure, farm interests succeeded in extending the program until 1964, 19 years after the war had ended. By that time, 90 percent of cotton was mechanically harvested. Most cotton was in Stage 4 of mechanization, and the workers were no longer needed.

The Bracero program—and its long-term extension—illustrates again the political influence that enabled cotton farmers to avoid competitive markets. The program went much further than simply easing immigration restrictions for U.S. farm work. Had the program stopped there, cotton producers still would have had to contend with the dreaded labor market. Even with the influx of Mexican labor, how would producers know that workers would be there when the cotton needed to be picked? Further, wage uncertainty in this volatile market posed an economic risk as well. Because all of a region's cotton had to be picked at the same time, "the market" might allow wages to be bid up to uneconomic levels to meet peak demand. Though there were a number of attempts by growers collectively to fix the price of Mexican farm labor, none of these attempts had any lasting effect. Attempts to restrict worker mobility to keep laborers from seeking higher wages on the next farm were also largely unsuccessful.[9] In brief, simply lifting the floodgates to allow Mexican labor onto U.S. farms still left the growers at the peril of a competitive labor market. They didn't like it then any more than they had before.

What the growers wanted was threefold. First, they wanted the labor they needed to be available on demand. Second, they wanted to know in advance what the labor would cost, and they did not want to compete with one another on the basis of price. Third, they wanted a guarantee that the labor would be productive. In other words, the growers wanted to assume none of the labor market risks that are normally associated not just with agriculture, but with business in general.

Congress gave the growers everything they asked for. Under the Bracero program, which was administered by the Department of Labor, the growers ordered a certain number of workers to be picked up on a certain day. The government guaranteed that the growers' order would be filled at a certain price. The laborers imported could work for only a single employer, so growers no longer had to worry about workers leaving in search of higher wages. Government workers also assumed the role of screening workers for health, likely productivity, and political ideology.[10]

Nelson and Ruth remember well the days of the Bracero program, the hundreds of Mexicans crawling through the cotton fields plucking the low Texas cotton. Whatever its effect on liberal sensibilities, they believe the program was a good one. How else could the cotton have been picked? How else could these workers have supported their families? Nelson and Ruth treated the workers fairly, and required their two sons to perform the same chores as the Bracero workers. Their older son, Lamar, remembers it this way, too.

Bureaucrats Push Out Sharecroppers

By the early 1930s, cotton prices had dropped to the lowest level ever observed (see Figure 3.5). While public policies had cushioned farmers' labor market risks since the beginning, with the federal price support programs of the early 1930s, the government also began to assume the risks of falling commodity prices. As the economic situation on Southern cotton farms became increasingly desperate, attention turned to Washington. For cotton farmers, the critical element of the New Deal's agricultural policy was the Agricultural Adjustment Act (AAA), which, for the first time, introduced government price supports for agricultural products, and also introduced the concept of paying farmers to take land out of production. The objective was for the government payments to put a safety net under rural poverty while at the same time helping commodity prices to stabilize.

A look at the winners and losers from farm price support programs, however, suggests a lesson about the beneficiaries of government policy. In practice, while growers such as the Reinsches benefited, landowners in

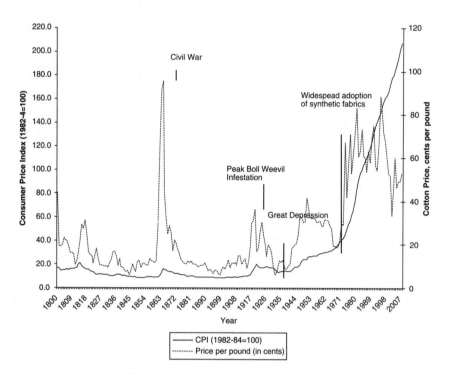

Source: Cotton prices from USDA. CPI 1800–1912 from International Historical Statistics: The Americas 1750–1993, CPI 1913–1998 from Bureau of Labor Statistics.

Figure 3.5   Cotton Prices

the Deep South typically chose to take the government check and then take their sharecroppers' acreage out of production, pushing farmers into the ranks of migrants who gradually went west into the pages of *The Grapes of Wrath*. Rarely did the sharecropper have the means to fight the landlord for his share of the government's payment.[11] In a cruel irony, it was the government programs designed to alleviate the sharecroppers' poverty that intimidated Ned Cobb out of cotton farming. Cobb had never intended to give up cotton farming. He had wanted to die growing cotton, and certainly was not about to be pushed aside by whites:

> I was born an raised here and I have sowed my labor into the earth and lived to reap only a part of it, not all that was mine by human right ... I stays on if it gives 'em satisfaction for me to leave, and I stays on because its mine.[12]

A short time later, Ned Cobb gave up. And he gave up because of, not in spite of, the government's efforts to help:

> ... the government took over this cotton business to a greater extent than ever before; I jumped out right there. Didn't want to fill out them papers every year, and a whole lot of red tape to it. I can't read and write; Josie can't either. And if I couldn't conduct my business myself, I weren't going to have nobody do it for me.[13]

And the final cruel joke: Many large farmers used their AAA payments to buy tractors, so many small sharecroppers were "tractored out" by World War II.

The cause of Ned Cobb's demise as a cotton farmer bears an important lesson for explaining the winners, both then and today. Cobb's biography shows us a brilliant man with a sophisticated and nuanced understanding of history, human nature, and science. But with the introduction of government price supports and the dozens of federal farm programs that soon followed, skill at navigating the bureaucracy and using the levers of political influence became prerequisites for survival. In 1999, the USDA acknowledged that decades of indifference and blatant discrimination against blacks in government farm programs had persisted well into the 1990s, and in 2008 the Government Accountability Office issued a report concluding that, nearly a decade later, things were not much better.[14]

For Ned Cobb, dealing with bureaucrats meant a brave new world: All of a sudden, if you couldn't read, you couldn't farm.

Machines that Don't Get All Discouraged

In the center pages of a catalog from Lands' End, a beautiful young girl beams into the camera from the center of a cotton patch. She is 17 or 18 years old, with long and shiny beauty-shop hair. She has peaceful and happy deep-pool eyes that say all is well in this place with the blue sky. And she has perfect teeth, lined up white and evenly, in a smile designed to bring forth your credit card. We are supposed to buy the polo shirt: It comes in many colors of the softest cotton. In the highlands of Peru, Maria picked the cotton by hand, fluff by fluff. It's better, says the catalog, than the machine-picked cotton.

Better for whom? In researching this book I met many people who had grown up handpicking cotton, but I didn't meet anyone who was nostalgic for it. Cotton farmers in almost all countries outside the United States still handpick their cotton; indeed, Terry Townsend of the International Cotton Advisory Committee (ICAC) told me that he did not believe that there was a mechanical picker in all of Africa. While handpicking cotton may be a job, it is not a job of choice. The Marias of the world don't get their hair done, and their teeth haven't been fixed. Surely they smile now and again, out there in the field, but it's not because they are picking cotton.

In 2005, I met Dr. Dick Auld, a chaired professor of Plant Genetics and Breeding at Texas Tech. He had grown up on a cotton farm, and had memories of coming home from school and handpicking and handweeding, the endless hours of backbreaking labor in the merciless sun. "Why I am here today?" he asked rhetorically about his academic career. "Why do I keep doing the research? Because no human being should have to work that way, or live that way, not here, not anywhere, not ever again."[15]

In 1999, Adrian Gwin still harbored a 75-year-old memory of picking cotton. It was only one day, long ago, but it was enough:

> There just ain't enough money in the world for me to do that again. I was a full-fledged, on-the-payroll cotton picker for one whole day about 70 years ago, and it cured me.... I've been there. It was about 1925 or 1926 that I got my cotton picking baptism, right out in a mile wide cotton field.... I'd seen other little boys making fortunes picking cotton, and I wanted some of that easy money. Cotton picking paid a dime a hundred. Ten cents for picking only a hundred pounds of cotton in the fields. I'd seen black boys and girls make 2 dimes a day.... To make that dime you had to loop a strap of mattress ticking around a shoulder, and drag behind you a six-foot ticking bag that would hold 30 or so pound of cotton. You went down the cotton row and grabbed the fluffy white cotton off the bolls and flipped it into the mouth of the bag. Before the sun was half up in the sky, I was convinced my bag had a hole in the bottom. My shoulders ached. My legs ached. My arms ached. My fingers ached. I was plumb sore all over before I got to the end of that first row.... I was ready to call it a day—but the day was hardly half-spent. And I wasn't yet halfway to that shiny bright dime I wanted. When Stentius blew his horn and twilight hovered over the cotton field, I looked back at my 100-pound bag diggin its feet into the ground as I dragged it—and it wasn't full yet.
>
> I remember so well. I didn't get a dime. I got a nickel. Five cents. The weighmaster at the gin was generous. I hadn't quite picked 50 pounds of cotton in my 14-hour day. Long years later, I remembered that day of cotton picking.... Never again would I drag a bag down a cotton row. Never again

that cotton pickin' cotton picking. Today, they have machines to do it. Great
big super-efficient machines that don't get tired all over and discouraged.
   Boy, I'm glad.[16]

Nelson and Ruth are glad, too. With a cotton-stripping machine, they
could drastically reduce once and for all their risky association with farm
labor. Whereas inventive farmers had tried various ways to mechanize the
harvest before, it was not until the 1920s and early 1930s that researchers
based in Lubbock, only a few miles from the Reinsch farm, began to
perfect the tractor-mounted cotton stripper in one of many applications
of the fruitful relationship among USDA cotton researchers, universities,
and farmers. The basic stripper technology, which survives today, consists
of a set of brushes that are pulled around the cotton plant, knocking the
bolls onto a belt and blowing them into a trailer. Though this essential
technology was developed in the 1920s and 1930s, widespread adoption
of mechanical strippers did not take place in west Texas until shortly after
World War II, and in the Deep South, much later.
   The mechanical march forward was halted first by the Depression, and
second by the necessity to adapt other phases in the production chain,
especially ginning, to mechanically picked cotton. And mechanical cotton
picking required farms of a certain size, as well. It was difficult to justify
an investment in cotton-picking machinery on a farm of under 150 or so
acres. While most Texas farms were easily large enough to benefit, the
small cotton patches across the Deep South were not. Today, the millions
of farmers across Africa and Southeast Asia also find it difficult to make
the leap to mechanical harvesting. Even if the farmers banded together
to share the machines, because of the whims of nature, everyone would
likely need the machine at the same time.
   It was 1953, Nelson believes, when the two-row International Harvester cotton stripper arrived at the farm and changed everything. The
machine could pick 10 bales a day, the work of 25 men in the field, and,
like Adrian Gwin said, it didn't get all tired and discouraged.
   But while the machine solved the picking problem, it created new bottlenecks. The cotton-picking weather windows in west Texas had always
posed a problem: a race to get to the cotton before the Texas elements.
The cotton needed water, yet it couldn't be picked wet. The hail would
come down and knock the fluff right off the plant, or the gusty wind would
blow it away, or the sand would make it dirty and lower its price. In the
three-month harvest season, Nelson needed windows where he could get

to the cotton after it had bloomed and dried but before the wind or hail or sand or rain. Unfortunately, the new stripper made this already-random challenge trickier yet.

With the mechanical harvester, Nelson had to wait for a hard freeze as well. The machine could not strip the cotton from live green plants. In order to work properly, the cotton stripper required that the plant be brown and brittle, as happened after a freeze, so that the cotton bolls could snap off easily. And worse yet, the picking day was shorter, because the stripper also did not do well in the morning dew. So into the already-impossible climate constraints on cotton picking came more things to wait for, while hoping the Texas weather monsters wouldn't get there first.

The result, for C.F., Hattie, and Nelson, and by now, for Nelson's young sons, too, was that when the stars were finally lined up right for stripping, the crew worked frantically. Harvesting the cotton required three to four workers: one to drive the tractor, the rest to ride in the trailer mounted behind the stripper. The riders' job was to move the cotton evenly around the trailer as it blew in, using pitchforks, and to tramp the cotton down to get better use out of the trailers. There was a definite hierarchy: Driving the tractor was better than riding the trailer. Nelson would drive the tractor and his sons Lamar and Dwade would ride in back, often with a hired hand. Because they couldn't strip the cotton until midmorning, they went until darkness was complete, until they had to stop because of the pitchforks.

Lamar's memory of riding the cotton trailer is permanently engraved, like Gwin's memory of cotton picking. It was hard, noisy, dirty work. Hard was okay, he was young and strong. Even though his hearing is still damaged, noisy was okay, too. But, dirty, well, you just can't imagine.

This is what he remembers: as darkness fell, being splattered with bloody rabbit pieces, from the ones that didn't jump quickly enough.

Lamar decided to go to college.

Pick Your Weather

Of course, in a given region, the hard freeze came at the same time for everybody, so while Nelson and his sons worked frantically, all of his neighbors were working frantically as well. This created a major bottleneck in getting the cotton to market. First, there were never enough trailers, and never enough time to tow them to the gin. In the middle of the harvest, Nelson needed empty trailers to catch the cotton, but to get them empty he had to stop work and tow them to the gin. And once he arrived there, his cotton trailer had to get in line with everyone else's, and wait its turn to get emptied into the gin. In those very brief west Texas weather windows, the cotton poured into the gins at a much faster rate than the system could handle.

In a pattern that continues today, one advance begot the next. Once the scientists and engineers created the mechanical stripper, they were forced next to address the challenges created by the innovation.

As the mechanical stripper closed the weather window, the virtuous circle turned to opening it. The idea was to let Nelson decide when the hard freeze would come—and, indeed, to let him decide which part of his field would freeze today, and which tomorrow. Scientists soon created chemical compounds that could make the cotton plant brown and crunchy, no matter what the temperature. Today, Nelson doesn't wait for the hard freeze. When the cotton is open and the weather stars are lined up, he freezes the cotton himself, with chemicals sprayed from behind his tractor. The plants turn as dead and crunchy as can be, whenever he wants them to. In fact, there isn't much that looks deader than a defoliated cotton field in west Texas. When I stood in the middle of the Reinsches' chemically frozen field, I felt like the earth itself was rusting away around me.

Actually, maybe the earth *was* rusting away around me. If a chemical kills the cotton plant, what does it do the rest of the natural world? Perusing the EPA-mandated Material Safety Data Sheet (MSDS) for a leading cotton defoliant left me more confused than alarmed.[17] On the one hand, the MSDS made it clear that the defoliant was dangerous to everything from humans to groundwater to rats to "non-target" plants. On the other hand, the EPA's reams of regulations and exhaustive rules for application and disposal, as well as its ongoing tests, seemed to construct at least a modicum of a safety net. It is hard to know whether to be alarmed by the toxicity of the chemicals or reassured by the thousands of pages of rules. But can we go backwards and ask cotton farmers to wait for God to send a freeze? Not likely; the growers' increasing control over both markets and nature—whether through politics, chemicals, or machines—was not to be a reversible trend.

Even with the stripper and the defoliants, there was still plenty of human labor involved in Nelson's cotton production in the late 1960s. Though the huge number of seasonal factory workers was no longer needed, Nelson, Lamar, and Dwade had plenty to do. The Reinsches described to me a system of team production, a real family farm where each member of the family had a job to do in getting the cotton to market.

Nelson and his sons were busy in the field, and Ruth and daughter Colleen kept the books, tended the garden and canned, kept the family fed, and sold eggs in town. The next chapter in cotton's story, though, beginning in the early 1970s, would change all this. The next chapter would let the children go off to the city and let Nelson do it all, hundreds of thousands of pounds, pretty much by himself.

The Reinsch Children Leave the Farm

Until the late 1960s, Nelson needed his sons, or at least reliable hired help, in every season except winter. In the fall, the cotton trailer needed two or three riders while Nelson drove the tractor and ferried cotton to the gin. In the spring and summer, irrigation was almost a full-time job for Lamar, as keeping the right amount of water going to the right places, through a system of wells and pumps and pipes, required pretty much constant attention. And in the spring, there were the weeds that threatened to overtake the young cotton plants, and somebody needed to drive up and down the rows, carefully chopping and burying them, for most of the season.

One by one, the USDA, the university scientists, and the large agribusiness companies invented these jobs away. First, in the early 1970s, new methods were devised that eliminated the need for riders during the harvest (no more rabbit pieces or pitchforks) and also did away with the need for Nelson to ferry his cotton to the gin. Nelson replaced his trailers with large baskets that caught the cotton but didn't carry riders. When the basket is full, Nelson simply tips it into a "module builder," a metal box with an open top, about the size of a large moving van. As the module builder fills, Nelson doesn't need his sons to tramp down the cotton. He has a hydraulic press, powered by the tractor, that turns the cotton into a gigantic snowy brick. When the brick is the right size, up to the top of the box with about 22,000 pounds of cotton, Nelson slides the box away, leaving the white brick in the field and the box empty and ready for more cotton. Workers from the gin drive a module truck over to pick up the cotton: A giant spatula slides under the cotton and lifts it up onto the truck. The cotton arrives at the gin only minutes later.

The irrigation man's job was the next to go. Though some of Nelson's cotton is still irrigated by pipes, most is watered by a giant computerized sprinkler that moves back and forth across the field like a big windshield wiper. It doesn't actually spray or sprinkle—west Texas is much too dry for Nelson to spray his water into the sky—instead, it drags hundreds of tiny dripping hoses gently across the field.

On a trip to Lubbock in 2007, I found that cotton harvesting had taken another leap into the future. In Levelland (a bit of west Texas understatement there)—just a few miles from the Reinsch farm—cotton grower Mike Henson is trying out the next-generation technology. Henson farms significantly more acreage than the Reinsches, and so has still been dependent during harvest season on a dozen or so workers. Henson repeated the cotton grower's age-old plight: Labor was his toughest challenge, he told me. Would he be able to find workers? Would they show up? Would they be back tomorrow?

Henson graciously invited me to hop aboard the new John Deere 7760 cotton stripper. He was pilot-testing the new technology on the last of his 2007 crop. Riding in the tractor cab with Henson was a bit like riding in a spaceship, with lots of computer programs running to tell us what was happening. The price tag of the 7760 is close to $600,000, but Henson thinks it will be worth it.[18] As the modules had eliminated the need for riders, the 7760 eliminates the need for modules. Once the 7760 has collected a certain amount of cotton, belts are activated that form the cotton into round bales and then wrap the bales in protective plastic. The grower no longer needs to stop harvesting to empty his basket into the module builder, and no longer needs to form and protect the modules. In the past, Henson might be stripping cotton with one tractor while workers formed modules with another. The 7760 allows the grower to simply drop the formed round module at the end of the row, make his U-turn, and continue harvesting with no interruption. With the new technology, Henson can strip about 75 bales before lunch. Nelson Reinsch's first mechanical stripper could strip three.

Henson believes that the 7760 will allow him to do the work of 10 or 11 men, and therefore almost dispense with seasonal workers. Other equipment will no longer be needed: no more boll buggies and module builders. From the perspective of the environment, the 7760 is a step in the right direction as well: Henson expects to save thousands of gallons of fuel per week with the new technology.

Old Enemies, New Friends

Throughout cotton's history, the fluffy plant has battled two enemies: insects and weeds. These battles continue today, yet in typical fashion the

Texas growers have an increasingly sophisticated repertoire of weapons against these natural enemies. The saga of these battles seems to be a tale of quick-wittedness and intrigue: Though the growers can never eliminate the weeds or the insects, they can, through science and technology, manage to stay a step or two ahead of them. While no one questions the resourcefulness of the farmers and the larger agricultural complex in battling these natural enemies, many question the long-run ecological consequences of the battles.

The traditional manner of keeping cotton "out of the grass" or free from weeds was to bury or chop the weeds. During the past century, this was done first by hoe, and then by implements pulled by mules and then tractors. Shortly after World War II, however, the battle against weeds went chemical.

The shift in tactics—from mechanical to chemical methods—began a battle of wits that continues today. One challenge is that herbicides by definition are substances that kill plants, and it is a continual challenge to design herbicide applications that kill the weeds (the "target plant") while sparing the cotton plant itself. A second challenge is the power of plant evolution to stay one step ahead of the scientists. While a chemical might kill most of a certain variety of weed, some renegade members of the weed's family will be resistant to the herbicide, and those weeds are of course the ones that will successfully reproduce. Some weeds, the growers found, developed resistance after just a few seasons. The chemicals, then, needed to stay a step ahead of the weeds' resistance, and so growers are dependent on private sector and university researchers to continually outwit the weeds as the plants develop resistance.

From an environmental perspective, substances that kill plants are unlikely to be good for the rest of us. Herbicides leach into groundwater and waterways, affect fish and wildlife, and contaminate adjacent areas. During the postwar era, a number of especially hazardous chemicals, including paraquat and arsenic, have been used to control weeds. Today, herbicides must pass stringent regulatory hurdles set by the EPA. I spent many hours reading the EPA's Material Safety Data Sheets (MSDSs) for common cotton herbicides. Threats, it seemed, were everywhere: to water, wildlife, air, and people. Herbicides could cause thyroid problems in rats, or liver problems in rabbits, or cancer in fish.

Fortunately for the planet and for the cotton growers, one of the most effective herbicides is the chemical compound *glyphosate*. Sold by Monsanto under the tradename Roundup, the compound is one of the most effective herbicides as well as one of the more environmentally benign.[19] In west Texas, Roundup came into widespread use in the mid-1970s. Roundup, however, was a nonselective herbicide, so, used incorrectly, it could damage the cotton plant as well as the weeds. The use of Roundup required the elements of the virtuous circle to work together: Only if the farmers received the right advice from Monsanto and from the scientists at Tech would the Roundup be sprayed at the right time, in the right place, and with the right method to spare the cotton itself. Roundup in the wrong hands was worse than no herbicide at all.

The virtuous circle became increasingly interdependent: The scientists at Monsanto and Tech created the herbicides, but the farmer then became dependent on the evolving and complicated advice from the scientists.

Ned Cobb, of course, battled weeds by relying on his hoe, his mules, and himself.

Designer Genes

In 1996, there was another leap into the future, a leap that some believe will one day be seen as momentous as the cotton gin or the mechanical stripper, but that others believe might turn out to be a dangerous corporate-led conspiracy. In that year, the first commercial crop of GM cotton was planted in the United States. Developed by Monsanto and called "Roundup Ready," the cottonseed was genetically engineered to allow the cotton plant to withstand "over-the-top" applications of Roundup herbicide. The delicate balancing act of how, when, and where to spray became immediately easier, because now the herbicide would attack the weeds but spare the cotton. Roundup Ready cotton and its subsequent improvements also meant that many farmers no longer needed to chop or bury weeds by machine. The cultivator—the tractor implement used to chop and bury weeds—began to go the way of the mule.[20]

For Monsanto, the combination of Roundup herbicides and Roundup Ready seed was a homerun: Each product created demand for the other. In addition to selling the cottonseed itself through a subsidiary, Monsanto also charged a "technology" fee for the use of the genetic trait. For the most advanced genetic traits, this fee was $136 per bag of seed in 2008. When added to the cost of the seed itself, this meant that the GM cottonseed cost growers about six times as much as conventional seed.[21] By 2007, thanks largely to the widespread adoption of Roundup Ready seeds, Roundup herbicide was responsible for more than 30 percent of Monsanto's revenues.[22]

Sales of Monsanto's herbicides increased by 85 percent in the second quarter of 2008 compared to the same period the year before, and between May 2003 and May 2008, Monsanto's stock price rose from $11 to $125.[23]

The new seed, however, was not just a new biological life form; it was a new business life form as well. Because Monsanto, not nature, had created the cotton plant, it was protected by patent. Since the dawn of agriculture, farmers had "caught" seed from each year's harvest to plant the following year. Monsanto prohibited this practice, however, and required the growers to buy new Roundup Ready seed each year.

Roundup Ready cottonseed was soon followed by seed that was genetically engineered to solve insect problems as well. Monsanto injected the gene of a natural bacteria—*Bacillus thuringiensis* (Bt)—into the cottonseed. Bt was toxic to several of cottons' most troublesome pests, particularly bollworms. The worms would eat leaves from the genetically engineered cotton plant, ingest the Bt bacterium, and a short time later would develop fatal holes in their guts. Once again, it appeared, the virtuous circle had developed a scientific solution to nature's risks. Bt seed was also protected by patent, and Monsanto again prohibited the "catching" of the seed for replanting. Within a few years, Monsanto was selling "stacked" varieties of cotton seeds that had been engineered to contain both the Roundup Ready and the Bt trait.

But no one—not Monsanto, not the scientists at Tech, and certainly not the cotton growers—can relax. The weeds and the insects on the one hand, and the virtuous circle on the other—continue to try to outwit one another.[24]

A tiny percentage of bollworms are resistant to the Bt cottonseed, and of course, while their friends wither from the poison, the resistant worms will reproduce. Left to themselves, these resistant worms could likely render Bt seed useless within a few years. Monsanto's solution to this challenge was to require the growers to plant a certain number of acres as "refuge." This acreage would be planted with conventional cottonseed, and would therefore allow some bollworms to live long enough to reproduce with their resistant neighbors. Since the resistance gene is recessive, the refuge system would keep the entire bollworm population from quickly developing resistance. The virtuous circle, in its ceaseless quest to control nature, was now trying to control the sexual partners of worms. At the same time, the cottonseed was being continually reengineered to respond to insect resistance, and Monsanto was strictly monitoring and enforcing the use of refuge. The technology agreements signed by the growers gave Monsanto's "seed police" power to inspect farms and punish those either replanting seed or failing to follow the company's refuge and other specifications.

Other challenges—real and potential—had to be met. The control of the bollworm meant that the insects that had previously been minor pests because they had been eaten by the bollworms, could now become major pests, so new treatments were needed control these "secondary pests." Other secondary pests could become major pests because they had previously been destroyed by the pesticides that had been targeting the bollworms. Furthermore, there were concerns that some "beneficial insects"—so-called because they fed on cotton's enemies but did not damage the cotton itself—might be harmed by an interruption in their food supply. In other words, the toxins directed at cotton's enemies might indirectly harm its friends.

The scientists at Monsanto and Tech, however, remain a couple of steps ahead, and continue to meet these challenges one insect and weed at a time. For Texas cotton growers, Monsanto's price premium and restrictions have been a small price to pay for the leap forward in their battle against weeds and pests. By 2007, nearly 90 percent of U.S. cotton acreage was planted with GM seed.[25] U.S. cotton farmers' incomes have likely increased by at least $1 billion as the result of GM technology, primarily through lower costs and higher yields.[26]

Back to Nature or Forward to the Future?

In traditional "high-input" industrial agriculture, there are growing environmental threats from increasing use of pesticides, fertilizers, water, fuel, and herbicides. While high-input agriculture has been the result of continuing scientific leaps, the scientific and chemical advances have come at a high environmental cost. The environmental effects of chemical-intensive agriculture are well-known, but there is a philosophical divide regarding the best way forward. One option is the "back-to-nature" response of organic farmers. Another, however, is to push forward with scientific advances that can solve environmental problems. In this view, the environmental problems created by scientific advances can be solved with more scientific advances. The back-to-nature and "scientific advance" responses to environmental challenges occupy opposite ends of the philosophical spectrum.

Today, GM technology is rapidly evolving so as to *reduce* chemical inputs required in agriculture. The GM technology, advocates argue, can address traditional problems such as weeds and pests while at the same time addressing environmental challenges. Bt seed already has drastically reduced the volume of pesticides applied to cotton in the United States (according to several farmers I spoke with, the reduction has been upwards of 90 percent), and the reduced application has the positive environmental effect of less fuel use from applications as well.[27] Somewhere, in the scientists' fantasy of the future, is a genetically engineered seed that takes care of insects without chemicals at all, that flourishes without chemical fertilizer, and that can coexist with weeds or benign herbicides. GM cotton and other crops are being created to use less water, to capture more solar energy to achieve higher yields, and to withstand both higher and lower temperatures. Indeed, Monsanto has pledged to double cotton crop yields by 2030, while at the same time reducing land, water, and energy requirements by 30 percent.[28] According to this version of the future, to doom genetic engineering is to doom the planet itself.

In an ironic twist, corporations are now genetically engineering seeds not only to reduce environmental damage but to withstand it. As of the spring of 2008, a small number of the world's largest agricultural biotech companies were seeking hundreds of patents worldwide for GM crops that would be able to withstand sustained global warming.[29]

Readers of a certain age will remember the queenly character in the 1970s TV commercial for Chiffon margarine. "It's not *nice* to fool Mother nature," she'd warn.[30] The list of things that *have* gone wrong with GM agriculture in the United States is relatively short and reassuring. Both weeds and insects have exhibited the ability to outwit Roundup and Bt seed traits, but this resistance was expected and, at least so far, has been managed by further GM advances.[31] The list of things that *might* go wrong, however, is more worrying. Could "superweeds" emerge and deprive growers of the use of the most effective (and environmentally safe) herbicides?[32] Could secondary pests and the emergence of new insects as pests reverse the scientists' gains? Could the widespread use of illegal and "pirated" seed grown "outside the rules" threaten the safety of plants, insects, and people? And what are the long-run economic and social effects of private ownership of a variety of life forms?

As GM seed is planted on increasing acreage, it has become more difficult to segregate GM crops from their conventional and organic counterparts because wind and water carry GM seeds from one field to another. While conventional and organic farmers bemoan the fact that their crops have been tainted by the GM seed, Monsanto has responded by suing these farmers for unauthorized use of the seed.[33]

I am not a scientist, and slogging through the research on GM agriculture was slow and confusing. Given the limited resources available, most research papers had limited scope: one country, one time period, one GM crop. I finally happened upon a definitive study. The paper looked at broad environmental and economic impacts of GM cotton over 10 years in 11 countries. The report was over 100 pages long, and the empirical methodology was clear, careful, and convincing. The conclusions were clear as well: GM cotton had been a boon, economically and environmentally, in each of the countries studied. It was only in footnote 9 that I saw that the study had been funded by Monsanto.[34] One does not need to be a cynic, or to doubt the integrity of the researchers, to wish that the science, commercial development, control, and evaluation of GM technology were spread around a bit more.

Yet the cotton growers I met around Lubbock seem still to be marveling at the good fortunes GM technology has wrought. So much less pesticide, so much less fuel, so much more free time, and so much more cotton! Criticisms of GM technologies sound to the farmers to be criticisms of progress itself, and of the 200-year-old success story of American cotton. The powerful position of Monsanto doesn't seem to bother the Texas growers, perhaps because Monsanto's power is part of the virtuous circle to which they, too, belong. Indeed, some research shows that the economic benefit from GM cotton has been larger for the growers than it has been for Monsanto.[35]

The growers are nothing if not practical. Roger Haldenby of Plains Cotton told me in 2008 that virtually 100 percent of the farmers in his area were planting GM seed in that year. He also told me, however, that almost every farmer has some old-fashioned conventional cottonseed tucked away in his barn, just in case.

Most of the farmers I met had an almost spiritual relationship with the land they farmed, and yet they also have little patience for environmental alarmists. Nelson Reinsch has a deep respect for land passed down by his father, and he takes seriously his obligation to look after the land for whomever will farm it next. Wally Darneille, president of the Plains Cooperative Cotton Association in Lubbock, put it differently. "Farmers are the original environmentalists," he told me. "Telling a farmer to take care of the land is like telling the ice cream man to keep his freezer plugged in." Wally has only disdain for the idea of farming organically—without chemicals or GM seed. He quoted his predecessor at the PCCA: "We tried that. We called it the Dust Bowl."

Nelson and Ruth Reinsch have no nostalgia for the Dust Bowl, or the old two-row stripper, or the days before Roundup Ready and Bt seed. The Reinsches still look forward, not backwards, because forward progress is the story of their lives on this farm. It is a narrative of discovery after discovery, advance after advance in a region of the country where the gears continue to engage among the USDA, Texas Tech, Monsanto, and the farmers. The virtuous circle of scientific discovery in American cotton farming continues to do away with risks—labor market risks, weed risks, insect risks, weather risks—each random element of the farmers' livelihood has gradually been brought under Nelson's control. And the virtuous circle, the growers believe, can address environmental risks as well.

The virtuous circle has not only done away with many risks, it has almost done away with farmers. Today, growing cotton in America is almost a one-man show.

Most days, Nelson Reinsch takes a nap after lunch.

ALL GOD'S DANGERS AIN'T THE SUBSIDIES

ALONE ON THE FARM BUT TOGETHER IN TOWN

The remarkable improvements in cotton production that Nelson Reinsch has witnessed—the machines, the chemicals, the GM technology—have occurred alongside equally remarkable advances in business practices. Just as Nelson gradually overcame his powerlessness against the Texas elements, he has overcome his powerlessness against the world markets as well. And, ironically, while advances in production methods have left Nelson out in the field by himself, advances in business organization, marketing, risk sharing, and political influence have led west Texas cotton farmers to band together as a united front against the markets that once dominated them. Little by little, as the farmers became more alone on the farm, they banded together in town.[1]

The journey of the Reinsches' cotton to China begins with a trip just a few miles down the road, to the Citizen's Shallowater Cooperative Cotton Gin. Though the number of cotton gins in the United States has been falling steadily since observers began to count, they are still located next to the cotton fields. It was not so long ago that growers were at the mercy of the local gin, which stood like a roadblock between farmers and their cash. Only a few gins served hundreds of farmers, so the economic power was with the gins rather than the farmers, and farmers desperate for cash lined up at the gin and waited and waited for a turn to pay whatever the ginner wanted.

On the surface, the power structure looks even more lopsided today. The market for cotton ginning is even more concentrated: From 1900 to 2004, the number of gins in operation in the United States fell by over 95 percent, from 20,214 to 896, and the capacity of the typical gin has risen by a factor of 40.[2] Cotton gins are big and profitable businesses now, driven to be larger and more productive by advances in gin technology and economies of scale. But as the gins became bigger and more profitable businesses, something else changed, too. Today, Nelson and Ruth are no longer at the mercy of the gin; instead, they own it. The Reinsches, along with about 300 other farmers, own the Shallowater gin, and their income from selling cotton is augmented by dividend checks from the cooperatively owned gin.

Backward to Seed and Forward to Denim: Farmer Profits at Every Step

Cotton growers have also shown an astounding ability to coax value out of cotton production by throwing nothing away and finding somebody, anybody, to eat it or buy it. Out of the 22,000 pounds of cotton that leave Nelson's farm in the module truck, only about 5,300 pounds is the white lint that will be turned into T-shirts. Everything else on the truck looks like garbage, and it was once garbage, but not anymore. Even the garbage produced by the garbage is now sold. The reusing, recycling, and repackaging that take place in Lubbock's cotton industry today would shame the thriftiest Depression-era housewives. And often, for Texas cotton farmers, the garbage is the difference between red and black at the end of the year. As with virtually all other aspects of cotton farming, substantial assistance has been provided by the U.S. government. While much agricultural research has been devoted to increasing the quality and quantity of cotton production, the USDA at the same time has been actively involved in research to find creative and profitable uses for everything else that arrives in the module.[3]

In addition to the 5,300 pounds of the module's contents that are destined to be spun into cotton yarn (which in turn could produce about 13,500 T-shirts), the module also contains 9,000 pounds of so-called gin trash—bolls, stems, leaves, and dirt—that have been sucked in along with

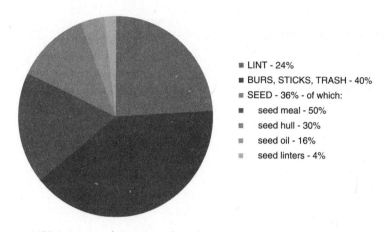

- LINT - 24%
- BURS, STICKS, TRASH - 40%
- SEED - 36% - of which:
  - seed meal - 50%
  - seed hull - 30%
  - seed oil - 16%
  - seed linters - 4%

Source: USDA, National Cottonseed Products Association.

Figure 4.1   Content of Seed Cotton

cotton by Nelson's stripper (see Figure 4.1). Once a little molasses is stirred in, much of this trash becomes cattle feed, trucked just a short distance to the feedlots dotted among the cotton fields. The gin trash is also being converted into briquettes (to be burned for fuel), building materials, fertilizer, and ethanol. With typical resourcefulness, the growers have turned a waste disposal problem into a revenue.[4]

Eight thousand pounds of the snowy white module is cottonseed. The cottonseed, like the bolls and leaves, once had an unprofitable fate as trash, dumped into gullies and streams, or burned in gigantic piles. The volume of cottonseed garbage during the 1800s became so problematic that a number of states passed laws to regulate its disposal.[5] But while the bolls and leaves were still trash, in the early 1900s, the seed began to move up the value chain to be used as fertilizer and animal feed. The cattle loved it, just raw, and cottonseed was soon found to improve the butterfat content of milk. After their cotton had been ginned, farmers would keep some of the seed for next year's planting, plow some into the ground as fertilizer, and use the rest to feed their cows. Now, however, the bolls and leaves are used as feed, but because the GM seed is not allowed to be replanted, it is off to the city to meet its own global market.

The tallest (actually, the only) mountains in the Lubbock area can be seen from miles around: In harvest season, the mountains at the Plains Cooperative Oil Mill (PCOM) contain about 20 tons of cottonseed apiece. The PCOM was born in the late 1930s as a desperate act of self-defense by west Texas cotton farmers, who at the time could hardly give their seed away. The west Texas seed had a reputation for poor by-products, and therefore brought low prices. Furthermore, the marketing of the seed was fragmented, with individual gins trying to negotiate with the likes of Palmolive, Wesson Oil, and Ralston-Purina. PCOM gradually proved to customers that west Texas seed by-products were in fact superior, not inferior, to those of its competitors, and also gradually consolidated the marketing efforts of the region's gins.[6]

The oil from the seed, about 16 percent of the seed's weight, is sold to buyers in Lubbock. It comes back into the Reinsch house in Snickers bars, Ragu spaghetti sauce, Peter Pan peanut butter, Girl Scout cookies, Certs breath mints, and almost any kind of crispy snack food (the biggest buyer of cottonseed oil in the world is Frito-Lay). CRISCO shortening (named for the acronym for Crystalized Cottonseed Oil), has come full circle back to cottonseed. Created in 1911 by Proctor and Gamble as hydrogenated cottonseed oil, CRISCO was reformulated with different ingredients over the years, but now once again contains primarily cottonseed oil, which is trans-fat free.

Cotton growers have also benefited recently from their competition from corn oil (which is getting more expensive due to demand for ethanol) and peanut oil (which is allergenic to many). Connoisseurs agree that when it comes to frying chips, cottonseed oil is best. In fact, gourmet chefs increasingly tout the benefits of cooking with cottonseed oil. The National Cottonseed Products Association (NCPA) offers recipes such as "Chocolate Banana Bread Pudding with Mascarpone Caramel Cream and Banana Beignets" to anyone who might be interested. In the sporting goods stores in west Texas, large jugs of cottonseed oil are positioned next to the turkey fryers. Cottonseed oil is also the primary input in the production of Olestra, a frying fat that glides through humans without leaving a trace of fat or calories, and is also an important source of vitamin E for pharmaceutical producers. And finally, the oil is also processed into "soap stock" that turns up in soaps and detergents of all kinds. Colgate-Palmolive is also a major customer. (See Figure 4.2.)

But while Nelson's cotton is exported worldwide, his cottonseed oil often gets stopped at the border. When the oil is intended for human consumption, or is contained in Pringles or Snickers, it becomes a food, and in many countries, particularly in Europe, U.S.–produced cotton-seed oil is a genetically modified food, subject to myriad restrictions and labeling requirements. U.S. cottonseed oil exports to Europe have fallen

Figure 4.2 Products Containing Cottonseed Oil Displayed at the Plains
Yazoo Cotton Oil Offices in Lubbock
(Author's Photo.)

from 5 million kilograms in 1989 to virtually zero for the 2004–2007
period.[7]

The meal of the cottonseed constitutes almost half of the seed's weight.
It contains high-quality protein and is now used to feed not just cattle,
but as Dave Kinard of the NCPA told me, "just about any critter at all,"
including horses, hogs, chickens, turkeys, sheep, and mules. Ralston Purina
is another major customer for cottonseed meal. And recently, researchers
in aquaculture (fish farming) have discovered that cottonseed meal makes
a high-quality fish food.[8] Catfish, in particular, appear to love cottonseed
meal, and will eat it even when offered fish meal instead. Because fish stocks
throughout the world are falling, driving up the prices of fish meal, and
cotton production is rising, driving down the price of cottonseed, feeding
cottonseed to catfish works for farmers of both cotton and catfish. And it's
convenient, too, as the catfish farms in the South are close to the cotton
fields. Dr. Lance Forster, a scientist at the NCPA, predicts that fish farms
may soon consume 10 percent of the production of U.S. cottonseed meal.[9]

And humans are critters, too. If current research in genetic engineering pays off, cottonseed flour will turn up in the bakery aisle in breads, cakes, and cookies. Even today, it is possible to produce a baking flour for human consumption from cottonseed meal. The problem, however, is that the cottonseed varieties that produce high-quality flour do not produce high-quality lint. As a result, farmers are unwilling to plant the flour varieties. As plant genetics research advances, however, industry scientists hope that it will be possible to breed cottonseed that produces superior flour, high-quality lint, and oil, so that almost every ingredient in a birthday cake can be produced with the leftovers from Nelson's cotton production.

Approximately 30 percent of the cottonseed's weight is in the hull, or outer covering. Like the cottonseed meal, the hulls show up in animal feed. But they are also used in the production of fertilizer, garden mulch, and soil conditioner. And in some regions, cottonseed hulls are processed into oil-drilling mud, a sticky, industrial-strength type of Play-Doh that is used to plug leaks in oil wells.

And finally, a ton of cottonseed will contain about 150 pounds of "linters," which are tiny bits of cotton fuzz that are stuck to the seed after ginning. The oil mill scrapes off the tiny fuzzy bits with microscopic saws and turns them into big bundles of fuzz to be sold. The fuzz turns up again in throw pillows, automobile upholstery, mops, candlewicks, blankets, mattresses, twine, rugs, and medical supplies. Linters are also used in the production of cellulose and viscose, which turns up in toothbrushes, ballpoint pens, picnic cups, and almost any item made of hard plastic. The cellulose from the linters is also found in cheaper brands of ice cream, where it is used to improve texture and reduce ice crystals. Linters are also used in hot dog and sausage casings, as well as writing paper, and in most countries, paper currency. And for those with sensitive skin, an environmental conscience, or both, "tree-free" toilet paper made from cotton linters is now available. The toilet paper, according to entrepreneur Willy Paterson-Brown, is "reassuringly expensive."[10]

In October 1999, PCOM merged with the Yazoo Cotton Oil Mill and the new entity, the Plains Yazoo Cotton Oil Mill (PYCO), markets about one-third of the cottonseed oil produced in the United States.[11] The Plains Cooperative Mill in Lubbock is the world's largest cottonseed oil mill, receiving about 1,200 tons of seed per day from the region's gins, and churning out the makings for peanut butter, soap, and throw pillows.

The PYCO oil mills have quite a monopoly on acquiring seed from the region's gins, which would appear to give the farmers little power in marketing their seed. But the Shallowater gin, along with about 175 other gins across the South, own PYCO, and the Reinsches, of course, own a piece of the gin. The income from the world's largest oil mill, then, is paid to the region's gins, which in turn pass it through in dividends to growers like Nelson and Ruth.

S o, Nelson doesn't throw away his cottonseed anymore. Instead, he gets a tiny dividend every time city folk spread peanut butter on their toast.

While his seed is trucked to the oil mill, Nelson's baled cotton lint is trucked to the Farmer's Cooperative Compress (FCC) not far from the cottonseed mill. In earlier times, cotton was compressed here, to reduce the space the cotton occupied in the ships bound for export markets. Now, however, most cotton is compressed at the gin, yet the FCC retains its name. The FCC is the distribution and warehouse point for Nelson's cotton. The FCC stores and insures cotton until it is sold, and then ships it by rail or truck, and for exports, by ship, to its destination. Cotton bound for Chinese mills typically leaves the FCC by truck for Long Beach, California, where it is loaded onto ships bound for Shanghai or Guangzhou. The FCC handles over 15 percent of the Upland cotton grown in the United States each year, and it paid out more than $210 million in dividends to its members during the five years ending in 2007.[12]

Surprise: Nelson owns a piece of the Compress, too.

And there is one more thing. In Littlefield, a short drive through the emptiness from the Reinsch farm, smack in the middle of the cotton fields, the farmers have built a denim mill.[13] The farmers made a deal in 1988: They promised to grow the cotton and Levi-Strauss promised to buy the denim. The established textile industry scoffed, called the mill "the farmer plant," and refused to help. And the things that went wrong—from rattlesnakes burrowing in the denim, to denim of such poor quality it couldn't even be sold as "thirds," to month after month of returns from the meticulous Levi-Strauss inspectors, to trying to find a workforce in the Texas emptiness—did not bode well for the farmers' foray into the textile industry. But by 1998, the Littlefield denim plant was winning Levi-Strauss quality awards. The Littlefield mill had started out producing a basic blue denim, but by 2007 it was producing more than 200 styles of fabric.

By the time I first visited the denim mill in 2007, the mill had upgraded its technology six times, and now employed the most advanced Belgian looms in the world. In the endless quest to address the labor challenges of the region, the new technology allowed each worker to man 50 looms, from 20 just a few years ago. The competition in the global denim market was fierce: Between 1988 and 2007 the selling price of denim had fallen by a third, and every one of the mill's domestic customers had disappeared. While Levis once had four apparel factories within 200 miles of the Littlefield mill, today it has none, and so all of the mill's denim is exported. Yet the mill buys more than 1 million pounds of cotton per week from the region's farmers, and turns it into 68 million square yards of denim to be sold all over the world.

No More Handfuls

Once all of the cotton is in from the fields, it would seem, the farmer deserves a rest. The next step, however, marketing the cotton, takes the farmer out of his element and subjects him to vagaries every bit as cruel and unpredictable as the weather. Nelson remembers well the days of trying to sell his own cotton. He would take his neatly tied bales down to Avenue A in Lubbock, where the cotton buyers all had storefronts. The buyer would poke his hand right into the bale and pull out a big fistful, look it over and name a price, take it or leave it. Usually the farmers had to take it. The season's bills had to be paid, and it was risky for the farmer to hang onto his cotton in the hope that the price would go up. It was the fistfuls that bothered Nelson, still do, thinking back. At the end of the season, Nelson suspects, the cotton buyers down on Avenue A had their own bales to sell.

Most older farmers I talked to had a similar memory. After months of work starting in March, after the planting, weeding, spraying, and harvesting, everything came down to one day, one handful, one man at the cotton buyer's office. Many farmers—40 years later—remembered his name.

Ned Cobb remembered selling cotton, too, hitching up the mules and taking a bale into town. But he tried not to take his cotton right to the buyer. He let a white friend do that, as he found that this made a big difference in the price:

> [C]olored man's cotton weren't worth as much as white man's cotton less'n it come to the buyer in a white man's hands.[14]

If cotton farmers everywhere had a tough time marketing their cotton each fall, nowhere was it tougher than in west Texas, where the cotton had a reputation, mostly but not entirely deserved, for poor quality. For one thing, the west Texas cotton was short fibered, averaging less than one inch; and for another, the fiber was weak. The cotton that was best suited to surviving the west Texas wind, hail, and sand was not, to discerning buyers from the textile mills, very good cotton. Many domestic mills wouldn't touch west Texas cotton, which meant that most had to go for export. And when the cotton did compete, it was only because of its steeply discounted price. It was possible for the west Texas farmers to grow better cotton, but they had no incentive to do so because west Texas cotton was priced by its origin and not by its quality. Buyers simply assumed that the cotton was shorter and weaker than its competition.[15]

The virtuous circle was as effective in advancing cotton marketing as it was in advancing science. Clearly, banding together to improve the quality and reputation of the region's cotton made sense. The Plains Cotton Cooperative Association was formed in 1953 with a $12,000 loan. In 1958, a media blitz on 2,100 radio programs and 50 area newspapers was directed at the west Texas farmers. The farmers were bombarded with the *whys* and *hows* of producing better, stronger, longer cotton. As the quality of the cotton improved, the PCCA took on the task of proving it to the textile world.

Most important, the "grab-a-handful" method of classing cotton gave way, under USDA leadership, to high-volume instrumentation (HVI) testing, in which samples from each bale were graded by computer for color, leaf content, fineness (or *micronaire*), strength, and length at the USDA classing office in Lubbock.

I visited the Lubbock classing office during the peak of the harvest season in late 2007. The classing facility was running 24/7, and grading approximately 45,000 cotton samples per day. I watched tufts of cotton pass through a sensor, where the cotton fibers were measured and graded into one of 20 length categories. The sensor also measured length uniformity: A bale containing very short fibers and very long fibers is less valuable than a bale containing mostly middle-length fibers. The strength of the cotton fibers is then measured by the weight it takes to break them, and the bales are graded into one of five categories for both uniformity and strength. A third, computer-driven technology is used to measure micronaire, which affects the ability of the cotton to hold dyes as well as the yarn manufacturing speed. Reflective technology is then used to measure the color of the cotton (how white? how yellow? how tinged? how spotted?) and to grade the color into one of 25 categories. Finally, optical scanners measure the amount of "non-lint" matter, such as leaf bits and bark, in each sample.[16] After accounting for the various combinations, west Texas cotton can be graded into about a hundred different quality categories.

The virtuous circles linking Tech, Monsanto, and farmers continue the quest for this year's cotton to "outclass" last year's, and each year, west Texas cotton is a little longer, stronger, whiter, and cleaner.

Each of the 12 USDA cotton classing facilities in the United States sends a few samples by FedEx each day to the Memphis USDA cotton classing headquarters. There, specialists compare the classing results across facilities. The object of the game is to make sure that cotton classed in Lubbock would receive the same grades if it were classed in Corpus Christi or Birmingham, Alabama.

As I traveled around the world visiting textile mills during the past several years, cotton buyers everywhere sang the praises of the PCCA in Lubbock. They loved the west Texans as people, and found them, as I did, to be unfailingly gracious and brimming with hospitality. They loved the west Texans as business partners as well: the quiet integrity, the professionalism, and the handshake mentality. But the buyers especially loved the USDA classing system. Every textile mill manager I spoke with seemed to have a nightmare cotton story of bales that had arrived from China or India or Uzbekistan—bales that were opened to reveal one unhappy surprise or another. Someone had "grabbed a handful" and classed the cotton, but it was dirtier or dingier or weaker or shorter than it was supposed to be. That never happened, the mill managers told me, with American cotton.

The PCCA also took on the task of selling cotton. In the mid-1970s, the PCCA launched TELCOT, an electronic cotton exchange linking buyers and sellers. Today, electronic marketing takes place through a system called TheSeam, an Internet-based system that provides buyers from all over the world access to west Texas cotton, and allows textile mills to examine on the computer screen the classing results for millions of bales. This all beats hitching up the mule, or driving downtown to Avenue A.

PCCA also gives the farmers the option of not worrying about selling cotton at all. Many farmers, including Nelson, put their cotton into the PCCA's marketing pool. The pool advances some cash as soon as the cotton is ginned, and then pools the cotton with that of other growers to sell throughout the year. Farmers receive periodic payments as cotton is sold from the pools. It is a risk-sharing arrangement that leaves no big winners or losers, as all of the farmers in the pool are assured of receiving "average" prices. Today, all Nelson has to do to sell his cotton is to tell

Barbara Burleson at the Shallowater gin to "put it in the pool." The next day, he gets his first check, and three more will come along as the cotton is sold. All told, the PCCA markets about 18 percent of the American cotton crop, about half of that through pools.

All This and Subsidies, Too

As we have seen, throughout American history, U.S. cotton farmers have solidified their political influence to manage virtually every business risk to shape the world in front of them. This political influence is striking, both in its repetitive pattern of protection from market risks and in the evolution of the relationships among researchers, government programs, and farmer resourcefulness. While farmers have long wielded significant political power in the United States, it seems that recently their power has grown even as the number of farmers has dwindled, especially in the case of cotton farmers. Texas cotton farmers had both a kindred spirit and a staunch ally in George W. Bush, who spent long weekends on his ranch in Crawford, Texas. Crawford lies 300 miles southeast of the Reinsch farm, an interminable drive but only a brief psychic distance from Texas cotton country.

According to at least some observers, the definitive source of U.S. cotton farmers' comparative advantage is their ability to get help from friends in high places.[17] On a per-acre basis, subsidies paid to cotton farmers are 5 to 10 times as high as those for corn, soybeans, and wheat, and subsidies for cotton are also 3 to 6 times higher relative to production than are subsidies for soybeans and corn.[18] Even by the normally generous standards of U.S. farm policy, the 2002 Farm Bill went over the top for cotton.

Under the 2002 Farm Bill, cotton farmers received a direct payment of 6.66 cents per pound of cotton regardless of the market price. In addition, under the commodity loan program, farmers are guaranteed minimum payment at the "loan rate" that was fixed in the Farm Bill legislation at 52 cents per pound. Finally, growers are also entitled to *countercyclical payments*, which kick in when the farmer's income per pound from the direct payment plus the loan rate (or market price, if it is higher) is less than the target price of 72.24 cents per pound.[19] In total, the 2002 Farm Bill therefore brought the cotton farmer's income up to a minimum of 72.24 cents per pound, though the world price of cotton for the 2002–2007 period ranged between 44 and 61 cents. For the 10-year period ending in 2006, the average U.S. cotton farmer received approximately 30 percent of his or her income from federal subsidies, though in some years the share was as high as 45 percent.[20] Thanks largely to the generous government payments, average annual household income for cotton farmers was $142,463 in 2003—approximately double that of non-cotton farmers.[21]

The 2002 Farm Bill and its antecedents protected cotton farmers from a wide variety of other business risks that most other industries must bear on their own, including bad weather, bad credit, bad luck, and tough competition. The Crop Disaster Program reimburses farmers for losses due to unusual weather or related conditions, while Farm Loan Programs provide financing to farmers who are unable to get credit from private sources. In addition, for cotton farmers, over 60 percent of crop insurance premiums are paid by the federal government.[22] The government offers a variety of "Agricultural Trade and Aid" assistance programs to help farmers export cotton, including guarantees against customer default.

The Reinsch farm is located in Hockley County, Texas, which has a population of just 22,000. During the 2003–2006 period, subsidies to Hockley County cotton farmers totaled more than $70 million, though this figure does not include conservation program payments, payments to cotton buyers, subsidies on other crops, and other forms of indirect assistance.[23]

The 2002 Farm Bill expired at the end of 2007, and, as expiration neared, it seemed that the gravy train for U.S. cotton farmers was pulling away. Voices from across the political spectrum called for a radical reform of the subsidy system. Indeed, as of mid-2007, it seemed that the 2002 Farm Bill had not a friend left in the world outside of the relatively small number of large commodity farmers, and that the 2007 Bill—to be authorized for another five years—would be a different animal, indeed.

Critics from the left, such as former President Jimmy Carter and "pro-poor" groups such as Oxfam and Bread for the World, argued for scrapping the subsidy system, both on the grounds of its largesse to the rich and its detrimental effects on the poor.[24] On the right, the libertarian Cato Institute, the conservative Heritage Foundation, and even President Bush put forth proposals for radical change, arguing that, at the very least, subsidies should be limited for very high-income farmers.[25] Environmental groups also lobbied vigorously for change, opposing the generous support for what they argued was environmentally damaging industrial agriculture.

The United Nations and the World Bank echoed these demands, as did coalitions of groups involved in health and nutrition. The farm subsidy program primarily supported large commodity "row" crops such as cotton, wheat, corn, and soy, and critics argued that support should be shifted to encourage production and consumption of fruits and vegetables, which were not eligible for most subsidies.

Every major newspaper in the United States jumped on the anti–Farm Bill bandwagon in early 2008, and each, it seemed, had a descriptive insult for the expensive subsidy programs embedded in the Farm Bill. The *New York Times* ("disgraceful"), the *San Francisco Chronicle* ("foolery"), the *Boston Globe* ("a cynical mess"), and the *Wall Street Journal* ("a scam") were on the same page on the issue.

Perhaps, however, the bicoastal big-city journalists were out of touch with the views of middle America? It appeared that this was not the case. Even in the cities close to the corn and cotton belts, the sentiments opposed the generous subsidy programs. Editorialists from the *Dallas Morning News* ("misguided"), the *Des Moines Register* ("Veto, Mr. President"), and, my favorite, from the *Birmingham News* of Alabama ("a steaming pile of political manure") seemed to agree on the program's merit.

Yet Des Moines and Birmingham were still sizeable cities, and perhaps the support for reform was limited to urban areas. But, for better or worse, the urban and rural interests were aligned: The *Lincoln Star* (Nebraska), the *Sioux City Journal* (Iowa), and the *Waco Tribune* (Texas) added their own derogatory adjectives to those of hundreds other small-town editorials opposed to the Farm Bill's so-called corporate welfare system.[26] Even the writers who argued for maintaining generous support were opposed to the high income caps ($1.5 million for married couples, not including up to $1 million in non-farm income) for program eligibility. And even Lubbock's *Avalanche Journal* couldn't quite bring itself to push for government payments to millionaires; it went only as far as to say that a "Viable Farm Bill Is Vital for This Region."

Pretty Pigs

As Congress debated the 2007 Farm Bill well into the spring of 2008, President Bush gave up on his initiative for radical reforms but threatened his veto unless the bill contained at least significant limits on payments to high-income farmers. As it turned out, the threat was a fairly empty one: Bush's veto was overridden by a comfortable margin in May 2008.

Though the 2007 bill had nearly twice the budget as the 2002 bill, the major provisions for cotton growers were virtually unchanged from the 2002 version. All of the subsidies and safety nets remained in place, and an important additional safety net was added. Under the new ACRE program, growers can now opt for protection against declines in revenues from falling crop yields. Under the 2002 Farm Bill, the growers were protected only against falling prices.[27]

How did the Farm Bill achieve overwhelming support from Congress in the face of such widespread calls for reform? The trick, according to Senator Charles Grassley, was to "smear lipstick on a pig."[28] In exchange for leaving support for the large commodity crop farmers in place, House and Senate negotiators packaged support for nearly everyone else into the bill. There were new programs to help producers of peanuts, mohair, fruits, vegetables, honey, and sugar. There was help for racehorse owners in Kentucky and salmon fishermen in Oregon and for the red-cockaded woodpecker in Georgia. And there were billions for nutrition programs, foodstamps, and environmental programs. In the end, most of the 2007 Farm Bill had little to do with farming. The lipstick went on the pig district by district, and state by state, until lawmakers who opposed the bill were in a distinct minority.

"It's not very pretty," an agricultural lobbyist told me. "But that's how we do it."

No Lipstick for Africa

Of course, the billions of dollars channeled to U.S. cotton farmers by the U.S. government seems like a cruel joke to cotton farmers in the poorest countries of the world, where such sums are fantastic enough to lose meaning. In West Africa, cotton is a principal cash crop and export, and provides more than one-quarter of export earnings for 11 countries.[29] While decades behind the United States in technology, productivity, and yields, because of low-priced or even free family labor, African cotton farmers can produce cotton at significantly lower cost than Texas growers.[30] Though West Africa has many more players—18 million cotton farmers to America's 25,000—the U.S. government's deep pockets virtually assure the continued dominance of the United States. On average, U.S. cotton farms produce more than 400 times the cotton than the typical African farm.[31] Remarkably, U.S. government subsidies under the cotton program—approximately $2.7 billion in 2006—exceed the entire GNP of a number of the world's poorest cotton-producing countries, as well as America's entire USAID budget for the continent of Africa.[32] U.S. agricultural subsidies—much like U.S. military might—are simply a force too big for small countries to reckon with.

The primary effect of U.S. government subsidies is to increase the supply of cotton grown in the United States and therefore to decrease the world market price of cotton.[33] Declines in world cotton prices in turn lower the income of farmers outside of the United States. Virtually all studies on the topic have found that U.S. subsidies do indeed affect the world price of cotton, and that the removal of direct subsidies would increase the market price of cotton by anywhere from 3 to 15 percent. The removal of subsidies would also weaken U.S. cotton exports, to the advantage of producers elsewhere.[34]

In the summer of 2004, the United States agreed to put agricultural subsidies generally, and cotton subsidies in particular, on the table for the current round of trade negotiations. In 2008, with the trade negotiations still stalled, virtually no progress had been made on the issue. But even if U.S. subsidies to U.S. cotton growers are cut dramatically, it is not at all clear that substantial benefits will then accrue to farmers in the poorest countries of the world, where the subsidies may be the least of farmers' challenges.

Where Is the Competition?

So, 200 years after the story began, American cotton farmers still have the comparative advantage they seized in 1792. This dominance jumps out from any list, any table of data, any pie chart on the topic. In 200 years, the United States has rarely dropped below second place in production and export of cotton, and is the clear leader in yields, technology, farm income, and farm size.

Yet in trying to understand this comparative advantage, the pie charts only tease us, giving us nothing at all about the *how*. And even the textbooks cannot help, as they explain the idea, but not the reality, of comparative advantage in a global industry. And the idea, as far as the international business textbooks can take it, is almost circular (a country exports what it has a comparative advantage in; look at all those exports—must be comparative advantage). Even when the idea is amplified, we are still in a circle, as it helps not at all to say that U.S. growers produce more cheaply, or that they are more productive. The *how* is not in the data; it is embedded in the story.

How did they do it? And what can American cotton's story reveal about today's globalization debate?

In *The Lexus and the Olive Tree,* author Thomas Friedman speaks about the winners in globalization as both lions and gazelles. The gazelles win by running faster and smarter than the competition, but the lions win by catching and eating their prey. U.S. cotton growers are both gazelles and lions, and sometimes have taken the high road but other times have not. We see the gazelles in the farmers' entrepreneurial spirit and creativity—in how they squeeze income out of every step in the production chain, and feed cattle, fish, and finally people with their leftovers. This is a complex recycling and value creation that other cotton-producing countries can only dream about. We see the gazelles, too, in the research and scientific progress that freed Nelson Reinsch's children from the farm, and that allows him to take a nap after lunch. We see the gazelles in the cotton farmers' business practices in which the growers' ownership of the gin, the oil mill, the textile factories, and the Compress gives the farmers power in their battle against world markets, and ensures that all of the extra pennies so creatively squeezed out of the cotton business flow into the farmers' pockets. And finally, we see the gazelles in the relationships among farmers, universities, and the U.S. government.

But many see lions rather than gazelles in the political power of the cotton farmers, which has shifted risks from weather to prices onto the U.S. taxpayer. We also see lions in the long practice of dominating in one market in order to suppress another. Since the beginning, the U.S. growers have been avoiding the labor market. Yet at least for the first 150 years, cotton production was among the most labor-intensive industries in the country. Most of American cotton's history—from plantation slavery to sharecropping to company towns to Bracero workers—is about yet another creative way of avoiding having to find workers and pay the market wage. Suppressing the labor market has been a central *how* of U.S. dominance in the global cotton industry. And in suppressing the labor market, basic freedoms were denied to generations of people—slaves, sharecroppers, and migrant workers. It was not the perils of the labor market but the absence of the market that doomed these generations of workers.

The subsidies to cotton farmers that have in recent years attracted so much attention are everything recent critics have charged: way too big, way too unfair, and embarrassingly hypocritical when practiced by the world's self-proclaimed free trade champion. But they are also not the whole picture.

   Competing with Nelson Reinsch requires a systematized method of factory cotton production. But cotton factories require capital, and profitable factories of any kind require functioning markets and both technical and basic literacy, as well as at least a semblance of the virtuous circle of institutions that support not just agriculture but broader development. At the close of the twentieth century, many poor cotton producers lacked capital, working markets, literacy, or all three. And in spite of our intuition, it is far from clear that cheap labor is an advantage at all. Labor costs are low when people have no choices, and people who cannot read have few choices indeed. It is worth remembering that Ned Cobb stuck it out through sharecropping and boll weevils and all God's dangers and even the arrival of tractors. Cobb ultimately gave up only when the government introduced programs that required that he be able to read. Labor costs are low for people who cannot read, but people who cannot read can only do hand-to-hand combat with cotton's enemies: weather and insects and picking and weeding—all of the enemies against which Nelson Reinsch has sophisticated weapons with complicated instructions. While critics of U.S. agricultural policy are quick to point the finger at U.S. cotton subsidies as the source of America's advantage, the removal of the subsidies would do little—at least in the short term—to develop the literacy, property rights, commercial infrastructure, and scientific progress required to take on Nelson Reinsch in world markets.[35] Activists at Oxfam would do well to take on these causes as well.

Vicious Circles

If Nelson Reinsch is embedded in a system that protects and enriches him, cotton farmers in West Africa are embedded in a system that exposes and impoverishes them. According to Terry Townsend of ICAC, the state often controls the distribution of inputs to these farmers, and sometimes seeds and fertilizer come to the village and sometimes they do not. Most of the farmers are illiterate, and when they are blessed with pesticides or fertilizers, they often send their children barefoot down the rows with the toxic chemicals, or prepare food or carry drinking water with the same implements that are used to spread and carry the poison. The farmers rarely wear the protective gear recommended by the manufacturers of the chemicals, and pesticide-related health problems are epidemic. In Benin, dozens of deaths were attributed to pesticides that had been sprayed on cotton but then drifted over to the maize, which the villagers ate, and in

Burkina Faso half of the cotton farmers surveyed by one researcher had pesticide-related health problems.[36]

Even scientists cannot avoid value-laden descriptors of the African cotton farmers' battle. According to agricultural specialists, the cotton farms in the poorest countries have a four-stage life cycle: subsistence, exploitation, crisis, and disaster.[37] According to Townsend, each cotton-producing village has a leader to deal with the cotton buyers: The leader can typically add and subtract, but not read, write, or multiply. The concept of percentages, then, critical to a range of activities in selling and growing cotton, is as foreign as a mechanical cotton stripper.

Lapierre-Fortin spent 10 months with cotton growers in Burkina Faso.[38] Surprisingly, the farmers did not blame U.S. subsidies for their challenges. Indeed, the farmers were admiring and impressed with the logic of government support of cotton farmers. "We would like such help," the reaction seemed to be.

In their view, the challenges facing the cotton growers were not subsidies paid in America but instead were the myriad injustices much closer to home. The notion that the government could be on their side was a radical concept to the farmers, who often experienced the government and other institutions as the problem rather than the solution. The farmers experienced a corruption that sapped their spirit and their livelihood in virtually every aspect of their lives. Truck drivers needed to be bribed to pick up their cotton on time, lest it lose value sitting exposed to the elements. Once the cotton was on the truck, things were not much better: One study found that truck drivers on the main transport routes in West Africa were stopped for bribes and illegal tolls an average of 48 times per trip.[39] Graders needed to be bribed to grade the cotton correctly. When farmers became trapped in a cycle of debt, they had to sell their animals or equipment, and could not get credit the following year. Farmers waited and waited and waited to get paid for their cotton.

There are only two prices paid to farmers for their cotton in West Africa: the A price and the B price, and buyers decide which to pay by the grab-a-handful method that Nelson Reinsch remembers well but has not experienced in decades. *Misgrading* by unprofessional manual and visual inspectors is the rule, and, as a result, West African cotton suffers from the discrimination common in Lubbock a generation ago.[40] A prices and B prices are set once a year by the government and, in recent years, have averaged about half of the price for which the cotton is sold in the export

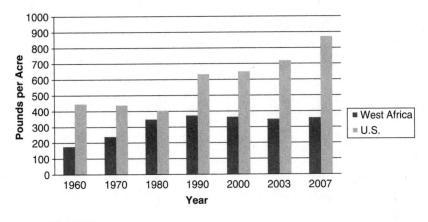

Source: UNCTAD.

Figure 4.3   West African vs. U.S. Cotton Yields

market.[41] In rough figures, then, if the international price of cotton is 50 cents per pound, West African farmers will receive 25 cents while U.S. farmers receive 72 cents per pound. Not only does this steep discounting impoverish the farmers and enrich the state-owned and private cotton traders, the exclusion from the market created by the A/B system gives the farmers no incentives to improve quality; all of the Eli Whitneys with better ideas have no reason to try. Cotton yields per acre in West Africa are barely half of those in the United States (see Figure 4.3).

While the PCCA (which is owned by the Texas farmers) is at work marketing the Reinsch cotton crop, most West African cotton is marketed by a handful of European companies that still enjoy the fruits of their colonial legacy. Indeed, all of the major cotton trading companies operating in West Africa are European, not African, and many have vertical monopoly power in ginning and other steps of the supply chain as well. Another set of monopolies supply inputs such as seed and fertilizer. Over and over again, with typical Texas understatement, farmers around Lubbock told me "the co-op's been very good to us." Over and over again, the institutions serving these purposes in West Africa are seen as the enemy: corrupt, inflexible, abusive, and opaque.[42]

For West African cotton farmers, then, the political and economic power balance between the farmers and the government and agricultural institutions has been and remains almost symmetrically inverted from that in the United States. While rich country subsidies clearly have a role to play in the farmers' difficulties, all God's dangers are quite a bit more complicated.

Too Poor to Pollute

The low labor costs that might give the poor farmers an advantage are in fact their undoing. For while there may be worse ways to make a living than to bend in the blistering sun all day, pinching worm eggs between your fingers, it is hard to imagine what they are. Yet if labor costs are low enough, it makes sense to hire worm-egg squishers rather than to battle the insects with more sophisticated methods. Or, as experts from the World Bank point out, apparently with a straight face: "Hand collection of pests is feasible only in countries with a plentiful supply of cheap labor."[43] Yet no matter how cheap and plentiful the egg squishers, it is difficult to imagine how they can have an advantage over Nelson's Texas Tech entomologists, his pesticides, his chemicals, and his machines. And if they cannot, then in the end the cheap and plentiful labor is the downfall, not the advantage, of Nelson's competition.

During the past several years, it seemed that there might be a silver lining in the cloud of poverty endemic to African cotton farmers. All of a sudden, a number of U.S. and European apparel companies began to request organic cotton from their suppliers. Marks and Spencer of the U.K., Levi-Strauss, Nike, and especially Patagonia all expressed an interest in sourcing organic cotton.

There are a handful of creative and contrary farmers growing organic cotton in west Texas, but they account for less than 1/3 of 1 percent of the cotton produced. ("It rounds up to zero," one conventional grower sniffed.) Kelly Pepper, Manager of the Texas Organic Cotton Marketing Cooperative, told me that organic farmers in the west Texas area numbered just a few dozen. Their motives varied: "We don't have any Greenpeace radicals," Pepper said, but some of the growers had an environmental conscience, some saw a market opportunity, and still others enjoyed the management challenge of keeping the cotton, weeds, and insects in a natural balance. Pepper himself had watched his father and other relatives die young of cancer or Parkinson's disease after a lifetime of applying agricultural chemicals. He does not believe the illnesses in his family were coincidence.

The organic growers in Texas have very few of the benefits of the virtuous circle. They do not use the chemical pesticides, defoliants, and

GM seed developed at Tech or Monsanto, and there are no well-funded experts to turn to for advice on the weed, weather, and insect challenges. Even with non-GM cotton-breeding techniques, cotton was bred to be compatible with the chemical inputs used in conventional farming, so organic farmers figure things out as they go. (It's "management-intensive," Pepper told me.) The organic cotton growers in west Texas are sometimes outside not just the virtuous circle but the social circles as well. In the tiny towns amid the cotton fields, the organic growers are talked about at the gin, at church, and even inside the family. ("They're growing boll weevils over on that farm.")

In organic cotton farming, the growers still face labor challenges. Organic growers must find workers to hand-hoe stubborn weeds, and to use mechanical methods of weed control. Pepper told me that organic growers may have just a two-to-three-day window to get control of weeds, whereas a conventional grower equipped with herbicides would enjoy a three-week window. Workers may also be required to inspect the fields for pests and respond with treatments of organic pesticides or beneficial insects. Without defoliants, nature, not the farmers, decides when the freeze will come, so labor requirements at harvest are unpredictable as well.

The growing demand for organic cotton seemed an opportunity made in heaven for many poor countries. Because even in the United States organic cotton farming was relatively labor intensive, the abundant and low-cost labor would give poor countries an advantage. More important, many farms in the poorest parts of the world were already organic. They had been, as one writer noted, "too poor to pollute."[44] The many de facto organic farmers had never used chemical pesticides because they couldn't afford them, and defoliants were not needed because the cotton had always been handpicked.

In yet another cruel irony, however, this opportunity, too, seems to have passed Africa by. While some fair trade programs have succeeded in developing the organic production of Africa's farmers, the majority of the world's organic cotton is from Turkey. The organic certification standards were written in Europe and the United States, and most de facto organic growers in Africa find it difficult to twist themselves into the rich country model of what an organic farmer should be. The growers cannot afford the fees to become certified, they cannot afford to meet the complicated certification requirements, and they cannot fill out the forms that even the Texas organic growers find intimidating.

Like Ned Cobb, the African growers know cotton farming. The rich world's paperwork is another challenge entirely.[45]

Bt Cotton Comes to China

In China, where the textile factories suck in more cotton than any country in the world, cotton production is much closer to Ned Cobb's world than to Nelson Reinsch's. In 2008, China was the world's largest cotton producer as well as consumer, but since the dismantling of the communes, virtually all of this production is at the level of the family, usually with an ox or maybe two, and about 10 acres, and typically no machines at all.

China was among the first developing countries to try the genetically engineered Bt seed, and adopted it on a large scale beginning in 1996. Hopes were high for the economic rewards and environmental benefits. One study found that before the adoption of Bt seed, the average Chinese farmer applied 20 chemical pesticide treatments per year, but within a few years of adopting Bt cotton, treatments had fallen to an average of just 6.6, and pesticide use by volume had fallen by over 70 percent.[46] This reduction in pesticide use led not only to environmental benefits but also to higher profits for the farmers. It seemed to be a case study on how poor countries could benefit from the science and technologies developed by the multinational corporations and universities in the West.

Shenghui Wang went to investigate this story as part of her doctoral research at Cornell University.[47] In 2004, she and a team of researchers traveled to China and interviewed nearly 500 cotton farmers. The happy story of Bt cotton in China disintegrated as Wang and her colleagues talked to the farmers.

The Bt seed had indeed been an effective weapon against one of cotton's most threatening natural enemies, the bollworm. Compared to the bollworm, many other pests—so-called "secondary pests"—were thought to be minor threats to the cotton plant. But as the Bt toxins did their damage to the bollworm in China, minor pests became major ones. In particular, Mirid insects—once kept in check by the pesticides targeted at the bollworm—now had free rein in the Chinese cotton fields.

Wang learned that because of the exploding secondary pest population, by 2004, China's Bt cotton farmers were spending 40 percent more on non-bollworm pesticides than their neighbors who grew conventional cotton. And the news got worse: Because Bt seed cost the farmers two to three times as much as conventional cottonseed, the Bt farmers were earning less than their conventional neighbors.

The environmental story was not much better. After bottoming out at 6 pesticide sprays per year in 1999, Wang found that by 2004 the pesticide applications for the Bt farmers averaged 18.2, nearly the same as the 20 applications used before the introduction of the Bt cotton. Neither the economic nor the environmental story was a happy one.

I spoke to Professor Per Pinstrup-Andersen, Wang's dissertation advisor at Cornell. He was and remains an optimist about the benefits of GM technology for developing countries, and he fully expected that Wang would find both increasing economic and environmental benefits for Chinese farmers. "When I saw her results, I said, 'This can't be,' and sent her back to go over the data again. But the results are very strong. There was a problem in China."

Why did a technology so economically successful in the United States (and at least arguably environmentally successful as well) fail to provide long-run benefits in China? Ned Cobb, I think, could answer. He'd say that without education and other elements of the virtuous circle, farmers are unlikely to understand the scientific complexity of introducing such technologies. Though Ned Cobb could not read or write, his biography shows a brilliant and intuitive understanding of nature's balance among plant, insect, and animal. But with sudden innovations such as Bt seed, this intuitive understanding, developed over a lifetime and the basis of a livelihood, no longer serves the farmer.

If Ned Cobb had been given Bt seed, it is difficult to imagine that this would be a gift rather than a curse. How would he know what other pests would emerge and how to fight them? How could he afford to plant a refuge crop when he was already on the edge? What if there is no one from Texas Tech around to explain how the new world works? What if there is no money or time to follow their directions, anyway?

Without the virtuous circle of education, public support, and proper training, technologies such as Bt provide further gains for the rich but can backfire on the poor. Indeed, without education and training, Wang and her co-authors concluded, technologies such as Bt cotton "may only serve to exacerbate problems associated with poverty and scarcity."[48]

Other researchers have also found that the GM technology so successful for U.S. growers has had mixed effects in developing countries. One team of researchers reviewing research to date found that in developing countries "the overall balance sheet, though promising, is mixed,"[49] and that the scientific merit of the technology is often compromised by weaknesses in politics and institutions. Reviewing results from Asia, Africa, and South America, Smale and her co-authors discuss a plethora of problems— unfamiliar to the growers in Lubbock—that compromise the promise of

GM technology: poor extension and farmer education, ill-functioning input systems and broken markets, and illegal and black-market seed. Some researchers estimate that half of the Bt seed planted in India is illegal. Extension services and technical support are absent for illegal seed, and yields are significantly lower.[50] While the scientific community is in general enthusiastic about the prospect for GM agriculture to improve both productivity and environmental profiles in the poorest countries, both access to and application of the technology remain significant challenges.[51]

While the virtuous circle connecting Monsanto, Tech, and the Lubbock growers has a good chance of staying one step ahead of the resistance of both weeds and insects to GM technology, each cotton-growing region has a unique ecology of weeds and pests, and resistance strategies that work in the United States cannot simply be exported to other countries, even if the farmers do have the capacity to implement evolving technical advice.[52] Most of the GM research has been targeted to the capital-intensive farming practices in wealthy countries, with relatively little directed to the unique circumstances of small farmers in poor countries. Because of the high degree of *agro-ecological specificity*, research done by universities and corporations in the wealthy countries has limited spillover potential for the poorest.[53]

Of course, we would expect that Monsanto would target its research dollars toward the wealthy countries. However, public sector support for agricultural research in poor countries is also weak. While traditional foreign-aid programs once targeted developing country agriculture, in recent years support for research directed at developing-country agriculture has fallen sharply.[54] In addition, research undertaken by the public sector is also heavily skewed toward wealthy countries. The World Bank reports that public agricultural research and development (as a percentage of agricultural GDP) in wealthy countries is more than four times as high as in poor countries.[55] In 2007, researchers reported that the fertilizer formulas being used in much of West Africa's cotton regions were more than 35 years old.[56] Poor countries simply do not have the equivalent of lifetime-loyal Texas Tech fans steering funding into cotton research.

The Worms Win

Though India and Pakistan are also large cotton producers, Nelson and Ruth Reinsch would also find very little that seems familiar on a South Asian cotton farm. Ned Cobb, again, would recognize almost everything:

the vise of the moneylender at 120 percent interest, the tiny number of acres, the illiteracy, the lack of government support or extension, the collapsed rural banking system, the backbreaking physical labor, and especially, life alone on the economic precipice, where little puffs of wind blow farmers right over the edge.

In 2001, for the first time in his life, Nelson Reinsch lost his entire cotton crop. It was June, the plants still young and tender, when a freak hailstorm showered icy bullets over the cotton fields around Lubbock. Nelson, ever the optimist, looked on the bright side. ("It melted. That'll be water for next year.") Nelson planted milo grain in the ravaged fields, which brought in some income to augment the government crop insurance and the disaster subsidy. In U.S. cotton farming, because of the variety of protections in place, disasters happen to cotton but not to people. Nelson Reinsch wasn't happy to lose his cotton, but he did not lose sleep and he did not miss a meal.

Disasters happen to people in other cotton-producing countries. A short time before Nelson Reinsch lost his cotton crop, more than 500 cotton farmers in the Andra Pradesh region of India committed suicide as worms ate the last of their cotton. Over the next six years, thousands more farmers would follow them.[57] The farmers could hear the worms chomping, with a sickening click-click sound that kept the villagers awake all night. Dealers had "furnished" the farmers with pesticides at 36 percent interest, but it was the wrong pesticide with the wrong directions, and the farmers couldn't read anyway. There was no government extension service to give the right advice, no federal financing to replace the moneylender, no public school where the farmers could learn to read, and, in the end, no way out. The pesticides so useless on the worms worked quickly as poison, and hundreds of farmers dropped twitching to the ground in the middle of the cotton fields. All of these cheap and plentiful people, working all day in the Andra Pradesh sun, just couldn't squish the worms quickly enough. They never had a chance against Nelson Reinsch, the USDA, and Texas Tech.

PART II

PART II

MADE IN CHINA

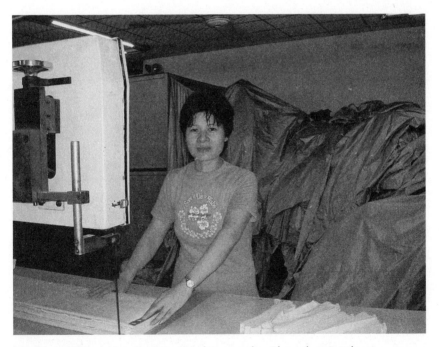

He Yuan Zhi at Her Cutting Machine at the Shanghai Brightness Factory. (Author's Photo.)

The Author with Tao Yong Fang, Manager of the Shanghai Number 36 Mill. (Author's Photo.)

COTTON COMES TO CHINA

N elson Reinsch's cotton leaves the Compress in Lubbock and turns left toward China. Usually by truck, but sometimes by train, the cotton heads through the blank space of west Texas, New Mexico, and Nevada, stopping finally at the Pacific Ocean in Long Beach, California. The cotton boards a ship and keeps going west, arriving a few days later at the port in Shanghai, and into the deafening pulse of China's weird new capitalism. Here, the Reinsch cotton is spun into yarn, knitted into cloth, cut into pieces, and finally sewn into a T-shirt. A "Made in China" label will be tacked to the collar. Thus transformed, the Texas cotton will return to America.[1]

Nelson and Ruth's son, Lamar, thinks it is funny that he never thought about the Reinsch cotton actually *going* to China. In fact, even as a professor in a business school, Lamar's cotton consciousness ended at the gin in Shallowater. He never thought about what happened next, where the cotton went, or how it got there. But there is a low buzz about China in Lamar's childhood memories. At the gin, or at church, or at the dinner table, China was one of the things grownups talked about, one of the topics that would make his parents sigh and shake their heads. To a child, the China conversations were like the weather conversations, or the cotton price conversations. China, cotton prices, weather: the wildcards in the life of a Texas cotton farmer. Lamar remembers only that China mattered.

China matters even more today. During the past several years, I found that it was impossible to get more than one or two minutes into a cotton conversation anywhere in the world before someone mentioned China and heads began to shake. Today, China is not only the largest buyer of American cotton, it is also projected to soon produce more than 40 percent of the world's cotton textiles.[2] Cotton was America's eighth largest export to China in 2007, and U.S. cotton exports to China more than tripled between 2000 and 2007. In a circular linkage that ebbs and flows (but mostly grows), demand by Americans for cheap clothing from China leads to demand from China for cotton from America.

As the Texas cotton is hoisted from the ship in Shanghai, it enters not just a new country but a new global industry. The production of textiles and apparel is almost as old as agriculture, and, since the beginning, agriculture and textiles have been linked: Whether wool, silk, flax, or cotton, whatever humans have spun or woven had to first be grown. Today, however, the agricultural and industrial chapters in a T-shirt's life often take place on different continents. It takes a little over a third of a pound of cotton lint to produce a T-shirt, maybe 15 cents' worth, so an acre of west Texas farmland can produce about 1,200 T-shirts each year. In a good season, then, Nelson could produce enough cotton for over a million T-shirts, and, as we have seen, he does this by supervising not people but land, capital, and technology. But to become a T-shirt, the cotton requires workers: cutters, spinners, knitters, and stitchers. While the labor component of American cotton production is almost too small to be measured, labor still accounts for more than half of the value added in the production of apparel. So Nelson's cotton travels to China, to where the people are.

Travelers who wistfully bemoan the homogenization of the world today will feel better if they travel between Lubbock and Shanghai. When I first traveled to Lubbock in 2000, the city had yet to open its first Starbucks, and I could buy ostrich leather cowboy boots but not a cappuccino. At the same time in Shanghai, Starbucks appeared everywhere, but so, too, did exotic goods such as ground rhino horn and bear bile. Today, globalization has brought the cities a bit closer together: There is now Texas-style barbeque in Shanghai (it's not great) and plenty of Chinese food (also not great) in Lubbock. Within a two-week period in

October 2004, both Shanghai and Lubbock got their first Hooters restaurants. Yet while cultures may be converging in Paris and New York, or L.A. and Hong Kong, it will likely be a while before one can buy ostrich leather boots in Shanghai or ground rhino horn in Lubbock. Physically, culturally, and temperamentally, the cities are planets apart. Yet the cotton textile industry is as important to Shanghai as the cotton agricultural industry is to Lubbock, so the very different cities are bound together by soft cotton fiber, and each city keeps a constant watch on the other.

The cities have been linked together by cotton fiber for nearly a century, but evolution in Lubbock has taken place alongside revolution in Shanghai. In July 1921, when the Texas cotton stood broiling in the first summer of Nelson Reinsch's life, before there really was a Lubbock, the Chinese Communist Party (CCP) was founded in a Shanghai schoolhouse. At this point, nearly half of the factory workers in Shanghai were employed in the cotton mills, and whatever labor tensions simmered in China boiled over in the Shanghai mills.[4] Throughout the 1920s, igniting events in the textile mills—beatings, wage cuts, murders—spilled up and down China's coast, mobilizing workers and paralyzing industry.[5] Labor activism in 1920s China was not for the weak of heart: As the workers stood up, the army squashed them, and many strike leaders in the textile industry were publicly beheaded as a lesson to others.

But as Shanghai's cotton textile industry bred the labor revolutionaries, it also generated the lavish wealth that transformed Shanghai into an X-rated Disneyland for the new industrialists. As cotton agriculture took hold in west Texas, Shanghai became known for its glittering and seamy decadence. The city offered the new industrialists opium dens, "singsong houses," and amusements for any appetite. And though it is not at all clear who counted or how, Shanghai in the 1930s reportedly had more prostitutes per capita than any city in the world.[6] Perhaps most illustrative of Shanghai during this period were the "pleasure palaces" to be found lining the main roads of the International Settlement. A wide-eyed American visitor remembers the Great World Pleasure Palace this way:

> On the first floor were gaming tables, singsong girls, magicians, pick-pockets, slot machines, fireworks, bird cages, fans, stick incense, acrobats and ginger. One flight up were ... actors, crickets and cages, pimps, midwives, barbers, and earwax extractors. The third floor had jugglers, herb medicines, ice cream parlors, photographers, a new bevy of girls, their high collared gowns slit to reveal their hips, and (as a) novelty, several rows of exposed (Western)

toilets. The fourth floor had shooting galleries, fan-tan tables, ... massage benches, ... dried fish and intestines, and dance platforms ... the fifth floor featured girls with dresses slit to the armpits, a stuffed whale, story tellers, balloons, peep shows, masks, a mirror maze, two love letter booths with scribes who guaranteed results ... and a temple filled with ferocious gods. On the top floor and roof of that house of multiple joys a jumble of tightrope walkers slithered back and forth, and there were seesaws, Chinese checkers, mahjongg, ... firecrackers, lottery tickets, and marriage brokers.[7]

With a 12-hour workday and often just two holidays per year, the cotton mill workers lacked both the price of admission and the time to visit this multistoried wonder. So, as the divide between labor and capital yawned wider, the Communists gradually and secretly infiltrated the cotton mills, where thousands of workers were locked in a steamy hell, ripening for revolution. In 1949, when Nelson's children were young and the Mexican migrants were still crawling through his fields, the Communists drove the mill owners from Shanghai, closed the pleasure palaces, and seized the factories for the people. Women cotton mill workers alone comprised more than one-third of the infamous Shanghai proletariat.[8]

And in the 1960s, as Nelson's sons rode the cotton trailer with their pitchforks, Mao Zedong and his Red Guards went mad in the Cultural Revolution, terrorizing the management of the spinning and weaving factories, forcing the lucky managers to confess to capitalist crimes, the less lucky to be jailed, and the least lucky to be executed or face starvation in the countryside. And finally, in the late 1970s, as Nelson's module builder freed his children from the farm, China reopened its door to the world. Shanghai grandparents, after a 30-year break, tasted chocolate and coffee again, and Shanghai parents tasted them for the first time. The blinding neon lights returned to Nanjing Road, the Great World Pleasure Palace was turned into a G-rated shopping mall, and China began to sell T-shirts to Americans.

Through all of the revolutions—Nationalist, Communist, Cultural, and now Capitalist—the cotton spindles have clattered on, an unbroken thread through the tumultuous times.

Comparatively speaking, things have been very quiet in Lubbock.

"Come to China," Patrick Xu told me when we first met in Washington. "I'll show you everything." In the spring of 2000, a few months after leaving Lubbock, I took Patrick up on his offer. During the next eight years, I returned a number of times. Like any frequent visitor to China, my most significant impression of the country is one of frenetic change: promising change, unsettling change, but most of all accelerating change. Whenever I returned to Lubbock, the terrain was pretty much as I had left it. This was not the case when I returned to China.

The Chinese Wall

After the first edition of this book was published in 2005, some of the most common questions I heard from readers were about how easy (or difficult) it had been for me to gain access to Chinese factories. And when I did visit a factory, readers wondered, how did I know whether I was seeing reality or a seeing a show? Would not the real conditions in the factories be kept hidden from visitors?

It is not hard to understand readers' reservations. Even people who have spent their careers in China are often confounded by various forms of secrecy in both business practices and public policy. China of course still maintains significant restrictions on freedom of the press as well as freedom of expression, and consistently ranks low on various measures of transparency.[9] The Communist Party excels at the control of information, in ways big and small, and censorship of all manner of inconvenient truths is the rule rather than the exception. How, in such an environment, could a professor from America expect to see the truth?

Yet, during the 2000–2006 period, I found that access to factories was easy to arrange and that both managers and workers were welcoming and forthcoming. Unfortunately, this changed somewhat after the first edition of this book was translated into Chinese in 2006. My reception changed, even though most readers found my treatment of China to have erred, if anything, on the side of the sympathetic. In retrospect, I see that my initial easy access to factories, workers, and managers was the result of the fact that I was both a Professor and a Nobody.

China has a centuries-old tradition of hospitality, even for Nobodies, and managers and workers during the 2000–2006 period were always generous with their time and insights. Chinese culture also has a deep respect for education, so I noticed that the fact that I was a Professor seemed to open doors as well.

After the first edition of the book was published in Chinese, however, I was no longer a Nobody and a Professor: I had instead become a Writer. When I asked to return to the two factories that I had discussed in the book, my requests were politely denied. Now that I had written a book, I was told, speaking to me could have negative consequences. "Things are somewhat complicated," one note read. "Please understand."

Alexandra Harney, the former *Financial Times* reporter, had similar difficulties in her role as a journalist. However, when Harney took a leave of absence from her job at the *FT* and accepted an academic post in Hong Kong, her access was immediately eased and she was able to complete her book, *The China Price*.

Interestingly, my experience in China as both a Nobody and a Writer was in sharp contrast to my experience in Texas and Washington. The hospitality in Lubbock is Texas-sized for everyone: Writers, Professors, Nobodies, and Somebodies. ("Well, if anybody is going to take the time to come all the way down here to see us, the least we can do is show them around," John Johnson said to me.) In Washington, life is a challenge for Nobodies, because while many people I contacted were gracious, many others had something more important to do than return a professor's phone calls. Once I was a writer, however, getting Washington to return phone calls was a piece of cake: Everyone wanted to be in the book. (After I spoke with one relatively powerful Washington type, a mutual acquaintance warned me, "You'd better put him in the book. Or else he'll throw a fit.") I was fascinated by the opposing dynamic: In Washington, authors are courted, and in China they are still feared.

Yet, during the past several years I have been able to continue to visit many modern, privately owned textile and apparel factories in China. Sensitivities seem to be raised only in traditional state-owned firms, and among older managers. However, because I was unable to return to the Shanghai Number 36 Mill or the Shanghai Brightness Garment factory after 2006, in the updates on these factories I have relied on secondary sources as well as my contacts in China.

Shanghai Number 36 Cotton Yarn Factory

The Shanghai Number 36 Cotton Yarn Factory is on the far-eastern outskirts of the city, reached by a one-hour drive through a crowded landscape that manages to be colorfully bleak. While the drive to the Reinsch farm is a journey through nothingness, the drive to the cotton yarn factory is a journey through an impossibly crowded jumble of alleys and high-rises, shacks and workshops, bakeries and tea shops, bicycles and pushcarts, water buffaloes and chickens. Mostly, however, southeastern China is a giant factory floor. Though some factories are new and gleaming, many are ramshackle and dusty workshops making things like hose fittings, engine parts, shoes, umbrellas, bicycles, toys, and socks.

Down a bumpy, unpaved road where people cook on the sidewalks and the buildings look close to collapsing, a quick left turn leads to a jumble of buildings. To the visitor who cannot read Chinese there is no hint at all about the purpose of the buildings until one arrives at a loading dock. There, in stacks perhaps 30 feet high, sit bales of Texas cotton.

Stepping into the Number 36 Cotton Yarn Factory for the first time was more than a sensory assault. The noise is a metal blanket, a deafening clatter of real machines, rather than the electronic buzzing or beeping emitted by factories in America. The metal noise blanket smothers not only conversation but thinking as well. Everyone and everything in the factory wears a light dusting of cotton flurries. For breathing, there is not air, but dusty steam, as the factory is kept moist to reduce the incidence of broken yarn. Perhaps the worst sensory assault, because there is no reason for it, is the color inside this factory. It might be titled Communist Green, and it is everywhere. I kept looking back at the walls to make sure that the color was really there: It was ugly enough to be astonishing. But to compensate for the awful color and deafening noise there is the feel and smell of the cotton itself. As the cotton is transformed from plant into yarn, it becomes softer and softer—impossible not to touch—and the musty-sweet smell of the cotton and yarn is comforting and mildly addictive. Coming from Texas, Shanghai smells foreign: green tea, frying dumplings, hairy crabs. But here in the factory, Shanghai smells like the Shallowater cotton gin.

The word *factory* conjures up an image of linear assembly, one thing attaching to another and another until an end product, a collection of parts made into a whole, appears at the end of the line. But nothing is assembled in the production of cotton yarn, and nothing is linear, either. The process is a transformation rather than an assembly, and almost every stage of the process is circular rather than linear: winding, twisting, spinning, coiling.

The cotton bales, still speckled with Texas leaf bits and rabbit fur, are hacked open, and the contents are sucked into a French-made vacuum cleaner. The vacuum cleaner's tubes are clear Plexiglas, and the clumps break up and whoosh through the tubes to clean whatever bits of Texas dirt and rabbit were left behind by the gin in Shallowater. Whereas the cotton had to be compressed to a brick for shipping, now it must be blown apart into a cloud in preparation for spinning. After it is blown apart, it is smoothed into a soft flat blanket. The blanket is a sheet of fluff, with soft tufts pointing in every direction. Next, the cotton is carded, tiny wire teeth forcing the fluff to lie down flat and face its fibers in the same direction. The now-flat blanket is drawn into a snowy rope perhaps an inch in diameter, called a *sliver* (pronounced with a long *i*).

The slivers are but a brief moment in the transformation from Texas plant to Chinese yarn, but for me they were the best part of the factory. The slivers are so transparent and gossamer that they are almost not there, like ghosts in a children's cartoon, and they are impossibly soft. My sensory experience in the factory was complete: I could not wait to escape the metal noise blanket and the appalling Communist Green walls, but I wanted to take the smell and the slivers back home with me to Washington.

The slivers are coiled around and around into tall metal cans, until they mound over the top like ropes of cotton candy. The ropes are then fed into the spindles and are twisted into yarn. In the final circular process, the yarn is wound onto bobbins, leaving a spool of yarn the size and shape of a motel ice bucket.

Supervising all of this circular motion was Tao Yong Fang, manager of the Number 36 factory. Tao stands not much taller than Nelson Reinsch's belt buckle, and she is so slight that she looks as if she could be picked up by a west Texas windstorm. But Tao walked and talked at double speed while seeing everything and knowing everyone in the factory.

The Number 36 Cotton Yarn Factory was built in 1944, five years before all factories were seized in the Communist Revolution. While much of China's textile industry has been privatized to some degree since the 1980s, the Number 36 factory remained in 2008 a classic Chinese state-owned enterprise (SOE), though it has recently put toes in the capitalist waters by entering into a joint venture with a Hong Kong firm. When Tao was assigned to the Number 36 mill in 1983, she did not move so quickly. Tao, the workers, and the factory itself were cogs in the wheel of China's central economic planning machine, with no room at all for initiative, no reason to be in a hurry. Well into the 1980s, the central planners delivered set quantities of cotton bales, machinery, and factory workers to the doorstep, and came back later to collect the production quota of cotton yarn.

Americans, and now Russians and Slovaks and Chinese, disdain such central planning for its inefficiencies. A system that ignores market signals, that provides no incentives, and that subsidizes losers cannot be efficient in producing goods and services. Central planners will produce the wrong goods, use the wrong inputs, set the wrong prices, hire the wrong people, and ultimately produce shoddy products, and not enough of them, anyway. But to meet Tao in the Number 36 factory was to realize that the real tragedy of central planning lies not in its inefficiency but in its crushing of the intellect, in 20 years of Tao's energy and intelligence laid to waste. For 35 years, the spindles in the Number 36 mill clattered, and no one working in the mill had to decide anything. So, today, there is determination but bewilderment as the managers of the Number 36 mill face the basic questions of running a business rather than turning a cog: what to produce, where to sell, whom to hire, what to pay?

In 2008, I learned that Tao had recently left the Number 36 mill and had gone to work for "a big private company." In this move, Tao had plenty of company. In the decade ending in 2004, the percentage of urban workers employed by SOEs fell by more than half, while the share employed by private companies quintupled.[10] Many industry experts with whom I spoke in 2008 viewed the state-owned Number 36 mill as a relic whose days were numbered.

The Shanghai Brightness Number 3 Garment Factory

On the opposite side of Shanghai's sprawl is another clump of buildings surrounded by farms. From the outside, the factory looks like a rural schoolhouse. On the inside, the Reinsch cotton is again transformed, this time from yarn into clothing.

The bucket-shaped spools of yarn are unloaded from a truck and placed on a knitting machine. As draping folds of fabric slowly and rhythmically fall from the machine, a lone inspector facing a large mirror simultaneously eyes both sides of the fabric for defects. On the second floor of the factory, the fabric is cut into pieces: sleeves, fronts, backs, and collars. In the United States, T-shirt pieces are cut largely without human interference, in a process that involves lasers, software, and a great deal of capital. At Shanghai Brightness, however, cutting is a peopled process, a bustle of workers manning big saws, little saws, and just plain scissors. The cut fabric pieces are piled into plastic laundry baskets and ferried to the sewing room.

In the production of T-shirts and other apparel, it is the sewing stage that has been most difficult to mechanize. Almost every other stage of apparel production has gradually replaced labor with capital, in a trend that mirrors cotton production in the United States. But despite millions of dollars in research in mechanization, people are still required to piece together fabric and feed it into sewing machines. The sewing stage of a T-shirt's life is also unique because it is sewing—not cotton farming, yarn spinning, or fabric knitting—that is most often associated with the evils of the sweatshop.

While both the Lubbock cotton farm and the Chinese textile mill had been completely foreign experiences for me, when I first walked into the sewing room at Shanghai Brightness I found an oddly familiar sight. Approximately 70 women were lined up in rows, each sitting at a sewing machine. It was relatively quiet, and on this sunny spring day the room was bright. Each woman performed just one operation, over and over again: sleeves, side seams, collars, or hems. At each worker's side is a plastic laundry basket, which the worker gradually fills as she completes her designated operations. When the basket is full, it is passed to the worker behind for the next operation. It only took a minute for me to realize what the setting reminded me of: Our Lady of Bethlehem Academy, La Grange, Illinois, 1969, seventh grade. We were all girls, lined up neatly in rows. We were doing what we were told, over and over again, and we were quiet. It is not that the experience was awful, far from it. But we watched the clock obsessively, waiting for recess. When we looked up, we saw a large crucifix and Sister Mary Karen's stern glare, so we usually looked back down. When the women at Shanghai Brightness look up, they see a sign on the wall:

Quality Has 3 Enemies: Broken Thread, Dirt, Needle Pieces

Then they look back down and continue working, waiting for recess, too.

As I visited cotton farms and textile mills during the 2000–2008 period, the technological advances seemed to be taking place before my eyes. Each time I returned, there had been another leap forward in the quest to produce better, faster, and cheaper cotton fiber, yarn, and fabric. Yet the garment stage of production has changed very little over the years, and the sewing factories that I visited in 2008 used manufacturing processes that looked pretty much like those I had seen in 2000: In China and around the world, stitching a T-shirt still involves a young woman and her sewing machine.

Shanghai Brightness was founded in the mid-1980s as a Town and Village Enterprise collective owned by the local government. Like Tao Yong Fang, Su Qin, the company's director, gained his early experience as a cog in the central planning wheel, assigned right out of school in 1976 to work in a state-owned garment factory. Also like Tao, he is gradually coming to terms with markets. Today, he has no guaranteed customers; instead he competes with over 11,000 T-shirt manufacturers in China alone, each trying to meet the relentlessly high standards of quality, delivery, service, and price in the international markets. Su does not remember any of these issues from his days in the state-owned garment factory, where he supervised the production of the utilitarian Mao-style jackets and trousers. He remembers no discussions at all about broken thread, dirt, or needle pieces. But today the T-shirts are commodities, and such details mean everything. Su remembers how surprised he was when he first heard a customer complain about needle pieces. But now Su has a metal detector, and every article of clothing passes through the detector on its way to the truck. Su's efforts are paying off. During the past several years he has expanded from one factory to seven and has more than tripled the number of employees. When I went back to visit Shanghai Brightness in 2003, Su had left T-shirts behind and moved up the value chain into high-end cotton knit children's wear. By 2008, Shanghai Brightness was operating eight factories, and employed 2,400 workers. The firm had again moved up the value chain and was producing apparel for U.S. major league baseball teams and for the Walt Disney company.

Shanghai Brightness funnels its knitted apparel to Shanghai Knitwear, the mammoth state-owned apparel export–import company that occupies the intermediary's place between Chinese producers and American importers. Shanghai Knitwear maintains a secure spot as one of China's top 100 exporters, and is among the top exporters of knit clothing in the country.[11] In 2007, China shipped nearly 365 million cotton knit shirts to the United States.[12]

Today, China dominates the global textile and apparel industries as the United States dominates the world cotton markets. In 1993, China became the world's largest exporter of apparel, a position it has held every year since.[13] Chinese apparel has significant markets in North America, Europe, and Japan, and Americans purchase approximately 1 billion

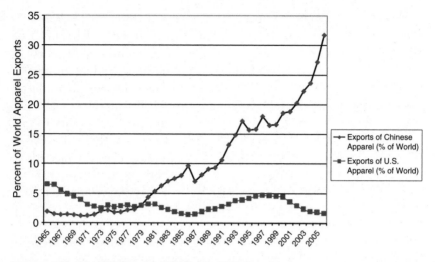

Source: UN COMTRADE, 84 (Clothing), SITC Rev. 2.

Figure 5.1   Chinese and U.S. Apparel Exports (as % of World Apparel Exports), 1965–2006

garments made in China each year, four for every U.S. citizen.[14] Since 1980, Chinese apparel exports have grown at an average annual rate of 30 percent, more than six times the rate of growth in merchandise trade.[15] By 2007, China's share of world apparel exports was approximately 30 percent (see Figure 5.1). Though the economic downturn that began in 2008 has affected Chinese producers, by most measures—production, exports, employment, or growth—China's textile-and-apparel complex leads this global industry today.

Yet as Americans snap up the cheap T-shirts along the beach, there is uneasiness in the United States about China's dominance in the labor-intensive textile and apparel industries. In a one-party state, where information is controlled, how can consumers or anyone else really know what is going on behind the factory gates? In her 2008 book, *The China Price*, Alexandra Harney argues that relentless pressure on costs has led to widespread cheating and deception in China's garment industry. The sweatshops, Harney contends, are skillfully and creatively hidden.

Could it be then that China's victory in this industry is really a failure? A failure for U.S. trade policy, a failure for American workers, and a failure especially for Chinese workers, who toil in poor conditions for pitiful wages in a quest to produce the cheapest shirts? In *The Race to the Bottom*, Alan Tonelson argues that the enormous "surplus" of labor in China imperils workers worldwide, as international competition puts incessant downward pressure on wages and working conditions, leading the apparel and textile industries to favor the cheapest and most Draconian producers who remain hidden behind the Chinese wall. If the means to victory in this industry are to provide the lowest wages, the poorest conditions, and the most restrictive regimes to apparel producers—all behind a veil of secrecy—then isn't the victory hollow at best? And does the race to the bottom *have* a bottom, or will the seemingly infinite surplus of unskilled workers in China lead to an incessant downward spiral into the depths of a Charles Dickens novel?

The "sweatshop" stories pour out of China almost as fast as the T-shirts, each more wrenching than the last. For example, the National Labor Committee found that apparel workers in China were:

> young women forced to work seven days a week, 12 hours a day, earning as little as 12 to 18 cents an hour with no benefits, housed in cramped, dirty rooms, fed on thin rice gruel, stripped of their legal rights, under constant surveillance and intimidation—really just one step from indentured servitude. . . . [16]

Globalization's critics continue to charge that the price of cheap T-shirts is high indeed. Sweatshops spawned by global capitalism exploit the poor and powerless, forcing people without alternatives to work in prison-like conditions for subsistence pay. The factory villages also destroy traditional family structures and cultures, and weaken indigenous agriculture. The powerless workers endure threats to their health and safety, as well as widespread cheating on payday.

As labor activists denounce the race to the bottom in wages and working conditions, environmental activists argue that the race is simultaneously destroying the environment. According to this argument, the incessant pressure to cut costs leads manufacturers to dump toxins into the air and water rather than to incur the costs of clean technology or compliance with regulations. The environmental catastrophe stories coming from China are every bit as sobering as the sweatshop stories. Of the 20 cities in the world with the highest levels of air pollution, 16 are in China, and the majority of the water in the country's largest river systems is unsuitable for human contact. [17]

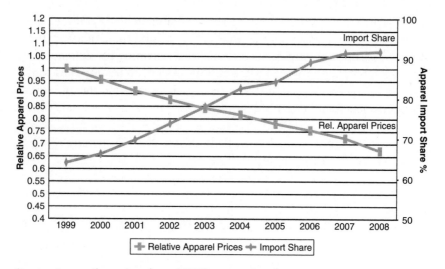

Source: Import share data from OTEXA; price data from BLS.

Figure 5.2   U.S. Apparel Prices vs. Import Share*

*Relative apparel prices computed by adjusting changes in apparel prices for changes in the CPI. 2008 data are annualized based on first half of year.

As U.S. apparel manufacturing has disappeared and imports have soared, the price of clothing in the United States has fallen markedly (Figure 5.2). Indeed, when I returned in 2008 to the same Walgreen's store where I had purchased my T-shirt for $6.00, I found that the store was selling T-shirts at 4 for $10. However, critics claim, the cheaper and cheaper T-shirts from China are a victory for U.S. consumers and for corporate profits, but a failure for workers and for the planet. To free trade advocates, the clothing flowing into U.S. ports are evidence that the system is working; but to critics, the swells illustrate what is wrong rather than what is right with global capitalism.

But whether we view China's dominance in textiles and apparel as a failure or victory, China's position at the top is strikingly different from the dominance of U.S. cotton producers. While U.S. cotton growers have held their position for 200 years, experience suggests that dominance in the textile and apparel industries has historically been a fleeting moment, a brief stop in the race to the bottom in this intensely competitive industry. To understand China's victory in the race today, to understand why American cotton travels so far to become a T-shirt, and ultimately to decide whether the race to the bottom (or perhaps the top) is a good thing or a bad thing, something to be stopped or facilitated, let us examine the course of the race itself: Where did it start? Where does it end? What happens to the winners and losers? And what about the air, the water, and the millions of young women eating thin rice gruel?

THE LONG RACE TO THE BOTTOM

Inventive Brits versus Thrifty Chinamen

The gaping divide between the poor sweatshop workers of the East and the rich consumers of the West is a relatively recent phenomenon. Kenneth Pomeranz has convincingly shown that until at least 1750, China rivaled Europe in virtually all measures of well-being and development.[1] Meticulously examining data ranging from life expectancy to technological development, to consumption of sugar and cloth, to the sophistication of markets, Pomeranz finds that China, if anything, was more favorably positioned for industrial development than even the most advanced regions of Europe until the middle of the eighteenth century. Early travelers to China agreed, finding the country superior to Europe in prosperity, politics, and art.[2] But though they may have been evenly matched at the starting line, Europe took a great leap forward in the late 1700s. Though scholars continue to debate the underlying causes of what Pomeranz has called "The Great Divergence" that occurred at this time, there is no debate that Europe's leap forward began with the Industrial Revolution, and the Industrial Revolution in turn was ignited by cotton textile factories that clothed much of the world in cheap, serviceable cotton garments that were similar in function though not in form to today's cotton T-shirts.

In China, most early textile production took place at the level of the family. Families were generally self-sufficient in textiles and clothing, and each phase of the process—spinning, weaving, cutting, and sewing—took place at home. In contrast, particularly in England, textile production by the 1700s had become at least somewhat specialized. While cotton and wool spinning remained auxiliary home industries, weaving in Britain gradually became a cottage industry. The "putting-out" system evolved wherein families would "put out" the yarn they had spun to professionals for weaving. A British visitor to China in the 1850s marveled at the self-sufficiency of the "thrifty Chinamen" and the ability of the household to engage in all phases of production:

> [A]ll hands in the farmhouse, young and old together, turn to carding, spinning and weaving this cotton; and out of homespun stuff, a heavy and durable material...they clothe themselves, and the surplus they carry to the nearest town.... It is, perhaps, characteristic of China alone, of all countries in the world, that the loom is to be found in every well-conditioned homestead. The people of all other nations at that point stop short, sending the yarn to the professional weaver to be made into cloth. It was reserved for the thrifty Chinaman to carry the thing out to perfection. He not only cards and spins his cotton, but he weaves it himself, with the help of his wives and daughters.[3]

The writer, marveling at the self-sufficiency of the Chinese household, went on to extol the virtues of the system. By engaging the wives and daughters in all phases of production, the system was innately more flexible and less prone to bottlenecks than the British putting-out system. The family production system meant that at almost all times of the year all members of the household could be productive in one way or another.

But what the writer had not appreciated was the value of bottle-necks. As Eli Whitney had shown, bottlenecks create a force behind them, attracting geniuses trying to go over, under, around, or through. Sometimes, bottlenecks blow the future apart. This is what happened in the late 1770s, when a choking bottleneck in the production of cotton cloth launched the modern world.

In traditional methods, the spinning of cotton was far more labor inten-sive than weaving, as it generally required between four and eight spinners to keep one weaver supplied with yarn.[4] Edward Baines noted in 1845 that:

> it was no uncommon thing for a weaver to walk three or four miles and call on five or six spinners, before he could collect (enough yarn) to serve him for the remainder of the day.[5]

The problem was exacerbated by the fact that spinning was a home-based industry, engaged in only to the extent that agricultural tasks had been completed. During the harvest season, it became difficult for British weavers to get any yarn at all. The bottleneck was made still worse by the technological progress that had occurred in weaving: The flying shuttle, widely adopted by the 1760s, multiplied further the number of spinners required to supply a weaver with yarn. In desperation, the British government began to sponsor competitions and award prizes to those offering solutions to the spinning bottlenecks.

James Hargreaves rose to the challenge and patented his spinning jenny in 1770. The first jenny contained eight spindles, immediately multiplying by eight the yarn that could be produced by a single worker. But by 1784, the jennies held 80 spindles, and by the end of the century, more than 100. Yet Hargreaves's was but one of many imaginative inventions to revolutionize the production of cotton cloth during the next 50 years, and they came with dizzying speed: the water frame, the mule, the steam engine. By 1832, the price of cotton yarn in Britain had fallen to one-twentieth the price it had sold for in the 1780s.[6] The race to the bottom had begun.

The spinning jennies gave rise to the factory system and to an entirely new economic order. Factory employment meant not only that workers gave up their domestic textile activities, but also that they gave up their agricultural activities and moved from farms to the new urban areas. The necessary business infrastructure, from finance and insurance to transportation and communications, soon developed to meet the needs of the new industrialists. And ancillary industries, from textile machinery to chemicals, steam, iron, and mechanical engineering, emerged as well. The new urban population in turn stimulated the development of the retail trades for food, drink, and medicine, as well as the clothing and housewares industries. Cotton spinning was also the first manufacturing industry to utilize the publicly subscribed limited liability company as a legal structure, which in turn formed the basis for the publicly held corporation as a form of ownership.

More broadly, innovation in cotton textile production was the ignition switch for the modern economy, leading to what economic historian W.W. Rostow has called "the takeoff," in which economic growth and continual improvement in the human condition came to be the normal and expected state of affairs. Indeed, prior to the revolution in Britain's textile industry, world economic growth had been barely perceptible. The importance of cotton textiles to Britain's economic development was such that Joseph Shumpeter has argued that the industrial history of Britain from 1787 until 1842 "can be resolved into the history of this single industry."[7]

Help Wanted: Docile and Desperate Preferred

Early cotton mill workers were pushed into the mills not by preference but by desperation and a lack of alternatives. Little skill was required for most jobs in the textile factories, so many workers were children from the "poorhouses" who were sent by the parishes to earn their keep. Work in the cotton mills meant that children could be economically self-sufficient from the age of five. The factories also drew labor, particularly women, from the agricultural sector. The enclosure movement of the 1700s had left much of the rural population without land, and increasing agricultural productivity meant that there was less wage work for rural laborers. Whether children without parents or farmers without land, an abundant and cheap labor force of desperate people powered the development of the factory system as surely as the steam engine.[8]

Children and rural women were recruited by early mill owners not only because of their abundance and low price, but also because owners found them temperamentally well-suited to the mind-numbing drudgery of early textile work. Manufacturers found men to be more difficult, whereas women and children were just as productive and a lot less trouble. An observer wrote that the master:

> finding that the child or woman was a more obedient servant to himself and an equally efficient slave to his machinery—was disposed to displace the male adult labor.[9]

Not only was women's labor cheaper than men's, women were "more easily induced to undergo severe bodily fatigue."[10] Married women with hungry children were best of all, as one mill owner explained that he:

> employs females exclusively at his power looms…[and] gives a decided preference to married females, especially those who have families at home dependent on them for support; they are attentive, docile, more so than unmarried females and are compelled to use their ultimate exertions to procure the necessities of life….[11]

Another factory owner concurred, noting that he, too, preferred females for their docility:

> Their labor is cheaper, and they are more easily induced to undergo severe bodily fatigue than men, either from the praiseworthy motive of gaining additional support for their families, or from the folly of satisfying a love of dress.[12]

The British cotton industry from the beginning developed an export bias, and by 1800 was shipping cotton cloth to Asia, Continental Europe, and the Americas. As a result, while the development of the industry fostered the growth of ancillary industries and broader economic development at home, it also fueled the engine of export-led growth. During the first half of the nineteenth century, cotton goods comprised nearly half of Britain's exports, and at the industry's peak Britain supplied nearly half of the world's consumption of cotton cloth.[13] And while the British monopoly of the world cotton trade began to decline in the later 1800s, Britain nonetheless remained the world's largest exporter of cotton textiles until the 1930s.

Yet the British recognized the precarious economic logic of an industry that imported cotton from the United States and India, only to sell cloth back to the poor of these countries. British dominance was assured only as long as they alone had the new textile technology. As a result, the British textile technology assumed the characteristics of smuggler's contraband. Britain forbade not only the export of textile machinery, but also the export of plans or drawings. To tighten the seal further, Britain also forbade skilled textile operatives, who might carry ideas abroad, to leave the country.

Today, China's defenders are quick to point out that America's industrial might began with intellectual property violations, and especially with a "stunning act of industrial piracy" committed by Francis Cabot Lowell, a blue-blooded Bostonian.[14]

In 1810, Lowell traveled with his wife and young sons to England. No one would have any reason to suspect him of industrial espionage. Instead, as historian Robert Dalzell writes, Lowell "must have struck the people he met as very much what he was: a well-connected, mild-mannered American merchant traveling in Europe...for reasons of health."[15] Only a few close friends knew his true purpose: a seemingly foolhardy scheme of industrial espionage that would bring textile factories to America.[16]

Using his significant mathematical aptitude, Lowell memorized the critical details of Edmund Cartright's power loom and returned home to Massachusetts. While Lowell's act was exceptional in securing for America the crown-jewel technology of the power loom, complementary technology also leaked into the United States during this period, most often in the minds of skilled artisans from Britain who had managed to evade emigration restrictions. By 1812, virtually all of the important technology related to cotton textile production had been transferred to New England.[17]

So, as it had in England, the production of cotton textiles led the Industrial Revolution in America, once again igniting parallel developments in urbanization, business infrastructure, and supporting industries. Enormous textile mills, the scale of which had not been seen before or since, soon lined the banks of the rivers throughout Massachusetts and New Hampshire. The U.S. mills produced a standardized and cheap cotton cloth, well-suited to clothing slaves in the South, farmers in the Mid-Atlantic, and settlers on the western frontier. The New England mills took the growing and profitable American mass market from England, leaving only the smaller market for fancy goods for the British. By the late 1800s, the world's largest textile mills were in New England. The biggest of all, the Amoskeag Mills on the Merrimack River, had 650,000 spindles and 17,000 employees, and produced 500 miles of cotton cloth per day.[18] By the early 1900s, the United States had surpassed Britain in cloth production, and British dominance of the international trade faded rapidly (see Figure 6.1).[19]

New England had emerged as the leader in the race to the bottom, and the golden era of British cotton manufacture came to a close. While the United States and Europe had absorbed nearly 70 percent of Britain's cloth exports in 1820, by 1896 they accounted for only 8 percent of these exports. Fortunately for the British, Asia would not mechanize textile production until much later, so much of the loss in American and European markets was made up in exports to India and China. But while Britain would maintain its preeminence as an exporter into the 1900s, its singular position at the top of the industry had come to an end. The profitability of cotton textile production in England fell steadily throughout the 1800s, and by 1912, exports of British cloth had peaked. Today, Britain is not a significant exporter of cotton textiles and clothing.

Like their British predecessors, the labor force of the New England mills was drawn from the ranks of "surplus" labor with no alternatives. Most of the early New England mill workers were young, single women from the farms of rural New England and Canada who could contribute

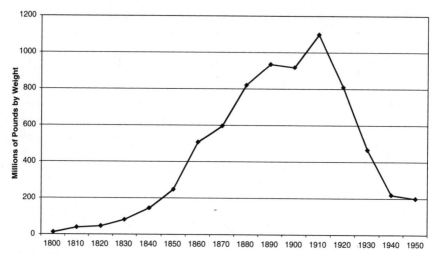

Source: Robson 1957, pp. 332, 333. Data reported for the initial year of each decade.

Figure 6.1   UK Cotton Piece Goods Exports (in Millions of Pounds by Weight, 1800 to 1950)

to their family's livelihood only by leaving the rocky farms and joining the swelling ranks of "mill girls." Working conditions were better than in Dickens's famed "Satanic mills," but not by much. The mill girls worked more than 70 hours per week in the steamy and suffocating heat with a bell to wake them at 4:30 A.M. and only short breaks for meals. Mills offering a 12-hour workday were lauded as humane, because such lenience "gave an opportunity for the girls to wash, mend, or read."[20] Even so, it was common practice to obtain more labor by falsely setting factory clocks.[21] Working conditions were compared unfavorably to life in jail, with a physician who had visited the mills noting that in prison work hours were shorter, lunch breaks longer, and ventilation much superior.[22] The workers themselves, in a petition filed in Lowell, Massachusetts, argued that the mill working conditions, through pain, disease, and privations, were hurtling the employees toward a premature death.[23]

Most New England mill girls resided in boardinghouses under the watch of hired matrons, and the limited time that they had outside of work was almost as closely supervised as their time in the mills. Church attendance was strictly enforced and moral purity a condition of continued employment. In one mill, causes for dismissal included levity, captiousness, impudence, or hysteria, and even a suspicion of immorality was sufficient for blacklisting by both fellow workers and management alike.[24]

Like their British predecessors, the mill owners had clear conceptions of the type of worker who was most desirable. Francis Cabot Lowell believed that young women, since they were "useless" on the farms, would be especially "docile and tractable," with the added benefit that keeping young women busy in the factory would reduce their chances of being tempted into impurity or other bad habits.[25] The New England mills later preferred the French Canadians, whom the owners found to be "docile, industrious, and stable," with the added advantage of their strict Catholicism and resulting large families.[26]

So, while the British mills had drawn upon pauper children and landless laborers, the New England spindles were powered by rural "mill girls"—also often children—and later, immigrants. In both cases, the growth of the cotton textile industry was dependent on a multitude of poor people with few alternatives, and in both cases the "ideal" laborer was hardy, docile, and uncomplaining. Early textile work and apparel work required neither creativity nor intelligence, but physical stamina and mental fortitude in the face of repetitive drudgery.

In the race to the bottom, New England's golden age in textile manufacture would be much briefer than Britain's. Between 1880 and 1930, cotton textile production gradually withered in New England and took root in the southern Piedmont region.[27] The main draw to the South was lower wages: Wages in the North Carolina textile industry during this period were generally 30 to 50 percent lower than those paid to textile operatives in Massachusetts.[28] While the Southern mill workers had slightly lower labor productivity, significant cost advantages remained for the Southern producers. The Southern labor cost advantages stemmed not only from differences in wage levels, but also from poorer working conditions. In addition, regulatory and cultural restraints on child labor and hours of work were significantly weaker in the South than in the New England mills. Child labor was more prevalent in textiles than in any other industry, and reliance on child labor was four times greater in the South than in the North.[29] Indeed, more than 60 percent of the females working in Southern cotton mills in the early 1900s were 13 years old or younger.[30] Finally, the Southern mill workers were more "docile and tractable," traits at least as important as wage levels in the comparative advantage of the industry.[31] In a precursor to today's call for global labor standards, the New England industrialists argued that their industry's only hope lay in convincing lawmakers to legislate working conditions and hours in Southern factories so that the lack of worker protections in the South could not be used to its competitive advantage.[32]

Like the New England mills of the early 1800s, the Southern mill workers and managers lacked the skills to compete at the higher end of the cloth market. As the more experienced New England and Mid-Atlantic mills increasingly specialized in fancier goods, the Southern mills seized the advantage in providing heavy and coarse cotton cloth to the U.S. market. But perhaps the South's most remarkable victory was in toppling British preeminence in Asia.

Southern mills from the beginning adopted a strong export orientation and by the late 1800s were systematically eliminating their British competition in Asia. Indeed, the Chinese export market was perhaps the single most important engine of growth for the Southern textile industry before 1900. Because the Asian textile industry had only begun to mechanize, and because of the Chinese preference for the durable, coarse cloth from the Southern mills, China presented to the South an immense market with insignificant competition from the higher-cost British exporters. In the decade ending in 1897, Southern textile exports to China more than doubled.[33] In the late 1800s, China purchased more than half of U.S. cloth exports, and more than half of U.S. exports to China were cotton textiles, with the great majority of this trade attributable to the Southern producers.[34] Many Southern mills sold virtually all of their output to China.[35] The Chinese market quite literally built the textile mills of the southern Piedmont region: A traveler in China reported back that in his wanderings through the country, "There was not a hole in the East where I did not find a Piedmont brand."[36]

The floods of cheap cotton clothing that flow today from China to the United States are almost a symmetric reversal of the trade flows of a century ago.

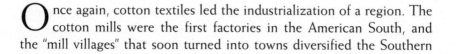

Once again, cotton textiles led the industrialization of a region. The cotton mills were the first factories in the American South, and the "mill villages" that soon turned into towns diversified the Southern economy away from agriculture and spurred the development of ancillary industries. Before long, the South had developed a capability in finer goods as well and had wrested the higher end of the domestic market from New England. For the 50 years ending in 1930, the New England mills gradually shuttered and reappeared in the South. By the mid-1930s, 75 percent of the yarn spindles in the United States were in the South.[37]

As had been the case in England and New England, most of the early Southern mill workers were drawn from ranks of the rural poor. Indeed, many of the Southern workers were former cotton sharecroppers, hard hit by low prices, the boll weevil, and the western movement of American cotton production to the factory farms of Texas. Melvin Copeland, a professor at Harvard in the early 1900s, described the Southern workers variously as "poor whites," "tackies," or "crackers" and appeared to hold his nose while describing the Southern mill workers who came from the surrounding farms and mountains. The mill workers:

> eeked out a meager livelihood from their squalid patches of barren soil and the fruits of their rifles. Their food was simple and not abundant, their clothing scanty, and their home a small cabin with a dirt floor . . . they pay scant attention to literature and entertainment . . . and the vast majority are improvident.[38]

While Copeland goes on to criticize everything from their cooking to their clothing and cleanliness, he conceded that, for the low-skill demands of the cotton mills, they would do: "Although lacking ingenuity, foresight, and ambition, they were, however, adaptable to factory life."[39]

In the early part of the twentieth century, Southern girls entered the mills as young as age 7 and worked more than 60 hours per week. They had little to no education, poor nutrition, crowded living conditions, and a hostile and sometimes violent working environment.[40] Four generations of Piedmont women might have worked in the town's cotton mill.[41]

But just as the Southerners were declaring a decisive victory against the aging mills in the North, a new competitor loomed in the race to the bottom. By the mid-1930s, Japan would have approximately 40 percent of the world's exports of cotton goods.[42] While Japan's lead came a full century after Britain's, the role of cotton textiles in the development of Japanese industry was as great in Japan as it had been in Britain. In the late 1920s, more than half of Japan's industrial workers were employed in textiles, and textiles comprised two-thirds of the country's exports.[43] While Britain's economy had long since diversified, cotton textiles was the only developed global industry in Japan prior to World War II. And while over 90 percent of Japan's spinning capacity was destroyed in World War II, Japan had regained its preeminent position by the 1950s.[44]

Following the now-familiar historical pattern, Japanese leadership in the industry was based on low labor costs and poor working conditions, and especially the prevalence of "night work," which doubled the productivity of the textile machinery.[45] In the early 1900s, researchers sent by the U.S. government to examine the Japanese textile industries found that wages for cotton mill workers in Japan were 20 to 47 percent lower than wages in the United States and England, even when they accounted for productivity differences.[46]

The first cotton mill workers in Japan were young women escaping a life of subsistence agriculture in the countryside, driven into the mills by both rural poverty and natural disasters. Indeed, recruiting agents regularly scoured the affected regions following the floods, famines, and earthquakes that struck rural Japan with tragic regularity, because such events led to especially fruitful opportunities to recruit desperate young women.[47] The rural migrants were much preferred to suburbanites, whom the mills found to be frivolous and without endurance. According to the Japan Cotton-Spinning Alliance, the ideal worker for a Japanese cotton mill was "unsophisticated, but honest, with great powers of endurance."[48] Or, as another manager put it, women from the rural areas were preferred because they were "naïve and diligent."[49] An American admirer observed the young women in the Japanese mills to be "docile, nimble, and deft."[50]

Female cotton workers in prewar Japan were referred to as "birds in a cage," given their grueling schedules—12-hour days and two days off per month—and captive lives in the company boardinghouses.[51] In most cases, the operatives were bound to the mills for a three- to five-year period, in a contractual arrangement not unlike indentured servitude. In the crowded boardinghouses the young women shared not only beds, but even pajamas, and they were confined to the premises by fences topped with bamboo spears and barbed wire. Food was scant, sanitation was poor, and disease was widespread.[52] Even as conditions improved in the postwar era, the cotton mills continued to employ a variety of techniques to control and to harness female labor.[53]

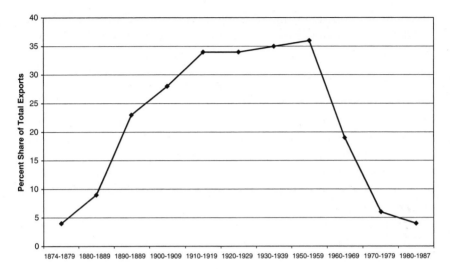

Source: Park and Anderson 1998, p. 170.

Figure 6.2 Textiles and Clothing as a Percent of Japanese Exports

Whereas textiles was in many respects a global industry as early as the 1800s, it was only in the 1950s that a similarly vigorous world trade began in clothing. Though Japan had leadership in both industries following World War II, by the 1960s, Japan's share of world trade in textiles and clothing had begun to fall and new leaders in the race to the bottom began to offer yet-lower labor costs and more docility (see Figure 6.2). By the 1970s, the Asian "Tigers" (Hong Kong, Korea, and Taiwan) had passed Japan in the race to the bottom and had assumed leadership positions in the textile and apparel industries.[54]

By the mid-1970s, Hong Kong was the world's largest exporter of clothing, with a manufacturing base designed for the low end of the Western apparel markets. In 1976, textiles and apparel comprised approximately half of manufacturing employment in Hong Kong as well as half of exports.[55] In 1980, the industry's peak employment year, nearly 400,000 workers were employed in Hong Kong's textile and apparel industries.[56] Hong Kong's cheap and largely unskilled labor force—many refugees from famine in the Chinese countryside—fueled the development of other light industries as well. Similarly, in Taiwan and Korea, young women poured from the rural areas into the sweatshops and spun, wove, knit, and stitched their countries' way to the Asian economic miracle.

In the mid-1970s, textiles and clothing comprised 35 percent of Korea's exports and employed more than 20 percent of the workers in Taiwan's export zones.[57] Once again, the industry's destiny was driven largely by labor costs: Wages for textile workers in these countries were about 7 percent of the level in the United States and perhaps 15 percent of the level in Japan.[58] And once again, both admirers and detractors marveled at the docility and industriousness of the rural women with no alternatives.

But not far away, Mao Zedong lay dying. China was waking and stretching from the nightmare of the Cultural Revolution, with wages perhaps 90 percent lower than those prevailing in Hong Kong. More important, China had millions and millions of young women—deft, nimble, desperate, and docile—who very much wanted off the farm.

Sisters in Time

FROM THE FARM TO THE SWEATSHOP
AND BEYOND

Docility on a Leash

Jiang Lan works eight hours per day, six days per week in the Number 36 yarn factory in Shanghai. Her job is fixing broken yarn. She sits on a hard metal chair that is attached to tracks on the floor in front of a row of spindles. By depressing the pedal at her foot, Lan glides left and right along the tracks, stopping wherever she sees a flashing red light, the signal of broken yarn. With a deft and intricate move of her fingers, she repairs the yarn, then glides left or right to the next flashing light. Lan does this all day, wrapped in the steam and cotton flurries, blanketed by the metal noise. At the end of the day, Lan steps outside to the surprising quiet and walks across the gravel road to the company dormitory.

Yes, she says. She likes her job.

Jiang Lan, of course, is China's comparative advantage. Yet while the sheer number of Jiang Lans, as well as their low wages, are often put forth to explain China's dominance in light manufacturing, the truth is that these economic factors—the supply and price of labor—take us only part of the way toward understanding China's leadership position in this industry. The whole story requires not only that we understand supply and price, terms that have meaning everywhere, but also that we understand Lan's life in China, its limits and its possibilities. Since the rise of industry in eighteenth-century England, ideal workers for low-end textile and apparel work have been those who endure repetitive drudgery not just cheaply, but willingly and uncomplainingly.

Researchers from a wide variety of backgrounds and nationalities, examining disparate regions and different centuries, come again and again to the *D* word in describing the ideal textile and apparel worker. *Docility* in turn in Lancashire, Massachusetts, South Carolina, Japan, Taiwan, and Hong Kong has been the product of a lack of alternatives, lack of experience, and limited horizons. Ironically, while the founding principles of the modern Chinese state rest on the rights of the working class, the Chinese government has at the same time engineered a system of laws virtually assuring an almost unlimited supply of docility. The Chinese government controls workers in ways that are bad for China's human rights record but very good for the production of T-shirts. Most Chinese textile and apparel workers are on a leash of sorts. It is not so much the labor market but the curse of anti-market forces in Chinese history that restricts the workers' lives and their possibilities.

Accidents of birth have always shaped destiny: race in America or class in England or caste in India. In China, the accident is *hukou*. To the worker, hukou is the leash, but to the textile industry, hukou is competitive strength, ensuring a stable and cheap labor force for the urban industry while at the same time ensuring that rural citizens bring their labor, but not themselves, to Shanghai. Roughly translated, *hukou* is a place of household registration. For a Chinese citizen today, the hukou specifies where you live, no matter where you actually are.

The hukou system was devised in the 1950s to support the economic development plans of the new Communist China.[1] The great majority of the country's citizens were assigned rural hukous: Those with rural hukous were required to remain in the countryside to produce quotas of food within their communes, and were normally barred even from traveling to the cities. Rural dwellers who did manage to make it to the city typically could not buy staple foods, however, since these goods required ration tickets that were only obtainable to those with an urban hukou.[2] Through the hukou system, China ensured a stable food supply for its cities while at the same time limiting the population of the urban areas. In reality, however, the masses in the countryside were "surplus labor," an academic term for people with nothing to do, people so "surplus" that their presence had no effect on the output of the commune. And while forcing the masses to remain idle in the countryside, China devoted its resources to the urban population, developing the cities' housing, education, health-care, and infrastructure while leaving the rural population to fend for itself. As the cities developed, hundreds of millions of unskilled, barely educated people were held captive in their rural villages by their hukou. One scholar has described the Chinese hukou system as "the broadest experiment in population control in human history."[3]

In the late 1980s, however, China began to gradually liberalize the hukou system, lifting up the land away from the coast and pouring the rural masses to the coastal areas to produce T-shirts and sneakers and plastic toys. But even today, each rural citizen rolling toward the coast is on a leash. They can visit the city but they cannot easily stay; they can bring their labor but not themselves or their families. These workers are *liudong renkou*, which translates roughly to "floating people." The migrant workers represent 70 to 80 percent of China's textile, apparel, and construction workers.[4] Human Rights Watch in China estimates that the rural migrant population in China's cities is between 60 and 120 million.[5] In 2003, the AFL-CIO charged that China's exploitive hukou practices constituted an unfair trade advantage.[6]

The rural hukou defines and limits the worker's life in Shanghai. Floaters work 25 percent more hours per week but earn 40 percent less than those with urban hukous.[7] Because they are not residents of Shanghai, they do not have access to what is left of the urban residents' "iron rice bowl" services such as subsidized housing, education, childcare, healthcare, and pension benefits.[8] Most of the Shanghai floating population lives at work, in dormitories, makeshift shelters, or in the workshop itself.[9] The typical dormitory room is an 8×12-foot space shared by 12 workers.[10] Some floaters are able to rent housing, but they pay six times as much as urban residents for half as much space. Toilets and kitchen facilities are the norm for the city dwellers and the exception for the migrants.[11] The workers come to the city alone; there is usually no living space, schooling, or healthcare for their spouses and children, and their rural hukous mark them clearly as second-class citizens.[12] The floaters are China's Bracero workers. In a more recent analogy, China labor specialist Anita Chan has likened the hukou system to South African apartheid.[13] Economists who have studied the hukou system believe it is a leading cause of income inequality in China, and even college graduates see an urban hukou as necessary for upward mobility.[14]

Sometimes China's floating workers show up in the city and hope for the best, but often the migrants have prearranged employment, especially in the textile and construction industries. Migrants risk not only economic failure but also detention and worse under China's regulations on "Custody and Repatriation" (C&R). Under these regulations, a rural visitor with the "three not haves" (*sanwu renyuan*)—no papers, no job, no address—can be forcibly detained in a C&R center, or sent home. At best, detention is costly (citizens detained must pay to be released); at worst, it is torturous.[15] And even those workers with employment live an uneasy life in the city, because the regulations governing migration to the cities are so byzantine that virtually every visitor is in violation of one rule or another. Depending on the city, a visitor might need an identity card, a temporary residence card, an employment registration card, a migrant identity card, a housing permit, and a family planning permit, each obtained from a different agency at significant cost.[16] In the cities studied by Knight et al., the permits necessary to avoid the C&R laws—if they can be obtained—cost more than half the monthly wage for the typical migrant worker.[17] Often, by the time the worker gets the final necessary document, the first has expired.[18]

In 2007, Amnesty International reported that in China:

> ... migrants are denied rights to adequate health care and housing, and are excluded from the wide array of state benefits available to permanent urban residents. They experience discrimination in the workplace, and are routinely exposed to some of the most exploitive conditions of work. Internal migrants' insecure legal status, social isolation, sense of cultural inferiority and relative lack of knowledge of their rights leaves them particularly vulnerable, enabling employers to deny their rights with impunity....[19]

Though China has recently increased migrant workers' protections under the C&R rules, many of these protections are only theoretical, because, as Anthony Kuhn found, often only those who surrender their protections are hired.[20] Even government officials acknowledge that migrants are often not paid: In one survey the government found that 72.5 percent of migrants were owed back wages by their employers.[21] In a tactic reminiscent of cotton sharecropping, withholding pay or requiring "deposits" from workers limits their mobility and protects the factories from open competition in the labor market.[22] And though the law requires that the migrants have employment contracts, the majority do not.[23]

The factories have an uneasy relationship with their floating workers. Managers report that the floating workers are critical to production, not only because they are cheaper than their urban counterparts, but, more importantly, because they "can bear more hardship" and are "more manageable."[24] Managers report that they hire floating workers for the simple reason that city workers will not take the dusty, steamy, noisy work of the construction and textile trades, and, even if they would, the city folk not only talk back, but are physically not up to the work.[25] Yet the factories' ability to hire migrants is restricted: Only some jobs are open to floating workers, and enterprises may have quota limits on the number of floating workers they may employ. The government uses the quota system as a labor market intervention, expanding the quotas during boom times and restricting them during times of urban unemployment. The rural workers are the variable cost, ebbing and flowing with the American appetite for T-shirts.

While there are frequent calls for reform of the hukou system, the Chinese government at the same time relies on the inexpensive and temporary laborers to sustain China's manufacturing might. In summary, as Professor Fei-Ling Wang writes, "It is the constant and continued sacrifice of the excluded majority that makes the Chinese economic miracle possible."[26]

Until today, each stop in the race to the bottom has been more fleeting than the last. Today, however, China's lead in the race to the bottom in textiles and apparel is the same yet different from that of her predecessors. The characteristics of the ideal worker—particularly docility and desperation—have not changed, the repetitive drudgery of at least most of the work has not changed, the relentless cost pressure has not changed, and the role of the rural poor in powering the factories has not changed. Yet China's sheer size, and especially the remnants of the state-engineered hukou system, ensure that the supply of docile young women from the farm will be much greater than it was for China's industrial predecessors. China, for the foreseeable future, will likely lead in the race to the bottom.

As was the case for slaves, sharecroppers, and Bracero workers, it is not the perils of the labor market that block the path for Chinese textile and apparel workers. Instead, as was the case for these prior generations as well, it is a state-engineered system that limits the ability of these workers to participate in the market as full citizens.

Sure Beats the Farm

Like their sisters in time, textile and clothing workers in China today have low pay, long hours, and poor working conditions.[27] Living quarters are cramped and rights are limited, the work is boring, the air is dusty, and the noise is brain numbing. The food is bad, the fences are high, and the curfews inviolate. As generations of mill girls and seamstresses from Europe, America, and Asia are bound together by this common sweatshop experience—controlled, exploited, overworked, and underpaid—they are bound together, too, by one absolute certainty, shared across both oceans and centuries: This beats the hell out of life on the farm.

In mid-1800 Britain, a 9-year-old girl not engaged in textile work instead was busy:

> ...driving bullocks to field and fetching them in again; cleaning out their houses, and bedding them up; washing potatoes and boiling them for pigs; milking; in the field leading horses or bullocks to plough...mixing lime to spread, digging potatoes, digging and pulling turnips...I loaded pack horses; went out with the horses for furze. I got up at five or six, except on market mornings twice a week, and then at three.[28]

Bertha Black was born in Trinity, North Carolina, in 1899, one of seven children of a rural family. Bertha's parents tried in vain to scratch a living from their 21 acres, and Bertha remembers well the family's exciting move up to the mill village, from picking cotton in the sun to spinning and weaving it in the shade:

> We all went to work in the Amazon Cotton Mill and we all worked there all our lives. We were all anxious to go to work because, I don't know, we didn't like the farming. It was so hot from sunup to sundown. No, that was not for me. Mill work was better. It had to be. Once we went to work in the mill after we moved here from the farm, we had more clothes and more kinds of food than we did when we was a-farmin'. And we had a better house. So yes, when we came to the mill life was easier.[29]

And today, literally millions of young Chinese women choose the factory over the farm, apparently preferring even the most grueling, worst sweatshop work to life in rural China. Liang Ying, a young woman interviewed by sociologist Ching Kwan Lee, remembered the day she escaped to the Shenzhen factory zone in southern China:

> That was the year when I turned sixteen. More than ten girls from my village planned the trip to Shenzhen. That day, we went to do the farm work in the fields as usual. We even went back for lunch with our parents. After our parents left for the field again, we took our luggage and left notes saying, "Dear parents, when you see this note in the evening, I will have already left for Shenzhen to find work. Please don't worry."[30]

For Liang Ying, almost anything was better than life on the family rubber farm and the choice between farm and factory was clear:

> It is really hard work. Every morning, from 4 A.M. to 7 A.M. you have to cut through the bark of 400 rubber trees in total darkness. It has to be done before daybreak, otherwise the sunshine will evaporate the rubber juice. If you were me, what would you prefer, the factory or the farm?[31]

He Yuan Zhi agrees with her sisters in time. Yuan Zhi has worked as a cutter at Shanghai Brightness for eight years. It was a good job for a girl from the farm, and it is an even better job now, she believes, as after several raises her pay in 2007 was nearly $300 per month. Yuan Zhi came to Shanghai from the mountainous area of Jiangxi province, because of the lack of opportunity at home in the village. She told me that she misses only two things about her home village: One is the spectacular scenery, and the other is her son, who is back in Jiangxi in the care of his grandparents. Everything else about life in Shanghai, she says, is better than that in the village. I have heard this sentiment, "My life is better now," from innumerable garment workers in China. Each had a story, it seemed, of the drudgery of farm life.

I remember in particular Japi Fong. Japi wore fashionably streaked hair, sequined jeans, and four-inch heels as she sat at her sewing machine at an apparel factory near Shanghai in 2005. She would never have been able to find, or pay for, such an outfit had she stayed on her parents' duck farm.[32]

The fact that low-skill factory work in textiles and apparel has represented a stepping stone from the drudgery of the farm is also illustrated by the manner in which many were denied the chance to step on the stone at all. In early New England, the Irish were denied any but the most menial work in the mills. In twentieth-century Shanghai, women from certain regions (in particular, Subei) who tried to make the move from night soil collector to cotton mill worker were openly discriminated against.[33] And in the American South, spinning and weaving jobs, albeit with separate toilets and water fountains, were opened to African Americans only in the 1960s. Whereas in most cases the exclusion of blacks was simply inviolate custom, in South Carolina it was law. To assure plenty of agricultural production as well as domestic labor, and also to maintain workplace segregation, South Carolina law prohibited "anyone engaged in cotton textile manufacturing to allow ... operatives ... of different races to work together in the same room."[34] The law was on the books until 1960, but African Americans continued to be systematically excluded from the mills until the Civil Rights Act of 1965.[35]

The Subei natives or the Irish or the African Americans could only walk by the cotton mills and think about what-ifs. At age 14, Billie Douglas started work, cooking and cleaning and looking after white mill workers' children. She would walk by the mill and think about what her life would be like on a mill worker's paycheck, where a day's work probably paid what she made in a week.[36] Johnny Mae Fields remembers a lifetime of obeying the white people, with her head down, in the postwar South. She used a simple philosophy of life handed down by her mother ("If the white woman want salt in her pie, put salt in her pie"). When the mills opened to black women, things were different.[37] Clest King remembered, too, "Before the mills opened up for black women, all they had was washing and ironing and cooking for white women."[38]

And in the late 1990s, Nicholas Kristof and Sheryl WuDunn, Pulitzer Prize—winning *New York Times* correspondents, found that for many poverty-stricken Asians working as garbage pickers, prostitutes, or not working at all, a job in a sweatshop, if beyond their reach, was an aspiration they held for their children.[39]

For He Yuan Zhi and her sisters in time, factory work has provided not only a step up the economic ladder and an escape from the physical and mental drudgery of the farm, but also a first taste of autonomy and self-determination, and a set of choices made possible by a paycheck, however small. For some, it was a choice to escape boredom, for others to escape a betrothal or a domineering father, for still others the chance to choose their own clothing. In the 1840s, a New England mill girl wrote home to a cousin to try to explain the variety of push and pull factors that had led her boardinghouse mates to the cotton mills. As the writer circles the dinner table in the boardinghouse, the new freedoms are almost palpable:

> I will speak to you of my acquaintances in the family here. One, who sits at my right side at the table, is in the factory because she hates her mother-in-law. The one next to her has a wealthy father but like many of our country farmers, he is very penurious.... The next has a "well-off" mother, but she is a very pious woman, and will not buy her daughter as many pretty gowns and collars and ribbons ... as she likes.... The next is here because her parents and family are wicked infidels, and she cannot be allowed to enjoy the privileges of religion at home. The next is here because she must labor somewhere, and

she has been illtreated in so many families that she has a horror of domestic service. The next has left home because her lover, who has gone on a whaling voyage, wishes to be married when he returns, and she would like more money than her father will give her. The next is here because her home is in a lonely country village and she cannot bear to remain where it is so dull. The next is here because her parents are poor, and she wishes to acquire the means to educate herself. The next is here because her "beau" came, and she did not trust him alone among so many pretty girls.[40]

In the early 1990s, sociologist Ching Kwan Lee went to live among migrant factory workers in southern China as part of her doctoral research.[41] For the young women from the rural villages, Lee found poor working conditions, limited freedoms, and a highly structured hierarchical labor system that limited the workers' conversations, their use of the toilet, and their diet. The conventional wisdom was that these women were an integral part of the family economy, sent to work in the city to send home money to keep the rural homestead afloat.

But as Lee gained the trust of the workers, much more complex motivations emerged. While the money sent home did indeed ease the burdens in the rural areas left behind, the women admitted, often embarrassed, that what had brought them to the factory towns was not so much money but autonomy of a kind that was impossible in the village, where they were dominated by fathers and brothers. Many, Lee found, were attracted to factories not only to escape agricultural work but to write their own destiny and to escape their parents' plan for their lives.

Chi-Ying, a young single woman from Hubei, was interviewed by Lee.[42] Though Chi-Ying makes seven to eight times as much money at the factory as her father does at home, money is not at the top of her list of reasons for leaving the village for the factory. Chi-Ying has delayed marriage and ultimately decided against the husband her parents had chosen for her. With her wages, she repaid the young man for the gifts he had given her parents. In the city, she feels modern, free, and young. She likes buying a pair of cheap earrings with her own money, seeing a movie, or visiting the shopping mall. Chi-Ying compares herself to her mother and grandmother, and the striking differences seem to her to be not income but horizons. Mom and Grandma never had their own jobs, or their own money. They never left the village, or saw a high-rise building. Actually, Mom and Grandma never saw a paved road.

The irony, of course, is that the suffocating labor practices in textile and apparel production, the curfews and locked dormitories, the timed bathroom visits and the production quotas, the forced church attendance and the high fences—all of the factors throughout industrial history designed to control young women—were at the same time part of the women's economic liberation and autonomy.

One payday, Lee went shopping with Hon-ling and Kwai-un, two migrant factory workers from the northern countryside. Walking into a boutique with money in their pockets, Hon-ling and Kwai-un were no longer peasants. Lee writes:

> A disposable cash income brought more than consumer items. It was a resource with which women workers from the north asserted their dignity in the face of society's imposition of an image of migrant peasant daughters as poverty-stricken and miserable.[43]

Lee found the young migrant workers eager to expand their professional horizons as well. Evenings were often taken up with night courses in business, typing, computers, and English, and many had entrepreneurial ambitions.[44]

More than 75 years ago, Ivy Pinchbeck closed her pathbreaking study of England's Industrial Revolution by concluding that its most significant legacy was the liberation of women. Similarly, researchers have found that the young rural women who powered South Korea's and Taiwan's economic miracle in the 1980s benefited from income but especially from increased autonomy and a chance at self-determination.[45] And 75 years ago, in Shanghai, young cotton mill workers banded together in groups called *pulochia*. Roughly translated, these were independent women who had their own money and refused to get married, often, like Chi-Ying, repaying the bride price paid by her family. And 150 years ago, in Lowell, Massachusetts, the mill girls also gravitated to self-improvement opportunities: lectures, plays, and, most of all, the lending libraries.[46]

In 1901, Sadie Frowne described her 12-hour days in a New York sweatshop. She made $7 per week, but at the price of frequent injuries, brutal bosses, and the exhausting pace of the piecework sewing system. At the end of each day, Sadie was so tired she wanted nothing more than to go to sleep. But she resisted the temptation:

[O]ne feels so weak that there is a great temptation to lie right down and go to sleep. But you must go out and get some air, and have some pleasure. So instead of lying down I go out, generally with Henry.

Sadie enjoys a good time, and especially enjoys the independence that comes with her paycheck. Though she is clearly fond of Henry, Sadie also likes to dance and to shop:

> I am very fond of dancing and, in fact, all sorts of pleasure. I go to the theatre quite often, and like those plays that make you cry a great deal....
>
> Some of the women blame me very much because I spend so much money on clothes. They say instead of $1 a week I ought not to spend more than 25 cents a week on clothes.... But a girl must have clothes if she is to go into high society at ... Coney Island or the theatre....
>
> I have many friends and we often have jolly parties. Many of the young men talk to me, but I don't go out with any except Henry. Lately he has been urging me more and more to get married.

But the New York sweatshop, while brutal in some ways, is liberating in others. Her paltry paycheck has given her a choice. She considers marrying Henry, but then decides:

> I think I'll wait.[47]

Exactly 100 years later, author Peter Hessler followed the fortunes of Ma Li, a young girl from rural China who had been in his English class when he served in the Peace Corps. Ma Li had left home and gone to the southeastern factory town of Shenzhen, where she worked in a jewelry factory with a lecherous boss and a night-time curfew. Hessler worried about how Ma Li was faring in the city and paid her a visit. He learned that:

> Since coming to Shenzhen, she had found a job, left it, and found another job. She had fallen in love and broken curfew. She had sent a death threat to a factory owner, and she had stood up to her boss. She was twenty-four years old. She was doing fine.[48]

Factory women the world over arrived at the factory with docility bred by a lack of alternatives, and it was docility rather than intelligence or creativity that was and is the defining character trait of the ideal sweatshop worker. Yet the factory work itself proffered alternatives to the young women: They could choose a new hat or a new boyfriend or no boyfriend, and, as they became more skilled, even a new job. And just as their docility had been bred by a lack of alternatives, the choices presented by their new worlds gradually melted their passivity away. In country after country, and factory after factory, the women stood up and stared down the bosses, expanded their horizons, made their own choices. In the process, they became less ideal workers for the textile trade, but better workers for the expanding industries requiring initiative, decision making, teamwork—industries that moved in as the race to the bottom progressed and the cotton mills closed.

Amazon.com and Dell Arrive at the Mill

In 1748, philosopher David Hume extolled the virtues of the race to the bottom:

> There seems to be a happy concurrence of causes in human affairs, which checks the growth of trade and riches, and hinders them from being confined entirely to one people.... When one nation has gotten the start of another in trade, it is very difficult for the latter to regain the ground it has lost because of the superior industry and skill of the former.... But these advantages are compensated in some measure, by the low price of labor in every nation which has not had an extensive commerce.... Manufacturers therefore gradually shift their places, leaving those countries and provinces which they have already enriched, and flying to others, whither they are allured by the cheapness of provisions and labor, till they have enriched those also, and are again banished by the same cause....[49]

Manchester, England, the birthplace of the Industrial Revolution, today produces little cotton cloth. Manchester is today a brash and slightly seedy place, producing hard-core music, and angry dances with names like trip hop and acid jazz. The young and raging underclass shoots up and sniffs and smokes in the boarded-up cotton mills. But there is an ego, an edge, to Manchester today. The descendants of the cotton mill workers learn in grade school that it all began here: factories, corporations, global industries, modern industrial capitalism. So today:

> Despite a century of decline and eleven years of Margaret Thatcher, despite lousy weather and even lousier prospects, despite the grim housing estates, the boarded-up buildings, the shallow obsessions of club culture, the drugs, the gangs, and garbage in the streets, Manchester still feels alive. That is an accomplishment, however long it lasts. The place survives through small acts of defiance. In and around the ruins of an empire, kids are dancing.[50]

Yet Manchester dominates a new industry today. It is the main home of the European "call center" business where touch-tone phones the world over will connect you to a young woman who cares about you, the customer. This industry now employs more than 400,000 Britons, mostly young women seeking flexible hours as well as job security. Some people liken the call center jobs to work in the early textile mills: relentless pace, unreasonable supervisors, too-short breaks. The comparison, thankfully, is nonsense.

Across the Atlantic in Manchester, New Hampshire, the economy is now dominated by technology, health care, and education. Manchester is the state's largest and most prosperous city, and frequently earns spots on national lists of "best places to live." But if the Internet now dominates Manchester's economy, the mammoth Amoskeag mills still dominate the skyline. In the mills are condos, offices, restaurants, and even a college campus. Today, what was the world's largest textile factory produces no cotton cloth at all. In fact, the largest textile complex in New England today is the American Textile History Museum, in Lowell, Massachusetts, the town named for the man who brought factories to America.

Charlotte, North Carolina, is also its home state's largest city. The former center of the Southern cotton mill kingdom today has one of the country's most robust growth records based on a diversified economy centered on the city's role as an international financial center. Bank of America and First Union Corporation, both headquartered in Charlotte, together employ more than 35,000 people, and IBM, BellSouth, and US Airways are also large employers. Charlotte has 23 colleges and universities in the surrounding area, and half a dozen advanced healthcare facilities. Just to the south, in Greer, South Carolina, is a new BMW manufacturing facility. The facility drew much of its labor force from the decaying cotton mills. Lane Jones, whose skin color would have kept her out of the cotton mills a generation ago, is an "associate" at BMW today, where she makes nearly $60,000 a year and drives a new BMW in the bargain.[51] Lane came to BMW from a denim mill: hot, dusty, boring, and work that never seemed to pay the bills. It Pittsboro, North Carolina, the old brick building that once housed the Kayser-Roth Hosiery factory is the new home for Biolex Therapeutics, a firm developing drugs for liver ailments. The lowest-paid technicians—many former mill workers—make far more than they had in the hosiery business.[52]

In Alabama, Honda, Toyota, DaimlerChrysler, and Hyundai have all built factories in former cotton mill country during the past decade, and there is little doubt that the former mill workers prefer the jobs in the auto factories. In Campbellsville, Kentucky, an old Fruit of the Loom plant was reopened, refurbished, and expanded in 1999. The new tenant is Amazon .com. And in 2008, both Ikea and Rolls Royce announced plans to open assembly and manufacturing facilities in the shadows of the defunct textile mills in southern Virginia.[53]

In Japan, the cotton mills around Osaka have made way for some of the world's most successful companies. Twenty-nine firms in the Fortune Global 500 are headquartered here, including Matsushita, Sanyo, Sharp, and Kyocera. Nearby is Toyota City, which began as a cotton-spinning factory but by the 1980s had revolutionized the global automobile industry.

And while Hong Kong remains a prodigious clothing exporter, the city's apparel industry has moved from the sweatshop to the high tech. TAL Apparel, Hong Kong's leading firm in the industry, is led by Henry Lee, who has a doctorate from Brown University. TAL has solved the age-old apparel problem of the puckering seam—caused by the fact that thread shrinks more than fabric—and has patented and licensed its "pucker-free" technology in countries throughout the world. The firm has not only seamstresses, but researchers committed to improving mechanical and chemical engineering in garment production. And as the firm perfects mechanical processes, it is also setting standards in logistics and supply chain management. As shirts sell from the shelf of JCPenney in suburban America, inventory data are relayed to Hong Kong, allowing TAL to restock a hot-selling product in 27 to 29 days, down from five months only three years ago. And the next major innovation in garment production—size customization for each consumer—is now close to a reality in Hong Kong. The world's best-selling garment-design computer program was developed in Hong Kong, and mass customization research is now under way at the Hong Kong University of Science and Technology. And Taiwan today dominates the computer industry, producing more than half of the world's laptop computers and more than one-quarter of its desktops. South Korea, too, has grown out of the sweatshop and into a world-class competitor in electronics, film, and automobiles.

The countries that have lost the race to the bottom are some of the most advanced economies in the world today, but they share a common heritage in the cotton mill and the sweatshop as the ignition switch for the urbanization, industrialization, and economic diversification that followed, as well as for the economic and social liberation of women from the farm. The now high-income workers have priced themselves out of work in the sweatshops, and these countries no longer have the desperate rural poverty that pushed and pulled women from the farms to textile and apparel factories. The workers are now neither cheap nor docile, and offer comparative advantages to other industries, in auto manufacturing, financial services, and information technology. While it was never a happy day when the mill closed, a padlocked cotton mill is also a sign that the economies, and the workers, by losing the race to the bottom, have emerged as victors.[54]

Of course, all is not rosy in the countries that have lost the race to the bottom. While some textile workers laid off in South Carolina will get a job in the BMW plant, many will not, and life after the mill closes often gets worse before it gets better, especially for the thousands who quit high school because their future in the cotton mills seemed secure. For the workers who are not equipped to move up to BMW or IBM, or those who do not wish to leave the mill towns that still pepper the South, the loss in the race to the bottom is of course not a victory. In Chapter 9, we will see the rather unbelievable lengths to which many will go to keep T-shirt production from moving on to the next stop in the race.

But of all the rallying cries of the anti-globalization movement, the call to "stop the race to the bottom" is both the scariest and the most nonsensical, especially when it comes from rich-country activists who owe their own prosperity to the very race they wish to halt for others. Who, we might ask, would these activists like to keep on the farm? Yet if some activists are misguided in their ideas about stopping the race to the bottom, others are a powerful force in changing the nature of the bottom itself.

THE UNWITTING CONSPIRACY

Writing the Rules of the Race

Globalization's skeptics are quick to point out that even if the conditions in apparel factories are a step up from those on the farm, it does not follow that workers in developing countries should simply accept their fate, working day and night in poor conditions, for pitiful wages and with limited rights. While free trade advocates may wish to isolate the activists as an uninformed fringe element, research shows that most Americans have reservations about the slippery slope in the race to the bottom and the working conditions in overseas apparel factories.[1]

Labor protection language is now written into U.S. trade agreements, "Global Labor Standards" has emerged as a topic on the agenda of the World Trade Organization, and the International Labor Organization (ILO) has endorsed a set of "Core Labor Standards" designed to serve as speed bumps in the race to the bottom. Yet many activists argue that the conditions for workers in Asian apparel factories are comparable to, or worse than, those found centuries ago in Europe and America. The dark Satanic mills have moved but not shut down. Even if the conditions in the factories are better than those on the farm, protestors argue, how can the conditions so deplorable a hundred or more years ago in the West now be acceptable in the East?

The truth, however, is that this comparison, too, is nonsense, as even a cursory review of factory conditions across time and space shows. Today's protestors have sisters and brothers in time as well, generations of activists who gave their efforts and sometimes their lives to improve the condition of the working classes. Generations of activists—today's included—have changed the rules of the race and raised the bottom, making it a much better place than it used to be.

While the competitive market forces powering the race to the bottom are strong, there have, since the first factories emerged, been opposing forces at work. As production spiraled down to lower and lower cost locations, there have been generations of activists to throw sand in the gears and erect speed bumps in the race. These opposing forces, forces of conscience, religion, and politics, have continually rewritten the rules of the race and changed the nature of the bottom, making it not a good, but a better, place to be. The forces, then and now, have been governments and labor unions, religious leaders and international organizations, student activists, and most centrally the workers themselves. As the factory experience itself melted away their docility, the workers have stood up and stared down the bosses, raising the bottom for themselves and the workers who followed them.

These opposing forces, competitive markets on the one hand, and political, religious, and labor activists on the other, have long been identified as enemies of sorts, eyeing one another suspiciously and even venomously. Today's trade skeptics identify the multinationals' pursuit of profit and free trade as the enemy of the poor and powerless, a greedy force to be stopped and never trusted. The business community in turn scornfully dismisses the skeptics and the activists as a lunatic fringe, a ragtag bunch of ill-informed obstructionists who are blocking the only path available out of poverty. The battle has been put in these terms—greedy inhumanity versus naive and reckless troublemakers—since the first textile factories emerged.

In a larger sense, however, global capitalism and labor activism are not enemies but are instead cooperators, however unwitting, in improving the human condition. As much as the CEOs would like to silence the activists and activists would like to silence the corporations, the fact is that the two sides need each other, and, most important, the workers at Shanghai Brightness Garment Factory and the Shanghai Number 36 textile mill need them both.

Activists Raise the Bottom, 1780–2008

Dr. Thomas Percival, a physician and social reformer in the late 1700s, proposed a radical reform for the Manchester, England, cotton mills. Percival's proposal was radical, first because it suggested that any sort of interference in the management of the cotton factories might be allowable, and second because it suggested that legislation might limit the hours (typically 14 per day at the time, including night work) that children were employed in the mills. Percival had in mind nothing so far-fetched as a ban on child labor, only a requirement that young children be given dinner breaks and be protected from working more than 12 hours per day.[2] Predictably, business interests charged that Percival and his allies were uninformed about the nature of their business, and thus began nearly a century of struggle in Britain, where successive waves of Factory Acts—in 1819, 1825, 1833, 1844, and 1878—gradually shortened children's working hours and raised minimum ages for work in the factories.

In the United States, Massachusetts, the birthplace of the American cotton textile industry, was the first state to limit the hours that children could work. Other states gradually introduced similar restrictions, and in 1916, President Woodrow Wilson signed the first Federal Labor Law restricting child labor. Yet representatives of Southern cotton mills battled the bill to the Supreme Court, where it was struck down by the now-familiar arguments regarding the proper role of the government in the affairs of business. In 1941, however, the Supreme Court upheld the Fair Labor Standards Act, affirming the right of Congress to legislate to protect working children. In Japan, legal protections for child workers came a full century after similar developments in Britain, and in China, the Compulsory Education Act, passed in 1986, prohibits children under the age of 17 from working, and requires minimum schooling for children.

So, just as the production of cheap cotton clothing ignited the Industrial Revolution in countries around the world, it also sparked the forces of conscience for generations of activists determined to protect the most vulnerable from the unrestrained forces of capitalism. While the race to the bottom fueled demand for the cheapest and most docile labor of all, the opposing forces, at first lone, alleged lunatics, and then mainstream citizens, and finally lawmaking bodies, were gradually successful in implementing protections for children from factory work, and fostering the now nearly universal belief that children belong in school.

Those who liken today's Chinese textile and apparel factories to those of a century or more ago in Britain and North America fail to note that however bad the current conditions, thanks to progressive activists around the world, the machinery is no longer powered by eight-year-olds.

Today, all of the world's significant textile and apparel producers have ratified the ILO's convention prohibiting child labor. Though child labor has by no means been eliminated from textile and apparel production, thanks to generations of noisy activists, the employment of children has moved from the ordinary and accepted course of business to the illegal, objectionable, and newsworthy. When investigative journalists in India found children working in a subcontractor's factory sewing Gap clothing in late 2007, the story appeared on the evening news worldwide within 24 hours. Thanks to the backlash, the story was breaking news—an outrage!—not business as usual.

And a job in textiles and apparel, however unpleasant, no longer presents appreciable risks of death or maiming. Thanks to textile machinery, missing fingers, hands, arms, and legs were so common a sight in Manchester, England, that Friedrich Engels likened Manchester to a place soldiers returned to after war.[3] In a two-month period in 1843, the *Manchester Guardian* reported that:

> 12 June, a boy died in Manchester of lockjaw, caused by his hand being crushed between wheels; 16 June, a youth in Saddleworth seized by a wheel and carried away with it; died utterly mangled. 29 June, a young man . . . at work in a machine shop, fell under the grindstone, which broke two of his ribs and lacerated him terribly. 24 July, a girl in Oldam died, carried around fifty times by a strap; no bone unbroken. 27 July, a girl in Manchester, seized by the blower (the first machine that receives the raw cotton), died of injuries received. August 3, a bobbin tuner died . . . caught in a strap, every rib broken.[4]

Even today, most older Southern mill workers recall machinery accidents as a common occurrence. Aliene Walser, who went to work in a North Carolina mill in the 1940s, remembers a coworker with long, beautiful blonde hair, scalped by textile machinery.[5] Machinery-related accidents that maimed or killed were also regular events in Japanese mills.[6] Thanks to activists from both the medical and labor communities, Britain began industrial safety inspections in the late 1800s.[7] In the United States, the Occupational Safety and Health Administration was formed in 1970 and today is advising an analogous body that is developing in China. Again, the point is not that industrial accidents no longer occur, but rather that, thanks to the efforts of generations of activists, workers in every country in the world have better health and safety protections than their predecessors.

Today, the most prominent health and safety issue in the apparel and textile industry is *ergonomics*. Repetitive-motion injuries such as carpal tunnel syndrome affect millions of workers each year, according to Eric Frumin, health and safety director for the largest union of textile and apparel workers.[8] Though the business lobby successfully blocked regulatory reform related to ergonomics during the Bush administration, if history is a guide, Frumin and his colleagues will eventually win, and textile and apparel workers will receive treatment, training, and compensation for ergonomics injuries. Business owners, of course, oppose the ergonomics regulations, echoing familiar objections voiced by their forebears centuries ago. But thanks to his activist ancestors, Frumin can devote his energies to the ergonomics fight, as workers don't get eaten by textile machinery anymore.

Rose Rosenfeld died at the age of 107, a few months before September 11, 2001. Had she lived a few months longer, she would have no doubt felt a déjà vu horror. A lifetime ago, in 1911, only a short distance from where the World Trade Center would later be built, Rose had watched her friends' bodies fall flaming out of the sky. In a garment factory known as the Triangle Shirtwaist Company, 146 people were killed in one of America's worst industrial fires, in a building with no alarms, no sprinklers, and no escapes. Rose made it out in time to watch her coworkers hit the pavement. Though the factory reopened within days of the fire, Rose never returned to work there. She spent the rest of her life as an activist, speaking to college classes, reporters, and labor rallies. At the age of 106, she said of the fire, "I feel it still."[9] Thanks to Rose and her compatriots, fire safety at work, like child labor restrictions and safe machinery, is accepted as a right the world over.

Bysinosis, or brown lung, is a disease that has been largely eradicated. Caused by the inhalation of cotton dust, it slowly asphyxiated generations of textile and apparel workers. The disease is now virtually unheard of, as OSHA-style cotton dust standards have been adopted in virtually all textile- and apparel-producing countries. And, of course, early mill workers not felled by brown lung or maimed by machinery might still fall victim to the myriad infectious diseases caused by poor sanitation, poor ventilation, and overcrowding. Life expectancy in Manchester, England, was under 30 in 1800, while 50 years later in Fall River, Massachusetts, it was 35. Today, life expectancy in Shanghai is 77, slightly ahead of that in New York City.

In the early 1900s, minimum wage legislation was virtually unheard of in the United States, though state-level legislation sometimes applied to women and children in certain industries. Only in 1938 did the U.S. Congress pass a national minimum wage law. Today, however, virtually all apparel-producing countries have legislated minimum wage levels, and have also placed limitations on hours of work and mandated overtime.[10]

And finally, a day's work in the cotton yarn factory is not at all what it used to be. Perhaps 100 years ago, children worked as "piecers," running from spindle to spindle watching for broken yarns. Spotting a break, they would climb up, tie the piecer's knot, and resume their watching. Less than 100 years ago, women in Shanghai performed the same task, not climbing but tottering on bound feet. Today, however, the Shanghai Number 36 mill has many simple devices—the red blinking light, the chair on tracks, etc.—that make all the difference to the experience of a day's work. And at the cotton mills in the American South today—as well as in many Chinese mills—piecers are now industrial history: On a walk through modern mills, one might see no people at all; the piecers are robotic devices that know where the broken yarns are and how to fix them. Gradually, the worst jobs in the production of T-shirts are fading into old photographs.

I n the mid-1990s, a variety of labor abuses came to light in factories that produced shoes and apparel for the Nike Corporation. Charges of underage workers, coerced or forced overtime, safety violations, and generally poor conditions began to surface, especially in factories in China and Indonesia. The factories, while supplying goods to Nike, were independently owned and operated. As a result, Nike argued, it bore no responsibility for conditions in its suppliers' facilities. Nike's general manager in Indonesia, while acknowledging that violations might exist, essentially argued that they were neither his nor Nike's affair: "I don't know that I need to know [about them]," he replied in response to questions.[11]

Nike was not alone in its practices. By the late 1980s, it had become common business practice for apparel companies to *outsource* the production of their clothing to manufacturers around the world, and indeed it became unusual for brand-name companies such as Nike and Gap to own any factories at all. The notion that apparel companies should be responsible for the conditions in their suppliers' factories—the so-called "supply chain"—was a novel and unwelcome idea to most companies. Indeed, the idea that a customer *could* be responsible for what happened behind the factory gates of its suppliers was unheard of.[12]

This changed radically over the next several years. Levi Strauss became the first U.S. apparel company to create and enforce a code of conduct for its suppliers, and other companies, under pressure from consumers, activists, and religious groups, began to follow suit.[13] Companies began to require that their suppliers commit to a variety of fair labor practices as a condition of their business relationships, and organizations emerged to help companies monitor conditions in their suppliers' factories. Verité, a nonprofit organization founded in 1995, assists dozens of multinationals in their efforts to oversee working conditions in supplier factories, and was recently honored as one of the country's leading "social entrepreneurs."

As with the struggles over child labor or minimum wage, the idea that large corporations should be responsible for workplace practices in their supply chains went from radical notion to mainstream business practice. Corporate codes of conduct for suppliers to the footwear and apparel industry are nearly universal in the United States today, and the mainstream business press now routinely advises large companies on how to address labor conditions issues in Asia.[14] Corporations are also investigating social issues "further back" in their supply chain. In the summer of 2008, a number of U.S. and European apparel firms announced that they would no longer allow Uzbeki cotton to be used in their apparel, because of concerns over child labor on the cotton farms.[15]

Nike today employs nearly 100 professionals in its "corporate social responsibility" activities (including several of my former Georgetown students) and publishes annually a comprehensive report related to labor and environmental issues in its supplier factories. The report includes factory names and addresses, code of conduct and monitoring details, and remediation efforts.[16] Nike publishes a separate report on its Chinese suppliers. An executive in Nike's social responsibility practice told me that while the company's early efforts were designed to protect Nike's reputation in the face of anti-sweatshop protests, today the firm is motivated also by the belief that "you can't make good products in bad factories."

And like child labor, fire safety, minimum wages, and occupational health, the activists' fringe-like demands continue to go mainstream and work their way into law. By 2008, it seemed clear that the United States would include labor protections in all of its future trade agreements.[17] By 2009, students studying in apparel, design, or textile programs had their first textbook exclusively devoted to social and environmental responsibility in the industry.[18]

Back at Georgetown, Bored Is Good

In 1999, when I encountered the protesting students at Georgetown, the "anti-sweatshop movement" was in full swing at many of the nation's largest universities. Most students were proud to be a part of their university community, proud to wear the T-shirts shouting Georgetown or Wisconsin or Duke. But if the T-shirt bore the name of their university, the students argued, we should know where the T-shirt came from. What if the Georgetown T-shirt *had* been stitched by a child chained to a sewing machine?

The students at Georgetown and elsewhere had a variety of demands: They wanted the companies that produced our T-shirts to disclose the names and addresses of the factories producing the clothing. They wanted the companies to adopt a strict code of conduct regarding factory conditions, and they wanted a system of independent monitoring in place that would check for compliance with the codes.

The companies at first protested, in an eerie echo of corporate response since the first factories emerged in England: The new generation of Thomas Percivals did not understand the industry, the business, or the supply chain, and the activists' demands were both unworkable and unreasonable. The companies argued, for example, that to disclose the locations of the factories was tantamount to giving away trade secrets.

At Georgetown, on February 4, 1999, junior Ben Smith left yet another meeting with university administrators, unhappy with the pace of change and the university's unwillingness to act. "I guess it's time for Plan B," he remarked to Andrew Milmore, a fellow student who served as President of the Georgetown Solidarity Committee.[19] The next day, about 30 students occupied the office of Georgetown President Father Leo O'Donovan. This was not your 1960s sit-in. For 86 hours, the students were peaceful and pleasant (one of my favorite students—Michael Levinson—wore a tie the entire time). But they refused to budge until the university had committed to an acceptable course of action.

In the 87th hour, the students and administration had reached a compromise plan for moving forward. Being a university, one of the first elements of the plan was obvious: We would form a committee.

I served on the newly formed Licensing Oversight Committee for six years, and this brief experience is a microcosm of the unwitting conspiracy at work. Early meetings were tense and often heated, the students on one side of the table and the faculty and administrators on the other. I remember clearly thinking that the students, however noble and impassioned, just weren't being reasonable. Names and addresses of all of the factories in this fleet-footed industry with its global supply chain? Unannounced visits by independent monitors? Who would these "monitors" be and what exactly would be they be monitoring? And why would the factories let them in, even assuming we did have names and addresses? And of course we would never get names and addresses, since every company producing the clothing had stated flatly that they would never release this information. I see now that my responses in these early meetings were very close to the responses the business community has had to social, environmental, or labor activists since the days of Thomas Percival: How could all of this possibly work? And how would we know we were doing more good than harm?

S ince the heyday of Georgetown basketball in the 1980s, the production and sale of Georgetown-logoed apparel has not been a billion-dollar business. Indeed, for companies such as Nike or Adidas or Puma, the Georgetown T-shirt business was a drop in the bucket, a drop so small that it certainly appeared that Georgetown would have no leverage to force companies to disclose their suppliers' factory locations. Yet, the new generation of student activists was armed with technology—cell phones, chat rooms, the Internet—technology that linked together students at Duke, Notre Dame, Berkeley, Wisconsin, and dozens of other schools. In aggregate, the university apparel business was more than a drop in the bucket and within a few months of the protests, the major apparel companies whose supply chains produced most university-branded apparel—including such powerhouses as Nike, had backed down and agreed to make public their suppliers' factory locations. By 2005, Nike—quickly followed by many other sportswear firms—had posted its global factory database on the Web, where it remains today. Recent research suggests that factory disclosure and student activism had benefited both the companies and the workers in their suppliers' factories.[20]

After a few months of meetings at Georgetown, we had agreed on a code of conduct for the firms producing Georgetown-logoed apparel. Briefly, the code meant that if a company wanted to produce T-shirts bearing the Georgetown logo, the company had to commit to enforcing our code of conduct in their suppliers' factories. The code bound the companies to a variety of fair labor practices, including prohibitions on forced labor and child labor, implementation of sound environmental and health and safety practices, and fair pay practices. [21]

Of course, the code carried little weight if it could not be monitored or enforced. By 2000, the Workers Rights Consortium (WRC) was founded by international labor rights experts, universities, and students. Funded by member universities as well as outside sources, the WRC began to perform in-depth factory investigations for code-of-conduct compliance, and began to issue public reports containing its findings. The WRC also committed to work with factories to help them comply with the codes. By spring of 2008, the WRC had 175 affiliate colleges and universities, ranging from Luther College and Middle Tennessee State to Princeton and Harvard.[22] A similar organization, the Fair Labor Association (FLA), had 200 member schools.

For most of the six years that I served on Georgetown's Licensing Oversight Committee, we met twice per month. In the early years, the issues were challenging, the debates often heated, as we hammered out the details step by step. I stepped down from the committee in 2006. For one thing, my schedule made it increasingly difficult for me to make the frequent early morning meetings.

With all due respect to my colleagues, however, there was another reason to step down: The meetings had become a bit—dare I say it—boring.

The meetings had become boring because the big battles were over. What had seemed in 2000 or 2001 to be a radical idea—that universities could control or at least influence how their apparel was produced in factories around the world—was by 2006 a widely accepted notion within university administrations and corporations. Supply chain codes of conduct, factory monitoring and disclosure, and a host of other practices had become standard business practice. Whether they like it or not, the students on the committee today are part of the establishment: They now meet every two weeks with LaMarr Billups, the new Assistant Vice-President for Business Policy, a job that exists because of the students' activism. At the meetings, students and administrators discuss the problems that have surfaced in various factories making Georgetown apparel, and how the university should respond to the problems. The students still keep pushing on a variety of fronts; the latest push is for a Designated Supplier Program (DSP) that would grant long-term contracts to model factories.[23] But there is no need to occupy anybody's office; the activists have a spot at the table. Actually, it's their table.

With a long historical perspective, it seems clear that when the meetings get boring, we have taken a step forward. Boring meetings mean that the radical has become mainstream, and that the establishment has changed its mind about the very nature of right and wrong. The struggles for bans on child labor, or for fire exits or minimum wage or factory codes of conduct, are never boring. But when the fight is won, the meetings get boring. While the battle rages for and against, it is interesting. But when the battle is over and the fight is no longer about *whether* to have fire exits but where to put them, not *whether* to have a minimum wage, but how to administer it, not *whether* to disclose factory locations but by what means and how often—when the establishment has changed its mind and we are just working out the details in (yet another) early morning committee meeting—it gets boring.

My boredom in the meetings was a very good sign for He Yuan Zhi and the many other garment workers I have met, as well as for all of the sisters in time who will follow them.

The saga of the collegiate anti-sweatshop movement would have rung familiar to Mahatma Gandhi. In encouraging an earlier generation of social and political activists, Gandhi described the historical pattern that has proven to be every bit as ineluctable as the race to the bottom: "First they ignore you, then they laugh at you, then they fight you, then you win."

Bad for Boy Rats

The race to the bottom in labor conditions that is fueled by globalization is not the only race that concerns trade skeptics. Increasingly, environmental issues have joined labor issues as a concern of social activists. During the anti-globalization protests of the early part of the decade, it was common for protestors to dress up as sea turtles, eagles, or other elements of nature that were allegedly at risk in our rapidly globalizing world.

Could it be that free trade is igniting a "race to the bottom" in environmental practices as well? As the relentless cost pressures push factories to the cheapest locations, will not corporations naturally seek out the locations in which the environmental rules are weakest? Indeed, some scholars see the battles to protect the environment in the face of trade and industrialization as part and parcel of the battle to protect workers. Historian Theodore Steinberg writes:

> Not only the conflict over the workplace, over wages and hours, but the struggle to control and dominate nature is central to industrialization. The face-to-face relations of power in the factory should be supplanted with a broader vision of conflict going on outside the factory walls. That struggle, at least in part, is over who will control the natural world and to what ends. Industrial capitalism is as much a battle of nature as it is over work, as likely to result in strife involving water or land as wages or hours.[24]

There is little doubt that without appropriate regulations in place, the production of T-shirts can be toxic to the planet, just as without labor laws and codes of conduct the race to the bottom will lead to children working in sweatshops. Environmental behavior is the classic case of an economic "externality" that necessitates regulation: Firms that dump toxins into rivers or burn cheaper fossil fuels for energy are able to reduce their own costs, but higher costs are borne by society at large. Just as a T-shirt can be used as a symbol of the evils of globalization, my T-shirt's life story can also be easily spun into a doomsday scenario for the environment: pesticides, herbicides, water, bleach, energy, fuel, and chemical dyes are all part of the story. Many readers have asked especially about the environmental effects of the transportation involved in my T-shirt's life story.

Shortly after the first edition of this book was published, researchers at Cambridge University released a study that presented an environmental case study of a cotton T-shirt.[25] The study assumed that the T-shirt was made of American cotton that had been shipped to China to be manufactured into yarn, fabric, and finally a T-shirt. The T-shirt was then shipped to the UK, where it was purchased by a consumer and ultimately disposed of.

The environmental impacts were many, but the bottom line of the study is that the energy use and climate change impacts of the T-shirt's life story were largely decided by each of us. The impacts of the "consumer use" phase of the T-shirt's life dwarfed the impacts of production and transportation. The location of production—that is, international trade—had virtually no effect on the energy profile of the T-shirt. Remarkably, the energy use and climate change impact of the T-shirt's life was reduced by 60% if the consumer made the simple shift from clothes dryer to clothesline and to a lower temperature of washing water. Another study found that the consumer phase of the T-shirt's life accounted for an even greater share of the environmental impacts. The study concluded "that the consumer holds the best possibilities for influencing the product's overall environmental profile."[26] While continued advances in green production processes are clearly important, those of us who wear T-shirts have a greater role to play in environmental sustainability than those who produce them.

I n 2008, I took another look at my T-shirt. The parrot on the front had become as familiar as an old friend. I had spent most of the prior decade researching, writing, or speaking about where my T-shirt had come from, but I suddenly realized that I had no idea where the *parrot* had come from. I soon realized that the parrot was just one example from my T-shirt's life story in which the question of "where it came from" led to an environmental quagmire.

The bright-red bird, I soon learned, was made of plastisol ink, and plastisol in turn is typically made by combining polyvinyl chloride (PVC) and phthalates. Phthalates are used to make plastics soft and pliable, and are ubiquitous in our everyday life. Phthalates are in our printed T-shirts, our rubber duckies, our plastic wrap, and our shower curtains.

Scientists agree that heavy exposure to phthalates is very bad news if you are a boy rat.[27] *Phthalate syndrome*, a term coined by EPA scientist Earl Gray, refers to the propensity of male rats exposed to phthalates to develop a range of reproductive difficulties, including deformities in their sexual organs, reduced fertility, and a variety of more feminine characteristics. In essence, boy rats exposed to higher levels of phthalates are more like girl rats, both in their physical characteristics and in their behavior. In 2005, a team led by Dr. Shanna Swan at the University of Rochester published a study showing that the same type of genital differences that had been found in male rodents were also present in humans. Baby boys whose mothers had been exposed to higher levels of phthalates had measurable *feminization* of their sexual organs.[28]

Of course, another problem is that unlike the T-shirt itself, which will eventually decompose somewhere, the parrot, made of plastic, will live forever. The phthalates are but one more element of the complex and evolving environmental story of the T-shirt's life: The science is advancing, the impacts are uncertain and evolving. Of course, our choice is not to destroy the planet and our health or to go naked. In textiles and apparel, as well as in other industries, clean technologies are increasingly available, though often at higher cost than traditional technologies.

Trade: Friend or Foe of the Planet?

In the debate over trade and globalization, the question is not whether the production and use of T-shirts is environmentally harmful, but whether trade in T-shirts makes the problem better or worse. The race-to-the-bottom logic (i.e., the "pollution haven" hypothesis)—that freer trade will spur production to flow to the cheapest locations, which are likely to be countries with lax environmental regulations—suggests that even if trade creates wealth and improves working conditions over time, this improvement will come at an ecological cost. In the race-to-the-bottom scenario, as consumers demand cheaper and cheaper T-shirts, companies and countries employing clean technologies will be shunned and the dirtiest T-shirts will win the race—to the detriment of the environment. At the same time, a related prediction holds that free trade will harm the environment through the *scale* effect: Trade increases the level of economic activity and therefore also increases the level of production and consumption of goods and services. Free trade in apparel leads to higher incomes, which in turn lead to more pesticides to grow more cotton to produce more T-shirts to be dyed with more chemicals. All of the T-shirts will then travel further, consuming more oil and emitting more air pollution.[29]

The doomsday scenario that links free trade with environmental degradation, however, is just that: a scenario. Significant research has been devoted to the relationship between trade and environmental quality during the past several years. While there are valid elements in the doomsday scenario, there are—just as in the race to the bottom in labor standards—opposing forces at work.

Most evidence to date points to the existence of the inelegantly named *environmental Kuznets curve*. This curve suggests that as countries first industrialize, they experience environmental degradation as economic activity moves from subsistence farms to cities and factories. However, as incomes continue to grow, citizens become more and more willing to pay for cleaner water and air, and environmental quality begins to improve as cleaner technologies are adopted.[30] In brief, "Poor countries appear relatively unpolluted, middle-income countries more polluted, and rich countries clean again."[31] As Copeland and Taylor write, "If higher real incomes generate a greater ability and willingness to implement and enforce environmental regulations, then the logical chain linking trade liberalization and environmental destruction is broken."[32]

Indeed, as international trade boosts incomes, the result is not a race to the bottom but instead to the top as wealthier countries are increasingly willing to pay for environmental quality. Arik Levinson found that for the 30-year period ending in 2002, total pollution emitted by U.S. manufacturers fell by 60%, even though real manufacturing output increased by 70%. Levinson concluded that the cleanup of American manufacturing was due largely to the adoption of cleaner technologies, while shifting polluting industries abroad played at most a minimal role.[33]

Of course, free trade also allows clean technologies to spread across borders: Recent research suggests that freer trade regimes have not only facilitated access to clean technologies but have also led to more rapid adoption of these technologies by poor countries.[34] In addition, trade allows rich-country consumer preferences to influence technology choice in poor countries. And there is reason to believe that trade enables a race to the top of another sort: In a globalized economy, companies will often design products to meet the environmental standards in the most heavily regulated market. (For a number of years, California has had emissions standards for automobiles that were the strictest in the United States. Companies exporting cars to the U.S. market must therefore "race to the top," i.e., produce to meet the strict California standards.) In mid-2008, the European Union was preparing to ban a number of chemicals that were legal in the United States. As a result, global firms were planning to shift production methods to meet the new European standards.[35] Without international trade, there would be no incentive for companies to adapt to the stricter standards outside their borders.

By mid-2008, it appeared that my red parrot was in trouble. Following negative publicity as well as street protests, Toys'R'Us, Wal-Mart, and Target announced plans to phase out phthalates and PVCs in a number of products, and big toymakers such as Mattel started to test plastics made from corn.[36] A quick walk around my local shopping center revealed phthalate-free baby products, water bottles, and T-shirts. Rather than wait for something to happen at the federal level, as of the spring of 2008, California had placed strict limits on the sale and manufacture of phthalates, and perhaps a dozen other states were considering similar rules.[37] Such limits were already in effect in Europe. Predictably, most apparel firms in China began to offer "phthalate-free inks" in their manufacturing processes. It seemed clear that the red parrot of the future would be greener. Also in 2008, the world's first carbon-neutral apparel factory opened. The factory, in Sri Lanka, produces underwear for U.K. retailer Marks & Spencer.[38]

The unwitting conspiracy, then, can work in environmental protection as it does for labor issues. While international market competition might appear to threaten the environment, it also creates the wealth that leads in turn to demands for environmental protection and for sustainably produced products.

Though the research continues to evolve, at least to date the evidence suggests that countries more open to trade have better environmental profiles, and that the environmental doomsday scenario linking globalization with environmental degradation has little empirical support. Researchers have failed to find evidence of the "race to the bottom," or pollution haven hypothesis.[39] Indeed, in reviewing this research, Jeffrey Frankel concluded that the net effects of trade on the environment were instead positive.[40]

These findings in no way minimize the environmental challenges facing the planet; they instead suggest that international trade is more likely part of the solution than part of the problem.

The China Challenge

The happy story that links trade and globalization to improved protections for both labor and the environment works better in some countries than in others. The argument that the economic development and income gains that result from trade will lead to better outcomes for labor and for the environment relies first on the assumption that higher incomes will lead citizens to demand these greater protections—a reasonable assumption that has empirical support. But it also relies on the assumption that someone is listening to the citizens' demands. In brief, without some way of making their voices heard, that is, in the absence of democracy, it is more difficult for citizen demands, whether for cleaner water or minimum wage, to work their way into law. The happy story of the unwitting conspiracy relies as well on other elements of a civil society. Well-functioning regulatory and judicial systems that are free from corruption are important, as is a free and active press.

In *The China Price*, Alexandra Harney documented the astonishing manner in which some Chinese apparel factories evade the code-of-conduct requirements of their American and European customers.[41] Harney discovered "falsification engineers" who helped companies deceive the social auditors, and also discovered software that could generate fake payroll, overtime, and benefits data for a large factory in under 30 minutes.[42] Perhaps most ingenious was the network of "5-star factories"— some companies have model factories open to the social auditors, while actually producing most of the goods in shadow factories that are unknown to even the local Chinese authorities.[43]

In 2006, Chinese government investigators went to visit the Fuan textile mill in South China.[44] The factory is owned by Fountain Set, the largest manufacturer of cotton knit T-shirt fabric in the world. The authorities had paid a visit because farmers nearby had protested that the river flowing downstream from the factory was dark red. (In a joke that was repeated to me many times, you can tell which colors are coming into fashion by looking at the rivers in southern China.) The investigators found a hole in a concrete wall. When they crawled through, they found a concealed pipe that was dumping 22,000 tons of dye water per day directly into the river. Though the factory had a wastewater treatment system, bypassing the system and dumping directly into the river shaved the costs in their highly competitive business. In another factory a few miles west, employees took boats out into the river and dumped dye neutralizer in an attempt to turn the water from red back to its brackish brown. The neutralizer was even more toxic than the dye, and dead fish bobbed to the surface. Local farmers were afraid to water their crops.[45] Elizabeth Economy has discovered similar widespread cheating all over China as companies attempt to evade environmental regulations.[46]

Economic growth alone will not generate labor and environmental protections; the other elements of civil society must function as well.[47] Ideally, citizens make their views known through a democratic process, and lawmakers respond with effective regulations. Abuses are brought to light by an independent press, and violators are dealt with by a noncorrupt regulatory and judicial system. In sum, protections are most effective in well-functioning democracies. Fortunately, most measures of democratization are improving for the world at large.[48]

Less fortunately, however, while China's economy is booming, its performance in these other spheres of civil society is not. It is not an accident, then, that China, a one-party state with rampant corruption, a party-controlled judicial system, and tight controls on journalists, has been a wellspring of environmental disasters and labor abuses. Yet even in China, the tide continues to turn.

The Race Moves On

The race to the bottom, the race to the top, and the unwitting conspiracy between social and market forces were all at work in eastern China in 2008. Even though China's record on a variety of civil and political liberties leaves much to be desired, as China has become wealthier its citizens have found a variety of ways to make their views known. Ching Kwan Lee writes that though the traditional view of the Chinese worker is as a "diabolically exploited, haplessly diligent, mindlessly docile, nondescript and disposable human being,"[49] the truth is that even by official Chinese government count there are now thousands of workplace protests each year by newly empowered workers demanding fair-pay practices and better working conditions.[50] A new Chinese labor law, in effect as of January 1, 2008, was responsive to many of the workers' demands, and represents a significant expansion of employee rights and protection in China.[51]

Chinese citizens are also increasingly making their voices heard on issues of environmental protection. The Chinese government itself has warned that environmental degradation is a potential source of social instability, and has released a report pointing to the "alarming" increase in environmental activism in both cities and rural areas.[52]

Chinese authorities have responded with a variety of laws strengthening protection for the environment.[53] Indeed, one industry expert argued that the stringency of the new environmental regulations would make it impossible to construct a traditional knitting and dyeing mill in southern China,[54] which is just as well, according to the newly wealthy surrounding communities, which prefer clean waterways to factory work. At the same time, pressures from the global community and especially from western companies for China to clean up both labor and environmental problems continue.[55]

The market forces were pushing in the same directions as the activists. Wealthier workers are increasingly likely to eschew garment factory work, and factories have responded by trying to woo workers with higher salaries and better perks, ranging from roller rinks to swimming pools. A worker in a South China shoe factory explained the transition simply: "Now it's not the factories choosing me. It's me choosing the factory."[56] And researchers continue to confirm the commonsense proposition that better working conditions are a market-led result of higher-skill industrialization.[57] Yet markets alone do not generate protections for workers or for the environment. Instead, as Peter Dougherty argues, it is often the protections demanded by the activists that facilitate the development of the markets.[58]

Labor costs in coastal China are increasing rapidly, and garment workers in this region now make approximately triple the wage as lower-cost producers such as Pakistan and Vietnam, as well as significantly more than the workers in the rural areas of China.[59] In 2008, stories abounded of firms moving apparel sourcing to less expensive areas of China and to other countries. All in all, the higher market wages, as well as the cost of complying with greater environmental and worker protections, have pushed light manufacturing costs up by 20 to 40 percent in recent years.[60] Garment factories in eastern China are shrinking, closing, and moving on to the next stops in the race—the inland areas of China as well as Bangladesh, Vietnam, and Pakistan.

The garment workers in Shanghai and south China may no longer stitch T-shirts, but there will be plenty to do. Chinese production of machinery, electronics, automobiles, and other high-end goods is growing, and the former seamstresses will take their new confidence and their new wardrobes to jobs at Coca Cola, General Motors, and Starbucks— or perhaps to Lenovo, which in 2005 purchased the personal computer business from IBM.

Other garment workers will take their savings back to the rural areas, where economic growth is now accelerating. The factory wages brought home are building houses, sending siblings to school, and starting businesses. In 2008, after a decade in Shanghai garment factories, He Yuan Zhi returned with her savings to Jianxi province.

A few years ago, I was given a coffee-table book of photos taken in Shanghai before the Communist revolution of 1949.[61] One section of the photo book is titled "Cotton Thieves," and the desperation, the fear, the abject poverty of the Shanghai mill workers nearly leapt from the pages. In one photo, children chase after a horse-drawn cart that was bringing raw cotton from the port into the mill. The children were hoping a fluff or two of cotton would fall from the cart. If they could grab a fluff, then perhaps they could spin a few inches of yarn themselves, to sell or to mend with, or perhaps the fluff could help to pad a jacket for the winter. In other photos, the mill workers themselves tried to tuck small fluffs into their clothing. The photographs show the bloody results for those who were caught.

We can try to imagine the desperation that would lead a mother to risk a bloody arrest for a small tuft of raw cotton, but we cannot, and neither can the garment workers in Shanghai today.

I thought of these photographs on a 2007 visit to the Number 8 spinning factory not far from downtown Shanghai. Using typical Communist flair, the Chinese government gave companies numbers, not names; the Number 1 cotton yarn factory, the Number 2 factory, and so forth, all the way up to number 40. Today, just six of these remain open, the rest razed and remodeled to make way for the new Shanghai as the race to the bottom moves on. The cotton mill I was visiting in 2007 was no longer a mill; it had been transformed into a complex of contemporary art galleries. Yet the bones of the mill were still in place, and plaques informed visitors that they were entering "the cotton receiving room" or "the spinning room." The complex contained perhaps a dozen buildings.

Of course, if the walls could talk they would tell of the workers killed in the Communist Revolution, and the managers who committed suicide during the Cultural Revolution. They would tell of the cotton thieves in the photo book and the mail slots where unwanted babies were dropped. They would tell of the hope of the reform era, when China began to sell cotton T-shirts to America. They would tell of the activists who fought for bathroom breaks or fire exits or overtime pay. They would tell of the race that stopped here for just a moment in time.

I sat near the old spinning room, which was now a chic café for the art gallery visitors. The waiter had a nose ring and streaked hair, and spoke perfect English. The "cotton thieves" photos had been taken near here just 60 years before, but it could have been a different universe. The race to the bottom had moved on, and in the cotton spinning room was not a sweatshop worker but a chef. She told me that she had come from the countryside to attend cooking school. Her mother had worked in a garment factory, which had paid for the tuition, but the garment factory had recently closed, and her mother was now comfortable in retirement. I asked the young woman whether she could sew. "No," she laughed. "But I can make tiramisu."

PART III

TROUBLE AT THE BORDER

Auggie Tantillo and Julia Hughes on Either Side of Matt Priest, Deputy Assistant Secretary for Textiles and Apparel at the U.S. Department of Commerce. (Author's Photo.)

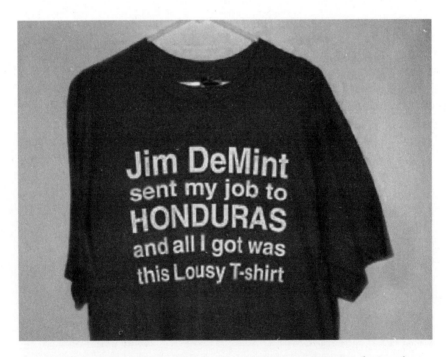

Textile Trade Issues Assume Prime Importance in 2004 South Carolina Senate Race. (Photo Courtesy of Tanya Sisk, South Carolina Democratic Party.)

RETURNING TO AMERICA

Chinese T-Shirts Versus American Jobs

The shipping container stacked with T-shirts boards the freighter in Shanghai and heads back across the Pacific.[1] The ship travels south along the western coast of Mexico and squeezes through the Panama Canal before heading north to the Miami port, and finally to the screen-printing factory at Sherry Manufacturing. At this point, the T-shirts enter the most complex and challenging phase of their lives: trying to gain access to the U.S. market. Chinese T-shirts and Chinese immigrants have similar experiences in attempting to get to America. In both cases, the journey is expensive, risky, and often illegal. There is an army waiting on shore, ready to fight the invasion. The U.S. apparel industry has lost the race to the bottom, and while this may be the result of a "happy concurrence of causes," as David Hume suggested in 1748, not everybody is happy about it. Most of the American South has moved onward and upward from textile production, but there are pockets across the Carolinas and Georgia where the mills are still at the center of the economy and the community. Losers in the U.S. textile and apparel industries are not going gracefully, especially not when losing to China. The textile and apparel trade is the most managed and protected manufacturing trade in U.S. history, or, as one writer noted, "the most spectacular and comprehensive protectionist regime in existence."[2]

Whether the regime has at the same time been a spectacular success or failure depends on one's point of view.

W hen Auggie Tantillo sees a T-shirt from China, he gets a bad feeling in his stomach, but his reflex is fight rather than flight. Auggie can go into Wal-Mart to buy soap or batteries, but he can't even walk by the clothing without the feeling coming back, so he avoids that section of the store entirely. Auggie is executive director of the American Manufacturing Trade Action Coalition (AMTAC), an advocacy group dedicated to preserving manufacturing jobs in the U.S. textile and apparel industries. Auggie represents not so much a "special interest" as a moral viewpoint. As the youngest of nine children in a traditional Sicilian family, Auggie is used to fighting for his fair share. He is soft-spoken, fiercely intelligent, and very sure that he is right. Auggie has spent his entire adult life on defense, trying to block or slow the waves of cheap clothing imports flowing into U.S. markets. For 35 years, the waves have been growing bigger, but he keeps bouncing back, ready to block and punch.

But Auggie thinks the fight with China could be the last. Between 2000 and 2007, the U.S. textile and apparel industries lost more than one-half of their remaining jobs, and looming on Auggie's horizon—and on the horizon of manufacturers everywhere—is the China threat, as well as a new set of rules to take force in 2009. Auggie believes that U.S. producers of yarn, fabric, and apparel have no hope of competing with China under the new rules, even as costs in China increase and the Chinese firms experience threats of their own. Unless somebody stops China, it will be all over, Auggie told me. Waves of T-shirts, socks, underwear, caps, sweaters, pants, and ties will come flooding in, and will drown the U.S. textile industry within the decade, along with the industries in dozens of other countries. Unless somebody stops China, there won't be another war to fight because there won't be an industry left to save.

Auggie used to have a bigger army in the war against apparel imports, but one by one his fellow soldiers have dropped out, or worse yet, defected to the dark side. The AKA (American Knitwear Association), ASA (American Sweater Association), and TIA (Trouser Institute of America) are all gone now, the industry associations having no *raison d'être* without an industry. In 1991, more than half of Americans' clothing was produced domestically, but in 2007, 95 percent of the 20 billion garments Americans purchased were produced overseas.[3]

In 2003, I met with executives of the American Textile Manufacturers Institute (ATMI), which for half a century had been the booming voice of the industry in Washington, where congressmen would answer their calls on the first ring, and even U.S. presidents made sure to stay friendly. When I went back a year later, the ATMI was gone, having shrunk and consolidated with other gasping textile associations into a shadow of itself, a shadow that often did not get its calls returned from Capitol Hill. Worse than the soldiers who have faded away, however, are the defectors. A Rolodex full of former government officials and even members of Congress are now across enemy lines, arguing not just for free trade in general but for free trade in T-shirts in particular.

Auggie understands the pull to the dark side. Increasingly, that is where the paymasters are, the rich retailers, the powerful China lobby, and all of the U.S. apparel firms that are now just importing machines. Auggie understands that there are more realists than idealists in Washington, though he himself isn't one of them. For most of his life, the manufacturing job news released every month has been bad news, and Auggie seems to take each layoff personally. But he also knows that without his relentless scuffles, there would be fewer jobs still, so he keeps going. Auggie also knows that, in the long run, he will lose. But on the way to losing there are victories, and these keep him energized. When Auggie can keep a factory open for a few more years, then a community will stay intact a while longer, a few more children will grow up with working parents, and a few more of them will be able to go to college. Every day a U.S. textile mill stays open is a win for Auggie Tantillo, and every day somebody keeps a job is a good day.

Though Auggie's army is smaller than it once was, the troops are rallying in the fight against China. After years of squabbling and splintering, there is a renewed unity and purpose in the face of a common enemy. In July 2003, the leaders of the ATMI, AMTAC, NTA, AYSA, AFMA, NCC, ASIA, ATMA, CRI, GTMA, THA, AFAI, NCMA, and TDA joined forces in a powerful alphabet army to demand that the Bush administration take action against China.[4] They demanded that the U.S. government institute "safeguard" quotas restricting Chinese textile and apparel imports, and also demanded that apparel from other countries be restricted in its use of Chinese fabrics. Weeks later, they fired off more specific requests, demanding immediate limits on Chinese knit fabrics, brassieres, dressing gowns, and gloves. In the meantime, a delegation from China flew to Washington to stop the madness, and the Bush administration had to decide whether to anger the Chinese—just when it needed China's cooperation on dozens of other issues, ranging from North Korea to semiconductors to intellectual property—or anger Auggie, just when it needed his help in the upcoming election. The Bush administration sided with Auggie and restricted the imports from China.

In 2004, another election year, Auggie turned up the heat. As President Bush rushed around campaigning in the swing states, AMTAC filed about a dozen more safeguard petitions to restrict Chinese imports of goods such as T-shirts, cotton pants, and underwear.[5] Unwilling to risk the wrath of the voters in the textile mills, the Bush administration again sided with Auggie.

When Auggie and I met again in the summer of 2008, he was again gearing up to use his election-year leverage. Observers expected about 10 tight Senate races throughout the textile South, and Auggie was plotting to extract China-related promises wherever he could.

Julia Hughes, Washington representative for the U.S. Association of Importers of Textiles and Apparel, is a leader in the opposing army, and has sat across the table from Auggie many times over the years. While Julia respects Auggie's integrity and commitment, she just thinks that Auggie is wrong, and that he and his troops should stop whining and join the twenty-first century. And besides, from Julia's perspective, almost everything has gone Auggie's way. As Julia sees it, Auggie's army has had unfair advantages for nearly 60 years. Where Auggie sees a flood of T-shirts from China washing American jobs away, Julia sees the Chinese T-shirts as underdogs with both hands tied behind their backs, hopelessly handicapped against the political power of Auggie's troops.

Most economists, of course, are on Julia's side. Under the widely accepted doctrine of free trade, the best course of action for both the United States and China is for everyone to clear the ring and let the best T-shirts win. This is the best course for the United States, where access to the best T-shirts at the best prices will boost incomes; it is the best course for Charlotte, North Carolina, which is now a regional hub in the global economy; and it is the best course for developing countries, where, as we have seen, exports of textiles and apparel provide a route from rural poverty and a first step onto the development ladder.

But free trade may not be the best course—at least in the short run—for Kannapolis, North Carolina, where nearly 2,500 textile workers lost their jobs on a single day in 2003 when the Pillowtex factories closed, or for the nearby town of Mt. Airy, where 1,000 jobs disappeared along with the Gildan Hosiery mills in 2007.[6]

My T-shirt's perilous journey home shows that the best economic policy from the perspective of the United States or even North Carolina does not make for the best politics, and that trade in T-shirts is not (yet) a contest of faster-better-cheaper on the part of competing businesses, but is instead a contest played out in the realm of politics. While the market forces powering the race to the bottom are strong, the political forces pushing back against the markets are strong as well, particularly in the United States. Trade flows in T-shirts are the result of economic forces but also the result of thousands of deals cut in Washington, Geneva, and Beijing, and politics are at least as important as markets in understanding the T-shirt's journey. Many of the firms still standing in the U.S. industry do not believe that they should have to compete with sweatshops that pay their workers 50 cents an hour, and especially not with China, where cheating of almost every type is rampant. Better to build a fence to keep out the lions than to run an unfair race that can't be won. The fence hasn't worked as well as many U.S. producers would have liked, but it has slowed the competition down. Most of all, it has confused them.

The effects of political barriers to Chinese apparel to the United States are readily apparent. While Chinese apparel has captured approximately 85 percent of apparel imports in several other industrialized countries, as of 2008, China's share of the U.S. apparel imports was approximately 30 percent.[7] China's victory in the race to the bottom is obvious when we examine its overall exports, but is far less striking when we examine its performance in the U.S. market (see Figure 9.1). My Chinese T-shirt, in particular, was one of the lucky ones. As Figure 9.2 shows, U.S. imports of cotton knit shirts from other regions have grown far more rapidly than have imports from China. As we will see, it is trade policy, not comparative advantage, that explains these patterns.

Auggie Tantillo and Julia Hughes spend their days in a Washington dance, following each other around the Commerce Department, the Congress, Customs, and the office of the U.S. Trade Representative, with Auggie trying to plug holes in the import dike and Julia trying to punch them open. Because Auggie and Julia are in constant motion, the trade policies governing apparel are in constant motion, as well. Textiles and

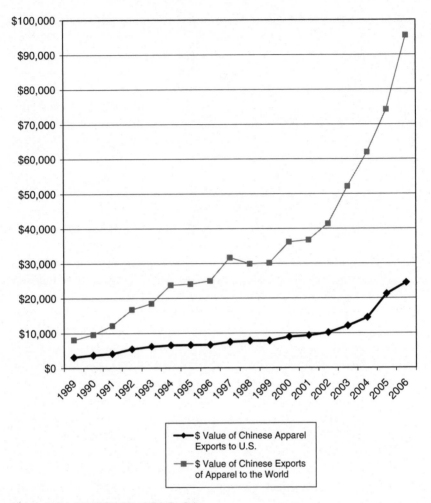

Source: UN COMTRADE, SITC.2, 84.

Figure 9.1   Dollar Value of Chinese Apparel Exports to World vs. Value of Chinese Apparel Exports to U.S. (in Millions of US $)

apparel are subject to not only a higher level of trade protection but also a higher level of trade protection complexity than any imports into the United States outside of agricultural goods.

During the time that I was writing and revising this book, the rules governing apparel imports into the United States seemed to change almost daily. The rules governing how many T-shirts of which types could be sold by which countries; the fabric the T-shirts could be made of under

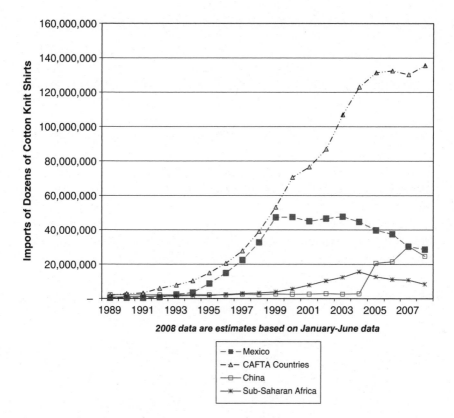

2008 data are estimates based on January-June data

— ■ — Mexico
— ▲ — CAFTA Countries
—◻— China
—✳— Sub-Saharan Africa

Source: OTEXA (apparel categories 338 and 339).

Figure 9.2   U.S. Imports of Cotton Knit Shirts

alternative regimes; whether a collar counted as a "component" or a "trim" (and whether it mattered); where the T-shirt's fabric could be dyed and "finished"; and, of course, tariffs, had all changed. In 1999, the rules did not look so bad for a Chinese T-shirt trying to enter the United States, but by 2003, the rules shifted against the Chinese in favor of producers in the Caribbean and Mexico. For a brief period in 2005, the rules were back on China's side, though this had reversed by the middle of the year to leave Central American producers on top. By 2009, however, it appears that the rules will be back on China's side, though not if Auggie Tantillo can help it.

Gary Sandler, the owner of Sherry Manufacturing in Miami, faces a daunting task in keeping apace with the rules governing T-shirt imports into the United States. Simply put, the rules are nuts, as even the people who made them readily agree.

A Taste of the (Crazy) Rules in 2008

Under the 2006 Central American Free Trade Agreement (CAFTA), Sherry Manufacturing may import apparel from El Salvador, Honduras, Nicaragua, Guatemala, and the Dominican Republic free from tariffs and quantitative limits.[8] In mid-2008, Costa Rica was expected to join the agreement soon.

However, in order for the apparel to have duty-free access to the U.S. market, it must generally meet the *yarn-forward* test, which requires that each step of apparel production from the spinning of the yarn "forward" take place in one of the member countries. For a T-shirt, the rule means that the yarn must be spun, the fabric manufactured, and the garment cut and sewn in a member country. In effect, the yarn-forward requirement is a boon for U.S. textile mills because it limits the ability of the Central American apparel producers to source yarn and fabric from elsewhere, and therefore creates a captive market for U.S. yarn spinners and fabric producers.

For some apparel, such as brassieres and woven boxer shorts, the *fabric-forward* rule instead applies. As a result, for this apparel a U.S. fabric manufacturer may source the yarn from Asia, for example, and ship the resulting fabric to a CAFTA country. When it returns to the United States as boxer shorts or brassieres, the import is duty-free. This provision tosses crumbs to U.S. fabric manufacturers, who often feel politically overpowered by the yarn-spinning companies.

If the apparel is manufactured in Nicaragua and made of cotton or manmade fabrics (but not wool), a limited amount of apparel may enter the United States freely even though it contains yarn and fabric from outside the region. However, an exception applies to trousers, for which manufacturers must use at least half U.S.-made fabric. For all apparel made of wool, a fabric-forward rule applies, which means, for example, that a U.S. knitting mill could use Australian yarn and the resulting garment would retain its duty-free status.

Certain categories of apparel are allowed to be made of Canadian or Mexican fabrics, not to exceed specified annual limits, and some apparel may also use certain nylon yarns from Israel. Mexico can import some apparel free of duty from the CAFTA countries, but only if the apparel is constructed of U.S.-made yarn and fabric. For knit fabric (not apparel), a *fiber-forward* rule applies. This means a U.S. fabric manufacturer who produces T-shirt fabric must use American-grown cotton in order to retain duty-free status (some crumbs for American cotton farmers). Apparel *linings* must also meet the fabric-forward rule for the clothing to retain its duty-free status. Special rules are in place for Honduran socks.

Finally, in 2008 a multi-year negotiation over the *pocketing provisions* of CAFTA was finally settled. In the original agreement, the fabric that comprised the "essential character" of the garment was required to meet the various tests. For blue jeans, for example, blue denim would represent the "essential character" and would be subject to the rules. However, in 2008, U.S. textile interests were successful in inserting a pocketing provision that required that pocketing fabrics also meet the yarn-forward origination requirements. In the summer of 2008, the U.S. Association of Importers of Textiles and Apparel was offering seminars to help retailers understand the new pocketing rules.

Julia, Auggie, and the alphabet armies negotiated for years over the CAFTA provisions, in a telling example of the dominance of politics over markets in T-shirt trade flows. Julia and the U.S. retailers, along with the Central American countries, wanted to simply lift the gates and allow free access to the U.S. market for whatever apparel the CAFTA countries produced. Auggie Tantillo and AMTAC, along with the textile and apparel workers trade union (UNITE), opposed any free access at all for Central American apparel, believing, both procedurally and sub-stantively, that "giving away" access to the U.S. market was bad policy. Some U.S. fabric manufacturers wanted a CAFTA fabric-forward rule that would allow them to produce with yarns from anywhere, while U.S. yarn spinners argued for the yarn-forward requirements. The complexity of the rules is perhaps inevitable, given the nature of these multiple oppos-ing interests. In the end, the rules were hammered out in the only way possible given the disparate interests involved: sock by sock, pocket by pocket.

Equally complex but different rules govern T-shirt imports from Sub-Saharan Africa, under the African Growth and Opportunity Act (AGOA), and from Bolivia, Columbia, and Ecuador, under the Andean Trade Preference Act (ADTPA). Under the North American Free Trade Agreement (NAFTA), still other rules apply to T-shirt imports from Canada and Mexico, and under the Caribbean Basin Trade Partnership Act (CBTPA) another set of rules applies to apparel from 18 countries in the Caribbean.

To Julia Hughes, the only thing more outrageous than all of these rules is to hear them referred to as "free trade" agreements. According to

Julia, a free trade agreement should make it easier, not harder, to trade. The poorest countries of the world, especially those in Africa, already handicapped on almost any dimension, cannot possibly succeed in such a byzantine tangle of rules, Julia believes, and many U.S. importers take one look at the rules and walk away. Trade from these areas is not free at all. It is easier and cheaper (at least once the time is factored in) just to pay the tariff and source from preference-free countries. Julia Hughes once tried to make sense out of the various free trade area provisions for her retail clients. She found, however, that she could not put them on a grid; they were all just too different. Auggie, for his part, believes that the retailers are responsible for the complexities: The complications, as Auggie sees it, are simply the result of all the exceptions that were made for Julia.

I n 2008, cotton T-shirts that did not meet the requirements for "preferential treatment," either because they came from countries outside the membership of AGOA, the CBTPA, ADTPA, CAFTA, or NAFTA, or because they did not meet the requirements regarding the origin of the fabric or yarn, were charged an import tariff of 16.5 percent, except if they were from Jordan, Israel, Bahrain, Peru, or Morocco. For these countries, bilateral agreements reduce the tariff to zero *if* the T-shirt passes certain tests, while for most Australian T-shirts, the tariff was 15.5 percent. As of July 2008, perhaps a half-dozen other free trade agreements were in various stages of negotiation or implementation, each, of course, with slightly different T-shirt rules.[9] Finally, Vietnam—the country many believed would be the next stop in the race to the bottom—was subject to a special "monitoring agreement" that allowed the United States to take unilateral action to reduce imports if U.S. textile or apparel manufacturers were threatened.[10]

Complexities are apparent in the tariff schedule as well. The 2008 tariff schedule contains 97 chapters and 543 pages of explanatory notes. The knit apparel chapter alone is 75 pages long, not including explanatory notes. For some apparel, the power of particular companies is evident. Tariffs are nearly 30 percent on some categories of clothing, including, for example, Harmonized Tariff Schedule category 6102.30.20, which is:

> womens' or girls' overcoats, car coats, capes, cloaks, anoraks (including ski jackets), windbreakers, and similar articles, knitted or crocheted, of

man-made fiber, containing less than 25% leather by weight and containing 23% or less wool or fine animal hair.

It might be hard to imagine such a garment, but it is clear from the tariff rate—nearly the highest of any on apparel—that someone in the United States manufactures them.

Until 2005, imports for an additional 40 countries were limited under the umbrella of the Agreement on Textiles and Clothing (ATC).[11] The ATC in turn is the phase-out mechanism for the Multifiber Agreement (MFA), which had set quantitative limits, or quotas, on clothing and textile imports from dozens of countries since 1974. The regime, as we will see, had many effects: good, bad, and mostly unintended.

Finally, as of 2008, import quotas, or limits, remained in effect for dozens of categories of textiles and apparel from China (see Figure 9.3).

Category	Description	Import Quantity Limit
222	Knit Fabric	21,482,908 KG
332/432/632	Socks	1,991,095,584 Pr.
338/339	Cotton Knit Shirts	26,938,606 Doz.
340/640	Woven Shirts of Man-Made Fiber or Cotton	8,724,590 Doz.
347/348	Cotton Pants	25,442,951 Doz.
349/649	Brassieres	29,479,266 Doz.
353/652	Underwear	24,302,011 Doz.
363	Cotton Towels	134,828,519 Units
443	Wool Suits	1,756,637 Units
447	Wool Trousers	280,581 Doz.
345/645/646	Sweaters	10,581,854 Doz.
847	Silk or Vegetable Fiber Trousers or Shorts	23,029,668 Doz.

Source: OTEXA.

Figure 9.3 Examples of 2008 U.S. Import Limits on Textiles and Apparel from China

Under the 2005 textile and apparel Memorandum of Understanding with China (MOU), these quotas were to be lifted on January 1, 2009, though what, if any, restrictions will replace them is the subject of the most recent scuffles between Auggie Tantillo and Julia Hughes.

I n the summer of 2008, I attended a seminar for apparel companies in New York City. The seminar's objective was to help the importing companies understand evolving complexities in apparel trade policy. Julia Hughes, as well as officials from various government agencies, gave presentations. I stepped outside for a few minutes, and when I returned I saw that a speaker from the Department of Homeland Security had taken the stage. The speaker, from the Office of Customs and Border Protection (CBP), displayed a PowerPoint slide that read:

> CBP's Mission: CBP's priority mission is keeping terrorists and their weapons out of the United States.

I wasn't sure why this was relevant to T-shirts. Brian Fennessey, the speaker, sounded vaguely threatening. "We know the bad guys are out there," he boomed. "We know what they are up to and we know their tricks. Make no mistake. We're going to track them down, and they will be sorry."

A moment later, I understood. Under pressure from the U.S. textile industry, the Department of Homeland Security had designated textiles and apparel as a "priority trade issue." Inspections specialists at the country's 300 ports of entry are responsible for keeping out terrorists and their weapons, but they had also been given special training and resources to stop socks and pockets that do not meet the complex rules. A leading law firm specializing in trade and customs matters advised apparel companies to stay calm if special agents showed up with guns and badges looking for fugitive socks.[12]

All in all, the restrictions and regulations governing apparel imports are written, administered, and enforced by hundreds of lobbyists and lawyers, as well as bureaucrats from the Department of the Treasury, the Department of Commerce, the Congressional Textile Caucus, the U.S. Trade Representative, and the interdepartmental Committee for the Implementation of Textile Agreements. In fact, a leading textbook illustrates the interlocking webs of government involvement in textile and apparel trade policy with a full-page map containing 11 boxes linked together by a dozen arrows.[13] While the United States is the largest offender, it is not alone. As Richard Friman has shown, other rich countries also employ complex patchwork approaches to protecting their domestic textile industries.[14]

According to many, when the Chinese quotas are finally lifted in 2009, it will be the last nail for the U.S. industry in the sad story of plant closings and job losses that has lasted nearly 60 years. It will also mean the last nail for Auggie Tantillo and the alphabet armies who have fought to save the U.S. industry from the waves of cheap imports.

"It's about time," many people told me. More than a few Washington insiders muttered "dinosaurs" when I asked them about Auggie Tantillo's troops. The Southern textile interests are living in the past, clinging to something that makes no sense in today's global economy, people told me over and over again.

The dinosaur label doesn't bother Auggie. When we first met in 2003, he told me, "We're not extinct. Not yet. "

When I went back to visit Auggie in the summer of 2008, he held out his hand with a battle-worn smile. "We're still here," he said.

DOGS SNARLING TOGETHER

HOW POLITICS CAME TO RULE THE GLOBAL APPAREL TRADE

How did the United States—as the self-anointed free trade champion of the universe—end up with such a dauntingly complex and downright silly mass of barriers to the import of T-shirts? Why, in an era of progressive trade liberalization and increasing deference to the market mechanism, has the role of politics remained so pervasive in this industry?

The first factor to explain the dominance of politics in the trade is the size of the textile and apparel manufacturing base, even today. While textile and apparel employment in the United States peaked shortly after World War II at approximately 2.5 million workers, the industries in 2008 employed about 500,000 people, which accounts for about 4 percent of manufacturing employment.[1] Given the size of the employment base, the unrelenting job losses related to the global race to the bottom have strengthened the political voice of the industry, as the "groans of the weavers" have become both louder and more sophisticated. Winning industries do not groan, and losing industries' groans become louder with the extent of their misfortune. The U.S. textile industry felt the first serious threat from imports immediately after World War II, and foreign competition since that time has been growing steadily and sometimes exponentially, which has led to compensating cries for help from Washington.

Yet the withering of America's competitive position in these industries is not sufficient to explain their political power, as industries from toys to bicycles to televisions have faded away with few rescue missions from Washington. Political response to industrial demise is the result of not only the demise itself, or even the size of the industry, but the strength of industry alliances and the access the alliances have to policymakers.[2] Or, as Jock Nash, perhaps the American textile industry's most colorful voice in Washington, reportedly advises, when a pack of dogs snarl together, people have to listen. The extent to which the industry can speak with one voice—or snarl together—goes a long way toward explaining its political influence.

Erik Autor, Vice-President for International Trade at the National Retail Federation, is continually frustrated by the "snarl together" phenomenon. Though retailers ranging from a beachfront tourist shop to Saks Fifth Avenue to Wal-Mart all benefit from access to cheaper T-shirts from abroad, such diverse groups of businesses find it difficult to speak with a single voice. Southern textile leaders, however, share a cultural and historical bond that allows them to speak together. ("They all know each other," Erik told me. "Their daddies all knew each other. Their granddaddies all built the mills, and they all knew each other, too.")

Related to the historical and cultural bond that strengthens their collective voice is the geographic concentration of the U.S. textile industry. More than 60 percent of apparel and textile manufacturing is located in Georgia, South Carolina, and North Carolina, and there remain many Congressional districts where the textile industry—or even a single firm— is the major employer. A geographic swath of congresspeople remains beholden to the industry, even as its fortunes wane. The U.S. retail industry, in contrast, while employing significantly more people than the textile and apparel industries, is not only unable to snarl in unison, it is spread across the country in a manner that leaves it nobody's Congressional priority.[3]

A third factor that lends support to the regime is that the American public is increasingly nervous about trade, especially trade with China, and especially when the trade is believed to have severe effects on small American communities. The "It coulda been me" syndrome leaves many American voters far more tolerant of complex trade protections than we might expect them to be. While North Carolina now has a diversified economy that has "moved up" from textiles, many towns, along with many less-skilled workers, have not moved up alongside Charlotte.

I was not able to find anyone in Washington and certainly no one in China who was happy with the rules governing imports of T-shirts into the United States, or indeed anyone who tried to defend these rules. Participants from across the spectrum agreed that the deal-making process often showed Washington politics at its worst. But observers on all sides also agree that access to the American apparel consumer is currency in Washington, and this currency, like any good money, can and has been traded for almost anything. Often, the currency has been traded for votes, which has left generations of congresspeople and even a few presidents indebted to the textile industry. Access to the American apparel consumer has also frequently been traded for foreign policy favors, from crushing Communism in Central America to crippling terrorists in Pakistan. Ironically, however, perhaps the most common use of the currency has been to pay Auggie Tantillo and his troops to move out of the way of broader trade-liberalizing initiatives. Beginning at least with Dwight Eisenhower, every U.S. president has paid the U.S. textile industry to be quiet so that America could get on with the business of free trade.

Auggie Goes to Washington

Auggie had thought little about politics and even less about trade policy as he neared his college graduation from Clemson University in 1980. He didn't know what his next step would be, and it was a fluke and a stroke of luck that led to a job as an assistant in Senator Strom Thurmond's office. Auggie left for the big city, having no idea what to expect. If he had opinions about politics, he doesn't remember them. Whatever illusions he might have had, however, were shattered at the ripe old age of 21, when he saw how Washington really worked. Auggie likens his Washington awakening to the day he discovered that Santa Claus was a fake. Santa Claus was President Ronald Reagan.

Strom Thurmond had figured critically in Reagan's 1980 election. Though the U.S. textile industry had a variety of trade protections in place at the time, Asian imports were gushing through new holes in the dike by the day. Between 1976 and 1979, textile and apparel imports into the United States had increased by nearly 50 percent.[4] In exchange for Thurmond's support, Reagan promised, if elected, to put a stop to it. In a letter to Strom Thurmond several months before the election, Reagan promised to limit the growth in textile and apparel imports to the growth in the domestic market.[5]

Thurmond kept his end of the deal and delivered a large Southern vote to Ronald Reagan. Reagan, however, shuffled his feet as Asian imports continued to soar. Auggie was just a note-taker and a gopher, but he remembers Thurmond's outrage as he raced around Washington meeting with Edwin Meese, George Shultz, and James Baker. He pounded the table, shoved the letter under their noses, as mill after mill closed and imports surged. "You've got to do something about this. *You promised.*"

Several people who had been involved with the negotiations in Washington told me that the infamous Reagan textile promise would have been impossible to keep, even with the best of intentions. It would have been a foreign policy disaster to renege on the deals already in place, which allowed imports under quota to grow at a rate of 6 percent, rather than the approximately 1 percent growth in the domestic market. It also would have required the United States to bring under quota many countries that had never been subject to export restraints, as well as to limit imports of many types of textiles and apparel that had also been without quota.

But to Auggie, Strom Thurmond, and the still millions of textile and apparel workers, a deal had been a deal. So, Auggie Tantillo's introduction to Washington was the broken Reagan textile promise. It was Auggie's first experience in the value of textile promises as currency, but it was not the last. Strom Thurmond, who died in 2003 at the age of 100, had played this game before and he would play it again. In fact, every post–World War II president has made his own version of the campaign textile promise to Strom Thurmond, and, beginning in the 1960s, to Fritz Hollings and Jesse Helms as well. Some of the promises have been kept, and some have not.

Since the end of World War II, every U.S. president has also publicly supported the doctrine of free trade. Indeed, scholars of presidential rhetoric cite free trade doctrine as a "remarkably consistent rhetoric" across both time and party lines.[6] For some presidents, free trade was a foreign policy choice, designed to keep Communists or war at bay. For others, it was a clear case of the best economic policy. For yet others, a free trade posture was a matter of moral consistency. The United States had been the architect of the postwar General Agreement on Tariffs and Trade (GATT), a set of rules with free trade principles at its very core. For more than half a century, the United States has been the world's self-appointed champion of free trade, in word if not in deed.

Regardless of what has motivated the free trade rhetoric of U.S. presidents, all have found it impossible to implement the rhetoric without paying the textile and apparel industries to get out of the way. While a long list of trade-liberalizing initiatives—from tariff reductions to NAFTA to CAFTA to China's WTO accession—has been championed by the United States, these initiatives have been politically possible only by making exceptions for Southern textile interests. In television appearances and public speeches, each postwar president has eloquently advanced the case for free trade on the grounds of freedom, prosperity, and morality.[7] But away from the cameras, in private phone calls, furtive telegrams, and secret meetings, each of them has assured the domestic textile industry that he had not really been talking to them.

In 2008, I mentioned this historical pattern to Steve Lamar, EVP for the (pro-trade) American Apparel and Footwear Association. Steve just sighed. "We deal with it all the time," he said. "We call it the 'wink and nod.'"

For nearly 60 years, U.S. policymakers have played a wink-and-nod balancing act with Auggie and his troops, trying to toss (or promise) them enough crumbs to get their votes and cooperation, but not so many as to make an obvious mockery of the free trade rhetoric. Almost every postwar president has needed help from the senators and governors in the Carolinas, who in turn needed help for their textile towns. Each special deal for the industry was labeled a temporary measure, but many of them, in one form or another, are still in place.

Making Deals and Making Exceptions

The first groans of the weavers came shortly after World War II, as cheap Japanese cotton goods took the lead in the race to the bottom. Though official U.S. policy was to open trade with Japan to encourage prosperity and thus stave off the Communist threat in Asia, the mill owners in both New England and the South felt a more immediate threat from the growing imports from Japan than they did from the Communists. The American Cotton Manufacturers Institute (ACMI) announced that a crisis was at hand:

> We are face to face with a life or death question of whether our own government will stand idly by and permit low-wage competition from Japan

to seriously cripple our industry. Must there be closed mills and bread-lines before the administration in Washington concedes the possibility of irreparable damage to our industry?[8]

In order to quiet the groans and especially to advance its broader trade-liberalizing agenda, the Eisenhower administration persuaded Japan to "voluntarily" limit its exports of cotton textiles to the United States to allow temporary breathing room for the U.S. industry. Like much else from the 1950s, from today's perspective the Voluntary Export Restraint (VER) agreement with Japan looks charmingly simple and innocent. The agreement was merely temporary, and it dealt with just one country, Japan. Only one alphabet troop, the American Cotton Manufacturers Institute (ACMI), had been involved, and the agreement covered only a narrow range of goods. Though Eisenhower saw no choice but to toss the crumbs, he was clearly not happy about it. In his diary, he later wrote of the "short-sightedness bordering on tragic stupidity" of the protectionists, and worried that unless the United States opened its markets, Japan would "fall prey to the Communists."[9]

In what would become a long epic of unintended consequences, the politics served to accelerate rather than slow the race to the bottom. The VER, which limited imports from Japan, supplied not so much protection for the U.S. textile industry as an opening for Japan's competitors in the race—especially Hong Kong and Taiwan—to supply the U.S. market. In a pattern that continues to this day, the effect of plugging one hole in the dike was to increase the force of imports gushing through others. Between 1956 and 1961, imports of cotton goods from Hong Kong rose by nearly 700 percent.[10]

The soaring imports led to predictable cries lamenting the imminent collapse of the U.S. industry.[11] In the 1960 presidential campaign, John F. Kennedy promised Governor Ernest Hollings of South Carolina that he would help. Kennedy fulfilled his promise by instituting the Short Term Arrangement on Cotton Textiles (STA) as temporary assistance to the industry. The arrangement allowed the United States to negotiate import limits from other countries—not just Japan—in cotton textiles. The effect was a bigger program, covering both more countries and more goods than the original Japanese VER.

Of course, a short-term reprieve was not enough to save the U.S. industry. In response to the continuing groans, on the expiration of the

STA the Kennedy administration created the Long Term Arrangement for Cotton Textiles (LTA), effective from 1962 to 1967. Just as the STA was a bigger VER, the LTA was a bigger STA, covering more countries, more products, and more years.

In exchange for protecting its own industry against imports, the ACMI dropped its fight against Kennedy's Trade Expansion Act and allowed the Kennedy Round trade liberalization to continue. The Kennedy Round resulted in tariff cuts on U.S. imports of 30 percent, but textile and apparel tariffs were off-limits in the negotiation. They maintained their already high levels and were, in the case of apparel, even increased.[12] Representative Carl Vinson of Georgia proudly wrote the ACMI that, "Thanks to their good friends in Congress, the industry had been singled out for special treatment by President Kennedy and his Cabinet."[13]

The "temporary" LTA was renewed in 1967 and again in 1970, each time as a bribe to allow Lyndon Johnson and then Richard Nixon to seek trade liberalization in other ways. By 1973, the LTA was restricting hundreds of categories of cotton textile imports from dozens of countries. With the passage of the LTA and its extensions, U.S. trade policy for textiles and apparel took the seemingly irreversible step to a complexity that left it unintelligible to all but a few.

However, just as blocking the flow of clothing from Japan had resulted in an even more forceful flow of imports from Hong Kong, blocking imports of cotton textiles and apparel also served to accelerate rather than slow the race to the bottom.

By limiting imports of cotton textiles and apparel, U.S. policy unwittingly encouraged its trading partners to upgrade their production and sales efforts to wool and to the increasingly popular synthetic fibers such as nylon and polyester. Predictably, imports of synthetic fiber apparel from Asia soon soared, with U.S. imports of these fibers from developing countries increasing 2,500 percent between 1964 and 1970.[14] Just as predictably, U.S. textile interests extended their groans to these other sectors. The ACMI morphed into the ATMI (American Textile Manufacturers Institute), and U.S. textile interests began an intensive campaign to extend the LTA to other fibers, calling for the implementation of a Multifiber Agreement (MFA).

In his 1968 presidential campaign, Richard Nixon promised Senator Strom Thurmond that he would seek to broaden the LTA into an MFA and would extend quotas from cotton to wool, synthetic fibers, and blends.[15] Once elected, Nixon faced the familiar challenge of reconciling his free trade rhetoric with his campaign promise. On the one hand, Nixon had a vision of trade as a path not just to economic growth but to political freedom. On the other hand, there was the MFA promise telegram to Thurmond that had been printed in newspapers all over the South. Nixon's rhetoric showed the balancing act, and was typical of rhetoric from Dwight D. Eisenhower to Barack Obama: Free trade was good, but there was a wink and nod for textiles:

> By expanding world markets, our trade policies have speeded the pace of our own economic progress and aided the development of others.... We must seek a continued expansion of world trade, even as we also seek the dismantling of those other barriers—political, social, and ideological—that have stood in the way of a freer exchange of people and ideas, as well as of goods and technology....
>
> [H]owever, the textile import problem, of course, is a special circumstance that requires special measures.[16]

In the end, MFA I, in effect from 1974 to 1977, was signed by 50 countries and covered approximately 75 percent of U.S. textile and apparel imports.[17] In painstaking bilateral negotiations, country after country hammered out with U.S. negotiators how much of which categories of textiles and clothing could enter the U.S. market. Though largely successful in satisfying the domestic textile interests, the MFA was, as William Cline wrote, "an embarrassing breach of the GATT principles," principles that the United States had authored and continued to espouse.[18]

In the 1976 campaign, Jimmy Carter promised to extend the "temporary" MFA. MFA II, which extended the arrangement through 1981, was more restrictive still in allowing access to U.S. and European markets. In the meantime, Carter and then Reagan also wished to maintain the free trade momentum on a new round of trade-liberalization talks—the so-called Tokyo Round. Once again, the textile and apparel industries were largely exempt: The United States cut its import tariffs on manufactured goods to an average of 6.5 percent, but apparel tariffs, while reduced from their postwar highs, remained at an average of 22.5 percent.[19]

Though Ronald Reagan had not kept his election-year textile promise to Strom Thurmond, Reagan had little choice but to toss some crumbs in the direction of the textile industry. Reagan would have to show his face in South Carolina in the 1984 campaign, as Thurmond kept reminding him. With MFA III, the temporary regime of textile and apparel quotas was extended yet again. In effect for the 1981–1986 period, MFA III was the most restrictive yet.

1985 to 1990: The Seed-to-Shirt Coalition

In what had become a predictable pattern, even with the stricter quotas under MFA III, the crisis continued in the U.S. industry and the groans of the weavers were unabated. Though the speakers had changed, the speeches had not. In 1985, Representative Ed Jenkins of Georgia told his House colleagues that the industry was experiencing its "last gasp," while a textile association president threatened that "in five years, the industry will cease to exist."[20]

The renewal of the MFA also did little to lessen the sense of betrayal that still stung from Reagan's unfulfilled promise to Strom Thurmond, and once Reagan had won a second term, the industry's hopes for justice were further dashed. Strom Thurmond's leverage over Reagan was gone, and White House aides had stopped picking up the phone. Ronald Reagan would not have to go back to South Carolina. Yet there was a silver lining in the betrayal: The injustice united the industry in a manner seen neither before nor since. Snarling together, they almost achieved the impossible.

If the White House would not listen, the Congress would have to. The mid-1980s were a golden era of sorts for the domestic textile and apparel industries. Though their fortunes were shrinking and their plants were closing, there was an energy and unity of purpose that propelled them forward. It was a pinnacle, according to Auggie Tantillo and many others with whom I spoke, where standing upon each other's shoulders they had made their greatest reach, coming within only inches of achieving justice. All of the alphabet armies in the U.S. textile and apparel complex, from cotton farmers to yarn spinners to fabric producers to apparel manufacturers— along with the unions representing the workers—began to snarl together. The wide-ranging alliance was dubbed the *seed-to-shirt coalition*.

Auggie Tantillo, still young but by now an expert in the areas of both textile trade policy and the ways of Washington, accepted a position to open the Washington office for Russell Mills, one of America's largest T-shirt producers. United, the seed-to-shirt alliance formed an industry coalition, the Fiber, Fabric, and Apparel Coalition for Trade (FFACT), to battle the imports.

Auggie and his troops sought legislation that would keep the Reagan promise. The Jenkins Global Quota bill would not limit the growth of imports from particular countries, but would instead place a global cap on U.S. textile and apparel imports, and also give the United States unilateral power to restrict imports, rather than requiring negotiations with each trading partner. The bill would roll back quotas for the largest Asian suppliers, as well as negate more than 30 existing bilateral textile and apparel trade agreements.[21] Ronald Reagan and his administration were nervous. Once Auggie and his troops got into the U.S. Capitol, there was no telling what would happen.

Though the framers of the U.S. Constitution placed responsibility for formulating trade policy on the shoulders of the Congress, during the past 50 years it has become increasingly clear—perhaps especially to Congress itself—that they are not up to the task of formulating rational trade policy.[22] Members of Congress seeking election or reelection are often forced into protectionist postures, but can obtain protection for their interests only by offering the same to their congressional colleagues. "The political logic of protection leads to protection all around," wrote an observer in 1935, because Congress's natural tendency is a spiraling protectionism extending trade barriers into the districts of each congressperson.[23] A vote for free trade, according to another early observer, is an "unnatural act" for a congressperson.[24] Only a very few die-hard constitutional literalists believe that the U.S. Congress should be in charge of trade policy.

Julia Hughes understands this all too well. While she has some free trade allies in Congress, she knows that nobody wins elections by promising free trade or help for the apparel consumer. Auggie, however, has comrades in Congress who will fall on their sword, or at least pretend to, to help the U.S. textile industry. From North Carolina through Georgia and Alabama, in town after town, the voters will choose the candidate who promises to keep the mill open. What members of Congress most want, however, is to make protectionist speeches without having to take protectionist actions. Indeed, as I.M. Destler notes, by surrendering power to make trade policy decisions, congresspeople are more freely able to spout protectionist rhetoric, secure in the knowledge that they will be unable to take action:

> A congressman, no matter how keen his desire to help the toy marble makers, does not want to be given the right of voting them an increase in tariff rates. He prefers to be in the position of being allowed merely to place a speech in

their favor in the Congressional Record...free to indulge the responsibility afforded those who do not participate in the final decision.[25]

But FFACT, having been spurned by the Reagan administration, began knocking on the doors of members of Congress. The Jenkins Bill passed easily in both the Senate and the House, where it had 230 cosponsors. But this victory was only the first step, as Reagan swiftly vetoed the bill. Some of those involved in the negotiations told me that at least some congresspeople were able to vote for the bill because they felt assured that Reagan *would* veto it. Dan Rostenkowski, chair of the House Ways and Means Committee, though sympathetic to the plight of the mill workers, saw the bill as being fraught with unworkable elements. "This bill is garbage," he allegedly remarked to Tip O'Neill. O'Neill, surveying the political landscape, replied, "Yeah, but move it along, Dan. Move the garbage."

The override received 276 votes, just 8 votes short of the two-thirds needed to undo Reagan's veto.[26] Yet it was a win of sorts. As Auggie Tantillo remembers, "We scared them good."

To many observers, the close vote was a terrifying brush with insanity, an example of the madness that can result if trade policy is left in the hands of elected representatives. Economist William Cline estimated that the bill would have cut back imports of textiles from Hong Kong, Korea, and Taiwan by nearly 60 percent, and would have cost U.S. consumers approximately $43,945 per U.S. textile job saved.[27] In addition, by the sheer force of its hypocrisy when placed against American free trade rhetoric, it would also have likely tied U.S. hands in pursuing other trade negotiations. And finally, swift and disabling retaliation against U.S. exports was virtually assured.

But, like Auggie said, they had been scared. They had seen the whites of Auggie's eyes, and were willing to talk. The USTR was willing to talk, Hong Kong was willing to talk, and even Reagan was willing to talk. The MFA IV, signed for a five-year period ending in 1991, was the most restrictive yet. For the first time, quotas were placed on fabrics not even produced in the United States, such as silk, ramie, and linen. The only fibers now exempt from U.S. quotas were jute and abaca, though U.S. negotiators warned that these, too, would be dealt with if imports surged.

In the meantime, Auggie Tantillo had moved up yet again. After serving a stint as Strom Thurmond's Chief of Staff, Auggie was appointed by President George H. W. Bush as Undersecretary of Commerce for Textiles and Apparel. The job was the top textile post in Washington, and carried with it the chairmanship of the Committee for the Implementation of Textile Agreements (CITA), an interdepartmental policy committee with representatives from the Departments of State, Labor, Treasury, and the USTR. Auggie was just 28 years old.

Snarling Back

From the pinnacle of political power they held in the late 1980s, the U.S. textile and apparel industries' influence declined rapidly in the 1990s. While their power remained the envy of virtually any other industry, compared to their influence in the heady days of the Jenkins Bill the troops were tattered and weakened. First, the seed-to-shirt coalition itself began to splinter, with infighting that weakened its collective snarl. More important, however, other political voices began to rise in volume, not drowning out but at least softening the snarls from the U.S. industry.

The "shirt" was the first to splinter off from the cause. Under the apparel industry's new business models, Auggie was starting to sound more and more like a dinosaur. For the firms who continued to produce apparel in the United States, access to cheaper and more fashionable foreign fabrics was a necessity. By limiting their access to foreign fabrics, trade restrictions were making it more, not less, difficult to keep their production in America. For other apparel firms, such as Warnaco and Liz Claiborne, it was becoming more attractive to source their clothing from abroad, partly because of the restrictions associated with gaining access to their fabrics of choice, and partly because of the increasing quality and price competitiveness of the Asian producers.

The American Apparel Manufacturers Association (AAMA) made a clean break with Auggie in 1990, when they refused to sign on to support the 1990 version of the global quota bill. They did not cross the line to the dark side at first, but instead made clear that they were not going to help. By the mid-1990s, however, the AAMA was the enemy, fighting in direct opposition to Auggie's efforts to contain textile and apparel imports. A short time later, with domestic manufacturing of both apparel and footwear increasingly irrelevant, and overseas sourcing increasingly important, the AAMA merged with the American Footwear Association to become the American Association of Footwear and Apparel (AAFA). The AAFA is today unabashedly pro-trade in its positions. The new acronym reflected the merger, but Keven Burke, AAFA's president, told me that some members of the new generation of U.S. apparel firms—with their far-flung international supply chains and no manufacturing at all—were hesitant to belong to a trade association containing the M word. Today, the notion of a large U.S. apparel firm that actually has M in the United States is almost as archaic as a cotton farmer with a mule.

The textile workers' union (UNITE), as well as the yarn and fabric sectors, also began to splinter into different directions. While the fabric producers wanted a freer rein to use imported yarn in production, the yarn spinners predictably preferred to limit the use of foreign yarn in U.S.-made fabrics. As trade agreements started to be negotiated, further splits appeared. The yarn and fabric guys squabbled over the provisions in the agreements, and the union workers generally opposed any agreements at all. Unable to snarl in unison, the industry became an annoyance rather than a threat on Capitol Hill.

As the seed-to-shirt coalition's united political front crumbled, other alphabet armies began to snarl in unison. For the first time, the U.S. retail industry formed a collective voice on the subject of trade in general, and apparel imports in particular. The Retail Industry Trade Action Coalition (RITAC) led by Sears, JCPenney, and Dayton Hudson, originally had been formed to counter FFACT on the Jenkins Bill, but soon took on the larger goal of doing away with all quotas.[28]

Retailers and importers were also successful in beginning to get their voices heard on trade disputes. Until the 1990s, CITA (the Committee for the Implementation of Textile Agreements, headquartered at the Department of Commerce) was in the domestic industry's back pocket. If the domestic industry wanted safeguard limits, or quotas, on certain goods from certain countries, they were only a phone call away. 'They were good ole boys in a Star Chamber," Brenda Jacobs, a leading trade lawyer, told me in 2008. (Ms. Jacobs was perhaps the fourth person to use the term *Star Chamber* to describe to me the early decision-making process at CITA, so I looked up the term: "A former English Court dealing with offenses against the Crown, notorious for its severity and arbitrary methods.") Today, CITA's membership represents importers' and retailers' interests as well, and safeguard quota decisions are made not in a Star Chamber but according to a specified and open process. The odds might still be with the domestic industry, as virtually all CITA chairpersons have roots in either the political or the business side of the domestic textile industry, but, as Brenda Jacobs told me, "At least there is a process in place and importers are allowed into the room."

Gone On Long Enough

Retailers were soon bolstered by another collective force as the developing countries that had been constrained by quotas also began to speak with one voice. The International Textiles and Clothing Bureau (ITCB), a coalition of developing-country textile and clothing exporters, began to echo the retailers' call for the end of quotas. In a foreshadowing of the collective clout they would display in 2004, poor countries banded together to shape the global trade agenda.

Many of the family businesses in Asia had first come under quota under Kennedy's administration, and some business owners remembered when their grandfathers had been assured that the quotas would be temporary. ITCB members were running out of patience in the globalized economy, where the MFA quotas appeared increasingly anomalous and hypocritical and were viewed as a rich-country plot that stood in the way of poor-country fortunes. In a twist on the well-worn historical pattern, America would now have to pay the developing countries to move out of the way of broader trade liberalization.

George H. W. Bush and then Bill Clinton were eager to see a successful conclusion of the Uruguay Round, the third major round of postwar trade liberalization talks. While both the Kennedy and Tokyo Rounds had focused on and achieved tariff reductions (though not for U.S. textile and apparel imports), U.S. aims for the Uruguay Round were more complex. In particular, U.S. negotiators wanted developing countries to liberalize rules for trade in financial and other services, and for foreign investment, and they also sought new agreements in areas such as intellectual property. The United States had little left to offer in return besides the MFA. Thanks to the successive rounds of liberalization, the United States maintained few trade barriers of any kind, save for those in place for agriculture and textiles, as tariffs for imports into the United States were close to zero for most goods outside of these industries. The developing countries made clear that they were willing to negotiate only if the MFA was on the table.

As Uruguay Round negotiations progressed, the MFA was extended twice more as the final agreement was hammered out. In the end, the negotiations took seven years and produced 22,000 pages of agreements.[29] With Auggie's troops in splinters, the new voice of the retail industry rising in the background, and, most important, the developing countries united for the first time in history, the rich countries agreed to abandon the MFA.

The Slow Unraveling

If there were doubts about the political staying power of the U.S. industry, they were dashed as it became clear that an agreement to end the MFA was not the same thing as the end of the MFA. While retailers and developing countries wanted to yank the yarn to unravel the regime in a few pulls, the textile interests pushed the other way, and ultimately made sure that the unraveling would proceed at a snail's pace. Negotiations over *whether* to end the MFA were simple compared to the negotiations over *how* to end the MFA.

Should the MFA be phased out over 5, 10, 15, or perhaps even 25 years? Should the poorest countries be freed from quotas first, or should the bigger exporters be allowed to go first? Or perhaps each category of clothing should be freed from constraint at the same time for all countries? The tortuous complexity that had characterized the administration of the MFA for decades was in the end trumped by the even more daunting complexity of the regime's undoing. Finally, the countries agreed to a complex 10-year phase out, with the fourth and final "tranche" of quotas to be lifted in 2005.

However, the term *phase out* is quite a misnomer, because the agreement did not phase out quotas steadily but instead left most in place until the "cliff" in 2005. Approximately 85 percent of quotas were still in effect on December 31, 2004.[30] Indeed, in the first tranche the United States lifted only one quota: that for work gloves from Canada.[31]

Julia Hughes and Erik Autor could only shake their heads at the beginning of the "phase out" in 1996 as nonexistent quotas were rescinded on parachutes, kelims, silk sport bags, and laparoscopy sponges. Thanks to the weakened but still snarling domestic industry, they had to wait another 10 years to see the quotas vanish on things that people actually buy, such as cotton T-shirts, underwear, or pants. Even then, as we will see in Chapter 12, the quotas did not actually vanish.

When I last saw Julia in the fall of 2008, she was older and she was wiser, but she was still waiting for the quotas to go away.

PERVERSE EFFECTS AND UNINTENDED CONSEQUENCES OF T-SHIRT TRADE POLICY

No More Doffers

What have been the effects of the dominance of politics over markets in world trade in apparel? The stated purpose of the protectionist regime was and remains to protect manufacturing jobs in the Western textile and apparel industries, and judged against this benchmark the regime's success has been quite limited. But the influence of politics in redirecting trade has had a number of other consequences—mostly perverse and unintended—but both positive and negative, for rich and poor countries alike. In addition, despite the limited success of the regime in protecting employment, the American public remains much more sympathetic to trade protection than we might expect. In mid-2008, barely half of Americans surveyed had a generally positive view of international trade.[1]

In the battle for the 2008 Democratic nomination, Hillary Clinton and Barack Obama seemed to be engaged in their own race to the bottom in anti-trade rhetoric as each candidate called for a cautionary approach to new trade-liberalizing initiatives and derided companies who "ship jobs overseas."[2] Both met sympathetically and photogenically (and repeatedly) with laid-off factory workers, and promised to "save jobs" if elected. Though these conversations were compelling in campaign soundbites, the truth is that while the protectionist trade regime has indeed saved thousands of jobs, the employment effect has largely been in Washington among the armies of lobbyists and bureaucrats who hold the regime together, as well as their counterparts in developing countries. Textile and apparel manufacturing jobs in the United States have been vanishing, and will continue to vanish, with or without protection from imports. John McCain had a more accurate but less popular assessment than Clinton or Obama during the 2008 campaign. Visiting struggling low-tech manufacturing communities, he said, "Those jobs aren't coming back."

Over the past 50 years, an entire vocabulary has become extinct in American textile mills as capital and technology have replaced labor in textile production. The *piece up* (yarn tying), *doffing* (removing full bobbins), and *draw in* (starting the warp threads) jobs are all gone now, the victims not of competition from China but of technological progress and mechanization. While employment in the U.S. textile industry fell by more than half between 1990 and 2007, production output has been relatively steady.[3] In 2007, U.S. textile workers produced approximately 60 percent more goods per hour of work than they had in 1990 (see Figure 11.1).

This pattern mirrors that of many other manufacturing industries in the United States: While employment is falling, production is steady or even rising. Indeed, for the 20-year period ending in 2007, U.S. manufacturing employment fell by approximately 20 percent, but manufacturing output increased by more than 60 percent.[4] While textile trade rules have had some effect in keeping *production* in the United States by increasing the price of imports, the stated goal of the regime—to save manufacturing jobs—has been undermined much more by mechanization and technological progress than by foreign competition.[5] Even if U.S. textile firms were completely protected from foreign competition, they would still have to compete with one another, and any firm choosing to preserve jobs rather than mechanize would soon wither from the better performance

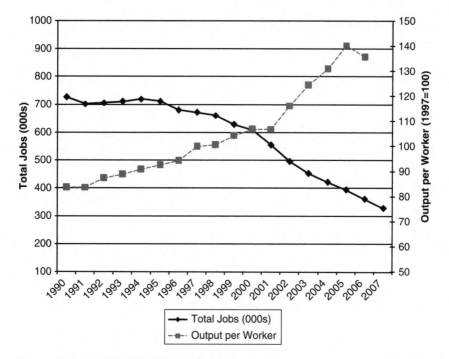

Source: BLS, NAICS 313, 314 combined.

Figure 11.1   Jobs and Productivity in the U.S. Textile Industry, 1990–2007

of its competitors. While the rationale for the series of "temporary" trade arrangements has always been to save jobs by giving U.S. industry breathing room in which to become competitive, the only hope for becoming competitive is often to get rid of the jobs.

The charge that America's textile jobs are going to China also must square with a remarkable and inconvenient fact: China is losing textile jobs, too, and losing more of them more rapidly than has ever been the case in North or South Carolina. According to a 2004 Conference Board study, China lost almost 10 times as many textile industry jobs as did the United States during the 1995–2002 period, and textile jobs losses were the most severe of any industry in China. While production, revenues, and exports are growing, employment is shrinking because of rapid advances in technology and labor productivity.[6] In short, textile jobs are not going to China; textile jobs are just going, period.

Own Worst Enemy

Not only has the regime failed to deliver its intended consequence—employment—it has also had the unintended consequence of reducing competitiveness across the U.S. textile and apparel complex, as members of the alphabet armies create higher costs for one another at each stage of a T-shirt's production. Or, as Erik Autor told me, the armies are often their own worst enemies. Cotton agricultural interests such as the National Cotton Council (NCC) have succeeded in erecting import barriers for raw cotton, which has increased the raw material costs for AYSA (American Yarn Spinners). The AYSA in turn lobbied for the tariffs and quotas on yarn imports, which have limited the ability of American fabric producers to obtain the best yarn at the best prices. And finally, the quotas and tariffs applied to fabrics not only increase costs for U.S. apparel producers, they also limit the ability of apparel producers to respond to the rapidly changing fashion whims of the U.S. consumer. The narrow successes of each step in the value chain in keeping foreign competition at bay have, collectively, imperiled rather than enhanced America's chances at remaining competitive across the production complex.

As we have seen, trade agreements contain innumerable side deals designed to protect U.S. producers. But these provisions often undermine rather than help the competitive position of U.S. firms. For example, free access under the CAFTA requires that apparel yarn or fabric be produced in a member country. This yarn-forward requirement actually often handicaps U.S. yarn spinners, who are discouraged both from exporting their yarn to more efficient fabric producers and from shifting production to more cost-efficient locations.

The regime has also introduced a regulatory risk into the already significant challenges of staying alive in this industry. Because apparel producers are never quite sure which types of textile trade policy currency will be traded away and for what, the risks inherent in forecasting policies are added to the already high normal business risks in the industry. For example, as a fabric "dyeing and finishing" provision was recently debated in Congress, firms had to consider for the better part of a year where and how to invest assets in printing technology in order to evade—or take advantage of—the new provisions. Trade agreements may be extended (or not) at the whim of the Congress, and if extended, the fabric provisions may (or may not) be modified. In attempting to carve out and preserve a piece of the pie for U.S. firms, the "preferential" agreements challenge an already debilitated industry to forecast not just markets but politics.

The economic costs of protecting the U.S. textile and apparel industries from imports have been estimated by many researchers. Though the results vary widely, most researchers conclude that the costs fall under the general category of Very Big Numbers. Surveying this literature in 1999, the U.S. International Trade Commission (USITC) estimated the annual cost of textile and apparel import quotas to be between $7 and $11 billion.[7] The USITC estimated that the removal of all textile and apparel quotas and tariffs would have resulted in an economywide gain of $10.4 billion in 1996, but at a cost of 117,150 U.S. jobs. Using these estimates, textile and apparel protection in the United States cost approximately $88,000 per year in the mid-1990s for each job preserved. Hufbauer and Elliott estimated the consumer cost of protecting an apparel job in 1990 to be $138,666, while a later USITC study estimates the cost of textile and apparel quota at between $7 and $12 billion.[8] Using the USITC's most conservative estimates, 2002 textile and apparel quotas cost $174,825 per job saved.[9] The costs of protection are not only high in dollar terms, they represent a regressive tax, which falls disproportionately on the lower-income workers that the regime is designed to protect.

Other self-defeating consequences result from apparel import quotas. The most predictable and obvious effect of the import limits has been "upgrading" by the exporting countries. When China, for example, is allocated a quota of 2,523,532 dozen cotton knit shirts or 211,076 dozen cotton dresses, producers in China have an incentive to use the quota for high-end rather than low-end products. Chinese producers are loath to waste cotton knit shirt quota by using it to sell a cheap T-shirt when the quota could instead be used to sell a high-end, combed-cotton polo shirt to L.L. Bean. The quotas have therefore encouraged China and other potential low-end producers to become high-end producers, and have in effect encouraged more high-margin, expensive clothing production to be shifted abroad. Again, my lowly $5.99 T-shirt was lucky to have made it in at all.

Friends with Benefits

The tariffs and quotas that allegedly protect the U.S. apparel industry cannot protect what today barely exists. In 2007, 95 percent of apparel purchased by U.S. consumers was imported, yet apparel tariffs averaged 16 percent, more than 10 times the 1.5 percent average tariff applied to other goods entering the United States.[10] If apparel manufacturing has nearly vanished from the United States, what exactly are the trade barriers protecting?

Today, the high tariffs levied on apparel mostly protect America's customers and its friends. The complex trade agreements create a captive market for U.S.-made yarn and fabrics, so the U.S. yarn and fabric makers have an interest in supporting their customers by maintaining trade barriers for apparel from other countries.

Perhaps more important, however, the trade barriers serve as a powerful tool with which the United States can reward its friends and allies. The high tariffs on apparel mean that countries that enjoy free access to the U.S. market have a 16 percent cost advantage over those that do not. The countries that have won this advantage have every incentive to keep their club as small as possible, and they therefore use their influence in Washington to argue for maintaining the high tariffs applied to their competitors. While the trade barriers do not protect the almost-nonexistent U.S. apparel industry, they do protect the apparel industries of America's friends. And as long as the high tariffs remain, the United States can dangle the carrot of free access to the U.S. market as a tactic to win over important friends, and indeed to negotiate for favors completely unrelated to trade. Recent research has shown that this carrot has significant value.[11] The spate of free trade agreements that have been negotiated recently in the Middle East—with Bahrain, Jordan, and Oman, for example—all have been intended to win friends in this sensitive region.[12]

Sometimes, of course, the desire to protect America's friends contradicts directly the interests of the U.S. textile industry. This conflict was thrown into sharp relief in the days after September 11, 2001.

Wal-Mart Backs Musharraf

In the days following the terrorist attacks on the World Trade Center and the Pentagon, world leaders arguably had more vital matters to discuss, but T-shirt imports into the United States were the subject of discussions at the highest level, including President George W. Bush, Secretary of State Colin Powell, Secretary of Commerce Don Evans, and U.S. Trade Representative Robert Zoellick.[13] Pakistani President Pervez Musharraf had aligned himself solidly behind the United States and was rewarded with an aid package worth billions. But Musharraf, as well as his commerce minister, Abdul Dawood, quickly made it clear in conversations with President Bush and Secretary Powell that perhaps the most important reward for Pakistan's solidarity with the United States would be a loosening of the restrictions limiting textile and apparel imports into the United States. Textile and apparel represented more than 60 percent of Pakistan's industrial employment and its exports, and the United States was by far the country's biggest customer. But even so, Pakistan's apparel and textile sales to the United States were restricted by tariffs as high as 29 percent and by tight quota restraints limiting imports of dozens of categories of textiles and of apparel. Even by September, many of the annual quotas were nearly full.[14] Musharraf argued that the war against terrorism would be best served if Pakistan's textile and apparel factories stayed open and the workers kept their jobs. This in turn would happen only if Wal-Mart, Target, and other U.S. retailers could more freely import cheap cotton clothing from Pakistan. Both George W. Bush and Colin Powell assured Musharraf that they would do what they could.

So, as the ruins of the World Trade Center still burned and America's military was mobilized for the war in Afghanistan, the alphabet armies mobilized for another type of war. The American Textile Manufacturers Institute (ATMI), the American Yarn Spinners Association (AYSA), the National Retail Federation (NRF), the American Apparel and Footwear Association (AAFA), the United States American Association of Importers of Textiles and Apparel (USA-ITA), and the Union of Needletrades, Industrial, and Textile Employees (UNITE) readied for a fight, bolstered on both sides by members of the U.S. Congress.

Ron Sorini, the chief textile negotiator under George H. W. Bush, represented Pakistan. Alongside him were Erik Autor of the National Retail Federation and other kindred spirits representing U.S. importers. They argued that U.S. firms such as Wal-Mart would continue to purchase clothing from Pakistan only if the quotas were lifted and the tariffs rescinded. Wal-Mart did not have to stay in Pakistan, Autor argued. There were a dozen other poor countries willing to meet the T-shirt orders at the click of a mouse. If the factories were to stay open in Pakistan, then the United States had to loosen the noose on Pakistani apparel imports.

Not so fast, said the other letters of the alphabet. Why should the U.S. textile and apparel industry be made to pay the cost of U.S. foreign policy? The ATMI pointed to its obituaries, showing the recent demise of more than 100 U.S. textile mills and 60,000 jobs across the American South. Members of Congress weighed in with letters detailing the dire straits of the U.S. textile and apparel industries, and urged the administration not to grant Pakistan's request. The textile industry's argument was that while assistance to Pakistan was a fine and noble goal, taking the assistance out of the industry's hide was not.

The two sides opened with extreme bargaining positions and began to wheel and deal. Pakistan requested the suspension of tariffs on all textiles and apparel through 2004, and a 50 percent quota increase for most categories of textile and apparel, as well as more flexibility in shifting unused textile and apparel quota to other categories. The U.S. textile industry opened with an offer to suspend tariffs on handmade carpets (then approximately 2 percent), period. The administration countered with a proposal to allow Pakistan to borrow from the following year's quota for T-shirts, pillowcases, underwear, pajamas, and mops. Not a chance, responded the textile interests. The wrangling started before the first U.S. bombs dropped on Afghanistan and was still going on as the new government took charge and the U.S. military tanks retreated. By mid-February, however, the alphabet armies had hammered out a deal, though both sides agreed that the final deal was much more responsive to the U.S. textile industry than it was to Pakistan.

Pakistan's request for tariff relief was rejected completely. Tariff rate changes would have required Congressional approval, and Bush knew as well as anyone the perils of taking trade matters to Congress. A few quotas were loosened so as to toss some crumbs to Pakistan, but these were for relatively low-volume goods. T-shirt quotas were not relaxed, and by April 2002, Pakistan had used up its entire year's T-shirt quota.

A year and a half later, the Bush administration unveiled another ambitious aid program for Pakistan. It contained no provisions at all on textile trade. "They knew better than to ask us for anything," an official at ATMI told me.

In the end, the concessions to Pakistan had amounted to little, and, in any case, the military phase of the "real" war in Afghanistan had concluded as the negotiations dragged on, so the original motivation—to help an ally in the war—was no longer so pressing. The political opposition to Pakistan's requests had been organized, swift, and powerful. At the end of the day, George W. Bush swallowed his rhetoric about the glories of free trade as well as his black-and-white moral rhetoric to do "everything possible" to help his key ally in the war against terrorism. He instead followed in the noble tradition of every U.S. president since Dwight Eisenhower: In staring down the U.S. textile industry, he winked.

Race to the Quotas

In most global industries, managers design their supply chains to obtain the best products at the most competitive prices. Such rationality has rarely governed apparel sourcing. By plugging the apparel import dikes from dozens of countries over the past generation, the United States encouraged myriad detours and otherwise irrational moves by firms that were forced to engage in what Andrew Tanzer has called "The Great Quota Hustle." Indeed, the astoundingly creative entrepreneurial maneuvers that have been undertaken to deal with the quota regime are as strong evidence as anything of the business acumen among Chinese managers. Managers who grew up learning to deal with the irrational regime of Mao Zedong have an advantage, it appears, in dealing with U.S. trade policy.

The Esquel Corporation, today the world's largest producer of cotton shirts, started in Hong Kong in the late 1970s, but, unable to obtain quota to sell to the United States, shifted production to mainland China.[15] When the United States tightened Chinese shirt quotas in the early 1980s, Esquel moved production to Malaysia. When Malaysian quota also became difficult to obtain, Esquel moved yet again, this time to Sri Lanka. The globe hopping continued, with the Chinese shirt producer setting up operations in Mauritius and Maldives. Other Chinese firms played the game as well, shipping Mongolian goat hair to tiny islands that had extra cashmere sweater quota. A difficulty with the system is that the countries with quota often had no expertise and few workers, so the firms were forced to ship Chinese workers to Mauritius and Chinese managers to Cambodia. The Chinese were still producing the clothing, though travel time and complexity had, of course, increased markedly.

The image of globe-trotting corporations often presented by anti-globalization activists as well as by textile interests in Washington demonizes corporations for their lack of loyalty, and especially for their fleeting moves to cheaper and cheaper production locations. While this race-to-the-bottom story is indeed descriptive, it is important to note that the globe hopping we observe in the textile and apparel industries is also the result of the very policies that have been erected by the textile interests. Indeed, it has been politics as much as markets that has fueled the race to the bottom, even as politics alters the course of the race. As the

Financial Times reports, the apparel industry has globalized in response to trade barriers rather than in response to open markets.[16]

Bob Zane, the Chairman of the U.S. Association of Importers of Textiles and Apparel, recently looked back at the decade he spent sourcing apparel for the Liz Claiborne company. He would have preferred to concentrate on building long-term relationships with high-quality suppliers, but because of the MFA, "All we did," he said, "was run around the world chasing quota."[17]

Under the many restrictive rules, cheating, by all accounts, is rampant. Though the United States employs hundreds of customs inspectors and regularly raids Chinese factories, billions of dollars in clothing made in China is labeled as if it were from other countries. One apparel importer told me that he had visited a factory of his Chinese supplier and seen "made in" labels for numerous countries on the sewing tables, and that his Chinese supplier had offered him goods "made in" Cambodia, Kenya, or Lesotho. In the summer of 2008, the Department of Homeland Security's border protection arm seized more than 1,000 containers of falsely labeled apparel that had in fact been made in China.[18] Though U.S. penalties for transshipment are severe, they make only a small dent in the illegal trade.[19] Many other countries cheat as well, given the myriad complexities of the various yarn-forward-type requirements.

A number of industry participants in China told me that the quota market was rife with speculation and manipulation, where, for example, a trader with "inside information" about a large shirt order from a U.S. retailer would buy up the necessary quota in advance and resell it at a profit. According to Roy Delbyck, an American trade lawyer, quota profits are found in Hong Kong's stunning skyline, where the riches from the quota trade have been invested in the property market.[20] While they may not have helped South Carolina's textile workers, the quotas have quite clearly helped Hong Kong's storied real estate investors.

As of 2008, quotas were in place on dozens of categories of clothing from China. Figure 11.2 shows examples of the prices at which Chinese apparel quota was trading in mid-2008. As the table shows, T-shirt quota (category 338/339) was selling for approximately $3.20 per dozen, though the quota price for knit shirts made of other fabrics was $4.20 per dozen. Quota costs added $3.30 to the cost of a dozen sweaters, and $15 to the cost of a dozen wool suits. Based on the market prices prevailing during the 2004–2008 period, the textile and apparel quotas granted to China

Description	Quota Price
Cotton Knit Shirts	$3.20 per Doz.
Sweaters	$3.30 per Doz.
Mens' Cotton Trousers	$6.20 per Doz.
Men and Boys' Wool Suits	$15 per Doz.
Man-Made Fiber Knit Shirts	$4.20 per Doz.
Wool Trousers	$10 per Doz.
Socks	$1.00 per Doz. Pr.
Swimwear	$3.00 per KG

Source: www.chinaquota.com.

Figure 11.2 Market Prices for Chinese Import Quota to the United States in August 2008

during that period represented a gift of approximately $1.5 billion to the Chinese government.[21]

It is hard to know where to start in discussing what is wrong with this picture. First, perhaps the chief complaint against China made by the U.S. textile industry is that the Chinese government subsidizes its textile industry, through subsidized inputs, easy bank loans, and tax credits. Indeed, the National Council of Textile Organizations (NCTO) counts 42 such subsidies.[22] But if the Chinese government is subsidizing its industry, then the United States is subsidizing the Chinese government with, as we have seen, a gift of 1.5 billion dollars. In exchange for this gift, however, few jobs have been saved in South Carolina, though they have clearly been saved for the bureaucrats around the world who administer the regime, and they have also been saved for workers in countries such as Bangladesh and Sri Lanka who supply the goods that China cannot when it runs out of quota. While the quota regime was allegedly put in place to protect the U.S. worker, it is difficult to construct a story that concludes that the Chinese quota saves U.S. textile jobs. And if the $1.5 billion in Chinese quota could be allocated instead to the 185,000 U.S. textile and apparel workers who lost their jobs between 2004 and 2008, each worker could be paid more than $8,000 in job retraining or other benefits.

But even if the nonsensical maze of U.S. textile trade policy—the tariffs and quotas and preference programs and origination requirements—*did* protect U.S. textile and apparel workers—which it doesn't—the question remains: Why do the 99.99 percent of Americans who are *not* textile and apparel workers put up with it?

Auggie and Aristotle Versus Wal-Mart

Needless to say, when free traders get going on textile and apparel trade policy, it is hard to get them to stop: The whole system is a blight on world trading, an island of reactionary irrationality in a forward-moving universe, and it is ineffective to boot. Today, the doctrine of free trade has virtually unanimous support among professional economists, a group almost without exception who scorn protectionism in general and quotas in particular.[23] Indeed, Douglas Irwin, the noted economic historian, suggests that the doctrine of free trade is not only a good idea but is even the best useful idea ever generated by economists:

> The case for free trade has endured because the fundamental proposition that substantial benefits arise from the free exchange of goods between countries has not been overshadowed by the limited scope of various qualifications and exceptions. Free trade thus remains as sound as any proposition in economic theory which purports to have implications from economic policy is ever likely to be.[24]

Nearly a century earlier, Frank Taussig noted that even the strongest political pressure cannot change the quality of an idea:

> [T]he doctrine of free trade, however widely rejected in the world of politics, holds its own in the sphere of the intellect.[25]

There is perhaps no other issue, however, in which the professional opinion of economists differs so markedly from the opinion of the American public. While economists are nearly unanimous on the superiority of free trade as policy, the American public has grave reservations.[26] Though the public is not necessarily supportive of U.S. textile interests, it is also not supportive of unrestrained gushes of cheap goods from China. During the 2008 election cycle, support for international trade was dropping precipitously.[27] What accounts for this gaping divide between professional and public opinion?

In general, economists judge policies by their effects on national wealth and income, or "global welfare," and it is inarguably true that this metric supports free trade over most, if not all, forms of trade protection. The American public, however, has other metrics in mind: metrics that are less well defined and certainly more difficult to measure. Whether the spigot pouring T-shirts into the United States from China should be closed, open, or left to dribble through an administrative maze is therefore a debate not about the best *economic* policy but instead about economic policy versus all of the other factors that weigh on policymakers' decisions. It is easy to be outraged about the dominance of special-interest politics over sound economic policy, but we must also recognize that it is not only special interests, but also the American public, that remain uneasy about free trade.

Trade has always made people nervous. Douglas Irwin writes that the ancient Greeks, in particular Aristotle, were highly suspicious of international trade, even as they acknowledged its economic benefits.[28] While conceding that trade brought more goods more cheaply, they were concerned about a number of negative influences on civil society. This same tension today is crystallized in the many and varied debates surrounding Wal-Mart, which supplies about 25 percent of the U.S. apparel market with goods that are virtually all imported from abroad. While Wal-Mart's provision of cheaper and cheaper imports is unquestionably a boon to the apparel consumer and to the economy at large, virtually every aspect of the firm's behavior has drawn protests, and the very behavior that gives consumers a windfall is at the same time the target of critics.[29] Protestors want Wal-Mart to stop its union-bashing, and to improve its pay and benefits for employees. The company is also criticized for its merciless squeeze on supplier pricing, and for its failure to effectively monitor the working conditions in the overseas factories that produce the apparel for its stores. The cheap apparel itself is blamed for the demise of South Carolina textile mills, and the laid-off textile workers complain that the only jobs left when the mills closed were as checkout clerks behind the enemy lines, because Wal-Mart had also squeezed out the smaller stores on Main Street.

Auggie Tantillo describes the Wal-Mart *squeeze cycle*, in which Wal-Mart's squeeze on its U.S. suppliers has bankrupted them, and led the firm to China where it squeezes Chinese suppliers, who in turn squeeze their own suppliers as well as their sweatshop workers. At the end of the squeeze cycle, we can buy our T-shirts for 25 cents less, so on average we are richer, but at what cost?

Auggie Tantillo has a moral view on the Wal-Mart squeeze, and he shares this view with a storied line of ancestors, beginning at least with Aristotle, as well as with an uneasy American public. A bit more stability, a bit more community, a bit more of a dike against the bashing waves from China are worth more than small savings for each of us on the cost of a T-shirt.

And while growth in consumer spending is often used to measure the health of the economy, Auggie and Aristotle also share a suspicion of the long-run effects of rampant borrowing and consumerism. In 2008, the United States had the biggest federal budget deficit—and the highest level of personal borrowing—in decades. Much of this borrowing was financed by China, which used its proceeds from selling goods to the United States to lend funds back to America. As the economy continued to stagnate in the year leading up to the election, the political response was to mail "stimulus checks" to approximately 130 million American families. Auggie was incredulous: "We're borrowing more money from China so that people will go to Wal-Mart and buy more stuff from China? How can we think the solution to our problems is *more shopping*?"

Another divide between professional and public opinion relates to differing perspectives: While economists view matters nationally or even globally, many Americans take a local perspective. While free trade increases global welfare, some local workers, companies, and communities are the losers; the economic benefits of free trade are diffuse, while the costs are typically concentrated. When the benefits of cheaper T-shirts for millions across the country are placed alongside the costs of job loss for a few thousand in a North Carolina mill town, the public's internal calculator often works much differently than does an economist's. Judging from the political rhetoric in the 2008 election, it is worth something, perhaps a lot, to keep the manufacturing jobs—or to try to keep the jobs—in a community that is on the edge. Even when it looks futile, Americans seem to want to try.

Economists do not deny that free trade may bring concentrated losses to certain industries and workers, but the solution, most economists argue, is the *compensation principle*. The best economic policy is not to erect trade barriers but instead to compensate the losers. The rationale behind a variety of Trade Adjustment Assistance (TAA) programs that have been undertaken in the United States is that by taxing the millions who have benefited from cheaper T-shirts and funneling the compensation to the thousands who have lost their jobs, we can both gain the economy-wide benefits of free trade and at the same time mitigate the negative local effects.

It works better in economic theory than it does in practice. While some towns in the textile South have moved beyond this industry and never looked back, others that used to produce textiles and T-shirts seem now to produce only news stories or documentaries on life after the mill closed. These stories have a common thread: It is not just that the jobs are gone, but that the communities are gone, too, and the future is uncertain and scary. The paycheck can be replaced by the compensation principle, but everything else, as the ad says, is priceless. Especially in low-tech industries such as apparel manufacture, the losers stay losers once their jobs are gone.[30]

Creative Destruction

Joseph Schumpeter argued that the essence of a market economy was the fluid dynamic of *creative destruction*, which saw the destruction of certain jobs and industries as a necessary evil for the creation of others. During the past several years, I have indeed seen the destruction during visits to many padlocked textile and apparel factories. In Alabama and North and South Carolina, my host would pull into the parking lot, and we'd take a walk around the shuttered factory. The overwhelming impression was always one of an eerie quiet, not unlike the silence of a cemetery.

The eerie quiet of the closed factories, however, contrasts markedly with the hum of activity elsewhere in the industry: As traditional textile and apparel manufacturing wanes, I have met dozens of people employed in the textile and apparel industries in the United States who hold jobs that did not exist a generation ago. Some of these jobs result from the new international business models of U.S. apparel firms; others result from the recent premiums placed by wealthy countries on environmental and social responsibility. In other words, concerns about the ravages of globalization have created their own opportunities. Finally, technical and scientific innovations are also creating opportunities. As traditional T-shirt jobs have dwindled, the T-shirt jobs of the future are emerging.

In New York, I met Michael Lambert, Director of Import Planning for Limited Brands. Michael's team of 12 professionals is in charge of facilitating the flow of goods from the company's far-flung international supply chain to store shelves. Every day that a shipment of apparel is held up in customs is a forgone profit, so Michael's team works to insure compliance with the complicated trade rules. In 2008, Michael's team was analyzing the regulatory risk associated with sourcing from various countries, as well as working to ensure that Limited Brands was in compliance with the emerging CAFTA rules. Limited Brands, like other major apparel companies, also employs hundreds in the area of "strategic sourcing." With dozens of countries and thousands of factories to choose from, how should a company trade off factors such as price, quality, time to market, reliability, and special trade advantages?[31] The fields of international supply chain management, strategic sourcing, and import planning employ thousands today in jobs that did not exist a generation ago.

Thousands more are employed in the fields of the social and environmental compliance of these international supply chains. In Washington, I met Caitlin Morris, Nike's Director of Compliance Integration. Caitlin's large and growing group did not exist a generation ago, but today employs nearly 100 people in monitoring Nike's international suppliers in the areas of labor, environmental, and social standards. Virtually all large apparel brands have similar operations in place. Independent organizations such as Verité and the Workers Rights Consortium that operate with similar missions also did not exist just a few years ago.

In California, I met Patagonia's Social Responsibility Manager, Nicole Bassett. All of Patagonia's cotton fabrics are produced with organic cotton, and Patagonia employs a sourcing team to obtain different grades of organic cotton from Peru, Turkey, and West Africa and deliver them to mills in Asia.

In Nebraska, I met Yiqi Chang, a scientist at the University of Nebraska. Yiqi is leading a team of researchers who are developing techniques to spin yarn from corn by-products. Perhaps soon, according to Yiqi, the same cornfield will be able to power our cars with ethanol, sustain our chickens with feed, and produce yarn for our T-shirts, all with a fraction of the water and chemical use employed for these purposes today.

In the traditional textile regions of North Carolina, innovative companies are also employing researchers to meet environmental challenges. Tuscarora Yarns began life as a cotton mill in 1899, but in 2008 announced an expansion that would enable expanded production of eco-friendly yarns made from corn, soy, bamboo, and post-consumer waste.[32] Not far away, textile industry leader Wellman Inc. is the world leader in processing plastic soda bottles into soft fleece. In the summer of 2008, I learned of perhaps a half-dozen industry conferences devoted to environmental innovations in the textile and apparel industries.

As creative destruction churns through the global textile and apparel industries, it churns increasingly through public policy, as well. In the fall of 2008, I spoke with Matt Priest, the top textile official at the Department of Commerce. Matt had been appointed by George W. Bush to the post, which was the same position held by Auggie Tantillo about 25 years before. Like Auggie, Matt was not yet 30 years old when he assumed the position. Auggie, Julia, and I met at Matt's office so I could take their picture. Auggie stood in his old office, and while the view of the Washington Monument was the same, much else had changed. For one thing, the office was smaller; renovations had chopped off square feet, which seemed to Auggie symbolic of the demise of the industry.

Yet Matt Priest's world was much more complicated than Auggie's had been. In the 1980s, the role of the Office of Textiles and Apparel (OTEXA) at the Commerce Department had been in effect to protect the domestic textile and apparel manufacturers from foreign competition. The battle lines were clearly drawn between domestic and international interests.

"It's not that simple, anymore," Matt told me. The "domestic" firms that still survived were not really domestic at all. Indeed, the U.S. textile firms that survive today have survived in part because they have international-ized: They were exporters and international investors, or they outsourced parts of their supply chain to more efficient international manufacturers. The battle lines, once so clearly drawn, now often seem barely legible.

Matt Priest also sees clearly the jobs created by trade in fields such as international supply chain management, logistics, and strategic sourc-ing. "Manufacturing jobs are important," he told me. "But these jobs are important, too."

The T-shirt jobs of the future are emerging in other wealthy countries, as well. On a trip to Europe, I met Mark Holt and Mike Betts of Better Thinking, a U.K. company that designed and sells the Perfect T-Shirt (perfect, that is, from an environmental and labor perspective). I also struck up an electronic acquaintance with Eric Poettschacher of Re-Shirt, an Austrian firm that enables new-age recycling: Customers buy T-shirts from one another online while sharing the life stories associated with those T-shirts. And Hiroshi Amemiya, one of the translators who brought the first edition of this book to Japan, introduced me to Ikeuchi Towel, a firm employing wind power to produce organic towels for the U.S. and Japanese markets.

In North Carolina, I met Eric Henry, whose firm, TS Designs, produces "all-American" organic and phthalate-free T-shirts in North Carolina, while Green Label, a Virginia firm, produces similar T-shirts for sale in Nordstrom and Whole Foods. Of course, the higher wages that have priced U.S.

companies out of plain-white T-shirt production are precisely the higher wages that create demand for TS Designs and Green Label T-shirts. In the summer of 2008, as the traditional T-shirt business in the United States struggled, Eric told me that his business was booming.

I also have visited perhaps a dozen textile factories in the American South that produce a variety of high-tech "fabrics of the future." These firms produce fabrics that can staunch bleeding on a battlefield, and others that can scramble enemy radar. A variety of high-tech industrial textiles are continually developed in U.S. universities and firms. The plain-white T-shirt factory may be gone, but tomorrow's T-shirts, developed in the United States, will be able to take a patient's vital signs and transmit them to a physician's computer. [33]

Interestingly, the "high-tech" textile company leaders with whom I spoke faced challenges that were much different from those faced by their colleagues at traditional textile mills. While more traditional companies—for example, those spinning cotton yarn or knitting T-shirt fabric—identified foreign competition in general and China in particular as their biggest threat, the high-tech companies almost without exception identified labor shortages as their biggest challenge. Eddie Gant, President of Glen Raven, one of North Carolina's high-tech textile leaders, told me in 2008 that his firm was chronically short of qualified workers.

That Glen Raven experiences labor shortages while Auggie Tantillo fights job losses is explained by the harsh reality of the global economy: In the dynamic of creative destruction, what is created often cannot help those who have been destroyed. The workers who lost their jobs when the old T-shirt factories closed are often not equipped with the skills or education needed to join the factories of the future.

Whither the Dinosaurs?

It won't be long now, political insiders told me over and over again in 2003, as if we were all standing over a comatose patient. Public opinion will shift to reflect the promise of the global economy, and the days of rampant textile and apparel protectionism and unintelligible trade barriers will soon be only in the history books. The old companies are dying, the venerable ATMI is dead, and the most legendary fighters are either dead or over 80. Strom Thurmond, the industry's most infamous soldier on Capitol Hill, died in 2003 at the age of 100. He had been a stead-fast ally since he entered the Senate in 1954, and had elicited textile promises in virtually every presidential election since then. Thurmond had not been much of a player while in his nineties, Auggie Tantillo told me, but at least they could always count on him for a vote. Jesse Helms retired from the Senate about the time of Thurmond's death, and Fritz Hollings—perhaps the only senator to proudly still call himself a protectionist in 2004—announced his retirement a short time later. Together, Thurmond, Helms, and Hollings had served as a triumvirate textile power bloc for 30 years. Some of the young guys have their hearts in the right place, but it is just not the same. According to Auggie Tantillo, U.S. textile interests today have about half as many die-hard supporters in Congress as they did in the late 1980s.

Though the industry's political and financial fortunes are waning, Roger Milliken, by all accounts, is still going strong. Milliken is the reclusive chairman of Milliken Industries and, according to Forbes, one of America's richest men. Milliken, like Auggie, believes in manufacturing in America, and believes that to surrender manufacturing to low-wage countries is to surrender our communities and our future. Milliken destroys his old textile machinery rather than see it shipped used to China, and supports organizations that see things his way on the subject of textile trade. Milliken is also the founding member and chairman of AMTAC, which Auggie directs. Auggie Tantillo and Julia Hughes—who agree on so little—agree on this: When Roger Milliken goes, things will be different. Milliken, while a force in the 2008 elections, turned 92 that year.

As the textile industry fades, the political power and influence of apparel retailers are growing rapidly. Wal-Mart's PAC donated $1.5 million in the 2004 elections, making the retailer the second largest corporate donor to federal candidates. As recently as 1998, Wal-Mart's Washington presence was negligible, but by 2003 the firm was spending $1.7 million a year to maintain three resident lobbyists in Washington, and in 2007, Wal-Mart increased its lobbying budget by 60 percent over the prior year.[34] Lowering trade barriers remains a crucial political objective for Wal-Mart, and it is joined in its efforts by Sears, JCPenney, Target, and other large retailers.

There is a moral to the story of the 2004 Senate election to replace retiring Fritz Hollings, surely the Senate's ranking protectionist. South Carolina had had the worst job record in the country during the several years leading up to the election, as mill after mill closed and manufacturing jobs evaporated. The remaining textile organizations—AMTAC, NCTO, and the NTA—wanted to force the candidates to commit on the issue of trade, to make public their positions on textile job loss, on China, and on the burgeoning trade agreements. The textile industry went to work backing Inez Tenenbaum, a traditional textile protectionist. AMTAC plastered billboards around the mill towns in South Carolina ("Have You Lost Your Job ... Yet?") and undertook a drive to register textile and apparel workers to vote.

Jim DeMint, the Republican candidate, broke ranks with every senator from the Carolinas in the past 50 years, and not only failed to support the protectionist position, but went to the other extreme and campaigned openly as a free trader. Trade was the most significant issue on which Tenenbaum and DeMint differed. As Tenenbaum promised to build trade walls, DeMint promised to tear them down. Free trade was the hope for South Carolina's future, said DeMint, in a message not heard in South Carolina in more than half a century. DeMint pointed not to the sputtering mills but to the other factories that had come to roost in South Carolina in recent years: BMW from Germany, Michelin from France, Pirelli from Italy, Fuji from Japan, and even Haier from China. He urged South Carolinians to look forward to the role that they could play in the global economy, not backwards to the wheezing textile mills.

DeMint beat Tenenbaum handily, in a trouncing that surprised virtually everyone. On inauguration day in January 2005, Ernest Hollings, the Senate's most ardent and unapologetic protectionist, was replaced by an almost rabid free trader.

It won't be long now, retailers and government officials told me over and over again in the summer and fall of 2003. A year later, though, the patient was perking up, and the last of the perverse consequences was emerging. Another whole army—actually, many armies—had come to shore up Auggie and his troops from the Carolinas. They came from Bangladesh and Mauritius, Turkey and the Philippines. The developing-country clothing exporters who had sided with Julia in her efforts to get the MFA quotas lifted were having second thoughts. In dozens of different languages, they began to snarl together with Auggie.

(Unintended) Winners

The master narrative, largely unquestioned since the early 1960s or earlier, was that rich-country protectionism for textiles and apparel was yet another example in the long history of rich countries tilting the playing field against poor countries through hypocritical policies. While pressing developing countries to liberalize trade and open markets, the United States kept in place a suffocating quota system and high tariffs that prevented the developing countries from sewing and weaving their way to prosperity. But as with all master narratives, this rich-versus-poor-divide story is only partly true.

U.S. tariff policies conform to the master narrative. Textile and apparel tariffs have been largely immune from the broad cuts that have characterized trade negotiations for the past 40 years. As a result, trade between rich countries is now close to tariff-free—but imports to rich countries from poor countries face disproportionate tariff barriers because of the heavy reliance of poor countries on textiles and clothing exports. Edward Gresser estimates that U.S. tariff "peaks" (i.e., tariffs exceeding 15 percent) are virtually never applied to U.S. imports from Germany, Norway, and Japan, but are applied to almost half of the primary imports from Bangladesh, Mongolia, and Cambodia. Indeed, the United States collects more tariff revenue from Cambodian underwear than it does from Australian wine or Japanese steel.[35] In 2007, textiles and apparel comprised 5 percent of the value of U.S. imports, but accounted for 43 percent of tariffs collected.[36]

Whether the various quota regimes are also consistent with the master narrative is a more complicated question. While the intent was to protect rich-country industries by limiting imports from poor countries, the effect of these import restraints has been neither uniform nor uniformly bad for poor countries. While the major cost-competitive exporters—Japan in the 1950s or China in the 2000s—have undoubtedly been constrained by the quota system, and while the global welfare losses for poor countries in aggregate have been great, the argument that the MFA has stood in the way of all developing countries' fortunes is less compelling.

With the introduction of textile and apparel quotas, and especially with their growing reach and complexity, the effect was to constrain the large competitive exporters, but also to divvy up the lucrative U.S. market and grant pieces to dozens of developing countries that might have never sold to the United States at all. It was quota allocations, not market forces, that granted U.S. market access to baby clothes from the Philippines, underwear from Sri Lanka, and men's shirts from Mauritius. And along with access to the U.S. market, the quotas also facilitated other forms of economic development. But the prediction that the end of the quota system will allow these countries to increase their fortunes is a shaky one: The end of the quota system will not so much allow the Philippines to sell more baby clothes as it will allow other countries to capture the baby clothes market that was once reserved for the Philippines. Observers on all sides of the debate now agree that however unsuccessful the MFA was in protecting the U.S. industry, it was successful indeed as foreign aid for dozens of small countries. Most large retailers plan to source their clothing from only five or six countries in the post-MFA world, whereas they were forced to find suppliers in more than 50 countries under the quota regime.[37]

As of mid-2004, the very countries that had argued—demanded, even—the removal of the quotas began to have second thoughts. Maybe not, they decided. Maybe this was a bad idea after all. One by one, they called and e-mailed Auggie Tantillo.

When the third tranche of products was lifted from quota in 2002, some of the poorest countries in the world got a frightening glimpse of the future. China had been admitted to the WTO in 2001 and for the first time would be eligible to have its apparel exports removed from quota. Not only did it appear that the Philippines or Sri Lanka or Mauritius would not get a bigger piece of the pie when the quotas were lifted, it appeared instead that China would get everybody's pie. Throughout the regime's history, observers had become used to the gushes that followed when holes had been poked in the dike, but no one had been prepared for the gushes from China.

In most of the categories that were released from quota in 2002, China's exports to the United States surged by more than 100 percent, with commensurate declines in the exports of the countries that had held the quota. For a number of textile and apparel categories, the gushes from China were more forceful than anything that had been observed in the postwar era. Chinese exports of baby clothes (category 239) surged by more than 2,000 percent, robes (category 350/650) by more than 1,500 percent, and knit fabrics (category 222) by an astonishing 21,000 percent.[38] Overall, China increased its U.S. import market share of the apparel released from quota from 24 to 86 percent.[39] At the same time, Chinese suppliers were slashing their prices, with wholesale prices often falling by more than half. Of course, the price declines were partly the result of the quota regime itself, as exporters no longer needed to purchase quota in order to sell to the United States. As Figure 11.3 shows, the gains for China meant losses for virtually everybody else.

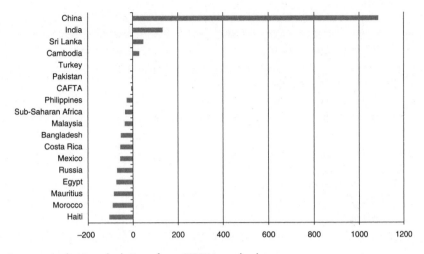

Source: Author's calculations from OTEXA trade data.

Figure 11.3 Percentage Increase or Decrease in U.S. Imports of Apparel Categories Released from Quota on January 1, 2002*

(*in Square Meters, 2004 Compared to 2001)

Retailers were giddy at the prospect of unrestrained sourcing from China. China was the gazelle of the global apparel industry: the fastest, the cheapest, the best. Firms ranging from JCPenney to Liz Claiborne announced plans to shift most of their sourcing to China.[40] Estimates varied on the degree to which China will dominate the global trade in the post-MFA world, but there was unanimity on the prediction that China would dominate. More conservative estimates predicted that China would triple its market share of U.S. clothing imports, from 16 to 50 percent, while some industry experts predicted that China could eventually supply 85 percent of U.S. apparel.[41] In mid-2004, the Esquel Corporation, which had been forced by the quota system to build factories in Mauritius, announced that it was closing up shop on the island and moving back to China.[42]

If the surges from China were feared in South Carolina, the prospects were far scarier in a number of developing countries. Textile and apparel exports comprised more than half of manufacturing exports for a dozen countries, including Bangladesh, Mauritius, Honduras, and Sri Lanka, where the industries also provide the largest number of manufacturing jobs (see Figure 11.4). In many of these countries, the majority of the clothing exports were to rich countries that had quota constraints on Chinese

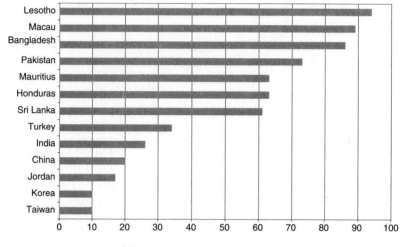

Source: USITC (2004) Table 1.1.

Figure 11.4   Textile and Apparel as % of Manufactured Exports, 2001

apparel.[43] The most dire predictions suggested that the end of the MFA could mean the loss of up to 30 million jobs in the developing world.[44]

In South Carolina, the lucky laid-off workers get jobs at IBM and the less lucky get jobs at Wal-Mart. The least lucky get unemployment benefits and trade adjustment assistance, and, if worse comes to worst, food stamps. In Bangladesh, however, there is little other industry and no safety net of any kind. Indeed, the closest thing to a safety net that Bangladesh has ever known was the secure market share provided by their MFA quotas. In 2002, Bangladesh's market share in the goods released from quota fell by nearly 90 percent, while China's share more than tripled. While economists predicted that the global welfare benefits from the removal of quotas were likely to be sizeable, these benefits are even more abstract in Dhaka than they are in Kannapolis, North Carolina.

Facing the impending China threat, an unlikely collection of bedfellows began to snarl together in mid-2004. Most developing countries had done an abrupt about-face and saw the quota system as their lifeline rather than as their nemesis. By July of that year, nearly 100 industry associations from 47 countries had signed the Istanbul Declaration, which called for an emergency meeting of the WTO to address the loom-ing China threat in the post-MFA world. The new coalition literally circled the globe, with members signing on from Argentina to Zambia.[45] "Not so fast," they seemed to say. The quotas and tariffs and crazy rules were nothing compared to what might happen next. The Chinese dragon was at the door, about to swallow North Carolina and Bangladesh and Turkey and Zambia, all in a single bite. Free trade was really, *really* not a good idea after all.

"See," Auggie Tantillo told me in late 2004, pointing out his new allies from around the world who were suddenly huddled under his umbrella of politics, seeking protection from the markets and especially from China. "We're not just a bunch of guys from South Carolina howling at the moon."

45 YEARS OF "TEMPORARY" PROTECTIONISM END IN 2009— NOW WHAT?

The Big Bang

Despite the scrambling by Auggie and his troops, as well as the support from his allies around the world, the final tranche of textile and apparel quotas was lifted as scheduled on January 1, 2005. The surges from China were everything Auggie had feared. As Figure 12.1 shows, for some categories released from quota, China's exports to the United States soared by more than 800 percent during the first four months of 2005, compared to the same period in the preceding year. The T-shirt, or cotton knit shirt category, showed import surges in excess of 1,200 percent. Overall, the average increase across all categories released was slightly more than 400 percent. It was a flood, and it did indeed appear that many firms in the United States and around the world would soon drown.

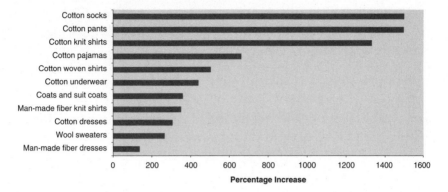

Source: Author's calculations from OTEXA trade data. Data in square meter equivalents.

Figure 12.1 Percentage Increase in U.S. Imports from China for Categories Released from Quota on January 1, 2005. January–April 2005 Compared to January–April 2004.

My first thought, as I followed the trade developments in early 2005, was that we were finally seeing—after decades of political control—what free trade in apparel would look like. Though there remained multiple complex agreements governing apparel trade, the most stultifying regime had ended and the market, it seemed, was finally in charge. And if this is what a "free market" looked like, it did indeed seem that critics who feared dramatic destabilization had much to fear.

As it turned out, however, the surges from China reflected not so much market forces as politically motivated tactics. Both the exporters in China and the importers in the United States had every reason to believe that Auggie and his troops would soon find relief somewhere in Washington. Julia Hughes told me that the surge from China was partly the result of fears among both Chinese producers and American importers that the China gate would not stay open for long. There would be but a brief window, they feared, so if anyone wanted to source from China they had best do it quickly. In yet another perverse and unintended consequence, Auggie's worst fears about the China surge were realized in part because of Julia's fears about what Auggie would do next.

A further complexity, according to a Chinese apparel executive with whom I spoke, was that the surge itself was in part a negotiating tactic. Whenever textile and apparel import limits are negotiated by the United

States and foreign governments, the practice is to negotiate the percentage *increase* in imports to be allowed over the current year. As a result, if limits *were* to be reinstated in 2006, as Chinese exporters and U.S. importers feared, it would be best to get the "base" up as dramatically as possible. If, during the brief open window in 2005, imports increased by more than 400 percent, the 2006 limits would still be more than 400 percent higher than they had been in 2004. In the end, the dramatic surges from China in early 2005 displayed more about politics than they did about markets.

The Big Wink and Nod

Many of the traditional ways in which Julia and Auggie conduct their Washington battles are risky, time-consuming, and expensive, and the complexity and the expense were adding up rapidly in early 2005. As the imports from China surged, Auggie and his troops filed numerous "safeguard" petitions, which, when successful, limited imports from China for certain types of textiles and apparel. The petitions required the U.S. industry to prove that domestic producers had been harmed, and to document each case with analysis and data. For Auggie and his troops, the cumbersome and expensive process was like trying to catch waves with a beach bucket; even as he slowed T-shirts or socks, that many more pants or skirts were flooding in around him.

Fortunately for the U.S. textile industry, however, at just about the same time, George W. Bush needed help, too.

Like every other postwar president, George W. Bush repeatedly made broad proclamations on the blessings of free trade while making complex side payments in response to the groans of the weavers. In 2002, Bush received the one-vote majority (215 to 214) he needed to obtain fast-track authority to negotiate trade agreements by promising Rep. Jim DeMint of South Carolina (ironically, the self-described free trade candidate in his Congressional race) that fabric used to make apparel in the Caribbean countries would receive preferential market access only if it was dyed and finished—as well as manufactured—in the United States. In just a quick whirl of the sausage machine, printing presses closed down in Honduras and powered up in South Carolina. While the dyeing-and-finishing deal was being worked out, the "sock dispute" stalled another trade measure as textile interests held up a tariff reduction bill in exchange for a requirement that toes be sewed shut in the United States in order for Caribbean-knit socks to gain preferential market access.

In 2005, the tried-and-true wink-and-nod was alive and well. While NAFTA had been Bill Clinton's signature Free Trade Agreement, the Bush Administration had pinned its hopes on the successful implementation of CAFTA, the Central American Free Trade Agreement. The Administration knew the Congressional battle over CAFTA would be a tight one, and knew as well that the agreement would be politically possible only if it contained protections for the U.S. textile industry. The Administration believed most Congressional Democrats to be hopeless causes. If CAFTA were to receive the 216 votes needed to pass in the House of Representatives, it would need the support of a number of "Textile Republicans."

Bit by bit, the White House winked and nodded. In exchange for the endorsement of NCTO (the National Council of Textile Organizations), CAFTA negotiators inserted significant protections for U.S. textile interests into the agreement.[1] The most important protection was the new *pocketing rule*, which required apparel linings and pockets to be made of "originating" yarn and fabric. While the support of the domestic textile industry might have seemed to give the Textile Republicans the cover needed to support CAFTA, there was much more to be gained by charging the White House one vote at a time.

In the days preceding the CAFTA vote, Bush visited textile districts in North Carolina as half a dozen Congressmen agreed to support CAFTA in exchange for more specific and arcane protections for the firms in their districts.[2] More promises were made about pockets and linings, and the amount of U.S. fabric that Nicaragua would purchase and the amount of Mexican fabric that they would not. Yet, on the days leading up to the House CAFTA vote, Bush was still short at least a few votes.

One more vote—that of Rep. Robert Alderholt (R-AL)—came on board in exchange for a variety of sock-related promises,[3] and then Rep. Robin Hayes (R-NC), whose spokesman only days before had described him as "a solid no" on CAFTA, switched his vote from no to yes, leaving the final vote in favor of CAFTA 217–215. Hayes's price was suggested in his letter to the Bush administration on the eve of the vote:

> I cannot stress to you how critical it is to reduce these damaging Chinese surges to help protect our domestic textile industry and its work force.[4]

A few days after the vote, the Bush Administration announced plans for a comprehensive agreement limiting textile and apparel imports from China.[5] The comprehensive agreement was to remain in effect until 2009. The quotas on China were back.

It had been a stunningly brilliant negotiation. Months before, the CAFTA agreement had been written to support the industry, and in fact had received the endorsement of the NCTO, which lobbied vigorously for its passage. Yet even though the industry supported the agreement, the Textile Republicans had held out, one at a time, for a better and better deal.

Steve Lamar, EVP at the American Apparel and Footwear Association, had stood alongside Julia Hughes in representing the apparel importers. When I spoke to him in the summer of 2008, he recalled the CAFTA drama of 2005. The domestic textile interests were indeed good negotiators, he told me. "They got paid to eat their ice cream," he said.

A Sigh of Relief

For the dozens of developing countries who had feared being swallowed by China, the events of early 2005 were cause for relief, even before the new restraints on China were announced. While many had feared that the surges from China would come at the expense of poor nations such as Sri Lanka and Bangladesh, it soon became clear that the U.S. consumer's penchant for shopping would leave plenty of demand for almost everyone. Remarkably, the surges from China in early 2005 occurred alongside healthy increases in sales for almost all major U.S. apparel suppliers

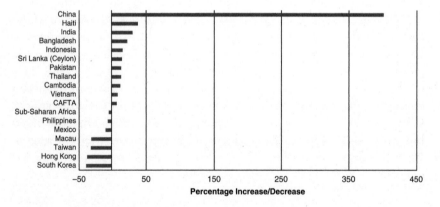

Source: Author's calculations based on OTEXA quota release and trade data. Data in square meter equivalents.

Figure 12.2 Percentage Increase or Decrease in U.S. Imports of Apparel Released from Quota on January 1, 2005 (January–April 2005 Compared to January–April 2004)

(See Figure 12.2). Indeed, the only dramatic losses were those experienced by the wealthy regions of Hong Kong, Macao, South Korea, and Taiwan. The T-shirts that had been sold by Hong Kong because of the quota system were now being produced in the poorer countries. This, most trade experts would argue, was as it should be.

Keven Burke, president of the American Apparel and Footwear Association, surveyed the situation in mid-2008. Finally, he told me, after decades of globe trotting in search of quota, the U.S. apparel firms were engaged in a "race to the top." U.S. firms were seeking out long-term relationships with high-quality suppliers, finally free of the need to buy wool coats from Mauritius because that was where the quota was. Finally, some semblance of comparative advantage appeared to be driving trade flows.

The Central American countries had the advantage of proximity to the U.S. market, and were attracting business for which speed to market was most important. Bangladesh was quickly becoming the supplier of choice for cotton trousers, while India and Pakistan were competitive for a variety of woven and knit apparel at moderate price points. Tiny Sri Lanka had carved a niche in high-end undergarments, and also was increasingly rewarded for its environmentally responsible production processes. Other countries, such as Cambodia, became known for their "sweat-free" labor practices. Vietnam was a rising star in a number of product categories.

The trade data for the 2005–2008 period suggested a more complicated picture (see Figure 12.3). While the worst fears of many developing countries had not been realized, there were indeed losers among the group, particularly in Africa. At the same time, however, there were many winners among poor countries as well, and the most significant losses were concentrated in wealthy countries.[6] As of mid-2008, even though China was still constrained by quotas, the quotas did not appear to be binding: China had plenty of quota left and quota prices were falling. In 2008, T-shirts were coming into the United States from more than 100 countries.[7]

What's Next?

On January 1, 2009, the landscape shifted once again when most quotas were removed for China. Not surprisingly, Auggie Tantillo and Julia Hughes disagreed on what would happen next. Julia believed the dramatic surges of the past were unlikely to happen again. Costs were rising

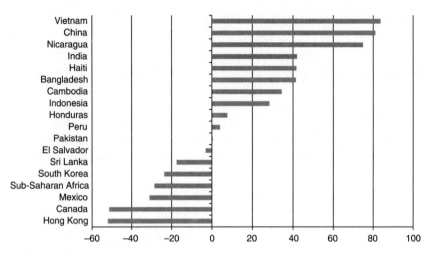

Source: Author's calculations based on OTEXA trade data. Data in square meters.

Figure 12.3   Percentage Increase or Decrease in U.S. Imports of All Apparel (Year Ending in June, 2008 Compared to 2004)

in China, and the higher wages meant that China could no longer undercut its competitors around the world. But both Auggie and Cass Johnson of NCTO believed that China remained a dangerous threat. The U.S. textile industry continued to dwindle, and was still defined by its miseries: job losses, bankruptcies, and plant closings. The miseries, according to Cass and Auggie, were about to get much worse. Both believed that China without quotas could quickly swallow the CAFTA countries, which were the most significant customers for the U.S. industry. Perhaps more important, however, Cass and Auggie both emphasized the myriad ways in which China simply does not play by the rules. From counterfeiting to currency manipulation and unfair subsidies, they believed that the deck is stacked in favor of China and against the American companies who play fair.[8]

In the summer and fall of 2008, Auggie and Julia were once again readying for a China battle. Brenda Jacobs, the trade attorney representing apparel importers, warned the firms sourcing in China to prepare for a fight. The domestic industry was "saber-rattling," Jacobs warned the importers, and was preparing to use all manner of political tactics to address the China challenge.[9] When I spoke that summer to a variety of people in Washington who worked with apparel importers, they all seemed to be engaged in the same game: guessing what Auggie Tantillo would be up to. What, exactly, were the sabers going to look like?

In mid-September 2008, Barack Obama and John McCain were unexpectedly in an apparent dead heat for the presidency. Julia and Auggie agreed that the tight race tilted the advantage to Auggie: Lining up trade protections for the textile industry was a tried-and-true vote-getting tactic. "The closer the election, the more they love us," Auggie told me.

I asked Auggie what exactly his sabers would look like. Would the industry press for monitoring agreements, import safeguards, punitive tariffs, or congressional action?

"Everything's on the table," he smiled.

Not exactly what Julia wanted to hear.

Friends and Enemies, 2008

Harry Truman famously remarked that the only way to have a true friend in Washington is to buy a dog. After following the T-shirt trade battles for a number of years, it was easy to see the wisdom in Truman's remark. In the life of a T-shirt, political alliances shift as rapidly as trade flows.

In 2004, dozens of developing countries had sided with Auggie as fears of the imminent China threat grew. In 2008, alphabet armies from around the world again arrived to shore up the American troops. ETGAMA (Ethiopian Textile and Garment Manufacturers' Association), LTEA (Lesotho Textile Exporters Association), and CANAINTEX (Cámara Nacional de la Industria Textil de Mexico), along with armies from more than a dozen other countries, were bombarding the Department of Commerce, the USTR, and the U.S. Congress with letters and lobbyists in the fall of 2008. The China wolf was again at the door, and desperate measures were called for.[10] In late 2008, it was not entirely clear what form this international coalition would take or how it would operate. "We'll be working with them," was about all Auggie could say of his international allies.

Yet other developing countries were on Julia's side. Julia was supporting the McDermott bill, or the "New Partnership for Development Act of 2007," legislation that would give duty-free access to goods from the world's poorest countries. Of course, the poor countries that would benefit were in Julia's camp, but those that were not quite poor enough to benefit, or those who already had free access and wanted to keep their club as small as possible, were siding with Auggie.

Some countries split their loyalties, siding with Auggie on protection from China and with Julia on duty-free access. It was hard to tell who were friends and who were enemies.[11] The battle lines were noticeably more blurry than they had been just a few years before.

Domestic alliances were increasingly fluid as well. The seed-to-shirt coalition that had been a reliable mainstay for generations had first begun to splinter in the early 1990s, when the shirts flipped to Julia's side. Yet in 2005, the seed-to-fabric bloc that remained was reliably solid on Auggie's side. The fact that the cotton growers in Texas and the textile producers in South Carolina could rely on one another for support in Washington went a long way toward explaining the generous coddling that both industries had long received. Textile producers and cotton growers had long been intertwined in the United States; in fact, in 2007, Wally Darneille, president and CEO of the Plains Cotton Cooperative in Lubbock, was elected vice-president of NCTO. "We try to look out for each other if we can," Wally told me when I visited Lubbock.

In 2005, the cotton lobby had sided with Auggie in seeking limits on Chinese apparel imports, and a few years later the textile lobby had returned the favor by throwing its weight behind the 2007 Farm Bill. The Farm Bill, as we saw in the first section of this book, had relatively little to do with farmers, and in fact included a number of valuable nuggets for the textile producers. In particular, under the 2007 Farm Bill, the U.S. government pays U.S. textile mills for each bale of cotton that they purchase, a provision that scratches everyone's back at once.[12]

An uncomfortable reality was threatening this cozy alliance in 2008, however. If Wally were going to side with Auggie again in the fight against China, the cotton growers would now be signing on to battle their own biggest customer. By 2007, China was purchasing more than twice as much U.S. cotton as was the U.S. textile industry.[13] If cotton growers signed on with Auggie to seek apparel import limits from China, the U.S. cotton growers would be crippling their biggest customer's ability to buy U.S. cotton.

It looked like an almost impossible position for Wally Darneille as president of the PCCA in Lubbock and vice-president of the NCTO. Wally laughed when I asked him about this. "I keep two baseball caps in my office," he joked. "Once says 'China' and the other says 'North Carolina.' I can change hats pretty fast."

How long the traditional loyalties linking Texas and North Carolina could remain in the face of the new global business reality was anyone's guess. A cold-hearted calculation seemed to suggest that the "seed" might soon go the way of the "shirt." Indeed, the cold-hearted calculation would have the seed and the shirt on the *same* side, battling with Julia to let the Chinese T-shirts in.

No one I talked to seemed to have a clear idea how it would play out. For many, it seemed highly unlikely that the fast-talking New York fashion types would come to roost in Washington with the Texas cotton farmers ("You should see them around the table together," Brenda Jacobs told me. "It doesn't work.") Julia Hughes believed that the traditions binding the U.S. textile producers and cotton growers together would be hard to break. For others, however, it was just as unlikely that the U.S. cotton growers would continue to shoot themselves in the foot by siding with their traditional allies. Perhaps the seed would just gradually drift away from the club.

Yet the very fact that the shifting or stable alliances were of such interest in 2008 proved that—whatever the outcome—apparel trade was still being worked out in the realm of politics rather than markets. Perhaps the markets were more in charge than they once were. But as I surveyed the Washington landscape of lawyers and lobbyists and quotas and trade agreements, of safeguards and trade associations and dumping petitions and shifting alliances, it looked to me like the best negotiators, not the best T-shirts, were still winning.

David Birnbaum, one of the industry's leading international sourcing experts, was sounding a warning in the summer of 2008. China would be an "unreliable supplier," he cautioned the importers. It wasn't price, or quality, or factories, or shipping costs that he was worried about. It was politics.[14]

Obama's Wink

By the end of October, Barack Obama seemed to have solidified his lead against John McCain in the 2008 presidential race. However, on the day of the election, virtually all media outlets were calling North Carolina—an important state in the race—a "dead heat" race for the presidency. Though North Carolina had voted Republican in 9 of the 10 prior presidential races, polls suggested that Obama would have a chance in the state.

The Obama campaign had devoted significant resources to the North Carolina textile communities, and Obama himself wore suits that were made in America throughout the campaign. In a TV ad airing in October, he referred to Carolina Mills, a North Carolina–based yarn spinning company. In the campaign ad, a somber narrator speaks over a close-up shot of a padlocked factory gate, which fades away into an American flag:

... Carolina Mills. Forced to shut down 17 plants; 2,600 jobs lost. Workers once proud to make thread for American flags have their jobs outsourced to Asia. Washington sold them out with the help of politicians like John McCain. He supported tax breaks and trade deals for companies that ship jobs overseas. North Carolina just can't afford John McCain.[15]

Ten days before the election, Cass Johnson of the NCTO received a letter from Barack Obama.[16] The letter was in response to a series of questions that NCTO had posed regarding the candidate's position on textile trade. NCTO had pressed Obama on six key issues, ranging from ambitious tactics to deal with Chinese imports to inserting yarn-forward rules in future trade agreements.

In his letter, Obama committed to pursue most of the aggressive policies requested by the industry. And he acknowledged that the textile industry was a special case: "...I am especially aware of the trade challenges faced by those working in our textile industries," he wrote. "I look forward to a productive working relationship with your industry."[17]

It was a wink. The wink was eerily similar to what I had seen in any number of online and library archives. The Obama textile letter sounded so much like the Reagan letter or the Nixon letter or the Carter letter that it was hard to imagine that several generations had passed. Obama's wink was announced to NCTO's members on October 29, five days before the election.

John McCain did not answer NCTO's questions. He did not need to: Everyone knew that as an avowed free trader, McCain would have given the wrong answers.

Though Obama was declared the national winner on the evening of November 4, it took two more days to decide the outcome in North Carolina. Obama's victory margin of just under 14,000 votes represented just 0.2 percent of votes cast in the state. As of 2008, North Carolina was still home to more than 60,000 jobs in the textile and apparel industry.

A few days after the election I asked Auggie Tantillo if the "Obama letter" had been a factor in the candidate's North Carolina victory.

"I think it helped," he said.

Julia and Auggie seem always to be consumed by the battle of the moment, without the time or inclination to look to the past. Yet like today's garment workers in China, Julia and Auggie have brothers and sisters in time, as well. The numbingly complex battles and trade barriers that govern textile and apparel trade today harken back not just to Ronald Reagan and Richard Nixon, however. Their long and colorful history in fact precedes even George Washington.

The labels that I often heard applied to Auggie Tantillo and his troops— *Dinosaurs! Protectionists!*—suggested that those who sought to slow or manage trade flows were somehow standing in the way of progress. Yet while the conventional wisdom associates free markets with forward progress and prosperity, barriers, too, can lead to progress. Sometimes a wall limits our fortunes; other times a wall can incite much more creativity than an open door. It was a barrier that led Eli Whitney to invent the cotton gin, and a different sort of bottleneck that led James Hargreaves to invent the spinning jenny. While the world in aggregate would have been richer without the trade barriers, the world also would have been a different place. Trade barriers, like other barriers, can blow the future apart.

What would the world look like today had the dinosaurs never roamed? It is impossible to know. Consider the following parable from long ago, when Auggie Tantillo's protectionist ancestors first tried to block the cheap cotton clothing flowing in from Asia.

Try This New Underwear

In the early seventeenth century, the English woolen industry had no rivals. The industry was highly successful both domestically and internationally, and it formed the backbone of entire communities in much the same way cotton mills dominated early twentieth-century North Carolina. Employment was also great in ancillary industries such as weaving and embroidery. Writers on the topic of English wool often became mired in what Thomas called "poetic ecstasy": The more restrained lauded English wool as the "foundation of English riches," while the less restrained compared English wool to Samson's locks.[18]

Poetic ecstasy notwithstanding, the term *English woolens* does not compel one to jump out of bed each morning to dress. Though the fabric was indeed central to the economy, the woolens were also expensive to the average consumer, so the English middle class had very little variety of dress. And then, as now, woolens were itchy, they were hard to clean and dry, and they were hot and clammy in the damp English summers. It is hard to imagine how even the most passionate patriot would, if given a choice, prefer woolen underwear to cotton.

The handmade Indian cotton calicoes and muslins that began to pour into British ports in the mid-1600s were a consumer boon not unlike today's cotton T-shirts from China. For socks, children's clothing, and frocks, there was a marvelous new alternative: It was cheap, it was light, and it was washable. It came in a variety of bright colors and prints, and it was soft instead of itchy. The directors of the East India Company wrote India in 1691 that any quantity, and any type, of Indian cotton cloth should be sent: "You can send us nothing amiss at this time when everything of India is so much wanted."[19] Daniel Defoe worried that the cheap cottons from India had:

> crept into our houses, our closets, our bedchambers; curtains, cushions, chairs, and at last beds themselves were nothing but Callicoes ... everything that used to be made of wool, or silk, relating to either the dress of women or the furniture of our houses, was supplied by the Indian trade.[20]

Readers can no doubt predict the response of the British woolen industry to the torrents of cheap cotton clothing flowing in from Asia. As consumers clamored for the soft and cheap clothing, the "groans of the weavers" quickly reached the British Parliament.[21] The mill owners told of crises and even starvation in the shadow of the shuttered woolen workshops, and of the unemployed fleeing to Holland and Ireland. Even the mills that stayed open had cut their employment drastically, and the related industries, as well as woolen district shopkeepers, also suffered and added their voices to the cacophony of groans. In many districts, unemployment was above 50 percent, leaving half the men, and most of the women and children, dependent on the parishes for support. And the cheap cotton imports cost not only jobs but lives. The 1700 *England's Almanac* reported that:

> Lord Godolphin's and Duke of Queensbury's sisters were burnt to death by muslin head-dresses and night-rails; the Lady Frederick's child burnt to death by a calico frock; a house belonging to St. Paul's School burnt by a calico bed and curtains, a playhouse at Copenhagen with 3 or 400 people burnt occasion'd by calico hangings.[22]

The new underwear was dangerous.

The war against cotton imports that raged through the English Parliament in the late 1600s pitted the woolen interests against the reasoned voices of those who argued that cotton was a superior fabric in some settings, especially in summer. Like snarling dogs today, the woolen interests tried to reserve some piece of the pie for the domestic industry. This act, introduced in Parliament in 1689, for example, reserved cottons for use in the summer only:

All persons whatsoever to wear no garment...but what is made of sheep's wool...from the feast of All Saints to the feast of Annunciation.[23]

Other attempts to shore up the market for woolens involved legislating the dress of particular groups in order to support the domestic industry. If the groups could be made big enough, perhaps wool could be saved. An act introduced in 1699 stipulated that:

all magistrates, judges, students of the Universities, and all professors of the common and civil law... [must] wear gowns made of the woolen manufacture [at all times of year].[24]

When this attempt to dictate dress failed, the woolen interests turned their attention to less powerful groups. It was argued quite shamelessly that even the poorest could afford a bit of wool in their wardrobe: An act at the same time introduced to Parliament required all female English servants earning five pounds or less to wear only woolen hats. As in today's trade agreements, there was an attempt to keep some piece of the pie for the domestic industry. If the woolens could have some part of the calendar, or some part of the population, then their well-publicized misery would be eased.

But in the end, by 1700, Parliament had granted woolen's wishes for only one group of consumers, a group that didn't get itchy in wool, the one group that was less powerful than female servants. An act, passed easily, stipulated that:

No corpse of any person...shall be buried in any shirt, shift, sheet or shroud...other than what is made of sheep's wool only.[25]

For this event, like many others, there was a little poem:

Since the living would not bear it
They should when dead be forced to wear it.[26]

Of course, each British citizen died only once, and once dead did not change clothes, so this limited market was not enough to restore the fortunes of the English woolen industry. With the landowners and the churches on their side, the woolen workers could not be easily dismissed. In 1701, Parliament responded with an astonishing rule for the living: Beginning on September 29, 1701, people simply could not wear this slight and tawdry cloth anymore. For all people, and at all times of year:

all calicos painted, dyed, printed, or stained (in Persia, China, or the East Indies) which are or shall be imported into this kingdom, shall not be worn or otherwise used within this kingdom of England.[27]

Notably, the act did not exclude simple utilitarian muslins that had not been dyed or printed.[28] Presumably, anyone with a legitimate "need" for cotton fabric could have it met with the plain muslins. The "calicoe madams," however, who had embraced the new fashionable prints, had best dust off their woolens. Yet while the Calicoe Laws of 1701 appeared at first to be a victory for the woolen interests, it became clear almost immediately that Parliament could not legislate the woolen industry's salvation.

Predictably, the barriers triggered entrepreneurial instincts. With consumer demand still rampant, and the plain, undyed muslins still flowing in at very low prices, entrepreneurs in England figured out quite quickly how to print and dye cotton cloth, and had soon mechanized the process. A new industry was born in England, and it was successful almost immediately. In 1702, barely a year after the act had gone into effect, the Commissioners of Trade and Plantations bemoaned the unintended consequences of the trade barriers:

> Though it was hoped that this prohibition would discourage the consumption of these goods, we found that allowing calicos unstained to be brought in has occasioned such an increase of the printing and staining calicoes here that it is more prejudicial to us than it was before passing the Act.[29]

In putting up a wall to keep out Indian printed cottons and save the domestic woolen industry, the protectionists had instead constructed a warm and profitable incubator for the cotton printing and dyeing industry in Britain. The woolen workers were behind where they had started. By 1719, they had taken their battle to the streets. Woolen weavers declared war, quite literally, against the calicoes that had stolen their livelihood. The woolen weavers—all men—not only began to "plunder" and protest in the streets of London, they began to attack the women. The news reports of the day are replete with references to "disorders" and "outrages and abuses" on bodies of persons wearing calicoes.[30]

The woolen weavers won the war, clearly and decisively. On December 25, 1722, it became illegal to wear—or to use in home furnishings—almost all imported cotton cloth.[31] And the law was not a brief insanity: The ban on cottons would not be lifted for decades, forcing a generation of Britons into hot, itchy, and expensive clothing, all in the name of saving the domestic textile industry.

But being forced into woolens in the damp English summers got people thinking, and before long, the British gushed forth with a stunning string of ideas about how to manufacture cotton cloth in England: power looms, spinning jennies, factories, the Industrial Revolution itself. By blocking access to cheap cotton clothing from Asia, protectionist dinosaurs had launched the modern world.

PART IV

MY T-SHIRT FINALLY ENCOUNTERS A FREE MARKET

THE GLOBAL TRADE IN CAST-OFF T-SHIRTS

A Just-Opened Bale of American Used Clothing Near the Manzese Market. (Author's Photo.)

Geofrey Milonge at His T-Shirt Stall at the Manzese Market in Dar Es Salaam. (Author's Photo.)

WHERE T-SHIRTS GO AFTER THE SALVATION ARMY BIN

JAPAN, TANZANIA, AND THE RAG FACTORY

Meet Me in the Parking Lot

In the wealthy and normally well-mannered Washington suburb of Bethesda, Maryland, the competition is heating up.[1] It is Saturday morning, and soccer moms are in a race to throw things away. First in line is a Lexus SUV, followed by a Town and Country minivan, and then a Lincoln Navigator. The first three vehicles alone cost well over $100,000, which would buy about one-tenth of a house in much of the surrounding neighborhood. The Salvation Army truck sits outside the Sumner Place Shopping Center, but the truck has only so much room, so it pays to be early and to be tough. The wait to dispose of last year's stuff is longer than the wait to buy more stuff inside the shopping center, and often, by 10:00 A.M., the van is full and the weaker competitors are turned away until the next week. Mostly, the moms are giving away clothing—large Hefty bags stuffed to bursting with perfectly fine clothing that someone is tired of. Some of the moms admit that later in the afternoon they would be headed to the mall to buy more stuff, and that next year they would likely be unloading that as well. A few of the moms express an altruistic motive for lining up behind the van, and all say that they will use the tax deduction. More than anything, though, the moms are here because they need to clean out their closets to make room for new stuff.

T-shirts? Yes, they agree, lots of T-shirts. They shake their heads, not sure how they ended up with so many T-shirts. It is easy to see the simple market dynamic of secondhand T-shirts in a wealthy U.S. suburb: all supply and no demand.

The high wages that have caused the demise of U.S. textile and apparel manufacturing have a flip side. The very wages that have stripped America's manufacturing might have at the same time led to a new comparative advantage: Rich Americans—or even middle-class Americans—excel at throwing things away, and the richer we become, the bigger the mounds of cast-off clothing swell. The Salvation Army at one time tried to sell all of the clothing in its stores or to give it away, but the supply now so far outstrips domestic demand that only a fraction of the clothing collected by the Salvation Army stays in the United States. There are nowhere near enough poor people in America to absorb the mountains of castoffs, even if they were given away.

America's castoffs, however, have customers the world over, and clothing thrown away by Americans forms the backbone of a dynamic global industry. While the United States has experienced an unbroken string of merchandise trade deficits for more than 30 years, recycled clothing has been a consistently successful export industry. Between 1995 and 2007, the United States exported nearly nine billion pounds of used clothing and other worn textile products to the rest of the world (see Figure 13.1), and the industry now has customers in more than 100 countries. During the past decade, the United States has in most years been the world's largest exporter of used clothing.[3]

Observers have sharply conflicting views about the global trade in cast-off T-shirts. Is the recycled clothing business a villainous industry—a shadowy network that exploits the goodwill of charities and their donors, and suffocates the apparel industries in developing countries under mountains of castoffs? Or is it a great industry, a model of nimble, free-market dynamism that channels charitable impulses into clothing for the poor? People who hold opinions about this business hold them strongly, but most people, of course, do not think about the industry at all, and while tossing T-shirts into the collection bins have only a vague and usually wrong idea of where the T-shirts might be headed and what will happen to them next.

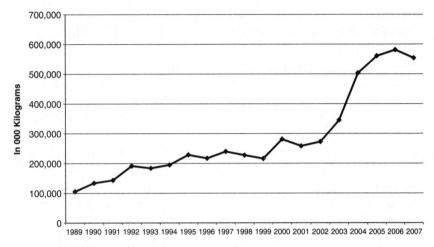

Source: USITC Dataweb.

Figure 13.1   U.S. Exports of Used Clothing (by Weight)

The industry is all but invisible except to insiders: It has no household names and no big global players. Firms go in and out of the business almost daily, and though there are some factories, there are mostly networks of small family businesses scattered around the globe. The networks are often linked by ethnicity or family ties, and most of the businesses have only fleeting advantages in demand or supply. It may look easy, a simple matter of funneling the mountains of clothing that rich people no longer want to the poor who never have enough. But there are multiple complications and many challenges with an industry that links the moms in the Bethesda parking lot with the moms in African villages. Each leg of the journey has another set of competitors, and it is impossible to know ahead of time what will get thrown away in Bethesda and who in Africa might want it. Both suppliers and customers are astoundingly fickle.

For now, I've decided to keep my T-shirt. But one day I will toss it into a Salvation Army bin, and it will encounter myriad new experiences. Most important, it is only in this final stage of life that the T-shirt will meet a real market. Unlike the U.S. cotton producers, the North Carolina textile mills, or the Chinese sewing factories, the clothing recyclers are on their own, without help, or even notice, from governments or lobbyists. There are no walls to keep out the lions, so successful players in the used clothing trade have no choice but to compete by punching rather than ducking, and each survives only by excelling in an exhausting race of faster-better-cheaper with hundreds of competitors, a race that leaves little time for politics. It is only in this final chapter of the T-shirt's life that world trade patterns are fashioned by economics rather than politics. While subsidies likely explain much world trade in cotton, and tariffs, quotas, and trade agreements explain much world trade in finished T-shirts, once the T-shirt is tossed into the bin its remaining life story is a story about markets and little else.

The global used clothing industry is also a fascinating study in the market for "snowflakes," as almost every item of clothing that enters the trade is unique. At the raw cotton stage, any bale of similarly graded cotton is interchangeable with any other, and once certain characteristics are specified, plain-white T-shirts, too, are interchangeable. But if the moms lined up in Bethesda toss away 100 T-shirts, each will be different, and this *snowflake factor* has important implications for how the industry is structured and what it takes to win. In brief, the snowflake factor means that the most successful firms in the industry are those with highly developed expertise in picking out special snowflakes, and with worldwide but personal relationships that allow them to match snowflakes with customers. It is hard to see how a big multinational could pull it off. Here, finally, is a global industry for the little guy.

Panning for Gold in New Jersey

The Stubin family of New York has been a player in the industry for more than 60 years. For most of that time, Trans-Americas Trading Company, the family firm, occupied a five-story warehouse and factory in the Greenpoint neighborhood of Brooklyn. For generations, Greenpoint was a first stop for generations of immigrants, especially from Europe. Morton Stubin, who arrived from Poland in 1939, was one of them. Family lore is a bit hazy on how Morton started in the used clothing business, but somehow he found buyers and sellers of used clothing and built a business bringing them together.

Ed Stubin, Morton's son, hadn't planned to join the business. His plan was to become an academic, and he went so far as to obtain his Ph.D. in psychology. But Ed found himself facing a weak academic job market and the demands of a growing family, so he joined his father in the business in the 1970s. Today, though Ed is completely committed to the business, and is considered by many to be the industry's leader and voice, he doesn't really believe he is a natural businessman, and he still thinks about what he might be able to do with his psychology training once he retires. Eric Stubin, Ed's son, also did not plan to join the business, but after college and a few years climbing the corporate ladder, he came back to Brooklyn and joined his father. Sunny Stubin, Ed's wife, also works at Trans-Americas. In 2006, with gentrification closing in, the Stubins sold their Brooklyn factory to a condo developer and moved their firm about 20 miles away to Clifton, New Jersey.

The U.S. textile recycling industry consists of thousands of small family businesses, many now in their third or fourth generation of family ownership, and Trans-Americas is both the rule and exception in the industry. Like its nearly 3,000 competitors, Trans-Americas is a family-run firm involving multiple generations in the day-to-day operations of the business.[4] Every year, the Stubins watch many of their competitors go belly-up, and every year the failures are quickly replaced by new and nimble players. In this fluid network of start-ups and failures, however, the Stubins stand out for their longevity. Ed Stubin repeats this often, usually with a tone of amazement: "We're still here," he keeps telling me, as if he can't quite believe it.

By 2008, the competitive landscape was far more intense than it had been just a few years earlier. "We have to run even faster to stay in the same place," Stubin told me. The Stubins buy clothing from charities within a 1,000-mile radius of New York, and on an average day their 85 employees will process about 70,000 pounds of clothing. The charities charge what the market will bear. Prices tend toward the higher end of the range when the castoffs come from wealthier neighborhoods, and toward the lower end in seasons that generate less desirable castoffs. In general, winter clothing has a more limited market than summer clothing, so prices trend down during periods when suburbanites are disposing of cold-weather clothing, and per-pound prices are higher in warmer climates. When I first visited Trans-Americas in 2004, the Stubins were buying unsorted truckloads of clothing from the charities for about 5 to 7 cents per pound. By the summer of 2008, this price had approximately doubled, thanks to competition from the increasing number of buyers. Interestingly, during this same period the price of new T-shirts from China fell by approximately half.

Used clothing buyers can't be choosy or averse to risk. They have no choice but to buy what has been thrown away and deemed worthless by somebody, and they never know exactly what will be buried in the truckloads from the charities. The most successful buyers are like successful stock traders, buying at low points, seizing timing opportunities, and hoping competitors are looking the other way.

Unfortunately, the best stuff has been picked off by the time the clothing reaches Trans-Americas. The larger charities—Goodwill and the Salvation Army—sort through donations for the goods that are saleable in their stores, so by the time the donations reach the Stubins, they have already been cast off twice, by the original owner and by the charity. But astute buyers not only know what types of goods get tossed to which charities and when, they also know which charities tend to skim off what.

Ed Stubin has seen a shift in the very nature of the business during the past generation. For many years, the business was essentially a sorting business. The tons of clothing pouring through the loading dock were sorted into three basic categories: for sale as clothing, wiping rags, and fiber. Each category had ready buyers, and, more important, each category was profitable. Whether the clothing coming into the warehouse was to be shredded into fiber, cut into rags, or worn as clothing, most of the prices paid for the raw material were sufficiently below the selling prices that the Stubins could make a profit. The business was simpler and easier then, and it was this appearance of easy profits that began to attract competitors.

Increasing competition in the 1970s led to a downward trend in selling prices that lasted more than 30 years. With selling prices falling and buying prices rising, it was no longer enough to sort and sell in the three categories, as most of the selling prices were below the Stubins' cost. The business changed from a sorting operation to a mining operation. Mining usually requires more skill than sorting, and also entails significantly more risk. While some firms in the industry simply "sort and sell," others, like Trans-Americas, have developed significant expertise in mining.

The clothing enters the Trans-Americas warehouse on a conveyor belt that moves quickly past the workers, who stand on either side of the belt.[5] Like an *I Love Lucy* rerun, the workers grab the clothing whizzing by and toss it into or onto one of a number of bins or conveyor belts. At this stage, little skill is required; the "rough sort" entails simply identifying the product and tossing to the appropriate place. The choices include, for example, skirts, men's pants, household materials, and jeans. T-shirt material has its own category, but includes not just T-shirts but also other articles made of cotton-T-shirt-like fabric.

Clothing in the T-shirt category slides onto another conveyor belt where it is again surrounded by a team of workers. The workers quickly examine each snowflake and decide its fate. The shift is subtle but distinct: The workers are now miners and graders, rather than sorters, and the job requires more skill and more attention, and is rewarded with more money. The workers also categorize the clothing by amount of wear, ranging from like new to slightly worn to unsaleable as clothing. As the workers grade and categorize, they are also panning for gold, because certain types of clothing, even that in poor condition, have an upscale and eager market. So-called *vintage* clothing has the highest value of all, though it is not easy to explain what exactly "vintage" is. If a worker identifies an article of clothing as vintage, the clothing is singled out for special treatment in a separate section of the factory, where Sunny Stubin matches special clothing with special customers. While it may not be clear what *vintage* means, what is clear is that the business depends on the workers' ability to spot it, because to let it whiz by with the flotsam is like flushing gold down the river along with the firm's profits. Spotting the snowflakes that have special value is a skill that management experts call "tacit knowledge." In other words, it's hard to explain. A skilled grader can decide a T-shirt's fate in approximately one second.

Some aspects of the panning business are easier than others. Everyone knows to watch for Levis and Nikes, because hip young Japanese have a penchant for these brands, and just the right pair of used jeans or sneakers can sell for thousands of dollars in Tokyo.[6] The Japanese also love Disney, and a perfect-condition Mickey Mouse T-shirt can be easily sold for 10 times the price of a less-well-adorned T-shirt. (Indeed, when I visited Tokyo in 2007 after this book was published in Japanese, I strolled in the Takeshita Dori neighborhood, where there were literally hundreds of $100 old American T-shirts for sale.) Because of its insatiable demand for trendy Americana, Japan is usually the largest customer for American used clothing.[7] However, Japan's demand is limited to high-end and quirky items; so while Japan is the largest-dollar-volume customer, the country absorbs only a tiny volume of America's castoffs. Most of the truckloads that are dumped into the Stubin factory have little of interest to the Japanese.

Once the likes of Mickey Mouse have been picked off, panning for gold in the T-shirt river becomes more inexplicable. The value equation might be flipped upside down, with worn items sometimes having greater value than new, and sometimes not. Old tie-dye, for example, is gold, new tie-dye is not, but the equation is reversed for sports team shirts. Somehow, Sunny Stubin just knows when she sees a T-shirt, whether it will appeal to one of her upscale customers, and somehow, the higher-paid workers are expected to know, too. How to explain to a worker from another culture that a ratty Led Zeppelin T-shirt (what is Led Zeppelin, anyway?) should be skimmed off while a newish JCPenney T-shirt should be sent down the chute? How to explain why some "event" T-shirts (David Faulkner Memorial 2001 Motorcycle Ride) have high value and others (Kidz in the Zoo Fun Day 2002) do not? Sunny Stubin shrugs repeatedly: You just have to know your customers, she says over and over again.

Certain T-shirts are hot right now, especially in Europe, New York, and Los Angeles. Sunny has customers willing to pay top-dollar for 1970s rock bands, for example, so the viability of the business depends on the workers' ability to spot such gold and send it onto the vintage belt for special handling. Sending an old Rolling Stones T-shirt to Africa is a lose–lose, as African consumers couldn't care less about the Rolling Stones and also do not like visible wear and tear. Just the right Rolling Stones T-shirt—from the band's 1972 tour, for example—can fetch about $300 at a hip vintage store.[8] If such a shirt ends up in an Africa-bound bale, then the Stubins have not only forgone profit from their vintage customers, but they have created an unhappy customer in Africa.

The T-shirts singled out for special treatment as vintage are matched with certain customers and are often sold by the piece, though sometimes by the pound. A nice Mickey Mouse can go for $3, and a rare rock band can bring much more. The vast majority of the T-shirts flowing onto the conveyor belts are not gold, however, and not bound for London, Los Angeles, or Tokyo. Like the leftovers from Nelson Reinsch's cotton production, old American T-shirts end up in surprising places.

T-Shirts in the Afterlife

Approximately half of the clothing arriving at Trans-Americas has another life to live as clothing. Where rich Americans see garbage, much of the rest of the world sees perfectly fine clothing that can be worn to work or even to weddings, and can clothe another child or two. Since the fall of Communism, American used clothing has found an eager market in the so-called "second world," and U.S. processors now ship large volumes of used clothing to the former Soviet bloc. According to the Department of Commerce, the United States ships used clothing to Poland, Ukraine, and Russia, and used clothing Internet message boards often contain expressions of interest from the poorer side of Europe. One advantage of the Eastern European market is its climatic similarity to the United States, as well as its similar fashion sensibilities. Interestingly, Ed Stubin told me that the wealthy countries of Western Europe have recently lost their used clothing industries to the poorer countries of Eastern Europe. Rather than sort clothing in Western Europe and then sell winter coats to Ukraine, the sorting and grading activities have shifted to the poorer countries in order to take advantage of the lower labor costs. Other common destinations for American used clothing include the Philippines, Chile, and Guatemala. Virtually all of the clothing shipped to these markets is in fine condition; the only thing wrong with most of it is that an American got tired of it.

But most of the clothing whizzing by on Trans-Americas' conveyor belts is headed to Africa, on a journey from the richest to the poorest place on earth. For many countries in Sub-Saharan Africa, used clothing represents one of America's leading exports (see Figure 13.2), and for several, it is often America's largest export.

The countries appear to have come from a list of World Bank basket cases, places where women still carry water and babies are born in mud houses. The basket-case imagery is often used by critics of the used

Benin	Dem. Republic of Congo	Republic of Congo
Guinea	Guinea-Bissau	Gabon
Gambia	Malawi	Mali
Mozambique	Niger	Senegal
Tanzania	Togo	Uganda

Source: UNComtrade.

Figure 13.2 Countries for which Used Clothing Was Among the Top 10 Imports from the United States, 2007

clothing trade, where observers like to describe how insult is added to injury when the poorest countries of the world serve as a dumping ground for America's rags.

Ed Stubin has traveled to many of these countries, traipsing through Niger, Mozambique, Angola, and Benin to meet with customers and drum up business. He is still haunted by images of swollen bellies and especially of land-mine amputees. But to Ed Stubin, Africa is not a dumping ground or a basket case but a customer, or rather hundreds of different customers, each with exacting demands for quality, service, and price. Stubin is mildly offended but mostly amused by the notion that he dumps castoffs into Africa. Such a business model would never allow him to survive, not when his competitors are eagerly trying to meet the demands of the African consumers.

As Americans continuously clean out our bigger and bigger but still-too-small closets so that we can head back to the mall to buy more, we create an exploding supply of used clothing that shifts the balance of market power to the African customer. Whether the African customer is seeking khakis, baby clothing, or T-shirts, he or she has hundreds of potential suppliers from the networks of exporters in the West, and Stubin survives only by figuring out what his customers want and delivering it in good time at a competitive price. The underlying principle is not original, but it is critical: The customer is king, and Stubin is in a faster-better-cheaper race to make the customers happy. Dumping ground, indeed.

Like clothing customers anywhere, Trans-Americas' customers in Africa want their clothing free of stains and tears. In addition, the hot climate means a preference for light cottons. But modesty is an important value in most of Africa, and so shorts have little appeal except for children. Miniskirts, too, are out, as is anything sexually suggestive. Most of Ed's African customers prefer darker colors, because they do not show dirt so easily. The Africans are every bit as fashion-conscious as the Americans, and know whether lapels are wide or pants have cuffs this year, and make their demands accordingly. T-shirts are perfect for the African weather, though the market is particular about the pictures or script on the shirt.

Most of Trans-Americas' clothing is baled according to customer specification and sold by the pound. Typically, the bale size is 500 pounds, though it can be smaller or up to 1,000 pounds. The bale's size and contents, as Stubin keeps telling me, are "whatever the customer wants." Stacked in the warehouse ready to leave the loading dock are literally hundreds of bales marked "women's cotton blouses," "baby clothing," "men's khaki pants," "cotton polo shirts," or just "socks." In their incessant quest to meet the exacting customer specifications, Trans-Americas today sorts clothing into more than 400 different categories.

T-shirts are their own mini-industry. In all, the Stubins sort T-shirts into approximately 20 different categories, for example, pocket tees, ringer collar tees, four-color pictures, script, two-color pictures, and sports teams. While some customers will order bales of mixed styles of T-shirts, others will specify in detail their T-shirt style preference. In 2008, the selling price of used T-shirts in good condition was about 80 cents per pound. Because T-shirts average three to a pound, this means that the Stubins sell T-shirts to their African customers for about 25 cents apiece. Ed Stubin likes to stress that he can send a nice T-shirt to Africa for less than the cost of mailing a letter. The cost is also approximately half of the value of the raw cotton in the shirt.

M y T-shirt from the Florida beachfront shop is well-suited to the African market. African customers do not like in-your-face logos (e.g., "Ya got a problem with that?") or suggestive messages (e.g., "Hot Chick"). But my T-shirt's colorful picture of the parrot and palm tree is cheerful and inoffensive, and the shirt could be worn by a man or a woman. The T-shirt is still in good shape, with no holes or stains. It has been washed a few times, but the print is still bright.

My T-shirt is among the lucky ones, however, because about half of the shirts that enter the Trans-Americas factory do not have another life as clothing, as there is virtually no demand from the world market for clothing that is torn, excessively worn, or stained. Of the clothing that is no longer wearable, T-shirts are among the most valuable: Most of them will end up as wiping rags in the world's factories. There are few better wiping rags than an old T-shirt, according to Ed Stubin. Suppose, he asks, you have a pile of old clothing at home and you spill your coffee: What would you wipe it up with—the jeans, the sweater, or the T-shirt?

Approximately 30 percent of the clothing entering the Trans-Americas factory is destined to become wiping rags. Trans-Americas provides bales of worn T-shirts for sale to rag cutters, who pay the firm about eight cents per pound. Many industrial processes require white rags, so white T-shirts are baled separately and sold for a higher price. At this stage, the value proposition reverses again, as a T-shirt with an elaborate four-color picture will sell for a lower price than a plain-white T-shirt, because the material used to make the print impairs the cloth's absorbency. Very dark T-shirts (whose dyes can react with some chemicals) and those containing some polyester (which impairs absorbency) can also sell for lower prices.

In order for an old cotton T-shirt to be saleable to a rag cutter, there must be enough left of the T-shirt so that the cutter can cut a rag of about 150 square inches. Some T-shirts are too ratty, or too covered with paint or prints, to be sold to the wiping-rag manufacturers. There is a gasp of breath left in such a T-shirt, however, as it enters yet another market to become *shoddy*.

A T-shirt becomes shoddy once it is shredded into bits by a machine called (aptly) a mutilator, in a process that is a bit like turning tree trunks into mulch. Shoddy has a market value of 2 to 4 cents per pound, and it also has customers across the industrial landscape. Bernie Brill, former executive director of the Secondary Materials and Recycling Textiles (SMART) Association, told me that used T-shirts are contained in, for example, automobile doors and roofs, carpet pads, mattresses, cushions, insulation, and caskets. Recently, shoddy has found a market in eco-friendly construction, where it is used as insulation.[9] And finally, in a fascinating full-circle story, high-quality cotton shoddy can be spun back into low-grade yarn and turned into cheap clothing again.[10]

Ed Stubin finds a use and a market for almost all of the textile articles thrown away by Americans. The high-end items with quirky appeal will be sold to vintage shops all over Europe and North America, and the Japanese will get most of the Levi's. Winter coats will go to Eastern Europe, and old cotton sweaters will go to Pakistan to be turned into new sweaters. Shoddy will go to factories everywhere and also to India, where it is transformed into cheap blankets that are passed out to refugees. Italy is a customer for old wool, where an industry is built on recycling fine cashmere.

The heart of the business, though, is the trade with Africa, where the exploding supply of castoffs from the rich meets the incessant demand for clothing from the poor.

How Small
Entrepreneurs
Clothe East
Africa with Old
American T-Shirts

Mitumba Nation

Poverty in Dar Es Salaam is a languid and sultry state that has settled on the city like a heavy wash of paint. Though Tanzania is one of the poorest countries in the world, the poverty is not one of frenetic wretchedness as one finds in Calcutta or Nairobi, but is instead a peaceful way of being, a slow-moving and purposeful means of navigating life's rhythms: sleep, eat, shop, laugh, smile, sing, be poor. Poverty is the weather in Tanzania. It is just there—there when the Africans go to sleep, and there when they wake up, there every day of their very short lives. Like the weather, poverty doesn't change enough to be a topic of conversation. Poor just is.

Tanzania's socialist dream is in shambles, crumbling like the colonial buildings left by the British. Julius Nyerere, the country's post-independence leader, had a dream for Tanzania of self-reliance: After generations of bowing to slave traders and colonial masters, Tanzanians would produce their own goods, grow their own food, write their own destiny. Nyerere's vision of "Socialism with Self-Reliance" was a road map to escape the past.

Under Nyerere's leadership, Tanzania in the late 1960s was the most committed of the socialist countries of Africa, and Nyerere was a spokesperson not only for socialism but for the poorest of the poor around the world. But like many of her African neighbors, Tanzania found that the socialist road led to dead end after dead end with factories that didn't produce, workers who didn't work, and farmers who didn't farm. Throughout the 1970s, incomes were falling, investment was contracting, and the majority of Tanzanians lived below the poverty line.[1] By 1980, Tanzania had the second-lowest per-capita income in the world. The Tanzanians, who had for so long been exploited by the British, were now exploited by an ideal—an ideal that could deliver pride, and perhaps a theoretical self-reliance, but could not deliver goods, food, jobs, or medicine.[2]

Today, free market economics is supposed to be the way forward for Tanzania, but this seems like an almost surreal prescription for this dusty, peaceful place of brilliant smiles. Children under five in Tanzania die at approximately 20 times the rate of babies in the United States, often from diseases that vanished from the West generations ago. AIDS has eviscerated villages and families, and has brought the average life expectancy in Tanzania down to 46, lower than it was a generation ago. The majority of the country's population survives by subsistence agriculture and still lives below the poverty line, and more than 40 percent of adults cannot read. How to define and measure poverty and well-being has been a challenge for development experts for generations, but it is not a challenge at all to see that by virtually any measure—income, calories, wealth, life expectancy, access to water, or brick housing—Tanzania holds down the bottom of the graph. During the past generation, as China's per-capita income has quintupled, Tanzania's has barely budged, and in 2006 reached just $1 per day.[3] Yet, in 2008, many were pointing to Tanzania as a bright spot in Africa. The country was at peace, the economy was stable, and the political system was working.

The most stunning scenery in Tanzania is not the savannah landscape but the African women. They stand taller and prouder than women anywhere, perhaps from years of carrying bananas and flour on the tops of their heads, perhaps from years of holding the country together. The white women—European backpackers, lunching wives of diplomats, missionary aid workers—fade away in comparison, graceless and silly in the shadow of the African queens. Many of the African women in Dar Es Salaam are draped in the brilliantly colored native cloth, graceful folds wrapping their strong bodies and stronger spirits. They are brilliantly colored splashes across the poverty and hardship of Tanzania.

The men are a muted background to this scenery. They work, or they sit under shade trees, not as proud, not as strong, not as busy. There are some men in Muslim skullcaps and a few in Indian dhotis, but none at all in traditional African dress. Almost all of the men and boys in Dar Es Salaam wear *mitumba*—clothing thrown away by Americans and Europeans, and many are in T-shirts. Julius Nyerere would turn over in his grave at the sight of it: Used clothing from the West was among the first imports banned under his prideful policy of Socialism with Self-Reliance. What could be less self-reliant or more symbolically dependent than a nation clothed in the white world's castoffs? Yet, it is difficult to see exploitation or dependence in the human landscape clothed in mitumba. I found that most of the men on the streets of Dar Es Salaam looked natty and impeccable.

In 2007, used clothing was America's third-largest export to Tanzania, and exports had increased by nearly 50 percent from 2006. Tanzania was one the largest customers for American used clothing, with competition from countries such as Angola, Mozambique, and Benin.[4] Though it would take an average Tanzanian perhaps 60 years to earn enough to buy the Lexus SUV in the Bethesda parking lot, thanks to a nimble network of global entrepreneurs, Tanzanians can dress well for very little money. In this small piece of the Tanzanian experience, the markets work just fine.

Two for a Penny

When I first visited Tanzania in 2003, the Manzese market in northern Dar Es Salaam was the country's largest mitumba market. The market occupied busy Morogoro Road for more than a mile and contained hundreds of stalls. Like a suburban shopping mall, the stalls were geared to different customers. Then and now, stalls specialize in baby clothing or blue jeans, athletic wear or Dockers, or even curtains. The higher-end mitumba stalls boast this year's fashions, tastefully displayed, but the perfect Dockers in 2003 were priced at $5.00 (and in 2008 were close to $8.00), so this high-end merchandise was far out of reach for the poor and accessible only to Tanzania's upper classes. Blue jeans, too, are high-end items, and the shoppers poring over the blue jeans are discerning consumers, often with a better sense of what is *in* (how many pockets? how much flare?) than the original purchaser. The young people in Dar Es Salaam are as fashion savvy as young Americans, with a flawless sense of the hip and unhip.

Georgetown student Henri Minion spent the summer of 2008 in Dar Es Salaam living with a host family and I asked him to study the role of mitumba in daily life. One of the first things that Henri noticed was that the mitumba-clad students at the University of Dar Es Salaam not only were well-dressed, but blended right in, fashionwise, with the American students visiting from Washington.

The market mechanism in African mitumba markets is considerably more flexible than in an American department store. The Dockers with waist sizes in the low 30s sell for more than those with sizes in the 40s, as Tanzanians in general lack Americans' paunches. Otherwise-identical polo shirts can vary in price as well, with more popular colors and sizes commanding a premium. Prices trend up at the end of the month when many workers get paid, but drift lower during periods between paychecks.

Perhaps the most interesting pricing behavior is evident in the divide between men's and women's clothing, as both supply and demand influences lead to significant price discrimination against the men. First, because Western women buy many more new clothes than men, they throw away many more clothes as well. Ed Stubin estimates that the truckloads arriving from the Salvation Army contain between two and three times as much women's clothing as men's. Women are also more particular about the condition of their clothing, so about 90 percent of what is cast aside by women is still in good condition. Men, however, not only buy less clothing but wear it longer, so only half of the clothing received by the used clothing exporters is in good condition. On the supply side, the bottom line is that world supply contains perhaps seven times as much women's clothing in good condition than it does men's. African demand exacerbates this imbalance, as African women's clothing preferences exclude much of Western fashion while men clamor for the limited supply of T-shirts, khakis, and suits that are in good condition. The end result of this supply-and-demand dynamic is that in the mitumba markets, similar clothing in good condition may cost four to five times as much for men as it does for women.

I first met Geofrey Milonge in 2003 at his T-shirt stall near the center of the Manzese market. Geofrey stands tall and shiny-black, with the languid pride and gentle manner that seem to be the national traits of the Tanzanians. Geofrey arrived from the countryside in the early 1990s, hoping to escape the rural poverty of his village in the interior. Geofrey had started out on the sidewalk with just a single 50-kilo bale of clothing, which he had purchased on credit. Within a few years, Geofrey had three mitumba stalls in the Manzese market, each catering to different types of consumers. His T-shirt stall was neatly laid out, with hundreds of T-shirts lining the walls on hangers. In 2003, Geofrey was selling between 10 and 50 T-shirts per day, usually for between 50 cents and $1.50. Almost all of Geofrey's T-shirts were from America.

The labels showed that most of the T-shirts were originally born in Mexico, China, or Central America, and most of the T-shirts also reveal something about their life in America. The college and professional sports team shirts (Florida Gators, Chicago Bulls) are ubiquitous, and winning teams' shirts fetch higher prices. Washington Redskins shirts move slowly, but Geofrey had earlier in the morning received $2 for the Pittsburgh Steelers. U.S. sportswear logos are popular, too—Nike, Reebok, Adidas— but Geofrey's customers can easily tell the fakes (cheaper, coarser cotton) from the genuine. Middle-American suburbia hangs neatly pressed as a backdrop to the more valuable sports logos. Across the back of the stall is a Beaver Cleaver caricature of America: Weekend activities (Woods Lake Fun Run 1999), family vacations (Yellowstone National Park—Don't Feed the Bears), social conscience (Race for the Cure), and neighborhood teams (Glen Valley Youth Soccer) are some of the customers' choices.

Because of the snowflake challenge, Geofrey is very careful about where he buys from. The sellers can hide all kinds of garbage in the middle of a bale, so it pays to know your suppliers and to make sure that they know that if they give you garbage you won't be back. Geofrey prefers to buy bales that have been sorted in the United States or Europe, rather than in Africa. The U.S.-sorted bales cost a bit more, but the jewels are less likely to have been skimmed off and you get a lot less junk. In the world of mitumba, an unbroken U.S.-sorted bale is a high-end luxury good.

In her study of the second-hand clothing trade in Zambia, anthropologist Karen Hansen found the perverse manifestations of the preference for castoffs fresh from American bales.[5] In the world of mitumba, Hansen found, consumers seek out "new" clothing that is wrinkled and musty-smelling. A fresh-pressed or clean-smelling garment cannot possibly have spent weeks or months in a compressed bale in a warehouse or shipping container; therefore, it is the more wrinkled and musty clothing that is likely to be "new" from America, while the fresh-pressed and clean-smelling clothing is more likely to be "old"—that is, worn or presorted in Africa.

Panning for Gold in Tanzania

Mitumba dealers told me repeatedly that 90 percent of a bale's value comes from 10 percent of the items. For every Gap shirt in perfect condition that might fetch $3 there will be a dozen pieces that will be hard to unload even at 50 cents. Once the few jewels have been skimmed, the bale's market value drops dramatically. As a result, successfully plying the mitumba trade is about keeping track of jewels. A bale consisting only of suburban activities will be a losing proposition for Geofrey. If the sports teams, Gaps, and Nike snowflakes have been pilfered, the Fun Run and family vacation T-shirts that are left will not allow him to cover his costs. In Dar Es Salaam, just as in Brooklyn, the business is all about snowflakes.

Geofrey told me that when he gets the chance to skim for jewels himself, he takes it. Many importers order clothing in larger bales, say 500 or even up to 1,500 pounds, which are too large for a single dealer to purchase. In these cases, the importer or wholesaler hosts a party of sorts, to which Geofrey and his peers will try to cadge an invitation. Sometimes, the dealers will pay 1,000 to 2,000 schillings ($10 to $20) to be invited. There are refreshments and a competitive camaraderie leading up to the highlight of the party: the breaking open of the bale. The bale breaking is a highlight, because only if mitumba dealers can see the breaking with their own eyes can they be sure that the jewels have not been skimmed, and in a large bale from the United States, the chances of valuable jewels are high. The mood is festive and raucous because of the surprise to come: You just never know what the Americans will throw away, and to be invited to the party to get first crack at the jewels can mean a windfall for the week.

The wholesaler breaks the bale and the melee begins. A 1,000-pound bale might contain up to 3,000 articles of clothing, and almost every bale will contain surprises. The dealers begin a competitive rummaging and quickly pull out the jewels. Multiple mini-auctions for the jewels take place simultaneously: The spotless Nike attracts offers of $1, which quickly rise to $1.50 and then $2. The baby overalls with the tags still attached draw bids of 50 cents, then 75, and finally $1.25. A special find is to uncover a group of identical items—six matching yellow sweaters, say, or a dozen blue twill shirts—the matching clothing has a ready and profitable market as uniforms for businesses.

The mini-auctions at the bale-breaking parties are close to a perfectly competitive market. There are many buyers; there is perfect information; there is, as an economist might say, excellent price discovery. And there is good fun. The element of surprise keeps it a fun market as well as a functioning one, and the party is a treasure hunt as well as a market. The hunt for treasure does not stop with the clothing but extends to the pockets, as Americans throw away not just perfectly good clothing but perfectly good money as well—U.S. dollars, no less.

The most valuable jewels will never make it to the crowded mitumba markets. Instead, the top-of-the-line jewels hang from trees in the commercial area near the harbor, close to Dar Es Salaam's handful of office towers and banks, and its second-floor walk-up stock exchange. These jewels—a perfect suit, say, or a like-new prom dress—hang like solitaires from the trees on the main boulevard, away from the pedestrian hubbub of the markets. A trader lucky enough to nab such a jewel will hire a helper to sit under the tree and guard the jewel until it is purchased, or until nightfall, whichever comes first.

The middle and upper classes often do not enter the crowds at the markets, though they too are dressed in mitumba. Just as a wealthier family might have help to shop for food, many Tanzanians also have relationships with mitumba dealers who know their size and style preferences, and keep a watch for just the right suit or dress shirt. Such personal shoppers make house and office calls when just the right jewels turn up in the bales.

When Geofrey Milonge emerges from the competitive market as a buyer, he almost immediately joins another perfectly competitive market as a seller. There are hundreds of stalls and thousands of T-shirts in Dar Es Salaam, and the consumers have nothing if not choices. At the other end of the spectrum from the jewels are the dregs, the clothing that is hard to unload at any price. Most mitumba dealers have a card table or two in the middle of their stall that is piled high with clearance items that haven't sold. While the vendors' better offerings will neatly line the stall on hangers, the dregs are simply piled up, mitumba's answer to the clearance table at Wal-Mart.

In the larger mitumba markets, many stalls have a worker with a microphone who drones on in a mesmerizing chant to entice shoppers to stop. As evening approaches, the competition intensifies because the shopkeepers would much rather unload a few more garments than pack them until the next day. The voices from the microphones form a cacophony that gets louder and louder as the afternoon wears on. The stall owners like Geofrey Milonge are especially loath to pack up the clearance-table items as darkness approaches. The Swahili chants ring out as the prices for items on the clearance table drop like a sharp curve along with the sun. By the end of the day, the clothing on the clearance table that sold for a dime at noon might go for two for a penny.

For Geofrey Milonge, the day ends in a seller's competition as intense as the buyer's competition with which he started the morning. If he rests in the morning, the competition will snag the jewels, and if he rests in the evening, the competition will snag his customers. The markets at the center of Geofrey's livelihood are more flexible—and closer to a "real" market—than anything the T-shirt has experienced before. With no barriers between himself and the market, Geofrey must adjust his selling prices by men's or women's, by size, by color, by weather, and by time of day and time of month, and he must adjust his buying prices at the bale-breaking party by trying to predict who will happen by that morning, what they will want, and what they will pay.

Finding Geofrey

I tried to track down Geofrey in 2007 and again in 2008. In 2007, the telephone number I had did not work and Google turned up nothing. I wrote to him at the address I had written down, but the letter was returned to me months later. I asked two people who had been helpful to me in Tanzania to see whether they could track him down, but I again came up empty-handed. In 2008, I gave Georgetown student Henri Minion the mission of finding Geofrey Milonge. Henri was studying in Dar for the summer. He would have six weeks.

While I remembered the approximate location of Geofrey's T-shirt stall (and of course had Geofrey's picture), this was no help because the Manzese market had closed and had in large part been replaced by other mitumba markets throughout the city. But the mission to find Geofrey seemed to be off to a good start. I had another contact in Dar Es Salaam who knew Geofrey (I will call him "Mike"—not his real name), and he quickly agreed to assist Henri. For weeks, Henri tried to connect with Mike. And for weeks, the meetings were canceled or postponed. The concept of

"Tanzania Time" is often used by western diplomats and businesspeople to describe life in Dar. And it was apt for Henri: Tanzania Time meant Maybe Later. Or Maybe Not.

As Henri's time in Dar Es Salaam was coming to a close, it appeared that the mission to find Geofrey would be unsuccessful. When Henri last tried to connect with Mike, he learned that he was in Amsterdam. Mike promised that his secretary would call Henri, but she did not. Ever resourceful, Henri received a tip from a friend about another person who would be willing to help. He called the gentleman, and agreed to meet at his office the next day. When Henri arrived, no one there had heard of the gentleman Henri had spoken with.

With just days left in Tanzania, Henri was not going to give up. Henri had gotten to know Elina Makanja, a freelance journalist and teaching assistant at the University of Dar es Salaam. Elina was an enthusiastic mitumba shopper, and she agreed to help. The day before Henri was to leave Tanzania, Elina found Geofrey Milonge in the market.

I thought of Henri's "Mission to Find Geofrey" a few months later, when I was chatting with Julia Hughes. We were discussing which countries might soon be competitive apparel producers for the U.S. market. "What about Sub-Saharan Africa?" I asked Julia. Julia sighed. "It's sad," she said. "It's just so hard to do business there."

Tanzania Time, or living life to a slow and unscheduled rhythm, can quickly become a charmed way of life for a visitor. For an apparel company needing to stock its shelves for the next season, however, Tanzania Time was a risk they were unwilling to bear.

Happily, in 2008, Geofrey's mitumba business was healthy and growing. Since 2003, he had opened four more stores, and now had a total of seven shops throughout Dar Es Salaam. Geofrey had also become active as a wholesaler. Where a few years before he had been purchasing clothing in bales, he was now importing shipping containers from the United States and Europe and selling bales to other mitumba dealers, and he often hosted his own bale-breaking parties.

As Geofrey gained experience in international trade, he was diversifying into other goods. By late 2008 Geofrey was importing building materials such as cement, and had also invested in real estate. When I first met Geofrey, he spoke only Swahili, but in late 2008 we were corresponding by e-mail in English. He wrote to me that he had recently spent a month in London, researching prices and drumming up suppliers.

Though the global supply of used clothing is increasing, Geofrey has observed steady increases in the prices at which he sells clothing. He estimates that the prices for good-quality clothing in the markets have approximately doubled during the past five years. The increase in the price of good-quality but basic T-shirts was lower but still healthy: Geofrey said that T-shirts that had sold for $1 in 2003 were selling for about $1.50 in 2008.

Ed Stubin and Geofrey Milonge describe this global industry with remarkably similar stories. In both cases, survival depends on their skill in spotting the jewels among the snowflakes and knowing their value in the market. Both men stress that they depend on personal relationships with suppliers and personal knowledge about their customers. On both sides of the Atlantic, the snowflake imperative keeps the businesses small and nimble, in close touch with suppliers and customers. Once you stop paying attention, or take your eye off the T-shirt river, or off your customer, you're finished.

Here, at the end of the T-shirt's life, is a global industry where it pays to be the little guy, where the power equation is flipped upside down away from the multinational corporations. Indeed, the grandfather and founder of the used clothing business in Tanzania was the victim of his own success. His far-flung empire, though built on profits from the used clothing trade, became much too big to keep track of snowflakes.

Too Big for Used Britches

Mohammed Enterprises Tanzania Limited (METL) is today one of the largest private companies in Tanzania, a conglomerate involved in manufacturing, agriculture, and trade. METL manufactures soap, sweeteners, cooking oil, textiles, clothing, and bicycles, and it owns 31,000 hectares of farmland producing sisal, cashews, and dairy products. METL is also a major trading house selling sesame seeds to Japan, pigeon peas to India, cocoa to the United States, and beeswax to Europe. METL seems to operate as a completely Westernized company today, committed to market awareness, customer focus, and corporate responsibility. Even METL's rise is a Western-sounding story.

As the family story goes, Gulam Dewji, METL's chairman, got his start in the 1960s by arbitraging onions in rural Tanzania. He drove a rickety truck across the crumbling non-roads, finding villages that had extra onions and connecting them with villages that had too much squash. He had a sense of market trends and impeccable timing, and he gradually added trucks and employees. In another place and time, Gulam Dewji might have run a hedge fund, but in 1960s Tanzania, Gulam used his market-timing talents on onions. Gulam remembers that the villagers, while poor, usually had enough to eat. They did not, however, have clothing, at least not to speak of. In rural Tanzania at the time, adults were mostly in rags and children were mostly naked.

Currency controls meant that hard currency was rarely available to import clothing, and mismanagement meant that the local textile industry was poorly equipped to supply the local market. There was special official scorn—and an outright ban—on mitumba. Though it was illegal to import used clothing, much made it through the porous borders with Mozambique and Kenya. But it was a furtive and haphazard trade, an underbelly business that was lubricated by bribes to border guards in the middle of the night.

In 1985, Julius Nyerere stepped down and the mitumba trade was legalized. Gulam immediately saw the business opportunity presented by the liberalization. From his decades of traveling through the rural areas he knew that people wanted decent clothing. It was not a matter of emulating Westerners, it was instead a matter of pride: Tanzanians had no desire to look like Americans; they wanted to look like well-dressed Tanzanians. Gulam went to America and began to meet with used clothing exporters.

During the next 10 years, METL's mitumba business grew rapidly and Gulam was soon importing 4,000 tons of used clothing per month into the port at Dar Es Salaam. Mitumba quickly reached not only the cities but far into the rural areas as well. A network of traders plied the backcountry as Gulam had once done with onions, and mitumba markets soon sprang up in every town.

Gulam purchased the clothing from American dealers in huge bales weighing up to 2,000 pounds apiece. Compared to the intricate sorting and mining processes that characterize the business today, the process was loose at best. Often the clothing had been sorted into just three categories: Category A contained only clothing that was in like-new condition; Category B clothing was in fairly good shape, a bit faded, perhaps, or missing a button; and Category C contained garments that were torn or stained. The bales were delivered to METL's cavernous warehouse, where they were broken up and sorted again and readied for market.

Just as Ed Stubin had once found it easier—most of the clothing he sorted was saleable at a profit—Gulam, too, found the early days to be the good old days. People in Tanzania had had so few choices and so little income that they welcomed almost everything from America. A bit of wear made little difference, especially in the countryside, as the clothing was usually a step up from the rags for the adults or the nakedness for the children. Gulam could sell almost everything that arrived in the bales from America, usually at a profit.

At the beginning, there were still many self-reliance ideologues who believed that the practice of wearing the white world's castoffs was shameful. Gradually, however, the ideologues toned down and began to dress in mitumba as well. Indeed, as Karen Hansen found in Zambia, the availability of mitumba was put forth as evidence of progress in the village. ("There is even mitumba now," residents would say, so as to point to the improved quality of life.[6])

But with widespread acceptance also came the maturing of the market and the erosion of Gulam's first-mover advantages. METL was growing and diversifying into other businesses, and the agility required to keep up with the mitumba trade was difficult to maintain. There were few barriers to entry, and it seemed that almost everyone had a friend of a friend in the United States or Europe who could begin to send over bales of clothing, so hundreds of nimble entrepreneurs emerged to buy and sell mitumba. The mitumba trade was an intensely personal business, built relationship by relationship as had happened with Gulam and his American suppliers. The relationships were needed to keep unhappy surprises in the bales to a minimum and happy surprises frequent enough to engender continued loyalty but not so frequent as to erase the black ink. The delicate balance required by the snowflake business required constant attention—attention that Gulam wanted to focus on other parts of METL's activities.

Another problem for Gulam was that customers were getting pickier. Not only had the market for Category C clothing all but disappeared, customers now wanted certain styles and certain colors at certain times. Without the time or attention to keep his ear to the ground in the marketplace, Gulam found it difficult to compete with the small entrepreneurs who spent their energies staying on top of consumer preferences. Gradually, Gulam ceded his mitumba business to smaller traders. You need to be small to do this, Gulam told me.

Partly because of his success in the mitumba trade, small was what he wasn't. But for the entrepreneurs to follow him, there were opportunities, and chances for little guys to participate in a global market.

MITUMBA: FRIEND OR FOE TO AFRICA?

I n both the richest and poorest countries of the world, critics of the used clothing trade are not hard to find. More than 30 countries effectively ban the import of used clothing, either through outright prohibitions (e.g., Botswana, Malawi) or impenetrable bureaucratic walls (e.g., Ethiopia, Morocco).[1] Even when imports are allowed, the barriers are often daunting, even by African standards. Tariffs can be prohibitive, and some countries require convoluted health certifications as well. The use by many African countries of preshipment inspection (PSI) companies—essentially privately run Customs authorities—has led to charges of overvaluation, corruption, and simple ineptitude.

The barriers to the mitumba trade have in large measure been erected by the groans of the local textile industry, which echo those of Americans threatened by Chinese T-shirts in 2008 or British threatened by Indian cottons in 1720. The industry's groaning obituaries and ominous employment trends are of course more poignant in Africa than in North Carolina, but the essential message of doom and gloom is the same. In Kenya, more than 87 textile factories closed between 1990 and 1998, and similar tales of industrial demise emanate from Zambia, Uganda, and Tanzania.[2] About 30,000 jobs in Zambia's textile industry have been lost in recent years, approximately the same number that have been lost during the same period in North Carolina.[3] In at least one case, a large fire was set in a mitumba market, allegedly by textile workers threatened by the trade.[4]

The fascinating twist, of course, is that while North Carolina has lost its textile industry to low-wage workers from China, the African textile industry has lost to the high-wage workers of America, who live in a land of such plenty that clothing is given away for free. How, indeed, can anyone, even China, compete with free? What's worse, critics charge, is that the swells of mitumba not only shrink employment in the textile factories, they also keep Africa from putting its foot on the development ladder offered by textile manufacturing—a ladder, as we have seen, that has lifted China, the United States, Japan, and countless other countries into the industrial age.

There is little evidence, however, that the African textile industries— at least in many countries—would be flourishing but for mitumba. The African press is riddled with derisive comments about the quality and price of locally made products, and with references to poor management and the failure of the local textile corporations to serve their customers. The Tanzanian textile industry, ironically, seems to have withered long before the flood of mitumba, and now is recovering even in the face of swells of used clothing imports. While protected from these used clothing imports— and indeed while protected from virtually all textile and apparel imports— output per worker as well as capacity utilization in the Tanzanian textile industry fell by approximately 40 percent.[5] Furthermore, as numerous cases show, producing for export rather than domestic production is the more effective industrial development ladder, and mitumba presents no threat at all to African export markets.

As for employment, while mitumba may destroy some jobs, it very clearly creates others. A drive through the large mitumba markets in Dar Es Salaam shows a level of economic activity unmatched anywhere else in the city and hundreds, perhaps thousands, of people who are very clearly working. The traders, importers, sorters, and launderers who people the mitumba trade show an astonishing variety of skills, and the tailors, in particular, are a marvel of the employment created by mitumba. Not only do the tailors adapt Americans' clothing to the thinner African figures, they create blouses and shirts to match "new" suits, and they turn curtains into dresses, socks into bathmats, and skirts into tablecloths and tablecloths into skirts. Though empirical estimates of the job destruction/creation patterns are impossible to come by, Gulam Dewji is convinced that the mitumba trade has created many more jobs than it has destroyed. In his peak years, Gulam Dewji had more than 100 people employed in sorting, grading, and distributing used clothing, more than had ever been employed in most Tanzanian textile mills.

The moribund textile industry in East Africa is testament not so much to mitumba but to the handicaps faced by African manufacturing in general, which are in turn similar to the handicaps faced by the African cotton farmers. While some of the blame must be borne by rich-country policies such as subsidies and trade barriers, textile factories are in trouble in Africa for the same reasons that factories of any kind are in trouble in Africa: corruption, political risk, low education levels, insecure property rights, macroeconomic instability, and ineffective commercial codes—in a phrase, bad governance.[6] To use Thomas Friedman's technology analogy, Africa has a better operating system than it used to (capitalism vs. socialism), and its hardware (roads, ports, communications) is improving. But much of Africa lacks the software (effective police and courts, enforceable rights and laws, transparent regulatory frameworks) necessary for factories to operate successfully.[7] A recent Oxfam report concludes that the challenges faced by the African industry are due less to the used clothing trade than they are to "supply-side" constraints such as "unreliable and expensive infrastructure; the cost and availability of materials; outdated capital stock and lack of access to credit; and inadequate training and management skills."[8]

Yet if the plight of the textile industry is testament to bad governance, the vigorous mitumba trade is testament to the entrepreneurial energy and resourcefulness of the African people. A decade or so ago, it was common for observers to draw a line between the "formal" and "informal" sectors of African economies, and to assume that the development of the formal was to be encouraged and the informal discouraged. Yet today, at least some countries realize that it is the informal sector that should be encouraged; this, after all, is the part of the economy that is working. Further, some experts have pointed out that so many types of activities are now lumped under the heading "informal," the category has lost much meaning, and our Westernized perspective has led us to label as "informal" most organizational forms that do not look American.

While it is clearly desirable for African countries to develop the institutions to support organized and formal economic activities, we should also laud the fact that the mitumba trade and other similar activities have provided a step out of the village as well as a step up the economic ladder for people who did not have factory alternatives. While Western business students study entrepreneurship, Geofrey Milonge lives it, and the entrepreneurial training ground provided by the mitumba trade can only bode well for the future of all types of economic activity in Africa. In just a few short years, Geofrey had evolved from a small-time trader to full participant in the global economy, complete with real estate investments, English language skills, and travel to London. More than any other person in this book, Geofrey's life had improved since we first met. It is a generalization, though not an absurd one, to say that the informal economy in Africa works better than the formal economy, and to suppress the part of Africa that is working seems to be a counterproductive prescription.

In fact, even as the mitumba trade has been liberalized, the state of Tanzania's formal textile and apparel sector has improved considerably. In 2002, Tanzania gained duty-free access for its apparel exports to the United States when it qualified for textile benefits under the African Growth and Opportunity Act (AGOA). Though success in the post-2008 quota-free world is by no means assured, the signs are encouraging, and Gulam Dewji believes that Tanzania can hold its own against China in a few niche markets. Apparel exports to the United States from Tanzania increased by more than 300 percent between 2003 and 2007 and exports of all goods to the United States nearly doubled.[9] Several mitumba dealers in Dar Es Salaam told me proudly that, for the first time, clothing produced in Africa is now showing up in mitumba bales from America. Gulam Dewji and his sons are bullish on Tanzania's textile industry: With profits from the mitumba trade they have purchased and refurbished several textile factories with an eye on the immense American market, and at its mill on the northern coast of Tanzania, METL is producing T-shirts for export to America.

Promise for the African industry, then, lies not in closing the doors to American used clothing but in opening the doors to the American market. AGOA, though riddled with provisions authored by the U.S. textile industry, is a step in the right direction.

Shadowy Middlemen and Economic Democracy

Many critics of the mitumba trade suggest darkly that if Americans only knew what they wrought by throwing away their clothing, fewer people would be lined up outside the Salvation Army trucks. News accounts invariably imply that the donors who drop off their clothing have no idea that the clothing will likely be sold to "middlemen" who will earn a "huge" profit from the donor's largesse. Of course, with so many sinister insinuations in the news, perhaps the secret is now out. But what is unclear is what the critics would have done with the donated clothing instead.

Some have argued that clothing donated for charitable purposes should simply be donated to Africans. The difficulty with this prescription is that it has proven impossible to suppress the mitumba trade even when commercial imports are banned. Donated clothing quickly makes its way to mitumba markets, though the trade becomes more illicit and hidden. Researchers in Sweden cite evidence from several countries that suggests donated clothing is unlikely to reach those who have a true physical need for clothing but instead is rapidly sent into the markets.[10] Researchers have also found that clothing intended for refugees in Asia efficiently enters the market. Clothing given away in this manner will still enrich a middleman, but it will be an illegal one.[11] And whether we like it or not, charities are no match for markets when it comes to giving people the clothing that they need or want. Trailer loads and shiploads of clothing are often donated following natural disasters such as hurricanes, but without people like Ed Stubin and Geofrey Milonge to match clothing with customers, most of these donations rot in warehouses. Charities are ill-equipped to provide the sorting, grading, and distribution functions so ably provided by Ed and Geofrey, and so most disaster-relief organizations nearly beg the well-intentioned not to send clothing to disaster areas.[12]

Banning mitumba imports, as, for example, South Africa has done, simply leads people to find ways around the barriers. Just as the British could not be forced into woolen underwear once they had tried cotton, denying mitumba to people who have tasted access to cheap and fashionable clothing is next to impossible. In countries where used clothing imports are banned, smuggling along porous borders is rampant, and used clothing is often found hidden in shipping containers. Banning the trade only drives it underground to enrich crooked border guards rather than legitimate businesspeople.

As for the huge profits, it is often said that huge markups are de rigueur, exploiting both the charity and the African customer. Critics point, for example, to the men's khakis that sell for $8 in the mitumba market but were purchased for perhaps 10 to 12 cents from the charity. Even a cursory look at the economics of the industry, however, seems to rule out the possibility of huge and easy profits. Ed Stubin estimates that the majority of the goods flowing into his business are sold at a loss, because the selling prices for clothing destined to become wiping rags and fiber (between 2 and 8 cents per pound) are significantly lower than the price paid to purchase the material (between 10 and 14 cents per pound). For Ed Stubin, for example, the "huge markups" on clothing destined for Africa must cover the losses he incurs on fiber and rags as well as his 80-person payroll and factory operating expenses, not to mention, for Tanzania, a 25 percent tariff. The fact that a "huge profit" is made on the pair of perfect khakis obscures the reality of just how unusual this snowflake is both for Geofrey Milonge and for Ed Stubin.

Media accounts of the used clothing trade also seem to have a magnetic attraction to the word *shadowy*. After spending time with the industry's players, however, I wonder whether it is judgmental observers rather than shadowy behavior—whatever that is—on the part of the players that is the more interesting phenomenon. The used clothing dealers I encountered were from varied backgrounds and ethnicities, and had in common nothing more shadowy than the quick wits and market awareness needed by gazelles who wake up to race every morning.

The notion that global trade is about powerful corporations peopled with well-tailored Waspish vice presidents is belied by the reality of the used clothing exporters, who are from Brooklyn, Brownsville, Pakistan, and India, in short, from Main Street rather than K Street or Wall Street. Far from shadowy, they represent a heartening parable about economic democracy: It is a positive, not a negative, that people from across the American experience can form the backbone of a successful global industry, and can play and win in a global game of faster-better-cheaper, and do so without the walls that protect their peers in many other industries.

The democratizing influence of the mitumba trade extends to Africa, as well. As John Quinn has argued, the policies adopted by most Sub-Saharan African countries following independence resulted in a concentration of political and economic power that has few parallels in modern history.[13] As is true for much of the cotton agriculture industry in Africa, state ownership and control excluded and impoverished those at the bottom of the power structure. The policies—especially state ownership—allegedly implemented to lift the masses instead funneled money and power to the top, where it was dispersed as largesse through a web of patronage and corruption.[14] State ownership of the textile industry by an unelected government enriched the few and excluded the many, and Geofrey Milonge and his present-day colleagues in the mitumba markets had little participation—either political or economic—in such a system. The mitumba trade, however, is run by the masses rather than the elite, and is governed by relationships among importers, customers, drivers, menders, and dealers rather than by what many observers have titled the "kleptocracies" still common in much of Africa. Mitumba not only has allowed ordinary people to dress well, it has let them into the club as well. Excluded from the elite clubs and without effective software to govern formal markets, African entrepreneurs rely on the relationships, trust, and social networks that have been created by the mitumba trade. Thanks to mitumba, Geofrey Milonge and his entrepreneurial peers are players now, and are finding their own way around Africa's challenges.

A final critique of the mitumba trade is the humiliation argument. How, critics charge, can Africa hold its head high while wearing clothing that has been cast off at least three times? While in Tanzania, I heard about ideologues who protested the humiliation wrought by Tanzanians wearing the white world's castoffs, but I did not meet any of them. Gulam Dewji and his sons told me that their numbers were dwindling rapidly, as most of the old ideologues were now clothed in mitumba as well; 300 years ago, even the English woolen workers eventually preferred cotton underwear. Gulam and his sons never had any patience for the humiliation argument. They pointed out, over and over again, that humiliation comes not from mitumba, but from having no clothes to wear.

There is something missing from both the critiques and the compliments of the mitumba industry in Tanzania: Whatever the economic costs and benefits of the trade, it is clearly true as well that mitumba is fun. I found that taxi drivers, shopkeepers, and high school students—far from being embarrassed—delight in talking about mitumba. The challenge and reward of shrewd shopping are as significant in Tanzania as they are in suburban America. Just as a sharply dressed soccer mom might drop her voice and whisper, "Can you believe it? I got it for $5.99 at Wal-Mart," Tanzanians delight in their fashionable mitumba finds. Over and over again, Tanzanians pointed out their natty clothing to me, and then dropped their voices, smiled, and said, "Mitumba." Shopping for mitumba is a fun and rewarding pastime in Tanzania for the same reasons that Americans enjoy trips to the mall. Yet the mitumba markets in Dar Es Salaam are more interesting, and much more full of surprises, than any suburban shopping mall.

While Americans have a relatively good idea what will be on display at the Gap, or at Sears, the mitumba shopper is not so much on a shopping trip as a treasure hunt: You just never know what the Americans will throw away next.

As Karen Hansen noted in her study of the used clothing trade in Zambia, the appeal of mitumba is not in emulating Westerners but is instead in the desire to be smartly turned out. Zambians, Hansen argues, make the West's clothing their own, and the ensembles they put together from shopping in mitumba markets reflect Zambian, not Western, cultural norms.[15] And while some would argue that mitumba fills basic clothing needs in much of Africa, Hansen finds that it is wants rather than needs that are satisfied by mitumba. An afternoon spent browsing the mitumba markets to piece together the perfect outfit is not about protection from the elements, or about trying to look American. It is, rather, about the fun and reward of being a smartly dressed and astute shopper.

Finally, it is hard to imagine a global industry with a more compelling environmental story to tell, and the used clothing trade stands to benefit considerably from increased attention to environmental issues. Without polluting chemicals or processes, the industry recycles virtually 100 percent of the textiles it receives, which are already considered a waste product. Today, most of the material comes from charities, but in the future, textile recycling may develop in the same manner as it has for glass, paper, and aluminum. In 2007, nearly 12 million tons of municipal textile waste was generated, and approximately 15 percent of this was recovered for reuse or recycling.[16] Though the percentage of textiles recovered has been increasing, it is nowhere near the 50 percent recovery rate for paper. The untapped opportunity—for Ed Stubin, for Geofrey Milonge, and for the environment—is vast. In the used clothing trade, what is good for business is also good for the planet.

Tanzania—indeed much of eastern Africa—has seen dramatic regime change over the past two decades as policies have shifted to market liberalization. In many cases, the policies have been less than voluntary, as many countries have had to adopt "Washington consensus" policies of liberalization in exchange for IMF and World Bank lending. Critics of the new policies feared that liberalization would lead to declines in already low standards of living, reduce the level of public services, and cause declines in farmer incomes. Unprepared and ill-equipped to compete in world markets, Tanzania, critics feared, would be pummeled by market forces that would leave the least well-off in even worse straits.[17] On the other side, the World Bank advanced the now-familiar argument that liberalization offered the best hope for Africa's poor.[18]

Tony Waters set out to settle the debate for himself.[19] Carefully researching conditions in a small rural village in western Tanzania, both before economic liberalization (in 1985) and after (1995 to 1996), Waters found that neither the alarmists' nor the optimists' predictions had come to pass. Things were not much better, and not much worse, in the tiny village. Even with the radical regime change, Waters found that life in rural Tanzania was about the same. The people of Shunga village are still ruled more by the earth's rhythms than by the regime in Washington, or for that matter, the regime in Dar Es Salaam. The houses looked the same, as did the school, the shops, and the roads. People seemed neither richer nor poorer, better off nor worse off. What happened in Washington and Dar Es Salaam did not seem to make much difference at all in rural Tanzania, and the more Waters searched for change the more things looked the same. Waters concluded that at least in this small remote village, nothing had really changed.

But there was one thing Waters noticed, almost as an afterthought: People were better dressed. This may seem a small thing to us, but because it is the only thing, it is important to the people in Shunga. Thanks to world trade, and thanks to Gulam, Ed, and Geofrey—who race like gazelles every day through the global marketplace—life was just a little better in a remote corner of one of the world's poorest countries.

Don't Look Now, but China Is Behind You

While relations among U.S. used clothing dealers are intensely competitive, the industry as a whole would seem to occupy a secure place in the global industrial landscape. Rich Americans buy more and more clothing each year and therefore unload more and more, as well. The falling price of new clothing—particularly from China—will only accelerate this trend. In addition, the growing penchant for recycling will likely divert increasing amounts of clothing from the waste stream. Together, then, continued rampant consumerism as well as changing waste disposal practices would seem to assure a growing supply of American used clothing for the global market.

Growing demand appears to be a safe prediction, as well. Trade barriers to used clothing continue to fall, thanks both to SMART's efforts and to the general trend toward import liberalization in most countries. Perhaps more important, the poorer countries continue to have high rates of population growth, as well as a growing attraction to fashionable clothing.

There is a natural economic success story here, a simple market dynamic that portends well for the future. At the end of the T-shirt's life, there is a refreshingly simple story of a winning business for America and for Tanzania, a link between Ed Stubin and Geofrey Milonge that is built on market logic rather than a web of political intrigue. While the U.S. textile and apparel industry is kept alive only by unnatural acts of life support in Washington, and U.S. cotton producers compete through politics, here is another business, mostly unheard of and largely ignored, whose promise lies in the simple matter of a compelling economic logic.

At the end of my T-shirt's life, it is refreshing, too, to see a real market in action, to see prices that move with the location of a collection bin or the time of day, where anyone with a bale is allowed to play. Such flexibility is the result of the faster-better-cheaper race that Stubin and Milonge engage in every day from opposite ends of the world, where everyone must keep their eyes on the markets and attend to numerous fluid relationships with customers, suppliers, and competitors. The used clothing trade is a dance of the gazelles with no protection from the lions. It is a marvel to watch.

Thankfully, here finally is a business that at least should be safe from low-wage competitors, especially from China. It is not a big industry or a sexy industry, but it is a secure spot for both Ed and Geofrey. China has only a limited tradition of charitable giving, and incomes are still far too low to allow for large volumes of castoffs. The comparative advantage of U.S. clothing recyclers lies in America's wealth and consumerism, both characteristics with staying power even given the challenging economic situation of 2008, and both characteristics in which China is far behind. And this relentless consumerism creates the supply that allows Geofrey to continually expand his business.

But in fact, by 2008 both Geofrey Milonge and Ed Stubin were very worried about China.

Every day, Geofrey sees more new clothing from China in the shops around Dar. Often the clothing is "seconds" from manufacturing runs destined for Europe or the United States, or just as often the labels and logos are pirated fakes. For now, customers still prefer the "old" clothing from America to the new clothing from China, Geofrey said, because the quality is believed to be better. But prices of new clothing from China have been falling while prices of old clothing from the United States have been rising, and Geofrey expects that over time the quality of the Chinese clothing will improve. And the relatively strong performance of the Tanzanian economy in recent years exacerbates the China threat. Geofrey worries that as incomes rise, the preference for new clothing will increase.

Ed Stubin's worries are a bit more complicated. After talking with Ed again in 2008, I realized that today, his business is now also a political creation of sorts, and that what politics creates it can also destroy. In a fascinating linkage, Stubin's business now at least partly depends on the Auggie Tantillos in China. Unlike the U.S. textile industry and cotton farmers, Stubin gets no help or protection from the U.S. government. Strangely enough, in yet another unintended consequence, Stubin's protection is now coming from the government of China.

Under pressure from its own textile and apparel industry, the Chinese government has long banned the import of used clothing into the country. While this ban might seem to threaten Trans-Americas' business, in fact the reverse is true.

Stubin's business creates value through its highly developed skills in grading and sorting. These skills can take a truckload from the Salvation Army in New Jersey and quickly get winter coats to Ukraine, T-shirts to Africa, blue jeans to Japan, and high-end vintage wear to shops in Manhattan's East Village.

The first leg of a T-shirt's journey from Trans-Americas to Africa begins with a truck ride to the port of New Jersey. It costs Trans-Americas about $700 to send 50,000 pounds of clothing on the short ride. The ride to Africa costs another $5,500, a journey of a month and a half with a stop in Europe. Container shipping is yet another industry ruled by clean market forces. When the supply of empty cargo ships at a given port swells, the price to load the container and send it on its way falls. America's rampant consumerism has implications not just for the supply of used clothing available to world markets, but for shipping costs as well.

Thanks to our penchant for consumption, in 2007 the U.S. merchandise trade deficit swelled to $711 billion. The billions spent on French wines, Chinese T-shirts, and German cars not only was unreciprocated, it also left hundreds of cargo ships at U.S. ports begging for something to ship back. At the broadest level, the merchandise trade deficit in the United States means that shipping stuff into America costs much more than shipping it out.

The price of shipping from America, however, reflects not just America's trade deficit, but also the demand for cargo ships elsewhere. Therefore, in cases where a country has a large imbalance with the United

States, shipping costs will be unbalanced as well. The U.S. merchandise trade deficit with China was $156 billion in 2007, with imports from China approximately five times greater than exports to China from the United States. While the 2008 trade deficit with China was expected to narrow with the economic downturn, a significant bilateral imbalance is projected for years to come. This means that shippers are keen to get ships from New Jersey back to the ports of Shanghai and Guangzhou in order to deliver more goods to America, but there are relatively few goods waiting to board the ships. In order to get ships back to China, the shipping companies in 2007 were dropping their prices to desperate levels: A 50,000-pound container of clothing could be shipped from New Jersey to China for approximately $800, about the same amount as it costs to send a truck from the Stubin factory to the New Jersey port. Even so, many containers return empty to China.

Given the shipping pricing trends that result from the U.S. trade deficit, Ed Stubin sees how at least some of the U.S. clothing recycling industry could shift to China. When I spoke to Stubin in 2004, he thought that it was possible that China would open its borders in the Export Processing Zones (EPZs) to used clothing. EPZs are an intermediate step between free trade and closed borders: Goods are allowed into the country for assembly or processing and subsequent re-export, but are not allowed into the domestic marketplace for consumption.

If used clothing were allowed into the EPZs, Stubin told me, Chinese firms could buy in bulk from the U.S. charities, ship to China for next to nothing, and do the sorting right there in the EPZs; the clothing would never even have to leave the port. The workers would make $1 per hour instead of $10, and all of the other costs would be a fraction of America's, too. The total shipping costs from the United States to Africa, even with the extra leg added onto the trip, could be lower than they are now. In other words, the low labor costs that give China an advantage in so many other industries could create an advantage in grading, sorting, and selling America's castoffs as well. Indeed, Stubin told me in 2008, much of the grading and sorting had recently moved to the EPZs in India; exports of American used clothing to India more than tripled between 2004 and 2007.[20] Because these goods were unsorted, the growing exports had bypassed U.S. firms such as Trans-Americas.

If China, too, opened its EPZs to American used clothing, the challenge would only be magnified. If cotton can travel from Texas to China to become a T-shirt, and then travel all the way back to the United States to be worn a first time and then to Africa to be worn a second time, then certainly a return trip to China would not be a major detour. Ed Stubin is not a cotton farmer or a textile mill owner, so it doesn't even occur to him to look to Washington for help in facing international competition.

But under this scenario, Stubin told me in 2008, there would still be a secure (even if smaller) spot for Trans-Americas. Stubin would still have the advantage of his worldwide network of customers who had come to rely on him for high-quality clothing, delivered quickly as the climate or fashion trends demanded. Perhaps most important, Stubin would have time on his side. Though China might beat the United States on labor costs, the extra month or so required for another trip to Asia would simply be too long to wait for many participants in this fast-paced market.

Remarkably, more than 2000 years ago, in *Politics*, Aristotle endorsed the concept of EPZs. Along with later writers from Rome, Aristotle had a fundamental mistrust of international trade. While he believed that some international trade was a necessary evil, he also believed that trade should take place behind walls, so as to influence the domestic economy as little as possible, and also to protect the citizenry from unhealthy influences. Ordinary citizens, Aristotle believed, should not even be allowed into the areas where trade took place.[21] Under the EPZ model, trade activity, in effect, should be quarantined. Domestic business, and domestic sensibilities, should be protected. I think of Aristotle whenever I visit Chinese EPZs today. Every one I have visited has had a military guard at the gate.

From ancient Greece to modern China, the EPZs have been a compromise between free trade and protectionism, between globalized markets and self-sufficiency. The EPZs are designed to allow small swells in, but to stop big waves. The full force of the global economy is stopped at the gate. The EPZs also represent a step toward globalization for countries such as India and China: A generation ago, most of the goods now allowed into the EPZs were not allowed in at all.

For now, Stubin is fully protected from Chinese competition, because America's used clothing is not allowed even into the EPZs. All of the Auggie Tantillos in China are protecting not only the Chinese textile industry but the American used clothing industry, as well.

But if Stubin believes that he could survive the opening of the EPZs in China to used clothing from America—because he could still excel at the game of faster-better-cheaper—he is also sure that under a true regime of free trade, Trans-Americas would be in trouble.

"Let me take that back," Stubin said to me in late 2008. "If China let everything in, we wouldn't be in trouble. We'd be gone."

China, Stubin told me, needs everything Americans throw away. With open borders, Stubin believes, the trucks would load unsorted mountains at the Salvation Army offices across America and put the containers directly onto ships bound for China. The enormous country covers the climatic gamut, so there would be demand for winter coats in the north and lightweight clothing in the south. The striking income inequality means that the tastes of over 1 billion people will run the gamut as well. The chic young people in Shanghai and Beijing would snap up the hip vintage goods and the Levis, and the poor peasants of the west would snap up the utilitarian blankets and boots. The factories could use the shop rags, and the shoddy would be turned into furniture and stuffed animals.

If China were to really open up, Stubin believes, there would be little left for Africa and nothing left for Trans-Americas.

The logic and the math play through Ed Stubin's mind sometimes. He thinks about everything he and his family have built, how his father Morton settled in Brooklyn as an immigrant, and how the used clothing business raised three generations of Stubins. He is worried that his son's generation will be the last.

Ed Stubin is a gazelle with no walls to keep out the lions, so he doesn't have much time to think about all this as he runs every day in a faster and faster race. But Stubin understands markets, and he respects them. He also understands that even though he is one of the industry's bigger players, he is actually very small. Stubin is confident that his family will continue to successfully navigate the markets for a while, just as it has for more than 60 years. He is confident that for a while Trans-Americas will continue to adapt and survive—thrive, even—in the global race of faster-better-cheaper. But Stubin feels the global winds blowing against the side of his new factory in New Jersey. The wind gets stronger every day, and it is coming all the way from China.

CONCLUSION

My T-shirt's story is really just an extended anecdote, and so is unable to confirm or discredit a theory, or to settle definitively a debate between opposing views on trade or globalization. My T-shirt's story also cannot be generalized to broad sweeps about globalization. The industries, the point in time, the product, and the countries are each unique. Yet the story of even this very simple product can illuminate, if not settle, a number of ongoing debates.

During the past decade, the backlash against trade liberalization that began in street protests in the late 1990s has evolved into more mainstream reservations about global trade on the part of citizens the world over. This evolution was abundantly clear in the economic downturn that began in 2008, as Americans were increasingly concerned about free trade agreements, the China threat, outsourcing, labor and environmental standards, and a host of related issues; it was even clear at the 2008 Olympics, as a broad coalition of activist groups protested against the alleged sweatshop conditions under which the athletes' sportswear and other Olympic-themed goods were produced.[1] As the business establishment and most economists continue to laud the effects of free trade and competitive markets, a wide array of other groups fear the effects of unrelenting market forces, especially upon workers and the environment. Yet the debate over the promise versus the perils of competitive markets is at least somewhat displaced in the case of my T-shirt: Whatever the positive or negative effects of competitive markets, in my T-shirt's journey around the world it actually encountered very few free markets.

My T-shirt was born in Texas because of a long tradition of public policy that has protected farmers from a variety of risks, including price risks, labor market risks, credit risks, and weather risks. While American growers have displayed and continue to display remarkable creativity and adaptability in both the technical and business sides of cotton agriculture, these tendencies are bolstered by the economic, educational, and political infrastructure of the United States, which fosters effective public–private partnerships that facilitate the growers' innovation and progress.

The rules of the game that govern global production of T-shirts are the result of the efforts of generations of activists, who continue to push back against the markets and rewrite both labor law and accepted corporate practice. My T-shirt was made in China under the state-engineered *hukou* system that still constrains labor mobility and limits the flexibility of labor markets. And while globalization activists' favorite targets are large U.S.-based multinational firms, most of the companies in my T-shirt's life story were relatively small family firms (Sherry Manufacturing, Shanghai Brightness, Trans-Americas, the Reinsch farm) rather than large multinationals, and the two biggest companies in my T-shirt's life story (Shanghai Knitwear and the Shanghai Number 36 Cotton Mill) were owned by the Chinese government.

My T-shirt's journey from China to the United States is engineered today by a web of highly political constraints on markets, in which both rich- and poor-country producers seek political protection from markets, and especially from the China threat. The China threat in turn, because of the political protections for industry (state ownership, the hukou system, subsidies, and a managed currency), is really a political threat rather than a market threat.

I now see that even the frenetic and market-driven used clothing trade is in part a political creation. While his own government gives Ed Stubin no protection at all from market forces, trade barriers in China have the unintended consequence of at least some protection for Trans-Americas.

In revising this book, I have kept in mind Hans Peter Lankes' evocative image of "circling the Buddhist stone garden." To circle, of course, suggests seeing from a variety of perspectives, and to circle again and again means to see new things each time. As I have circled, my conclusion regarding the importance of politics in understanding my T-shirt's life has only strengthened. It is political reactions to markets, political protection from markets, and political involvement in markets, rather than competition in markets, that are at the center of my T-shirt's life story. To either glorify or vilify the markets is to dangerously oversimplify the world of trade. To paraphrase James Carville, "It's the politics, stupid."

We might view all of these protective political maneuvers as an "artificial" interference with the market mechanism. Indeed, it has become fashionable to equate the market mechanism with biological processes such as survival of the fittest, in which nature is best left alone. But while interference may be less than optimal as economic policy, it is surely not unnatural; in fact the reverse is true. What could be more natural than seeking protection from a world of Darwinian survival?

My T-shirt's story, then, is not a tale of Adam Smith's market forces, but is instead a tale of Karl Polanyi's double movement, in which market forces on the one hand meet demands for protection on the other. This call for protection is not just from textile workers or cotton farmers, but from citizens everywhere who feel a growing unease about globalization even as incomes rise. In some cases, the political protections make things worse for the poor (U.S. cotton subsidies), while in other cases, they make things better (minimum labor standards). In all cases, however, they are central to the story.

Neither trade nor theorizing about trade began with Adam Smith. There was trade in textiles and clothing, and debates surrounding this trade, long before there were economists. For centuries, trade was a subject of moral and religious debate, rather than a subject for economic analysis. Indeed, in perusing the early Christians' debates over trade, I am struck by the complete absence of economic discussion.[2] While economists often despair that noneconomic factors influence debates over trade policy, with a long historical view we see that it has been only relatively recently that economic factors entered into trade discussions, let alone became central. That moral discourse continues to pervade debates about trade should not be surprising.

My T-shirt reveals that the moral and political discussions are critical today if the double movement is to have widespread blessings. Some players in my T-shirt's life story—Nelson Reinsch, North Carolina textile workers—have some protections. A few—Ed Stubin and Geofrey

Milonge—are either winning or at least afloat by competing in the markets, or benefiting from the indirect protection given to others. Neither side of the double movement, however, has reached millions. Most African cotton farmers, for instance, are granted neither political protections nor market opportunities nor access to technical or even basic literacy. In China, while most sweatshop workers are happy to have escaped the farm, these young women are second-class citizens in a country where even first-class citizens lack political voice. It is not the cruelty of market forces that has doomed millions of African farmers and Asian sweatshop workers. It is instead exclusion from opportunities found in market competition, political participation, or both.

This exclusion occurs both at the hands of developing country governments who either retain the spoils from the markets (African governments) or fail in various ways to give their citizens voice (Chinese government), and at the hands of rich-country governments that continue to maintain a shameful double standard in trade policy (U.S. government). Fortunately, positive change is afoot. Cutting agricultural subsidies, democratization, and giving poor countries a place at the table at trade negotiations are all steps in the right direction.

Since completing my travels, I have come to believe in a moral case for trade that is even more compelling than the economic case. After observing two world wars, former Secretary of State Cordell Hull wrote in his memoirs that he had come to believe that trade was an instrument of peace:

> I saw that you could not separate the idea of commerce from the idea of war and peace. You could not have serious war anywhere in the world and expect commerce to go on as before.... And [I saw that] wars were often caused by economic rivalry.... I thereupon came to believe that ... if we could increase commercial exchanges among nations over lowered trade and tariff barriers and remove international obstacles to trade, we would go a long way toward eliminating war itself.[3]

As I followed my T-shirt around the globe, each person introduced me to the next and then the next until I had a chain of friends that stretched all the way around the world: Nelson and Ruth Reinsch, Gary Sandler, Patrick and Jennifer Xu, Mohammed and Gulam Dewji, Geofrey Milonge, Auggie Tantillo, Ed Stubin, Su Qin and Tao Yong Fang. How can I type this list of names without agreeing with Cordell Hull? The Texans, Chinese, Jews, Sicilians, Tanzanians, Muslims, Christians, whites, blacks, and browns who passed my T-shirt around the global economy get along just fine. Actually, *much* better than fine, thank you very much. All of these people, and millions more like them, are bound together by trade in cotton, yarn, fabric, and T-shirts. I believe that each of them, as they touch the next one, are doing their part to keep the peace.

Some early Christians believed that God did not want us to trade. St. Augustine was unambiguous in his disdain: "For they are active traders...they attain not the grace of God."[4] Indeed, the very existence of oceans was taken as evidence that trade was contrary to God's will. St. Ambrose advised that we could go fishing, or enjoy the view, but never should we use the sea for trade:

> ...God did not make the sea to be sailed over, but for the sake of the beauty of the element. The sea is tossed by storms; you ought, therefore to fear it, not to use it ... use it for purposes of food, not for purposes of commerce....[5]

Others, however, had a different view of God's will. Perhaps, instead, trade was a part of God's plan to help us get along with those different from ourselves. Libanius, writing nearly 2,000 years ago, believed that:

> God did not bestow all products upon all parts of the earth, but distributed His gifts over different regions, to the end that men might cultivate a social relationship because one would have need of the help of another, and so He called commerce into being, that all men might be able to have common enjoyment of the fruits of the earth, no matter where produced.[6]

As I watch the many far-flung members of my T-shirt's extended family continue to "cultivate a social relationship" with one another, I can only agree with Libanius. While some observers of the 2000–2008 period of world history will see primarily war and intolerance, my T-shirt continues to forge bridges of understanding: The bonds formed by my T-shirt can only be a force for good.

So, what do I say to the young woman on the steps at Georgetown University who was so concerned about the evils of the race to the bottom, so concerned about where and how her T-shirt was produced? I would tell her to appreciate what markets and trade have accomplished for all of the sisters in time who have been liberated by life in a sweatshop, and that she should be careful about dooming anyone to life on the farm. I would tell her that the poor suffer more from exclusion from politics than from the perils of the market, and that if she has activist energy left over it should be focused on including people in politics rather than shielding them from markets. And I would tell her about the shoulders she stands on, about her own sisters and brothers in time and the noble family tree of activists, and the difference they have made in a day's life at work all over the world. I would tell her that, in just a few short years, I have seen the difference her own generation has made, and that someday people will stand on her shoulders, too. I would tell her that Nike, Adidas, and GAP need her to keep watching, and so do Wal-Mart and the Chinese government. I would tell her that I have met dozens of seamstresses in Chinese factories who need her, and that future generations of sweatshop workers and cotton farmers need her as well. I would tell her to look both ways, but to march on.

Yet, as we have seen, the hardest work of this generation of activists is finished now. Not all of the work is finished, but the hard work of shifting the very paradigm by which the global apparel industry operates is finished. The work that remains is important, but it is work at ground level—factory-by-factory work related to *how*, not *whether*, large multi-nationals should be responsible for conditions in their far-flung supply chains. The current generation of campus activists continues to make progress on these issues. This progress reminds us that globalization is not a faceless monster over which we have no control. Human beings write the rules of the game, and the rules are changing every day.

But there is a new generation of protestors on Georgetown's campus today, and on campuses everywhere. One of Georgetown's most active student groups is now Eco-Action. Almost all of the apparel company executives I spoke with during the past several years believed that environmental issues will be—indeed are —the newest challenge facing their global industry. While the topics change with the generations, the pushback against global capitalism takes a remarkably similar form. It is the "double movement" all over again—market forces on the one hand versus demand for protection on the other. Whether the protection is for air, or water, or worker safety, or child labor, the unwitting co-conspiracy is alive and well as global capitalism adapts to the demands of the activists and then the broader citizenry. *Environmental responsibility*, as a corporate creed, has gone mainstream in a remarkably short time.

Whether the issue is labor conditions or clean air, as I continue to circle it becomes harder and harder to be a pessimist. It is not that I wish to gloss over the problems, but rather that I find them to be so much less interesting than the solutions. As I continued to circle the stone garden during the past few years, I saw a multitude of environmental challenges in my T-shirt's life. But each time I circled I saw a new solution as well—wind-powered spinning mills and soy-based dyes and organic cotton and GM cottonseed and yarn from corn and windmills in the Texas cotton fields. The solutions seem to be coming at dizzying speed, each one more innovative and remarkable than the last. The scientists and entrepreneurs behind these innovations were invariably optimists, and globalization increasingly links them together. While economic activity clearly creates environmental challenges, globalization and continued prosperity also make possible the innovations that hold promise for the ecological future of our planet.

In late 2008 I met Michael Shellenberger at a meeting held at a Washington think tank, and several months later we spoke again by phone. Michael had begun his career in the 1990s as an anti-globalization activist, and had spent several years targeting Nike's alleged sweatshop practices in Asia.

When we spoke in 2008 Michael had changed his mind about many things, and he felt both older and wiser. He had recognized himself in the opening pages of the first edition of this book, and had identified with the protestor on the steps at Georgetown. "I thought that trade and globalization were evil," Michael told me. "I thought the companies were evil and the IMF was evil and that the World Bank was evil. I thought that the poor got the raw end of the deal from globalization."

"I had this nostalgic view of rural peasants," Michael continued. "I didn't realize that they did not actually want to be on the farm. They wanted to be in the cities like the rest of us. And I didn't see how globalization was a way out of their grinding poverty."

"I'm pro-globalization, now," Michael told me. "I see that it is a force for good, and I want to improve it rather than stop it. But it is still important to advocate for change. You can be pro-globalization and still want companies to improve."

Michael concedes what he thinks of as his youthful confusion but he has no regrets about his anti-sweatshop activism. He continues to see the long- lasting impacts that he and his fellow activists had. "I'm very proud of the work we did," he told me.

In the early 2000s, Michael shifted his focus from labor to environmental issues. In 2004, he and Ted Norhaus published an essay titled "The Death of Environmentalism" that took the world by storm. The ideas were also published in their 2007 book, titled *Breakthrough: From the Death of Environmentalism to the Politics of Possibility*. In short, Michael and Ted argued that the environment was too important to be left to the environmentalists. The environmentalists' dominant paradigm held that economic growth was a *cause* of environmental problems, and that solutions were to be found in the "politics of limits"—in words such as "stop," "restrict," or "regulate."[7]

Michael believes that the "politics of limits" has it backwards. Though he is a Democrat and identifies himself as "progressive," Michael since his anti-sweatshop days has developed a fundamental respect for the ability of economic growth and investment to solve problems, particularly ecological ones. Prosperity brings out the best in human nature, Michael believes, and economic growth can be the *solution* to our environmental challenges. Michael and Ted "…called on environmentalists to replace their doomsday discourse with an imaginative, aspirational, and future- oriented one."[8] Investment and innovation in clean energy and technologies are *enabled* by economic growth, and will create the prosperity of the future, just as past infrastructure investments in highways, railroads, microchips, and the Internet created the prosperity of the present. In late 2008 Barack Obama named Steven Chu, the Nobel prize–winning physicist, to head the Environmental Protection Agency. Chu is a forceful advocate for investment and innovation to solve environmental challenges. Indeed, Obama has proposed "green" jobs and investment as partial solutions to America's economic and environmental problems, and many of Michael's and Ted's ideas are now reflected in Obama's environmental and economic policies. In 2008 the two young activists were named "Heroes of the Environment" by *Time* magazine.

If Michael and I had met 10 years ago, we would have disagreed about almost everything; an anti-globalization activist on one side of the table, a business school professor on the other. We have both changed our minds a lot since then, and I'd guess that now we likely have no important disagreements at all.

We are both optimists, for one thing. I still have my red parrot T-shirt, but it is looking more and more like an antique, a relic of a different era, an era with pesticides and phthalates and without codes of conduct and factory monitors. To watch the dizzying innovations of the last few years, I can only believe that tomorrow's T-shirt will have a better story still. The future isn't perfect, but it is brighter than it used to be.

EPILOGUE

DEVELOPMENTS 2009–2014

I: American Cotton Is Still King

Cotton Subsidies Redux

The Agricultural Act of 2014 (or "Farm Bill") was signed into law two years late in February 2014. At 956 pages and with a nearly $1 trillion price tag, it was, like the 2008 Farm Bill (discussed in Chapter 4), the result of painstaking deal-making across multiple constituencies ranging from catfish farmers to food stamp recipients to the National Rifle Association to traditional "Big Ag" farmers of cotton, wheat, soybeans, and corn. In general, the agricultural community was happy with the outcome, while anti-hunger advocates were less happy, primarily because of cuts in food-assistance programs.[1]

Cotton subsidies had a much more complex role to play in the deliberations than did other crop programs, however. In addition to the disparate domestic constituencies that were active in all of the negotiations, the cotton industry had the additional burden of addressing the WTO complaints by Brazil. U.S. cotton subsidies had been found in violation of global trade rules as early as 2004, and the ongoing dispute had become a thorn in the side of broader U.S.–Brazil diplomatic and business relationships. Many had lost patience with the long saga, and Brazil had been assured that their concerns would be addressed explicitly in the new Farm Bill. In effect, cotton would need its own Farm Bill.

"Everyone knew that cotton would have to be peeled off," Darren Hudson of Texas Tech told me in April 2014. "Cotton was causing problems everywhere, and we needed to help solve them."

Since 2002, Brazil had argued that U.S. cotton subsidies unfairly stimulated U.S. exports and production and depressed world cotton prices.[2] The WTO found in favor of Brazil in 2004 and in 2007, and though the United States made modifications to some cotton subsidies, in 2009 the WTO ruled that the changes had not been sufficient and authorized Brazil to retaliate against the United States.

It became immediately clear, however, that traditional trade "retaliation"—which authorized Brazil to impose punitive tariffs on imports from the United States—would mostly harm Brazil. Many of the goods that Brazil imported from the United States were capital goods or critical inputs into their own exports, and, in addition, imposing tariffs on imported consumer goods would be inflationary and unpopular in Brazil. Brazil therefore requested permission to "cross-retaliate," which would allow the country to impose penalties other than tariffs on U.S. goods. The WTO granted Brazil's request, and authorized the country to violate normal intellectual property rules, or so-called TRIPs (Trade-Related Intellectual Property Rights), as well as rules governing services trade (GATS, or General Agreement on Trade in Services). The effect of the ruling was to allow Brazil to suspend some intellectual property protections for goods such as pharmaceuticals and engineered seeds, and to instate trade protections for Brazilian services firms. The cross-retaliation authorized by the WTO therefore shifted the costs of the cotton subsidies to other American industries and firms, including giants such as Microsoft, Monsanto, and Intel. The wider business community in the United States now took notice of the cotton subsidies.

On April 5, 2010, one day before the "cross-retaliation" measures were to go into effect, U.S. and Brazilian negotiators reached a settlement. The most significant aspect of the settlement was an agreement by the U.S. government to simply pay Brazilian cotton farmers $12.275 million per month, with assurances that the next Farm Bill would address the violations.[3] If the solution was expensive for the American taxpayer, it worked for cotton farmers in both countries: The U.S. government agreed to pay subsidies to Brazilian cotton farmers in order to continue to pay subsidies to U.S. cotton farmers. The WTO had estimated that the illegal

U.S. subsidies had led the world market price of cotton to be 9.38 cents per pound lower than it would have been otherwise, and the monthly payment was designed to compensate for Brazilian farmers' share of the resulting losses.[4]

Over the preceding decade, the WTO had ruled that many—but not all—provisions of U.S. cotton supports were in violation of global trade rules. In general, programs that either subsidized exports (such as export credit guarantees) or were judged to increase world supplies of cotton and reduce prices (such as the "countercyclical payments" that protected farmers against price declines, discussed in Chapter 4) were found to be "distorting" and in violation of the rules. However, the U.S. cotton industry had also won several rounds in the fight. "Direct Payments," which were per-pound payments based on historical production, as well as subsidized crop insurance, were found by the WTO to be permissible subsidies, despite Brazil's objections.

But direct payments were not politically feasible at home. The payments, which were paid to owners of land that had once produced cotton, were the poster child of all that was wrong with agricultural policy. Journalists delighted in finding wealthy Manhattan dwellers collecting 7 cents per pound for cotton they had never grown. The *New York Times* had referred to the direct payments program as "one of the worst abuses in the federal budget."[5]

In the end, of all of the major programs supporting U.S. cotton farmers, only crop insurance was both palatable at home and legal under the trade rules. The solution: "Put everything in insurance." The cotton industry went to work to design a new crop insurance program that would re-create as much as possible the protections and economic value that were to be eliminated along with the direct payments and the countercyclical payments.

Designed by the National Cotton Council (NCC), the new Stacked Income Protection Plan (STAX) in the 2014 Farm Bill is "stacked" onto traditional insurance. Both traditional and STAX insurance protect the farmer from revenue declines resulting from falling yields, falling prices, or both. In combination, STAX and traditional insurance put a "floor" under farmers' income, and therefore achieve an effect that is similar to that of the subsidy programs that were replaced. The approximate level of this floor is 80 percent of expected income, with the STAX insurance covering the top 20 percent of this amount. The critical distinction between STAX insurance and conventional insurance is that insurance payments for STAX are based on the experience of the county, rather than the individual farm, a provision that shifts additional risk onto the farmer. The insurance premium for STAX policies is subsidized at the rate of 80 percent, while the insurance premium for traditional insurance carries different subsidies depending on policy specifics, but can also reach a maximum of 80 percent.[6]

During my spring 2014 visit to Lubbock, I found virtually everyone I spoke with relieved by the provisions of the 2014 Farm Bill, which would apply through 2018.[7] At Texas Tech, and the Plains Cotton Growers and the Plains Cotton Cooperative Association (PCCA), I got the same answer when I asked about the 2014 Farm Bill: "We did as well as we could have hoped," everyone said.

The Brazil–U.S. cotton dispute was a Goliath-versus-Goliath drama, pitting two of the largest and most advanced cotton producers in the world against one another. Indeed, many of the farmers in Brazil are American.[8] Both countries have advanced technology, powerful political lobbies, and the resources and expertise to fight a 12-year battle. And the global trade battle between Brazil and the United States over cotton subsidies may not be over. "These changes are significant, and we believe the matter is resolved," said Wally Darneille, the Chairman of the NCC.[9] But in the spring of 2014, Brazilian officials were considering returning to the WTO, reopening negotiations, or both, and had charged that the new cotton provisions continued to distort the global market.[10] More generally, critics of the 2014 Farm Bill charged that it had accomplished only a "bait-and-switch," substituting one form of subsidy for another.[11]

What About Africa?

As early as 2003, anti-globalization activists and others had framed the debate over U.S. cotton subsidies as a David-versus-Goliath battle, focusing on the effects of U.S. cotton subsidies on the poorest farmers in the world, mainly in West Africa (see Chapters 1 and 4). In the end, however, the long battle between rich farmers in one country and rich farmers in another ended well for both groups, but had little effect on producers in the poorest countries. The so-called Cotton-4 countries (Benin, Burkina Faso, Chad, and Mali) did not have the means or risk tolerance for an extended battle with the United States, and they had relied on negotiation rather than confrontation. They had relied in particular on U.S. negotiators' 2004 commitment to tackle cotton subsidies "ambitiously, expeditiously, and specifically" in the Doha Round of multinational trade negotiations (see Chapter 1).[12] But a decade later the Doha Round of trade negotiations remains stalled.

IDEAS, a Swiss NGO, had originally mobilized the Cotton-4 countries around the subsidy issue, and had served as a lead advisor to the countries. In 2013, IDEAS announced that its *Cotton Newsletter*, which chronicled the saga of the Cotton-4 countries' quest to reduce cotton subsidies, would terminate with its February 2013 issue after 11 years.[13] Oxfam's cotton subsidy activism has also largely ceased. By 2014, anti-poverty activists around the world had moved on to other causes.

In any case, the U.S. subsidies remain the least of worries for West African cotton farmers, as the power structures in place for cotton producers are still reversed from those in the United States. While cotton farmers near Lubbock own the gins, seed mills, and cotton warehousing and distribution facilities while at the same time wielding disproportionate political power, West African cotton farmers remain impoverished by poor governance, poor infrastructure, and supply chain relationships in which oligopolies provide inputs and oligopsonies purchase cotton. Throughout this book I have illustrated the ways in which the poor and powerless often suffer more from the suppression of competitive markets than from competition itself, and the case of cotton farmers in Africa remains a case in point. While there has long been significant attention to external factors such as trade barriers and U.S. subsidies, during the past several years a number of researchers have begun to examine the effects of internal market structure and governance issues on poverty levels among African farmers. Perhaps predictably, the effects are significant: In Burkina Faso, for example, a single state-owned firm, Sofitex, controls 85 percent of the country's ginning capacity. Guido Porto and his co-authors estimate that splitting Sofitex into two competing firms would raise Burkina Faso's cotton farmers' income by 12.5 percent, while more vigorous competition among equal-sized firms could raise their incomes by more than 20 percent.[14] Additional recent research in Burkina Faso documents consistent patterns of corruption and bribery in cotton classification, late payments to farmers, and deep-rooted mistrust of the large cotton processing firms. In 2011, farmers uprooted their crops in protest of the continued abuses.[15] A broader 2014 study of farm size and productivity in developing countries concluded that internal country policies often keep poor countries in a "small farm" trap, which in turn dramatically limits farmers' productivity and profits.[16]

West Texas Wind

In April 2014, I returned to the Reinsch farm with Nelson Reinsch and his son, Lamar. Nelson and his wife Ruth had moved in 2011 to a retirement community closer to Lubbock, but Nelson still frequently makes the drive out to the farm and keeps a close eye on the land he now rents to another grower. Ruth Reinsch died in July 2014 at age 93, just a few weeks before the couple's 70th wedding anniversary.

Mother Nature had not been kind to West Texas cotton for several years. The weather wildcards—wind, rain, hail—had each taken their toll. In spring of 2014 the region was entering its fourth year of serious drought; the 2011 drought was the worst experienced since the 1950s, and the region's cotton production had been the lowest seen in decades. In June 2013, more than 29,000 acres of young cotton had been lost in a hailstorm, and a year later Hockley County—the location of the Reinsch farm—saw baseball-sized hail.

The wind has long been the most consistent weather enemy in this region. As we drove out to the farm in spring of 2014, Lamar remembered the Texas dust storms of his childhood in the 1950s. An approaching dust storm looked like a dark black cloud against the blue sky. Drivers would turn on their lights and slow to a crawl as visibility dropped. Ruth would try to protect the interior of the house by taping windows and covering valuables, but it would be no use. Lamar remembers dust on the furniture and books and dishes and food.

But Nelson remembers the real Dust Bowl of the 1930s. After a bad dust storm there could be a sand-dune as big as a truck on the side of the house. Over the course of a day the wind could move the entire dune to the other side of the house.

The wind and dust were cotton's enemy. With low rainfall always a challenge, wind dries out the soil even more. And even when the cotton bolls survived the wind, which they often did not, the sand would blast into the boll and damage the crop. The world's textile mills were willing to pay little or nothing for sandblasted cotton.

But in the familiar story of the virtuous circle described in Chapter 4, Lubbock area farmers and the supporting research enterprise have made significant progress in protecting the value of the cotton crop from the wind and dust. Land was put into conservation, and plantings held the soil in place during the windstorms. Tougher, more resilient cotton was bred, and "sand-fighting" technology was used to clean the sand from cotton.

Yet while the wind has become less of a threat than it was in earlier decades, growers in Lubbock still face the risk of gusts that will dry the soil, destroy their cotton, and lower the value of the crop.

But during my return trip to Lubbock in 2014, I heard a surprising new term. Growers were talking about the area's "wind resources," suggesting new ways that wind might create rather than destroy value for west Texas farmers. The developing story of west Texas wind resources has many of the ingredients so familiar in the history of the region: Once again, a challenge is being transformed into an economic opportunity, and once again, the farmers are banding together in an "all for one, one for all" model with philosophical ties to agricultural cooperatives.

John Billingsley, now 75, had grown up handpicking cotton near Lubbock but had gone on to have a varied and successful career in financial services, real estate development, banking, and manufacturing. Billingsley still owns the family's cotton-producing land, where some of the acreage is devoted to organic cotton. In the early 2000s, Billingsley was approached by a firm wishing to lease the right to place wind turbines on his farm.[17]

Billingsley took issue with the standard business arrangement between the wind energy companies and the farmers, however. For one thing, profits were destined to leave the community, while Billingsley thought that local ownership could better stimulate and diversify the local economy. In addition, the outcome in which some neighbors won (because turbines were erected on their property) and others lost violated the spirit of the community.

Billingsley founded a new company, Tri Global Energy, to address both of these concerns. Under the Tri Global business model (which had a patent pending in spring of 2014), west Texas cotton farmers banded together in much the same way that they had once joined forces to take on cotton marketing, cotton research, and denim production.

Tri Global assists communities in forming locally owned wind energy corporations in which the farmers themselves own shares so that both the risks and rewards are shared within the community. The eventual profits will also stay close to home. Individually the farmers had had little power against the large wind energy companies, but together they held all of the cards to form companies themselves. In the summer of 2013, Tri Global announced the formation of the Hale Community Energy, the world's largest community-owned wind farm, on 120,000 acres north of Lubbock.

Mike Price, a local cotton grower, is President of Hale Community Energy. Price, in his late 50s, has spent his life growing cotton. The random elements of his livelihood have taken their toll. Price spoke of the ongoing drought, the volatile crop prices, the falling water-table, the global consumer shift toward synthetic fabrics, and the random policies from Washington. Price sees the community wind resources as a permanent path toward supplemental income, lower risk, and tax revenue for a region that can no longer afford to rely only on the random fortunes of cotton faming.

Steve Verett, President of Plains Cotton Growers, told me in the spring of 2014 that the wind had been worse for cotton growers than usual that spring, quickly drying up the sparse rainfall and precious water from irrigation. But Jeff Clark, executive director of the Wind Coalition, had a different view of the area surrounding Lubbock: "It's some of the best wind in the world," he said.[18]

What's Next?

During the 15 years that I have spent following the west Texas cotton industry, the core competitive advantages of the region have not changed. The culture of integrity in business practices that inspires trust around the world, the exceptional skill in acquiring and using political influence, the symbiotic relationships between business, government, and universities, and the entrepreneurial creativity—all of these factors seem to be as native to this landscape as the tumbleweed. At the same time, however, there are also seismic shifts underway that suggest challenges in the future.

Perhaps most importantly, global consumption of cotton is falling relative to manmade fiber. While advances in cotton science continue to improve fiber quality, at the end of the day cotton is a plant subject to nature's whims, and technology, research, and engineering are advancing even faster to improve the performance and cost of manmade fabrics. In the United States, manmade fiber apparel imports were in 2014 set to exceed cotton apparel imports for the first time in 20 years, and cotton's share of worldwide fiber consumption has been falling since 2006.[19]

The farmer-owned Plains Cotton Cooperative Association (PCCA) in Lubbock remains America's largest handler of U.S. cotton. In 2009, the PCCA acquired Denimatrix, an apparel manufacturing facility in Guatemala. Denimatrix supplies jeans to Abercrombie and Fitch, Michael Kors, Lacoste, and other high-fashion brands. West Texas cotton is transformed into denim in the Littlefield textile mill, and the denim is then shipped to Guatemala for cutting, finishing, and sewing. With the acquisition of Denimatrix, the PCCA formed the first firm in the Western Hemisphere that was vertically integrated from cotton farm to apparel manufacture. In June 2014, however, the PCCA sold both Denimatrix and the Littlefield denim mill to American Textile Holdings, a firm formed by private equity investors.[20] For the first time, I encountered a topic that my friends in Lubbock did not really want to talk about. I assume, though I do not know, that the denim mill and garment factory had been struggling along with the rest of the American textile and apparel industry.

The U.S. government's safety net for cotton growers is largely intact through 2018. It is difficult to imagine, however, that the net is secure in the longer run. A significant number of "Tea Party" farm state Senators voted against the 2014 Farm Bill, including members from Alabama, Texas, Kansas, and Iowa. Though the agricultural interest groups are gearing up to punish these Senators in the next election, the systemic budget pressures, together with international trade disputes and the swing in voter sentiment toward support for other forms of agriculture—particularly fruit and vegetables production—may suggest an uphill battle for traditional Big Ag subsidies in the future.

In 2014, however, American cotton was still winning in the global marketplace and in Washington. The United States remains by far the world's largest cotton exporter, and cotton yields per acre continue to climb as the virtuous circle creates further scientific advances. For now, at least, American cotton is still king.

II: The Race to the Bottom Speeds Up

On April 24, 2013, a shoddily and illegally constructed building collapsed outside Dhaka, Bangladesh. The building, Rana Plaza, housed garment factories that produced apparel for dozens of Western apparel retailers, including Benetton, JCPenney, Carrefour, and Primark. The day of the collapse, newspapers reported that at least 142 people had died. But day by day over the next month rescuers worked in the rubble and the estimate of the number of dead rose—to 348, 446, 650—finally settling at 1,129. More than 2,500 people were injured, and many had lost limbs. The collapse of Rana Plaza was the single most deadly event in the global history of the garment industry. The day before the collapse an engineer had warned that the building was unstable and should not be occupied, but factory owners forced garment workers to return to the building, saying production deadlines had to be met.[21]

China remains the world's largest apparel exporter by a significant margin: At approximately 40 percent, China's share of the U.S. apparel market in 2013 was larger than the next eight exporters combined.[22] Chinese dominance in the global textile and apparel trade is still powered by the continued waves of migrant workers who have limited rights and second-class citizen status.[23] Yet the effects of higher Chinese wages continue to reverberate, and the rate of growth in Chinese exports is slowing. Even with slower growth, however, China is likely to remain the world's leading apparel producer for many years to come. At the same time, a common and important question is which countries are rising in the long race to the bottom described in Chapter 6.

Until the collapse of Rana Plaza, Bangladesh was poised to be a significant next stop in the race. Between 2005 and 2012, Bangladeshi apparel exports grew by nearly 200 percent, a rate exceeded only by Vietnam. In addition, by 2013, Bangladesh was the world's second largest apparel exporter and more than 80 percent of the country's non-farm exports and employment were comprised of apparel.[24] In the post-quota world, apparel production was pulled to Bangladesh by the lowest wages in the world: At the time of the Rana Plaza collapse the minimum wage for garment workers in Bangladesh was $38 per month, less than one-fifth of the minimum wage in the southeastern provinces of China.[25] Yet, along with the great floods of apparel exports, by 2014, Bangladesh had clearly surpassed China in producing alarming sweatshop stories: Fires, building collapses, and abusive bosses were all part of the Bangladeshi narrative.[26]

The origin of the Bangladeshi apparel industry is a familiar story. In the late 1970s, Bangladesh was an impoverished rural country still recovering from war. About two thousand miles away, however, South Korea had used up its apparel quota, which had quickly become binding under Richard Nixon's promises to protect the U.S. textile industry.[27] South Korea sent capital, machines, and training to Bangladesh as a way around the choking quota limits. Bangladesh's first manufacturing industry was born, and millions of women began to migrate from rural areas to urban factories. Like their sisters in time before them, they came to pay debts, to save for marriage, to educate siblings, to escape the village, to write their own futures.

A particularly tragic circumstance common in rural Bangladesh results from the system of arranged marriage and dowries, wherein young women are married off by their parents, who must also pay substantial sums to the grooms' families. A cruel twist is that dowries required for adult women over 16 are higher than those for young girls, so the economic incentives to marry off daughters early is strong. A job in the garment industry, however, confers new power to young women to move to the city rather than to engage in the rural system of arranged marriages and dowries. Research has shown that women working in the Bangladeshi garment industry marry later, have fewer children, and provide higher levels of education for themselves and their families than the women who stay in the village. In 2013, the garment industry employed approximately 4 million workers, the great majority of whom were young women.[28]

Fast Fashion and Factory Fires

There were other key differences, however, in the Bangladeshi story, differences that made it clear that the familiar cycle of industrialization and broader development that had run its course in other countries might play out differently in Bangladesh. First, for the first time since the 1960s, trade in apparel was free of the quotas discussed in Part III of this book. To be sure, the apparel trade in 2014 was still far from free, as high tariffs and complex trade agreements remained. But the certainty that a country would sell set quantities of specific types of apparel to the West was gone. Whatever the negative consequences of the quota regime—and there were many—the system had provided orderliness and predictability to the apparel trade for decades.

A second difference between Bangladesh in 2014 and China in 2000 or Japan in 1955 lies in the evolution of the consumer-driven "fast-fashion" supply chain. Particularly after 2005, global firms in the apparel industry began to compete aggressively on speed as well as price. While the department stores of an earlier era stocked spring and fall merchandise a few times per season, in 2014 fast-fashion retailers such as Inditex (owner of Zara) and H&M had new items in the stores weekly. Inditex, the industry leader in fast-fashion logistics, can now move apparel from designer to the consumer in as little as two weeks, and the design and delivery process is driven by real-time consumer data from stores.[29]

Together, the demise of the apparel quota system and the rise of fast-fashion retailing meant that overall demand as well as the structure of that demand became highly unpredictable, particularly after the end of all China quotas in 2008. With the rapid growth in demand for Bangladesh-produced apparel, the "good" factories, particularly those in the Export Processing Zones, were often operating at full capacity. In order to meet the tight deadlines for unpredictable orders from retailers, production was often pushed out to second- and third-tier subcontractors where working conditions were poorer and safety provisions questionable.

Beginning in the 1990s, anti-sweatshop activists had largely been successful persuading Western brands and retailers to adopt supplier codes of conduct, and while virtually all codes of conduct prohibit the use of unauthorized subcontractors, the tight deadlines imposed by their customers often left factory owners with no option other than declining the orders. The takeoff of the Bangladeshi apparel industry and the unpredictable demands for fast and cheap clothing has led to ceaseless time pressure: Trucks marked "Emergency Export Duty" in Bangladesh have the same privileges as ambulances;[30] workers are often forced into overtime, and, most tragically, were forced to return to a shaking building in order to keep sewing. And the surges in demand also led to illegal and unsafe stories being added onto existing buildings in order to quickly add capacity.

Activists, Workers, and Governments Respond

The institutions in Bangladesh were ill-equipped to deal with these surging and unpredictable market forces from the West. Sohel Rana, the owner of Rana Plaza, was a thug involved in the drug and guns trade. He had seized the land for the building illegally, and paid off building inspectors with bribes as he brandished falsified deeds. The police, inspectors, and other alleged civil protectors were in Rana's pocket.[31] Workers had no effective means of organization, and labor activists were routinely roughed up by government security forces. The garment industry owners are well-represented at all levels of political power, including Parliament. In brief, the myriad institutions that should protect all citizens—police, politicians, building inspectors, and unions—have failed and continue to fail millions of garment workers in Bangladesh. While poor governance is common to many countries—China certainly among them—for the first time relatively open competition in the quota-free apparel trade now coexists in a governance vacuum that is not equipped to protect its citizens.

The collapse of Rana Plaza brought not only a new urgency but also new dimensions to the debate surrounding the role of western apparel companies in the working conditions in supplier factories. During the past two decades the labor laws and policies on the books in developing countries have gradually converged to an international standard.[32] At the same time, however, weak governance, corruption, power imbalances, and lack of resources in many countries mean that enforcement is often lacking. As a result, western brands and retailers have continually increased their role as "government substitutes" by monitoring factories for a wide range of problematic practices. These practices have generally related to issues such as discrimination, underage workers, and pay practices. The collapse of Rana Plaza, however, opened a new dimension to the role of western brands: Now global corporations best known for designing and marketing apparel in wealthy countries were called upon to take responsibility for the structural integrity of suppliers' factory buildings.

Responses to the disaster came from rich-country activists, Bangladeshi workers, western clothing brands and retailers, and the Bangladeshi government. By mid-2014, these collective responses began to resemble the unwitting conspiracies that had unfolded throughout industrial history (see Chapter 8), and hope began to emerge that the Rana Plaza disaster might have a transformative impact on business prac- tice and public policy, in much the same way that the Triangle Shirtwaist fire had mobilized change more than a century earlier.

Garment workers in Bangladesh staged crippling strikes for myriad demands in the year after the disaster. By late 2013, a 77 percent increase in the minimum wage had taken effect, and a new labor law removed many of the barriers to collective action by workers. Workers had argued that stronger unions would facilitate safety improvements and lessen intim- idation by factory bosses.[33] Both the EU and U.S. governments had threatened to withhold trade privileges unless the laws were modified.[34]

Major Western firms that sourced from Bangladesh responded with two collective programs. The "Accord on Fire and Building Safety in Bangladesh" was signed by more than 150 companies, dominated by the major European brands.[35] Chaired by the International Labor Organiza- tion, the Accord requires building and fire safety inspections of factories producing for member companies, and requires closure of unsafe factories as well as remediation. Members of the Accord also agree to maintain their production in Bangladesh for a five-year period, and to require that workers continue to receive salaries when factory buildings are closed for safety reasons. By mid-2014, the initial round of inspections was complete, and the results were posted on the Accord's website. At George- town, the student-led Licensing Oversight Committee voted to require all companies producing Georgetown-logoed apparel to sign the Accord. Georgetown was joined by eight other U.S. universities.[36]

The Accord represented a new level of commitment for Western firms not only because it addressed issues related to buildings and structural integrity, but especially because the Accord is legally binding in the legal system of the brands' home countries. For most American companies, however, the Accord was a leap too far. Concerned about legal liability and financial commitment, the major U.S. brands formed a parallel organization, the "Alliance for Bangladesh Worker Safety." Led by Wal-Mart and Gap, the Alliance also provides for structural, fire, and safety inspections. The Alliance had completed more than 600 factory inspections by July 2014.[37]

In 2013, Richard Locke published a path-breaking book in which he analyzed nearly 30 years of efforts by Western companies to promote labor standards among their suppliers in developing countries.[38] Locke had access to thousands of factory inspection reports, and he and his graduate students visited apparel, electronic, and shoe factories around the world. Locke documents the evolution and maturation of a variety of approaches to supplier labor issues in developing countries, from codes-of-conduct "compliance"-based systems to capability initiatives and public–private partnerships. Though he observes significant improvements over the past generation and his conclusion is fundamentally hopeful, Locke also documents the inherent tension created when Western companies' demands for the cheapest and fastest production are juxtaposed with their simultaneous demands for safe and humane workplaces. In Bangladesh both the Accord and the Alliance face this tension.

For some Western firms, an alternative response to the workplace issues in Bangladesh was to leave the country altogether. The Walt Disney Company, the world's largest licensed apparel producer, announced plans to withdraw production from Bangladesh shortly before the Rana Plaza collapse. Nike, citing worker safety concerns, also has minimized its reliance on Bangladesh, and by spring of 2014, the trade data suggested a marked slowing of Bangladeshi apparel exports following the Rana Plaza collapse. Industry sources attributed the trend to concerns over safety, worker unrest, and poor governance.[39]

The Cops Are Just Not There

What do the events in Bangladesh during the past several years suggest about the conclusions of *Travels of a T-Shirt*? While I believe that these events confirm the general conclusions in the second section of the book,

at the same time it is also clear that some past patterns will not be repli-
cated. On one hand, the long race to the bottom in apparel production
continues, with all of the advantages and disruptions for young women
and for economic and human development. On the other hand, the end
of the quotas and the rise of fast-fashion changed not just the direction
but the speed and predictability of the race. The conclusion that "the
bottom is rising" at each subsequent stop in the race is now more questionable; it certainly appears that working conditions and other standards
in lower-tier factories in Bangladesh are often weaker than they were in
China a decade ago. More broadly, recent events confirm a central theme
of *Travels of a T-Shirt*: The most vulnerable have more to fear from power
imbalances and weak institutions than from competitive markets, and,
indeed, markets depend for their survival on a set of basic institutions and
values that protect the most vulnerable. The decline in apparel exports
from Bangladesh following the events of 2013 is one such response of
"markets" to institutional vacuums.

In 2014, *New York Times* columnist David Brooks argued that our focus
on creating market-led economic growth in the developing world is misguided or at least skipping a step. Issues of scarcity, poverty, and economic
growth are of primary interest to us but are secondary in many parts of
the world:

> We in the affluent world live on one side of a great global threshold. Our
> fundamental security was established by our ancestors. We tend to assume
> that the primary problems of politics are economic and that the injustices of
> the world can be addressed with economic levers...
>
> But people without our inherited institutions live on the other side of the
> threshold and have a different reality. They live within a contagion of chaos.
> They live where the primary realities include violence, theft, and radical
> uncertainty. Their world is governed less by long term economic incentives
> and more by raw fear. In a world without functioning institutions, predatory
> behavior and the passions of domination and submission blot out the long
> term economic logic.
>
> The primary problem of politics is not creating growth. It's creating
> order.[41]

Brooks notes that in the District of Columbia, the government spends
$850 per person per year on police, while in Bangladesh the comparable
figure is $1.50: "The cops are just not there," he writes.

This was not a problem for Sohel Rana, however. He traveled surrounded by his own biker gang of armed guards.[42] In Bangladesh the

powerful had created their own institutions to protect themselves from markets, from fear, and from political competition. But as the weakening export performance of Bangladesh makes clear, market-led growth cannot be sustained in a system where people fear for their physical safety when reporting to work.

III: The Alphabet Armies March On

Julia Hughes and Auggie Tantillo each had new roles when I visited with them in mid-2014. Julia's firm had been renamed and rebranded as the U.S. Fashion Industry Association, while Auggie had assumed the presidency of the National Council of Textile Organizations (NCTO). Roger Milliken, the textile magnate who had led protectionist efforts for 60 years, died in 2010 at the age of 96, and AMTAC, the organization he had founded (and which Auggie had led) was folded into the NCTO. However, while affiliations or company names may have changed, in many ways Auggie and Julia were where I had left them after our conversations in 2008 and 2003. Their offices were blocks away from one another in Washington, and each was still engaged in numbingly complex sock-by-sock battles alongside a variety of alphabet armies. Julia, representing the increasingly global U.S. apparel industry, remained committed to liberalizing trade policies to allow apparel imports freely into the United States while Auggie remained on the side of U.S.-based textile manufacturers.

From Quotas to Trade Agreements

On January 1, 2009, the remaining quotas limiting imports from China into the United States were removed, and as of spring of 2014, the effects of a quota-free world could be observed. As expected or feared, China was the big winner, supplying 41 percent of U.S. apparel imports by 2013, up from 12 percent a decade earlier. Between 2003 and 2013, China's apparel exports to the United States nearly quintupled while overall apparel imports into the United States increased by 31 percent. Other strong performers in the post-quota period included Vietnam, Indonesia, Bangladesh, Cambodia, and Honduras.[43]

Yet while trade in T-shirts is no longer limited by quotas, a wide range of trade protections remain in place. Though only about 2 percent of Americans' clothing is made in the United States, tariffs remain among the highest of any manufactured goods.[44] Average tariffs applied to apparel in 2012—at 13.2 percent—were approximately 10 times the rate applied to all U.S. imports, and the tariff rate applied to T-shirts remained at 16.5 percent.[45] In 2014, tariff "peaks" of over 30 percent remain common for apparel.

More important and more complex than tariffs, however, are the burgeoning free-trade agreements (FTAs) that increasingly influence trade flows among countries. In 2014, most of the battles between Julie Hughes and Auggie Tantillo revolved around these trade agreements. According to the World Trade Organization (WTO), as of 2014 there were 377 trade agreements in effect throughout the world, representing 377 separate sets of rules negotiated by governments and alphabet armies.[46] The set of agreements is often referred to in trade circles as a "spaghetti bowl"— sets of rules linking pairs or groups of countries together. The growing number of agreements is largely attributable to the failure of broader WTO-led multilateral negotiations. The "Doha Round," launched in 2001, has been stuck for 13 years, faced with the imponderable task of trying to forge consensus among 160 members.

In 2014, the United States was focused on completing negotiations for the Trans-Pacific Partnership (TPP), a free trade agreement among 12 countries that together account for more than 40 percent of the world's GDP.[47] Auggie Tantillo, wise in the ways of Washington, seemed almost tired when we discussed TPP. "It's a typical second-term thing," he told me. "Obama needs a foreign policy success, a global geopolitical success. Obama wants to go out with this kind of win. Remember Nixon and China? Bush and NAFTA? It's the same thing." In the summer of 2014, it was not at all clear that Congress would support TPP, even if negotiations among the member countries were successful.

The current debate over TPP has clear echoes of the globalization debates—and anti-globalization protests—of a decade ago. While business groups and U.S. policymakers laud the prospects of liberalized trade to boost incomes and create jobs, critics are concerned about a variety of issues ranging from the closed door and secret negotiations to employment, pharmaceutical access, and food safety and labeling. The Peterson Institute for International Economics has estimated that the TPP will yield income gains of $78 billion annually for the U.S., while analysis from the Center for Economic and Policy Research suggests that virtually all of these gains will accrue to the richest Americans, and that the gains themselves are minimal.[48] Anti-TPP protests have broken out in the United States, Malaysia, New Zealand, and Japan.

At one level, the debate over TPP revolves around lofty issues such as foreign policy and economic inequality, but for Julia Hughes and Auggie Tantillo, TPP is about boxer-shorts and bras. In particular, when I met with Julia and Auggie in mid-2014, both were in fight mode over the TPP implementation of the *yarn-forward* rule, a seemingly arcane provision with staggering complexity but even more staggering importance to U.S. clothing companies and the U.S. textile industry. Julia wanted maximum flexibility in the rule, while Auggie argued for airtight implementation.

As discussed in Chapter 9, the yarn-forward rule, contained in most U.S. trade agreements, requires that, in order for apparel to enter the United States free of tariffs, all steps in the production process beginning with the manufacture of yarn must take place in member countries. The yarn-forward rule is therefore a "triple transformation" requirement (fiber into yarn, yarn into fabric, and fabric into clothing). Even Auggie agrees that no other U.S. industry is protected by such restrictive rules; a single transformation rule is a typical standard

For Julia Hughes and her allies in the U.S. retail industry, the fact that the yarn-forward rule remains in a so-called "twenty-first-century" trade agreement is evidence of the antiquated thinking that allowed quotas to survive for nearly half a century. To Julia's dismay, the U.S. trade negotiators committed early in the TPP negotiations to support the rule, after intense lobbying from Auggie's troops and a letter supporting the yarn-forward rule signed by 167 members of Congress and the NCTO.[49] Julia argues that a strict yarn-forward rule is unworkable in the modern-day global apparel industry. To meet the demands of consumers, apparel companies must be free to utilize the most competitive "global value chains," in other words, product designers must have access to the best yarns, fabrics, pockets, and elastic no matter where produced. Without such access, according to Julia, FTAs are not "free trade" agreements at all; instead they are simply disguised trade protection. Adding insult to Julia's injury, textiles alone are singled out as a separate industry in the summary of the U.S. negotiating position.[50]

Ironically, while FTAs should be especially valuable to U.S. apparel retailers and importers because of the high level of apparel tariffs that might be avoided, instead these FTAs seem to be increasingly ignored by the industry. The American Apparel and Footwear Association reports that the use of FTAs by apparel importers fell by more than 25 percent between 2003 and 2012, even as the number of FTAs has more than doubled. Only 20 percent of apparel imports utilized FTAs in 2012 (predominantly

CAFTA), and average tariffs paid on apparel imports are increasing. In other words, as the number of FTAs increases, apparel trade appears to become less free.[51]

Apparel importers increasingly bypass FTAs because they believe that sourcing flexibility is key in delivering the quality, speed, and value demanded by apparel consumers. It is especially difficult to exclude China from apparel sourcing and design, as many of the most competitive yarns and fabrics are produced there. In addition, importers are also scared off by the stunning complexity of the rules governing apparel imports under FTAs. While yarn forward appears to be a simple rule, the myriad different exceptions for the various agreements are a record-keeping and compliance nightmare.

For most apparel importers, paying the tariff is more than worth the flexibility, speed, and freedom to source inputs from anywhere, and to avoid the risk of non-compliance and penalties. "It's like a toll road," Julia told me. "People will pay a lot to use the fast lane and not get a ticket."

Unintended Consequences All Over Again

When I first met Auggie Tantillo in 2002, he and his armies were engaged to fight the China threat that was emerging with the end of the quotas, and in 2014 their fight over the yarn-forward provision in TPP was in effect a China fight as well. Since the end of the quotas, Vietnam, a TPP member, had emerged as a leading U.S. apparel supplier. Though far behind China in volume terms, Vietnamese apparel exports to the United States had quadrupled between 2005 and 2013.[52] However, the Vietnamese yarn and fabric industries are still relatively small, and Vietnamese apparel producers are highly dependent on yarns and fabrics from China. With a yarn-forward rule under TPP, Vietnam would have duty-free access to U.S. apparel consumers only if they gave up their key yarn and fabric supplier. To Auggie, a TPP without strict yarn-forward provisions is tantamount to giving away access to the U.S. market to China while receiving nothing in return. With yarn-forward, however, Vietnam would be a less competitive threat in particular to Central America, a region that is a major customer for U.S. yarn and fabrics. "Remember the Istanbul declaration?" Auggie asked me in 2014, referring to a coalition of countries that had banded together against the China threat in 2003 (discussed in Chapter 11). "It's the same thing all over again. It's not only about American companies—China could take out Haiti and Honduras, too."

Yet as discussed in Chapter 11, textile and apparel trade protection has led to perverse unintended consequences for centuries, and it is likely that this will continue into the foreseeable future. While the intended consequence of trade protection had always been to preserve domestic production, in the postwar period, the textile and apparel industries had instead globalized in response to trade protection, as "quota chasing" led production to dozens of new countries. In 2014, the likely unintended consequences of TPP were becoming clear: Chinese investors were flocking to Vietnam to establish yarn and fabric factories.[53] Even with a strict yarn-forward rule under TPP, Chinese firms could produce yarn and fabrics in Vietnam and gain duty-free access to the United States, Japan, and other high-income countries. In protecting themselves from yarn spinners in China, U.S. firms had simply created an incubator for yarn spinners to establish factories in Vietnam. Auggie Tantillo acknowledged the likely perverse consequences. "It still buys us time," he told me.

Indeed, Auggie's battles have always been about buying time, and by that measure he has had much success. The performance of the U.S. textile industry had stabilized during the 2009–2014 period, and many even spoke of a turnaround. Though employment in the industry continued its downward trend, industry production had stabilized and productivity was at record levels.[54] In addition, the U.S. textile industry was attracting foreign investors: Firms from India, China, and Canada had all recently invested in yarn spinning mills throughout the South. Traditional economic factors such as excellent infrastructure and access to cheap electricity were certainly part of the equation explaining the industry's attraction, but the primary factor was the yarn-forward rule that was expected to be a part of U.S. trade agreements for the foreseeable future.[55] By producing yarn in the United States, foreign firms could sell to customers around the world as the number of FTAs grew, and the resulting apparel would have duty-free access to the huge U.S. market. In other words, trade protection in the U.S. was leading textile producers from India and China to globalize, another echo of the long epic of perverse consequences that had begun in Britain nearly 300 years ago. In 2014, foreign investors were still betting on Auggie Tantillo.

"Someday," Julia Hughes told me, "T-shirts will have the same rules as everything else. But not yet."

IV: Competition Heats Up in the Used Clothing Business

Used Clothing Entrepreneurs Discover Politics

In 2013, the United States sold nearly 800 million kilograms of used clothing to customers around the world, an amount nearly quadrupled from the year 2000.[56] In Clifton, New Jersey, Eric Stubin had taken over leadership of Trans-Americas, the clothing recycling firm founded by his grandfather. The dynamic competition in the used clothing business has only increased during the past several years, and it had become clear to Eric that the traditional business model that had sustained the firm during his grandfather's and father's generation would no longer be viable. Eric is reinventing the business, and even the industry, in the face of global competition in multiple markets.

The recession of 2008 struck Trans-Americas on several fronts. First, clothing donations dwindled, as consumers held onto their older clothing rather than donate it. At the same time, however, cash-strapped consumers became more likely to shop in charity thrift shops, so, in combination with the shrinking donations there was even less clothing available for sale to export-bound recyclers such as Trans-Americas. Eric told me that the tightly constricted supply for the export market saw raw material prices— that is, the market price for unsorted clothing—nearly double, from 15 cents to 30 cents per pound, which squeezed Trans-Americas' profit margins as well as its business opportunities.

As the economy recovered in 2010, however, the firm's business was challenged from another angle. Entrepreneurs from around the globe, but particularly concentrated in Pakistan, India, and the United Arab Emirates, began to enter the U.S. raw materials market and purchase unsorted raw materials directly from U.S. charities. The firms ship the unsorted clothing into export processing zones in South Asia and the Middle East, and then grade and sort the clothing for export to Africa and beyond. Even with the additional leg of travel on the journey from the United States to Africa, the new firms were undercutting Trans-Americas because of sharply lower labor costs in sorting and grading the clothing. While Ed Stubin had been worried in 2008 about potential competition from China, the threat had instead come from even lower-wage locations. "Wage levels, health-care costs, employee benefits—we can't compete with India and Pakistan," Eric told me.

As if labor costs and dwindling raw material supplies were not challenges enough, a different China threat emerged for Trans-Americas. As incomes grew in Africa, consumers began to have more and more choices in new clothing, particularly from China. At the same time, the Chinese middle class began to dispose of clothing, too, and cast-off clothing from China began to enter the global market.

By 2013, then, Trans-Americas faced heightened competition in the labor market, the raw materials market, as well as the product market, and the firm's profit margins were under threat as an employer, as a buyer, and as a seller.

"I realized we needed a paradigm shift," Eric told me in the summer of 2014. "We have to take a long view." Trans-Americas' new multi-pronged strategy, Eric hopes, will create a new future. To increase the supply of raw materials, Eric has led the formation of a new coalition, the Council for Textile Recycling, which aims to divert the supply of discarded textiles and clothing from landfills. The Council recently held its first meeting, and Eric was optimistic. The new Council, and its website, www.donatewearrecycle.org, aims to change the behavior of the next generation of apparel consumers.

Eric is also working with a number of apparel companies to enhance their "end-of-life" practices. These practices might range from simply encouraging consumers to recycle their garments by providing recycling information on clothing tags, to setting up collection processes. One of Trans-Americas' partners is Nice Laundry Socks, which provides consumers with envelopes with which to return and recycle their socks.

At the same time, Eric and others in the U.S. used clothing business are also actively engaging with municipalities around the country to form partnerships in establishing textile recycling programs. "We are like a lot of American industries," Eric told me In June 2014. "We can't compete on labor costs. We have to re-engineer the business."

The U.S. used clothing industry remains characterized by near-perfect competition among multiple small players. Barriers to entry are low, used clothing is a commodity product, and those involved in the business have historically had little use for collective action or politics. My primary conclusion after following my T-shirt around the world was that only in this final chapter did I encounter a textbook example of a competitive market.

However, my discussion with Eric Stubin in 2014 suggested an evolution: Interestingly, Tran-Americas' evolving strategies involve political engagement, collective action, and coalition building, all terms that I had come to associate much more with Auggie Tantillo and Julia Hughes than with Trans-Americas.

In her 2011 book, *Recycling Reconsidered*, Samantha MacBride investigated a puzzle: Post-consumer glass recycling has become widespread practice throughout the United States, even though the activity is of minimal environmental value (glass is environmentally inert and relatively clean to produce) and is also economically irrational (municipalities spend more on glass recycling than they earn). In other words, the most commonly recycled substance creates little (or negative) economic or environmental value. At the same time, textile and clothing recycling in the United States is minimal, even though it creates significant economic value as well as environmental benefits. Either a rational economist or a rational environmentalist "should," it seems, prioritize textile recycling over glass. MacBride concludes—perhaps not surprising those who have followed my T-shirt—that the disparate practices are explained in significant measure by politics and especially by business lobbying.

As chairman of the new Council for Textile Recycling, the organization he helped to found, as well as CEO of Trans-Americas, Eric now wears two hats. He knows he needs to stay focused on the intensely competitive business of buying and selling used T-shirts. But at the same time, he also recognizes the value of politics and coalitions with consumers, apparel brands, retailers, and governments. The new Council is a small step compared to the giant political machines of cotton farmers, textile mill owners, or the beverage industry, but it is a step nonetheless. Like the Plains Cotton Cooperative Association, or the National Council of Textile Organizations, the Council hopes to influence the rules of the game.

Mitumba in East Africa

In 2013, Georgetown student Aristides Serlemitsos met with Geofrey Milonge near the Kariakoo market in Dar Es Salaam. Geofrey had turned 40 years old, and now had five children. From his beginnings as a small-time informal street trader of used clothing, Geofrey had built a "real" business, Chata Investments, Ltd. Geofrey now kept formal accounts, employed an accountant, and operated multiple shops. Geofrey was proud of his business success, and stressed that his income had increased each year since he had launched his business as an informal street trader. Geofrey normally purchased a container—roughly 50,000 pounds—of used clothing every few months. His acumen in grading, sorting, and marketing used clothing has increased every year.

Yet many of the same competitive forces that affect Eric Stubin are felt by Geofrey Milonge 8,000 miles away. Geofrey noted that supply is an ever-increasing problem, with growing competition for the limited amount of clothing from the United States and U.K. Competing goods from China—both new and used—threaten the traditional mitumba trade between Africa and the West, and the new suppliers in India were disruptive as well. Geofrey is not optimistic about the long-term viability of his business model sourcing from the West: He predicts that tightening supplies will drive up costs, and competition from China will erode profits. Geofrey has a plan, however. With the profits from his mitumba business, he has recently bought a cattle ranch. Geofrey believes demand for meat will grow with rising incomes in Tanzania. Soon Geofrey Milonge will transition from mitumba entrepreneur to ranch operator.

Meanwhile, Gulam Dewji, who began his career in the 1970s as a small-scale trader and had been among the first to bring mitumba to east Africa, is today one of Africa's wealthiest men.[57] Gulam's son, Mohammed, is now president and CEO of METL, the family's conglomerate, as well as a member of Parliament. Mohammed is frequently honored as one of Africa's young business leaders. METL remains a fast-growing diversified company operating in textiles, agricultural products, mobile telephony, and financial services, and now employs 24,000 people and accounts for more than 3.5 percent of Tanzania's GDP.[58] In 2014, the seeds from humble entrepreneurial beginnings in the mitumba trade continue to blossom in East Africa.

ACKNOWLEDGMENTS

My first thanks are to the people in this story. In my travels around the world I have been blessed by hospitality, kindness, and insights from people on three continents who have welcomed me into their homes and businesses, and patiently explained things to me. As a tenured professor at an American university, my livelihood is as immune as it is possible to get from the gale-force winds of global economic and political change, so I humbly concede that to live this story is a far greater challenge than to write it. My respect for my many friends who get up every day to face these challenges is immense. My thanks and admiration are especially due to Nelson and Ruth Reinsch, Gary Sandler, Su Qin, Tao Yong Fang, Patrick Xu, Mohammed and GulamDewji, GeofreyMilonge, AuggieTantillo, Julia Hughes, and Ed and Eric Stubin.

Georgetown University has been my second home for 30 years, and I have benefited from innumerable conversations with my students and colleagues. Special thanks are due to our student activists, who first sparked the idea for this book, and who have changed my mind more than once. Their energy and engagement are inspirational, even when we disagree, and I am tremendously proud of them and the difference that they continue to make in the course that globalization takes. Many of the ideas in this book were discussed at meetings of the university's Licensing Oversight Committee, which has been chaired successively by Jim Donahue, Michael Garanzini, Dan Porterfield, and LaMar Billups.

A number of capable research assistants and administrative assistants have helped me in the course of this research. Thanks are due to Brooke Barber, Lan Feng, Russell Jame, Renee Jiang, Dana Omahen, Jeffrey Pardini, Ann Pitchayanonnetr, Jessica Dybfest, and Emma Thompson.

My students and faculty colleagues on the fall 2003 voyage of Semester at Sea also deserve thanks for our many conversations and shared experiences that helped me to sharpen the ideas in this book. Semester at Sea also made possible additional field research in China and Tanzania.

I have now interviewed hundreds of people about the topics in this book, and it is impossible to thank them all by name. I hope that the notes throughout the book can serve as thanks to many for now. However, I would be remiss if I did not mention the extensive help and Texas hospitality of John Johnson of the PCCA. For China-based research I owe a special debt to Professor Lijun Qu, and for helpful discussions and valuable data and analysis to Nate Herman and Steve Lamar of the American Apparel and Footwear Association. For field research in Tanzania thanks are due to Elina Makanja, Henri Minion, and Aristides Serlemitsos.

It was an honor to work with the NPR *Planet Money* team in 2013 as they followed their own T-shirt around the world. I am especially grateful to Adam Davidson of NPR, who plucked the first edition of this book from his large pile of review manuscripts in 2005, and who initially brought the T-shirt's story to the radio.

Pietra Rivoli
July 2014

NOTES

PREFACE

1. Polyani, *The Great Transformation*.
2. Dougherty, *Who's Afraid of Adam Smith?*
3. Pew Research Center, "Beyond Red vs. Blue."
4. For a recent examination of the relationship between trade and inequality, see Helpman et al., "Trade and Inequality."
5. For an exposition of this position, see Stiglitz, "Inequality Is Not Inevitable," *New York Times*.
6. The Accord on Fire Safety and Building Safety in Bangladesh is an agreement signed following the Rana Plaza collapse. Details are at www.Bangladeshaccord.org.

PART I

CHAPTER 1 (pgs. 3–8)

1. See Gillham et al., *Cotton Production Prospects*, as well as data reported at www.usda.gov/nass/.
2. Porter, *The Competitive Advantage of Nations*,15.
3. See Oxfam, "Fairness in the Fields" and "Cultivating Poverty."
4. Williams, "Talks Unravel over Cotton."
5. De Jonquières and Williams, "Top WTO Nations Hail Deal on Doha."

CHAPTER 2 (pgs. 9–23)

1. Quoted in Dodge, *Cotton: The Plant That Would Be King*, 40–41.
2. Data are from Bruchey, *Cotton and the Growth of the American Economy*, which also contains an in-depth discussion of the U.S. cotton industry during this period.
3. Earle, "The Price of Precocity: Technical Choice and Ecological Constraint in the Cotton South, 1840–1890."
4. Wright, *The Political Economy of the Cotton South*.
5. Callender, "The Early Transportation and Banking Enterprises of the States in Relation to the Growth of Corporations," 118.
6. Wright, *The Political Economy of the Cotton South*, 28, 52.
7. Breeden, *Advice Among Masters: The Ideal in Slave Management in the Old South*, contains a number of rich sources on the planters' management of slave labor.
8. DeBow, reproduced in Bruchey, *Cotton and the Growth of the American Economy*, 84.

9. Whitney's letters are compiled in Hammond, "Correspondence of Eli Whitney Relative to the Invention of the Cotton Gin."
10. Bruchey, *Cotton and the Growth of the American Economy*, Tables 1a and 1c.
11. Landes, *The Wealth and Poverty of Nations*, 157.
12. Ibid., 157.
13. Ibid., 342.
14. Ibid., 342.
15. Ibid., 336.
16. Ibid., 342.
17. Andrews (1853), reproduced in Bruchey, 71. Other Western European colonies, of course, also relied on slave labor. Production on plantations in the Caribbean and South America was devoted especially to sugar and rubber.
18. Hammond, "Speech Before the U.S. Senate, 1858," *Congressional Globe*, March 4, 1859, p. 959.
19. Ibid.
20. A recent study of this topic is Schmidt, *Free to Work*. See also the discussion in Daniel, *Breaking the Land*.
21. In *The Cotton Plantation South*, Aiken discusses the implication of crop lien laws during this period.
22. Johnson, Embree, and Alexander, *The Collapse of Cotton Tenancy*, 25.
23. Rosengarten, *All God's Dangers*, 106.
24. Johnson, Embree, and Alexander, *The Collapse of Cotton Tenancy*, 12.
25. See Daniel, *Breaking the Land*, Chapter 1, for a discussion of the government's attempt to manage the boll weevil and the disparate effects on rich and poor farmers.
26. Street, *The New Revolution in the Cotton Economy*, 38.
27. Rosengarten, *All God's Dangers*, 144.
28. Ibid., 223.
29. Foley, *The White Scourge*, 120.
30. Aiken, *The Cotton Plantation South*, 109.
31. Material on the Taft Ranch is from Foley (1996 and 1997).

CHAPTER 3 (pgs. 24–48)

1. Chapters 3 and 4 are largely based on interviews conducted in Lubbock and the surrounding area during eight visits between 2000 and 2008. Interviewees include Nelson, Ruth, and Lamar Reinsch; Wally Darneille, Bryan Gregory, John Johnson, Grady Martin, Joseph Tubb, Lonnie Winters, and Jack Kenwright of the Plains Cotton Cooperative Association; Don Harper and Ron Harkey of the Farmers Cooperative Compress; Randy Kennedy and Barbara Burleson of the Citizens Shallowater Cooperative Gin; Michael Henson, Levelland cotton grower; Craig Moore of PYCO; Kenny Day of the USDA Lubbock classing office; Roger Haldenby of Plains Cotton Growers; Professors Randy Allen, Dick Auld, Donna Davis, and Dale Duhan of Texas Tech University; Ralph and Naomi Hoelscher, organic cotton growers; Kelly Pepper of Texas Organic Marketing Cooperative; and Craig Moore of PYCO Industries. In Washington, Hunter Colby, Stephen MacDonald, and Carol Skelly of the USDA were helpful on several occasions. I conducted telephone interviews with Dave Kinard of the

National Cottonseed Producer's Association, Gail Kring of PYCO, Terry Townsend of the International Cotton Advisory Committee, and Ed Price of the USDA.

2. The proposed seal can be seen in Blackburn, "Cotton Stripped from Texas Tech Seal," available at www.lubbockonline.com/stories/050505/loc_050505026.shtml.

3. Blackburn, "Cotton Stripped from Texas Tech Seal."

4. Day, "The Economics of Technological Change and the Demise of the Sharecropper." Other classic studies on the mechanization of cotton production include Sayre, "Cotton Mechanization Since World War II," and Street, *The New Revolution in the Cotton Economy*. See also Ellenberg, *From Mule South to Tractor South*.

5. Rosengarten, *All God's Dangers*, 466.

6. In *Mule South to Tractor South*, historian George Ellenberg traces both the history and the social significance of the shift from mules to tractors in the Deep South.

7. Quoted in Grove, "The Mexican Farm Labor Program," 309.

8. Foley, "Mexicans, Mechanization, and the Growth of Corporate Cotton Culture," 285, 295.

9. Grove, "The Mexican Farm Labor Program," 307.

10. Ibid., 312–313.

11. Daniel, *Breaking the Land*, 94–95.

12. Rosengarten, *All God's Dangers*, 500.

13. Ibid., 492.

14. Dewan, "Black Farmers' Refrain: Where's All Our Money?" and Fears, "USDA Is Called Lax on Bias."

15. Dick Auld also makes this point in his interview with National Public Radio for "The World in a T-Shirt," produced by Adam Davidson. The program is available at www.npr.org/templates/story/story.php?storyId=4620285.

16. Gwin, "Looking Back: No Cotton Picking for Me, Thanks."

17. The MSDS for Bayer Crop Science's Ginstar cotton defoliant is at www.bayercropscienceus.com/products_and_seeds/regulators/ginstar.html.

18. A video of the John Deere 7760 in action may be seen at www.deere.com/en_US/ag/feature/2007/product_intro/7760cotton_picker.html.

19. Pollock, "Widely Used Crop Herbicide Is Losing Weed Resistance."

20. Laws, "Growers Say: Flex May Revolutionize Weed Control."

21. The cost multiple is my estimate, based on communications with Roger Haldenby of Plains Cotton Growers.

22. Sales data are from Hoovers Online, accessed 5/14/2007. Though the chemical formulation in Roundup herbicide no longer enjoys patent protection, Monsanto employs a number of strategies to keep growers from switching to generic versions.

23. Stock prices obtained from www.cnnfn.com, accessed May 18, 2008. Also see Anderson, "Monsanto's Dominance Continues."

24. A nontechnical description of Bt cotton challenges is Barnett, "Economic Challenges of Transgenic Crops: The Case of Bt Cotton."

25. USDA, "Adoption of Genetically Engineered Crops in the U.S.: Cotton Varieties."

26. Studies on the economic impact of GM cotton include Frisvold and Reeves, "Economy-Wide Impacts of Bt Cotton"; Blackshear, Johnson, and Gum, "Profitability and Cost of Production of Roundup Ready versus Conventional Cotton Varieties in the Southern High Plains of Texas"; Brookes and Barfoot, *GM Crops: The First Ten Years*.

27. Wally Darneille of the Plains Cotton Cooperative told me that the typical west Texas grower might perform up to 15 insecticide sprays per season with conventional cotton and only one or two with Bt cotton. This is consistent with research that shows that insecticide use has dropped sharply with the adoption of Bt cotton. See, for example, Becker, "Insecticides Reduced in Runoff from Bt Cotton."
28. Richardson, "Food Shortage Recasts Image of 'Organic.'"
29. Weiss, "Firms Seek Patents of 'Climate Ready' Altered Crops."
30. Readers of a younger age can see the commercial too: www.youtube.com/watch?v=LLrTPrp-fW8:.
31. Roberson, "Herbicide-Resistant Weeds Plague Cotton, Peanut Growers"; Pollack, "Widely Used Crop Herbicide Is Losing Weed Resistance."
32. ICAC, "Biotechnology Applications in Cotton: Concerns and Challenges," www.icac.org/cotton_info/speeches/Chaudhry/2007/pakistan_march_2007.pdf.
33. See Hartley, "Grain Farmer Claims Moral Victory in Seed Battle," and Simon, "Monsanto Wins Patent Case on Plant Genes."
34. Brookes and Barfoot: GM Crops: The First Ten Years.
35. Traxler and Falck-Zepeda, "The Distribution of Benefits from the Introduction of Transgenic Cotton Varieties."

CHAPTER 4 (pgs. 49–73)

1. In Cotton's Renaissance, Jacobson and Smith provide a careful study of marketing innovation in the industry.
2. See Anthony and Mayfield, Cotton Ginners Handbook, 6 and USDA, "New Technologies for Cotton Gins Combine for Big Savings."
3. For a survey of USDA involvement in this research, see Finlay, "The Industrial Utilization of Farm Products and By-Products: The USDA Regional Research Laboratories."
4. Sansom, "From Trash to Treasure."
5. Wrenn, Cinderella of the New South, xvi.
6. Lichtenstein, Field to Fabric, 33.
7. USITC Dataweb, accessed 5/16/2008.
8. Hayes, "Aquaculture Gets Hooked on Oilmeals," 1.
9. Ibid., 1.
10. Buckley, "Starting at the Bottom," 2B.
11. www.deltabusinessjournal.com/archives/7-99, accessed 1/25/04.
12. Personal communication with Mr. Ron Harkey, President of the FCC, May 16, 2007.
13. This discussion of the cotton farmers' early foray into the textile industry is based on Lichtenstein, Field to Fabric. The material on the current operations of the mill is based on my discussions with Bryan Gregory, VP of Textile Manufacturing for Plains Cotton Growers, in December 2007.
14. Rosengarten, All God's Dangers, 190.
15. Lichtenstein, Field to Fabric, 38.
16. USDA, The Classification of Cotton, contains a description of HVI cotton-testing processes.
17. Oxfam, Cultivating Poverty, discussed throughout.

18. Agricultural Outlook reported in "Cultivating Poverty," 33; Hart, "Agricultural Situation Spotlight," Figure 1.
19. This description of the 2002 Farm Bill is necessarily simplified. In particular, I abstract from the "base acreage/base yield" complexities, which link the farmers' direct payment and the countercyclical payment to their historical cotton acreage and yields, rather than to current production. Farmers may receive these payments even if their land is not planted in cotton, or even if it is not planted at all. Subsidies therefore technically depend on historical acreage and yields rather than current acreage and yields. Also, the "loan rate" is adjusted for cotton quality. For a detailed description, see Westcott, Young, and Price, *The 2002 Farm Act*.
20. Meyer, MacDonald, and Foreman, "Cotton Backgrounder," 21–22.
21. Ibid., 17.
22. Ibid., 21.
23. Environmental Working Group Farm Subsidy database at http://farm.ewg.org/sites/farmbill2007/progdetail1614.php?fips=48219&progcode=cotton.
24. Carter, "Subsidies' Harvest of Misery"; Oxfam, "Fairness in the Fields"; Bread for the World's Campaign directed at the 2007 Farm Bill is described at www.bread.org.
25. James and Griswold, "Freeing the Farm: A Farm Bill for All Americans"; Reidl, "Seven Reasons to Veto the Farm Bill." The Bush Administration proposed that government payments under the crop subsidy programs be limited for farmers earning over $200,000 per year. Related press releases are at www.whitehouse.gov.
26. The Environmental Working Group has compiled more than 400 newspaper editorials opposed to the 2007 Farm Bill. See www.ewg.org/farmeditorials.
27. The formal title of the "Farm Bill" is the Food, Conservation, and Energy Act of 2008.
28. Grassley, "Smearing Lipstick on a Pig."
29. FAOSTAT, cited in Oxfam, "Cultivating Poverty," 9. Additional detail for African producers is in Baghdadli, Cheikhrouhou, and Raballand, "Strategies for Cotton in West and Central Africa."
30. Chaudhry, *Update on Costs of Producing Cotton in the World*.
31. ICAC and Estur, "Africa's Cotton in the World."
32. U.S. cotton subsidies by year are reported by the Environmental Working Group: http://farm.ewg.org/sites/farm/progdetail.php?fips=00000&progcode=cotton.
    USAID assistance to Africa in 2006 was $1.6 billion. See USAID's "Greenbook" at http://qesdb.usaid.gov/gbk/query_historical.html.
33. Under pressure from the WTO and other cotton-producing countries, the United States plans to continue to decouple production from subsidies so that subsidies do not lead to higher production. However, because of the specialized assets associated with cotton production, subsidies—even when decoupled from production—often encourage higher cotton production.
34. Econometric studies of the effects of cotton subsidies include Anderson, Martin, and der Mensbrugghe, "Doha Merchandise Trade Reform: What Is at Stake for Developing Countries?"; Pan, *The Impact of U.S. Cotton Programs*; Poonyth et al., *The Impact of Domestic and Trade Policies on the World Cotton Market*; Sumner, *A Quantitative Simulation Analysis of the Impacts of U.S. Cotton Subsidies on Cotton Prices and Quantities*; and Tokarick, *Measuring*

the Impact of Distortions in Agricultural Trade in Partial and General Equilibrium. See also The World Bank, *World Development Report 2008*, Chapter 4.

35. This point is developed in several articles compiled in Moseley and Gray, *Hanging by a Thread: Cotton, Globalization, and Poverty in Africa.*

36. For Benin, see Bingen, "Genetically Engineered Cotton." For Burkina Faso, see Gray, "Cotton Production in Burkina Faso."

37. See the sources cited in Eisa et al., *Cotton Production Prospects*, 26. On the challenges facing African cotton farmers, see Carr, *Improving Cash Crops in Africa;* Baghdadli, Cheikhrouhou, and Raballand, "Strategies for Cotton in West and Central Africa."

38. Lapierre-Fortin, *Constructing Fair Trade from the Bottom Up: An Examination of Notions of Fairness in the Conventional Cotton Trade of Burkina Faso.*

39. See the research discussed in Baghdadli, Cheikrouhou, and Raballand, "Strategies for Cotton in West and Central Africa," 41.

40. Ibid., 46.

41. Bassett, "Producing Poverty: Power Relations and Price Formation in the Cotton Commodity Chains of West Africa," 54.

42. Lapierre-Fortin, *Constructing Fair Trade from the Bottom Up: An Examination of Notions of Fairness in the Conventional Cotton Trade of Burkina Faso*, 56. On the monopoly power of cotton traders and input suppliers, see Bassett, "Producing Poverty: Power Relations and Price Formation in the Cotton Commodity Chains of West Africa."

43. Eisa et al., *Cotton Production Prospects*, 28.

44. Kutting, "Globalization, Poverty and the Environment in West Africa: Too Poor to Pollute?"

45. On the challenge of organic cotton production in poor countries, see Dowd, "Organic Cotton in Sub-Saharan Africa: A New Development Paradigm?" and ICAC, "Limitations on Organic Cotton Production." A more optimistic view is Lakhal and H'Mida, "The Economics of Organic and Conventional Cotton Cultivation in Mali: Country and Farmers Analysis."

46. Huang et al., "Bt Cotton Benefits, Costs, and Impacts in China."

47. The results are summarized in Wang, Just, and Pinstrup-Andersen, "Bt Cotton and Secondary Pests."

48. Wang, Just, and Pinstrup-Andersen, "Tarnishing Silver Bullets," 8.

49. Smale, Zambrano, and Cartel, "Bales and Balance: A Review of the Methods Used to Assess the Economic Impact of Bt Cotton on Farmers in Developing Economies," 209.

50. For a discussion of the research related to illegal cottonseed in India, see Frisvold and Reeves, "Economy-Wide Impacts of Bt Cotton."

51. For the specific case of Africa, see Paarlberg, *Starved for Science.*

52. ICAC, "Executive Summary of the Report of the Second Expert Panel on Biotechnology of Cotton."

53. See Delmer, "Agriculture in the Developing World: Connecting Innovations in Plant Research to Downstream Applications"; The World Bank, *Agriculture for Development*, Chapter 7; Kiers et al., "Agriculture at a Crossroads."

54. Bradsher and Martin, "World's Poor Pay Price as Crop Research Is Cut."

55. The World Bank, *Agriculture for Development*, 167.
56. Baghdadli, Cheikhrouhou, and Raballand, "Strategies for Cotton in West and Central Africa."
57. Karp, "Deadly Crop," 1A; Sengupta, "On India's Farms, a Plague of Suicide." A Frontline video on this topic, "Seeds of Suicide," is available at www.pbs.org/frontlineworld/rough/2005/07/seeds_of_suicid.html.

PART II

CHAPTER 5 (pgs. 77–91)

1. In addition to the secondary sources cited, I have relied on interviews and factory visits in China during eight visits between 2000 and 2008. The most extensive interviews were conducted with Patrick Xu, Hong Yan, Tao Yong Fang, Su Qin, Li Guo Ping, He Yuan Zhi, Mike Mikkelborg, Lijun Qu, and Manfred Tsai. A number of workers and managers with whom I spoke declined to be named.
2. Laws, "China Cotton Consumption Trends Up."
3. United States International Trade Commission Dataweb, accessed 5/28/08.
4. See Honig, *Sisters and Strangers*, Table 1, 24. A detailed study of the labor–management relations in the early cotton textile industry in eastern China is Köll, *From Cotton Mill to Business Empire*.
5. The classic account of the Chinese labor movement during this period is Chesneaux, *The Chinese Labor Movement*.
6. Honig, *Sisters and Strangers*, 10.
7. Quoted in Ling, *In Search of Old Shanghai*, 93.
8. Honig, *Sisters and Strangers*, 1.
9. Reporters without Borders ranks China 44 out of 48 countries in freedom of the press, while the Milkin Institute ranks China 58 out of 71 in its "Opacity Index."
10. Giles, "China's Labor Market in the Wake of Economic Restructuring."
11. Chinese Chamber of Commerce for Export and Import of Textiles, accessed 6/2/08.
12. Import data are from OTEXA, for apparel categories 338 and 339.
13. World Trade Atlas, accessed 5/28/08.
14. www.nlcnet.org/china, accessed 3/7/01.
15. Author's calculations from UN Comtrade data, based on SITC code 84 (apparel).
16. National Labor Committee (1998), p. 1; www.nlc.net.org/China, accessed 6/21/00.
17. For a comprehensive treatment of China's environmental challenges, see Economy, *The River Runs Black*.

CHAPTER 6 (pgs. 92–104)

1. For comparative indicators of development, see Pomeranz, *The Great Divergence*.
2. See Blue, "China and Western Social Thought in the Modern Period."
3. Chao and Chao, *The Development of Cotton Textile Production in China*, 28.
4. Quoted in Dodge, *Cotton: The Plant That Would Be King*, 21.
5. Ibid.

6. Deane, *The First Industrial Revolution*, 92.

7. Quoted in Deane, 87.

8. A recent discussion of labor policies in early British textile factories is in Rose, *Firms, Networks, and Business Values*.

9. Pinchbeck, *Women Workers and the Industrial Revolution*, 188.

10. Ibid., 190.

11. Ibid., 194.

12. Ibid., 190.

13. Robson, *The Cotton Industry in Britain*, Table A2, 334; Bazely (1854), cited in Farnie, *The English Cotton Industry and the World Market*.

14. Dalzell, *Enterprising Elites*, 5.

15. Ibid., 5.

16. Ibid.

17. Rose, *Firms, Networks, and Business Values*, 41.

18. www.psnh.com/AboutPSNH/EnergyPark/Amoskeg.asp, accessed 1/27/04. See Hareven and Langenbach, *Amoskeag: Life and Work in an American Factory City*, for oral histories from former Amoskeag workers.

19. Rose, *Firms, Networks, and Business Values*, 198.

20. Cited in Ware, *The Early New England Cotton Manufacture*, 249.

21. Ibid., 250, 252.

22. Ibid., 252.

23. Ibid., 251.

24. See Josephson, *The Golden Threads*, for an early treatment of the social controls on New England mill girls. Additional insight may be gleaned from the letters collected in Dublin, *Farm to Factory*.

25. Josephson, *The Golden Threads*, 23.

26. Hareven and Langenbach, *Amoskeag*, 20.

27. Kane, *Textiles in Transition*, presents a careful study of the movement of the U.S. cotton textile industry from New England to the South. A more recent study is English, *A Common Thread*.

28. For analyses of wage differentials between Northern and Southern mills, see Wright, "Cheap Labor and Southern Textiles," and Kane, *Textiles in Transition*.

29. Holleran, "Child Labor and Exploitation in Turn-of-the-Century Cotton Mills."

30. Saxonhouse and Wright, "Two Forms of Cheap Labor in Textile History."

31. Hearden, *Independence and Empire*, 125.

32. Ibid., 102–103.

33. U.S. Department of State, cited in Hearden, 66.

34. Ibid., 129.

35. Ibid., 128–129.

36. Ibid., 129.

37. Michl, cited in Rose, *Firms, Networks, and Business Values*, 204.

38. Copeland, *The Cotton Manufacturing Industry of the United States*, 40–41.

39. Ibid.

40. Byerly, *Hard Times Cotton Mill Girls*, 45.

41. Ibid., 3.

42. Robson, *The Cotton Industry in Britain*, 4.

43. Destler, Fukui, and Sato, *Textile Wrangle*, 29.
44. McNamara, *Textiles and Industrial Transition*, 36–37.
45. Chokki, "Labor Management in the Cotton Spinning Industry."
46. Moser, *The Cotton Textile Industry of Far Eastern Countries*, 13.
47. Tsurumi, *Factory Girls*, 107.
48. Ibid., note 1, 121.
49. Cited in Chokki, "Labor Management," 8.
50. Moser, *The Cotton Textile Industry of Far Eastern Countries*, 16.
51. See Chokki, 160, and Tsurumi, Chapter 8.
52. For numerous accounts of working conditions in early Japanese textile factories, see Tsurumi, *Factory Girls*.
53. These techniques are discussed at length in Macnaughtan, *Women, Work and the Japanese Economic Miracle*.
54. Superb analyses of the geographic movement of the textile and apparel industries in search of lower costs are in Anderson, *New Silk Roads*.
55. Beazer, *The Commercial Future of Hong Kong*, 61, 67.
56. Berger and Lester, *Made by Hong Kong*, 142.
57. Song, *The Rise of the Korean Economy*, 105; Scott, "Foreign Trade," 337.
58. Scott, "Foreign Trade," 360.

CHAPTER 7 (pgs. 105–119)

1. For a complete historical treatment of China's hukou system, see Solinger, *Contesting Citizenship in Urban China*.
2. Mackenzie, "Strangers in the City."
3. Ibid., p. 1.
4. Lu, "Balancing Rural-Urban Relations for the Sake of Rural Residents," cited in Lee, *Against the Law*, 6.
5. "Human Rights in China," *Institutionalized Exclusion*.
6. See www.aflcio.org/issuespolitics/globaleconomy/china_petition.cfm.
7. Wang and Zuo, "Inside China's Cities: Institutional Barriers and Opportunities for Urban Migrants."
8. Liang and Ma's "China's Floating Population: New Evidence from the 2000 Census" provides a survey of the hukou system and its effects. For a study specific to Shanghai, see Feng, Zuo, and Ruan, "Rural Migrants in Shanghai: Living under the Shadow of Socialism."
9. Ibid., 277.
10. Wu, "Migrant Housing in Urban China," cited in Lee, *Against the Law*, 57.
11. Ibid., 278.
12. Wu and Treiman, "The Household Registration System and Social Stratification in China."
13. "Off to the City," *The Economist*.
14. Whalley and Zhang, "A Numerical Simulation Analysis of (hukou) Labor Mobility Restrictions in China"; Démurger et al., "Geography, Economic Policy, and Regional Development in China." Similarly, liberalization of the hukou system has been found to reduce inequality. See Hertel and Zhai, "Labor Market Distortions, Rural–Urban

Inequality and the Opening of China's Economy," and *China Daily*, "Graduates Prefer Hukou over High Salary."

15. Woodman, "China's Dirty Clean Up."

16. Ibid.

17. Knight, Song, and Huaibin, "Chinese Rural Migrants."

18. "Off to the City," *The Economist*.

19. Amnesty International, "People's Republic of China: Internal Migrants: Discrimination and Abuse—The Human Cost of an Economic 'Miracle.'"

20. Kuhn, "Migrants: A High Price to Pay for a Job," 30.

21. Ibid., 30.

22. Amnesty International, "People's Republic of China," 12.

23. See the studies cited in Amnesty International, "People's Republic of China."

24. Knight, Song, and Huaibin, "Chinese Rural Migrants," 92.

25. Ibid., 91–92.

26. Wang, *Organizing Through Division and Exclusion: China's Hukou System*, 120. On the role of the hukou system in China's economic development see also Zhu, "China's Floating Population and Their Settlement Intention in the Cities: Beyond the Hukou Reform."

27. For a survey of China labor issues, see Chan, *China's Workers under Assault*. For a recent account of the lives of young women in China's factories, see Chang, *Factory Girls*.

28. Pinchbeck, *Women Workers and the Industrial Revolution*, 17.

29. Byerly, *Hard Times Cotton Mill Girls*, 64–65.

30. Lee, *Gender and the South China Miracle*, 78.

31. Ibid., 78.

32. Photos and audio of Japi are available at "Behind Shanghai's Boom Is a Simple T-Shirt," produced by NPR's Adam Davidson. See www.npr.org/templates/story/story.php?storyId=4621936.

33. Honig, *Creating Chinese Ethnicity*, 62–63.

34. Hall et al., *Like a Family*, 66.

35. See Minchin, *What Do We Need a Union For?* for an in-depth treatment of the integration of the Southern textile industry.

36. Hall et al., *Like a Family*, 157.

37. Byerly, *Hard Times Cotton Mill Girls*, 141.

38. Ibid., 94.

39. Kristof and WuDunn, *Thunder from the East*, 128.

40. Josephson, *The Golden Threads*, 64.

41. Lee, *Gender and the South China Miracle*.

42. Ibid., 5–9.

43. Ibid., 134–135.

44. Ibid., 130.

45. For Korea, see Kim, *Class Struggle or Family Struggle?* For Taiwan, see Kung, *Factory Women in Taiwan*.

46. Josephson, *The Golden Threads*, 92.

47. Frowne (1902), quoted in Stein, *Out of the Sweatshop*.

48. Hessler, "Letter from China."

49. Hume (1748), quoted in Anderson, *New Silk Roads*, xvix.

50. Schlosser, "Urban Life," 22.
51. Pressley, "The South's New-Car Smell," A1.
52. Goodman, "In NC, a Second Industrial Revolution."
53. Mui, "Ikea Helps a Town Put It Together," A1.
54. For a discussion of the role of the apparel industry in broader development, see Schrank, "Ready-to-Wear Development? Foreign Investment, Technology Transfer, and Learning by Watching in the Apparel Trade."

CHAPTER 8 (pgs. 120–139)

1. See discussions in Varley, *The Sweatshop Quandary*, and Pollin et al., *Global Apparel Production*. Dickson (2000) discusses the effects of social issues on apparel consumers' behavior.
2. Hutchins and Harrison, *History of Factory Legislation*, provides a full account of early British factory legislation.
3. Engels, *The Condition of the Working Class*, 170.
4. Ibid., 173.
5. Byerly, *Hard Times Cotton Mill Girls*, 85.
6. Tsurumi, *Factory Girls*, 44, 168.
7. Hutchins and Harrison, *History of Factory Legislation*, 248.
8. Losciale, "Rules May Ease Aches."
9. McCracken, "The Lives They Lived."
10. U.S. Department of Labor, *Wages, Benefits, Poverty Line*.
11. Spar and Burns, "Hitting the Wall," 5.
12. Supply chains in the apparel industry, especially in relation to working conditions, are discussed in a number of articles compiled in Hale and Willis, *Threads of Labour*, as well as in Bonacich and Appelbaum, *Behind the Label*. The classic business guide to apparel supply chains is Birnbaum, *Birnbaum's Global Guide to Winning the Great Garment War*.
13. The anti-sweatshop movement of this period is described at length in Bonacich and Appelbaum, *Behind the Label*.
14. See, for example, Rosoff, "Beyond Codes of Conduct." A number of case studies of U.S. corporations' current practices are in Hartman et al., *Rising above Sweatshops*.
15. Saidazimova, "Central Asia: Child Labor Alive and Thriving."
16. Nike, *Innovate for a Better World*.
17. Aaronson and Rioux, "Striking a Proper Match? Strategies to Link Trade Agreements and Real Labor Rights Improvements."
18. Dickson, Loker, and Eckman, *Social Responsibility in the Global Apparel Industry*.
19. Sinderbrand, "From the Start, Sit-In Was a Concerted Effort."
20. See Doorey, "Can Factory List Disclosure Improve Labor Practices in the Apparel Industry?" and Harrison and Scorse, "Improving the Conditions of Workers? Minimum Wage Legislation and Anti-Sweatshop Activism."
21. Georgetown's code of conduct for supplier factories is at www8.georgetown.edu/admin/publicaffairs/loc/code.html.
22. WRC' university affiliates, factory reports, and governance structure are available at www.workersrights.org.

23. Featherstone, *Students against Sweatshops*, chronicles the development of the student-led anti-sweatshop movement in the United States. Recent developments, such as the DSP, may be followed at www.workersrights.org.

24. Steinberg, *Nature Incorporated: Industrialization and the Waters of New England*, 15–16.

25. Allwood et al., "Well-Dressed?" For discussions of the environmental impacts of the textile and apparel industries, see also Chen and Burns, "Environmental Analysis of Textile Products"; Slater, *Environmental Impact of Textiles*; and Hethhorn and Ulasewicz, *Sustainable Fashion: Why Now*.

26. EDIPTEX, "Environmental Assessment of Textiles," 30.

27. This discussion of phthalates is based on Chapter 3 in Schapiro, *Exposed: The Toxic Chemistry of Everyday Products and What's at Stake for American Power*.

28. Swan et al., "Decrease in Anogenital Distance...." *Environmental Health Perspectives*.

29. This argument is developed in Speth, *The Bridge at the End of the World*.

30. Though the "Environmental Kuzets Curve" has strong empirical support, the causal relationship between economic growth and environmental quality could take a number of forms. For example, it may be that as countries become wealthier they are better able to put in place efficient regulatory structures; that the marginal cost of containing pollution falls as the economy reaches a certain size, or simply that richer countries are more willing to trade income for environmental quality. Israel and Levinson, "Willingness to Pay for Environmental Quality," examine these possible causal relationships in depth.

31. Israel and Levinson, "Willingness to Pay for Environmental Quality," 1.

32. Copeland and Taylor, *Trade and the Environment*, 3.

33. Levinson, "Technology, International Trade, and Pollution from U.S. Manufacturing."

34. Lovely and Popp, "Trade, Technology, and the Environment: Why Have Poor Countries Regulated Sooner?"

35. Layton, "Chemical Law Has Global Impact: E.U.'s New Rules Forcing Changes by U.S. Firms."

36. Pereira, "Protests Spur Stores to Seek Substitute for Vinyl in Toys."

37. Reuters, "California OK's Phthalates Ban on Children's Products."

38. *The Economist*, "Get Your Green Pants Here."

39. See Ederington, Levinson, and Minier, "Trade Liberalization and Pollution Havens."

40. Frankel, "The Environment and Economic Globalization." See also Frankel and Rose, "Is Trade Good or Bad for the Environment? Sorting out the Causality." For additional studies of the relationship between trade and the environment, see Copeland and Taylor, *Trade and the Environment*, and the research cited therein.

41. Harney, *The China Price*.

42. Ibid., 202.

43. Ibid., 35.

44. Spencer, "Ravaged Rivers."

45. Ibid.

46. Economy, *The River Runs Black*.

47. Frankel (2005) develops this point in the context of environmental issues.

48. Annual reports by Freedom House, Reporters without Borders, and the Milkin Institute provide data on political and civil liberties, press freedom, and measure of corruption over time. All are updated frequently and are available online.

49. Lee, *Against the Law: Labor Protests in China's Rustbelt and Sunbelt*, ix.
50. Ibid. See especially Chapter 5.
51. Cha, "New Law Gives Chinese Workers Power, Gives Businesses Nightmares."
52. See the sources cited in Economy, *The River Runs Black*, 87–88.
53. Batson, "China's Eco-Watchdog Gets Teeth."
54. Fong and Canaves, "South China's Factories Lose Edge as Costs Climb."
55. Spencer, "Ravaged Rivers."
56. Cha, "New Law Gives Chinese Workers Power, Gives Businesses Nightmares."
57. See Moran, *Beyond Sweatshops*, for a survey.
58. Dougherty, *Who's Afraid of Adam Smith?* See especially Chapter 3.
59. *Emerging Textiles*, "Apparel Manufacturing Labor Costs in 2008."
60. *China Daily*, "Hit the Door."
61. Birns, *Assignment Shanghai*.

PART III

CHAPTER 9 (pgs. 143–155)

1. Chapters 9 through 12 rely on numerous interviews during 2001 to 2008 in Washington; New York; Alexander City and Florence, Alabama; North Carolina; and Shanghai. Erik Autor, Phyllis Bonanno, James Bryan, Kevin Burke, Christopher Champion, Michelle Eubanks, Anna Flaaten, Eddie Gant, Nate Herman, Jennifer Hillman, Julia Hughes, John Jackson, Brenda Jacobs, Cass Johnson, Donna Lee McGee, Steve Lamar, Michael Levy, Carlos Moore, James Moore, Paul O'Day, Ralph Reinecke, Coleman Rich, Michael Ryan, Ronald Sorini, Richard Stetson, Auggie Tantillo, Mike Todaro, Earl Whipple, Patrick Xu, and Tom Young were particularly helpful. For current developments on textile trade policy, I relied especially on electronic updates from Sandler, Travis, and Rosenberg, P.A. Telephone discussions were held with Jack Albertine, Ross Arnold, Michael Hubbard, Jeff Martin, and David Trumbull.
2. Underhill, *Industrial Crisis*, 4.
3. American Apparel & Footwear Association, "The U.S. Apparel and Footwear Industries: A Primer."
4. Joint Textile Industry letter on China to President Bush at www.atmi.org, accessed 5/20/03. The letter was signed by American Textile Manufacturers Institute, American Manufacturing Trade Action Coalition, National Textile Association, American Yarn Spinners Association, American Fiber Manufacturers Association, National Cotton Council, American Sheep Industry Association, American Textile Machinery Association, Carpet and Rug Institute, Association of Georgia's Textile, Carpet & Consumer Products Manufacturers, Hosiery Association, Industrial Fabrics Association International, North Carolina Manufacturers Association, and Textile Distributors Association.
5. For an account of the pre-election safeguard campaign, see Blustein, "Textile Makers Fight for Limits." The status of China safeguard petitions is reported at ww.otexa.ita.doc.
6. Data on plant closings and job losses are from www.ncto.org.
7. OTEXA trade database, accessed 7/1/08.

8. CAFTA is sometimes referred to as CAFTA-DR, because the Dominican Republic is not geographically located in Central America. A nontechnical summary of the textile and apparel provisions of the agreement is at http://otexa.ita.doc.gov.

9. Status and texts of free trade agreements and trade preference programs are available at http://otexa.ita.doc.gov.

10. The status of various textile monitoring agreements may be followed at the OTEXA web site.

11. www.customs.gov/xp/cgov/import/textiles_and_quotas/archived/.

12. STRtradenews, "When Customs Knocks."

13. Dickerson, *Textiles and Apparel in the Global Economy*, 399.

14. Friman, *Patchwork Protectionism*.

CHAPTER 10 (pgs. 156–170)

1. Includes employment in NCAIS categories 313 (textile mills), 314 (textile product mills), and 316 (apparel). See www.bls.gov for employment data by industry.

2. Friman, "Rocks, Hard Places, and the New Protectionism," 691.

3. On the effects of geographic concentration on political influence in trade policy, see Schiller, "Trade Politics in the American Congress," or Metcalfe and Goodwin, "An Empirical Analysis of the Determinants of Trade Policy Protection."

4. Aggarwal, *Liberal Protectionism*, 164.

5. The Reagan letter is excerpted in Brandis, *The Making of Textile Trade Policy*, 56.

6. Conti, *Reconciling Free Trade*, xiv.

7. See Conti for an analysis of presidential rhetoric related to trade.

8. Quoted in Rosen, *Making Sweatshops*, 82.

9. Quoted in Rothgeb, *U.S. Trade Policy*, 102.

10. Aggarwal, *Liberal Protectionism*, 53

11. Ikenson, *Threadbare Excuses*, 9.

12. Cline, *The Future of World Trade in Textiles*, 163.

13. Vinson's letter is excerpted in Brandis, *The Making of Textile Trade Policy*, 25.

14. Aggarwal, *Liberal Protectionism*, 111.

15. Aggarwal, 69.

16. Nixon, "Special Message to the Congress on United States Trade Policy."

17. Brandis, *The Making of Textile Trade Policy*, 46.

18. Cline, *The Future of World Trade in Textiles*, 150; GATT principles prohibit quantitative restraints, or quotas, as well as market access that discriminates across countries.

19. Cline, *The Future of World Trade in Textiles*, 163.

20. Ikenson, *Threadbare Excuses*, 10.

21. Dickerson, *Textiles and Apparel in the Global Economy*, 365.

22. The classic exposition of the role of the U.S. Congress in trade policy is Destler, *American Trade Politics*.

23. Quoted in Rothgeb, *U.S. Trade Policy*, 21.

24. Quoted in Destler, *American Trade Politics*, 4th ed., 5.

25. Quoted in Conti, *Reconciling Free Trade*, 22.

26. Dickerson, *Textiles and Apparel in the Global Economy*, 366.

27. Cline, *The Future of World Trade in Textiles*, 213.

28. In *Making Sweatshops*, Rosen provides a complete treatment of the political rise of the retail industry on the subject of trade.
29. Schott and Buurman, *The Uruguay Round*, 5.
30. USITC, "The Economic Effects of Significant U.S. Import Restraints," 61.
31. Dickerson, *Textiles and Apparel in the Global Economy*, 378.

CHAPTER 11 (pgs. 171–195)

1. Pew Global Attitudes Project, 2008.
2. James, "Race to the Bottom? The Presidential Candidates' Positions on Trade."
3. Based on employment and output data for NCAIS 313 and 314. See http://data.bls.gov/servlet/SurveyOutput/Servlet.
4. Employment and output data are available at www.bls.gov.
5. Disentangling the import effect on employment from the productivity effect is, of course, complex. The USITC estimates that the demise of the quota system will have relatively small employment effects in the United States, ranging from 1 percent in textile products to 6 percent in apparel. See USITC, "The Economic Effects of Significant U.S. Import Restraints," fourth update, Table 3-5.
6. Spiegelman and McGuckin, *China's Experience*. The authors found that China lost 1.8 million jobs in the textile sector during the 1995–2002 period, while the United States lost 202,000. During the same period, Chinese labor productivity rose by over 300 percent.
7. USITC, "Economic Effects of Significant Export Restraints," second update, 1999, 29.
8. Hufbauer and Elliott, *Measuring the Costs of Protection*, 13.
9. USITC, "Economic Effects of Significant Export Restraints," fourth update, 2004. The study's worst-case estimate for job losses due to the elimination of quotas is (in 2002) 40,040 jobs, while its lowest estimate for economywide costs is $7 billion. See p. 71 and Tables 3-1 and 3-5.
10. Brian Fennessey, remarks at USA-ITA Conference, June 25, 2008.
11. Limão, "Are Preferential Trade Agreements with Non-Trade Objectives a Stumbling Block for Multilateral Liberalization?"
12. In *Termites in the Trading System*, Bhagwati argues that the proliferation of free trade agreements poses a significant threat to the world trade regime, primarily because they institutionalize "discrimination" in trade relationships.
13. This account is based on accounts from www.insidetrade.com during September 2001 to February 2002 and from personal discussions with Ronald Sorini of Sandler, Travis, and Rosenberg; Erik Autor of the National Retail Federation; and Cass Johnson of ATMI during spring 2002. See also Blustein, "A Pakistani Setback."
14. Import quotas, as well as fill rates, may be found at www.customs.ustreas.gov/quotas/.
15. This account is based on Tanzer, "The Great Quota Hustle."
16. De Jonquières, "Clothes on the Line."
17. Remarks at USA-ITA meeting, June 25, 2008, New York.
18. Morrissey, "Customs Finds Illegal Chinese Apparel Shipments."
19. In July 2004, Kenyan authorities set ablaze 16 containers of clothing from China that were destined to be transshipped through Nairobi. Ali, "Clothes Worth Sh960m from China Set Ablaze."

20. Tanzer, "The Great Quota Hustle," 124.
21. My estimate is based on the quota prices reported by the Hong Kong Trade and Development Council at http://tdc-link.tdc.org.hk/quota/China/china.asp and the quota allocation to China at www.customs.gov/xp/cgov/import/textiles_and_quotas/textile_status_rpt/.
22. National Council of Textile Organizations, "Government of China Subsidies Applicable to the Textile Industry."
23. Irwin, *Against the Tide*, 3.
24. Ibid.
25. Ibid, 1
26. See Aaronson, *Trade and the American Dream*, as well as *Taking Trade to the Streets* by the same author, for full accounts of research related to public opinion on trade.
27. For current data on public sentiment related to trade, see the Pew Global Attitudes Project, updated annually.
28. See Irwin, *Against the Tide*, for a discussion of early views on trade.
29. For a description of a variety of anti–Wal-Mart sentiments, see Walmartwatch.org. *The Los Angeles Times* was awarded a 2004 Pulitzer for its coverage of Wal-Mart's business practices and their effects.
30. See the discussion in Irwin, *Free Trade Under Fire*, 103–104. The evidence suggests that laid-off textile and apparel workers have poorer reemployment than laid-off workers in other industries. See also Cline et al., "Socioeconomic Impacts of Manufacturing in Selected Arkansas and Texas Communities."
31. The standard manual for "strategic sourcing" is Birnbaum, *Birnbaum's Guide to Winning the Great Garment War*.
32. See www.tuscarorayarns.com/newcolor-green.
33. On high-tech textiles, see McGrane, "Smarter Clothes," and Newman, "Dreamweavers."
34. Political contributions and lobbying expenditures are available at www.opensecrets.org.
35. See Gresser, "Who Gets Hit?" and "It's Expensive Being Poor."
36. Presentation by Brian Fennessey, USA-ITA meeting, June 25, 2005, New York.
37. De Jonquières, "Clothes on the Line."
38. Calculations are based on square meter equivalents and measure the change from 2000 to 2003. See www.ita.otexa.doc for trade data by category.
39. I have based these calculations on 2001–2003 trade data for the categories that were fully released from quota in 2002. See http://otexa.ita.doc.gov/scripts/tqsum2.exe.
40. De Jonquières, "Clothes on the Line."
41. For studies on the likely market share effects of the quota phase-out, see USITC, "Textiles and Apparel," and Nordas, "The Global Textile and Clothing Industry." See also Malone, "Low-Wage Nations Import Share to Surge."
42. Malone, "Low Wage Nations Import Share to Surge."
43. Nordas, "The Global Textile and Clothing Industry," Chapter 4.
44. Magnusson, "Where Free Trade Hurts."
45. See www.fairtextiletrade.org/istanbul/declaration.html, accessed 7/1/04.

CHAPTER 12 (pgs. 196–211)

1. *Inside U.S. Trade*, "NCTO CAFTA Endorsement Based on Three Promises to Help U.S. Industry."
2. Andrews, "White House Makes Deals for Support of Trade Pact"; *Inside U.S. Trade*, "Opponents, Supporters See Textile Republicans Supporting DR-CAFTA."
3. *Inside U.S. Trade*, "Bush Officials Win Hayes, Aderholt Votes with Assurances on Textiles."
4. Sparshott, "U.S. Eyes Textile Pact with China."
5. See *Inside U.S. Trade*, "Bush Officials Win Hayes, Alderholt Votes with Assurances on Textiles," and Andrews, "U.S. to Seek Curbs on Chinese Clothing Exports."
6. Data in square meters is not always a reliable indicator of trade performance. Sri Lanka, for example, now specializes in high-end lingerie for which dollar value is high but square-meter-equivalent measures are low.
7. OTEXA trade data for categories 338/339, accessed 8/1/08.
8. NCTO, "Government of China Industry Subsidies." For current information regarding the question of currency manipulation, see http://chinacurrencycoalition.org.
9. Brenda Jacobs, remarks at USA-ITA Seminar, June 25, 2008, New York.
10. National Council of Textile Organizations, "International Textile Groups Urge U.S. Government Monitoring of Chinese Apparel Exports."
11. On developments related to the McDermott bill, see Islam, "LDCs Duty-Free Access: New Trade Bill Worries U.S. Textile Bosses"; *Emerging Textiles*, "Duty-Free Access for Bangladesh and Cambodia Offered by New U.S. Bill."
12. Morrissey, "Textile Manufacturers Have Stake in Farm Bill."
13. Brandon, "Exports, China Dominate Cotton Outlook."
14. American Apparel Producers Network, July 31, 2008.
15. The ad may be viewed at www.youtube.com/watch?v=n1KJwHvOhcs.
16. National Council of Textile Organizations, "Obama Backs Key Textile Provisions."
17. The Obama letter is reproduced in NCTO, "Obama Backs Key Textile Policy Positions."
18. Thomas, *Mercantilism and the East India Trade*, 49.
19. Thomas, 44.
20. Quoted in Lemire, *Fashion's Favourite*, 16.
21. Thomas, *Mercantilism and the East India Trade*, 50.
22. Ibid., 47.
23. Ibid., 62.
24. Quoted in Lemire, *Fashion's Favourite*, 25.
25. Lemire, 24n.
26. Thomas, *Mercantilism and the East India Trade*, 62.
27. Lemire, *Fashion's Favourite*, 31.
28. Also allowed under the various acts were the domestically produced "fustians," which combined linen and cotton.
29. Quoted in Lemire, *Fashion's Favourite*, 32.
30. See Lemire for colorful accounts of the "calicoe protests."
31. For details of the ban, see Lemire, Chapter 3.

PART IV

CHAPTER 13 (pgs. 215–226)

1. Chapters 13–15 rely especially on interviews from 2003–2008 with Ed Stubin, Sunny Stubin, and Eric Stubin of Trans-Americas Trading Company. I also rely heavily on discussions in Dar Es Salaam and subsequent correspondence with Mohammed Dewji, Gulam Dewji, Geofrey Milonge, and Mehdi Rehmtulah. The 2008 updates from Tanzania are based on field research by Henri Minion and Elina Makanja. Finally, I have benefited from discussions with Bernie Brill, formerly of Secondary Materials and Recycled Textiles (SMART); Anna Flaaten at the U.S. Department of Commerce; Said Ngosha Magonya of the Tanzanian Embassy; and members attending the SMART Association meeting in Miami in August of 2004.
2. http://dataweb.usitc.gov, accessed 8/1/08.
3. Ibid.
4. Estimates vary widely regarding the number of firms engaged in the business. I asked government officials, association officials, and businesspeople how many firms were active in the industry and was told repeatedly that "nobody knows," though most guessed several thousand. The 3,000 figure is from Brill, "Textiles."
5. Videos of Trans-Americas' operation may be seen at www.tranclo.com/.
6. Tracy, "Out with the New." Actually, I found that used jeans sell for up to $100 just a few blocks from my Georgetown office, at a shop called "Deja Blue."
7. USITC dataweb, accessed 7/22/08. Technically, Canada in some years imports more American used clothing than does Japan, but virtually all of this is then sorted and baled for subsequent re-export.
8. Zinman, "Vintage T-Shirts."
9. Jones, "Eco-Friendly Homes Are Moving into the Mainstream."
10. Lucy Norris has studied the export of shoddy from the West to India, as well as the used clothing trade in India. For fascinating accounts of both, see "Creative Entrepreneurs" and "Cloth that Lies."

CHAPTER 14 (pgs. 227–238)

1. See Reed, *Economic Change*, 47.
2. Coulson, *Tanzania: A Political Economy*, contains an assessment of Tanzania's post-independence economic policies. See also Temu and Due, "The Business Environment in Tanzania after Socialism."
3. Data for income, life expectancy, and literacy are from the World Bank, *World Development Report 2008*.
4. USITC dataweb, accessed 7/22/08.
5. Hansen, *Salaula*. Hansen refers to *salaula* (the term for used clothing from the Zambian Bemba language) rather than *mitumba* (from Swahili).
6. Hansen, 90.

CHAPTER 15 (pgs. 239–252)

1. The count of countries that ban or effectively ban used clothing is not fixed. My estimate of 30 is based on data provided by SMART, and from discussions with Anna Flaaten of the U.S. Department of Commerce.

2. See Barasa, "Cheap Imports Killing Kenya's Textile Industry"; and Dougherty, "Trade Theory vs. Used Clothes in Africa."
3. Jeter, "The Dumping Ground."
4. Tervil. "Millions Go Up in Smoke as Fire Guts Huge Market."
5. World Bank, *A World Bank Country Study: Tanzania at the Turn of the Century*, 76–78.
6. *The Economist*, "A Survey of Sub-Saharan Africa."
7. See Fafchamps, *Market Institutions*, for a comprehensive study.
8. Baden and Barber, "The Impact of the Second-Hand Clothing Trade on Developing Countries," 2.
9. USITC dataweb, accessed 7/23/08.
10. Wicks and Bigsten, *Used Clothes as Development Aid*.
11. Norris, "Cloth that Lies."
12. See, for example, w.ucc.org/disaster, accessed 9/3/04.
13. Quinn, *The Road Oft Traveled*.
14. Danielson and Skoog, "From Stagnation to Growth," discusses the case of Tanzania in this context.
15. Hansen, *Salaula*, 196.
16. EPA, *Textiles: Common Wastes & Materials*, 1.
17. In *T-Shirt Travels*, filmmaker Shantha Bloeman sees Africa's used clothing trade as symbolic of the problems created by IMF and World Bank programs.
18. The debate over the efficacy of World Bank programs in Africa is an extensive one. For an African perspective, see the papers collected in Mkandawire and Soludo, *African Voices on Structural Adjustment*.
19. Waters, "Beyond Structural Adjustment."
20. OTEXA Trade Data, accessed 7/24/08.
21. The material on these early views of trade is from Irwin, *Against the Tide*, 12–14.

CONCLUSION (pgs. 253–261)

1. Weisskopf, "Targeting the Olympic Sweatshop."
2. For a review of this literature, see Irwin, *Against the Tide*.
3. Quoted in Rothgeb, *U.S. Trade Policy*, 17.
4. Quoted in Irwin, *Against the Tide*, 17.
5. Ibid., 18.
6. Ibid., 16.
7. Nordhaus and Shellenberger, *Breakthrough*, 7.
8. Ibid., 2.

EPILOGUE (pgs. 262–285)

1. Nixon, "Farm Bill Compromise Will Change Programs and Reduce Spending."
2. For reviews of the Brazil–U.S. cotton dispute, see Baffes, "Cotton Subsidies, the WTO, and the 'Cotton Problem,'" and Schnepf, "Status of the WTO Brazil–U.S. Cotton Case."
3. The Brazilian government set up the Brazilian Cotton Institute to receive the payments. See discussion in Schnepf, "Status of the WTO Brazil—U.S. Cotton Case."
4. Schnepf, "Status of the WTO Brazil—U.S. Cotton Case," 4.

5. "The Farm Bill Could Have Been Worse," *New York Times*.
6. This brief description excludes many details. A full description of STAX may be found in Section 11017 of H.R.2642, The Agricultural Act of 2014.
7. I had many helpful conversations regarding the 2014 Farm Bill. These include interviews in spring 2014 in Lubbock and Washington with Mary Jane Buerkle and Steve Verett of Plains Cotton Growers, Darren Hudson of Texas Tech, John Johnson of Plains Cotton Cooperative, and Tom Sell of Combest and Sell.
8. Elizondo, "U.S. Farmers Scramble to Buy Brazil's Farmland."
9. *Cotton Grower*, "NCC Believes Brazil WTO Case Resolved."
10. Baragona, "Brazil Says Farm Bill Violates Trade Rules."
11. Nixon, "Farm Bill Compromise Will Change Programs and Reduce Spending."
12. World Trade Organization, "Sub-Committee Set Up on 'Cotton.'"
13. IDEAS Centre Geneva, "Cotton Newsletter 101—Last But Not Least."
14. Porto et al., *Supply Chains in Export Agriculture, Competition, and Poverty in Sub-Saharan Africa* (Washington: World Bank, 2011), 177. On the general topic of the effects of internal governance and market structure factors on African farms, see also Jouanjean, "Targeting Infrastructure Development to Foster Agricultural Trade and Market Integration in Developing Countries: An Analytical Review."
15. Dowd-Uribe, "Engineering Yields and Inequality? How Institutions and Agro-Ecology Shape Bt Cotton Outcomes in Burkina Faso."
16. Adamopoulos and Restuccia, "The Size Distribution of Farms and International Productivity Differences."
17. This discussion is based on an April 17, 2014, interview with David McCulley of Tri Global Energy, and Mike Price, President of Hale Community Energy. See also Sakeleris, "Wizard of Wind Power: Entrepreneur Bets He Can Make Alt Energy Pay."
18. Sakeleris, "Wizard of Wind Power: Entrepreneur Bets He Can Make Alt Energy Pay."
19. See Wexler, "Cotton's Crown Threatened by Manmade Fibers, " and
    U.S. Department of Agriculture, "Cotton Losing Share to Man-Made Fiber."
20. Prentice, "Plains Cotton Sells U.S. Mills as Textile Boom Continues"
21. For a summary of the Rana Plaza event, see Bolle, *Bangladesh Apparel Factory Collapse: Background in Brief.*
22. U.S. apparel import data is accessible at www.otexa.ita.doc.gov/msrpoint.htm.
23. A recent treatment of the effects of the *Hukou* system on Chinese economic performance is Dollar and Jones, "China: An Institutional view of an Unusual Macroeconomy."
24. For world apparel trade data, see the WTO Statistics Database at http://stat.wto.org/Home/WSDBHome.aspx?Language=E. For additional trade and employment data for Bangaldeshi garment industry, see Bangladesh Garment Manufacturer and Export Association at www.bgmea.com.bd/home/pages/TradeInformation#.UzMFMIWflc4.
25. For data on apparel production costs in China, see "China Textile & Clothing Production Costs Country Report," in *Emerging Textiles*. A comparative analysis of wages across leading apparel exporters is "Global Wage Trends for Apparel Workers, 2001–2011" (Workers' Rights Consortium and the Center for American Progress, 2013).

26. Deaths in the Bangladeshi garment industry have been attributed to fires, stampedes, and building collapses. Many fires have gone unreported. CBC News has chronicled the major events since 2005: www.cbc.ca/news2/interactives/timeline-bangladesh/.

27. In 2013, NPR reporter Zoe Chace interviewed the Korean and Bangladeshi businessmen who designed the 1970s collaboration: www.npr.org/blogs/money/2013/12/05/247360903/nixon-and-kimchee-how-the-garment-industry-came-to-bangladesh.

28. On the influence of the garment industry on young women in Bangladesh, see Heath and Mobarak, "Supply and Demand Constraints on Educational Investment: Evidence from Garment Sector Jobs and the Female Stipend Program in Bangladesh "; Pramanik, "Poverty and Ready-Made Garment (RMG) Workers in Bangladesh"; and Ghosh, "Despite Low Pay, Poor Work Conditions, Garment Factories Empowering Millions of Bangladeshi Women."

29. Bjork, "Inditex Builds for the Future."

30. See Zoe Chace, "Where a Truck Full of T-Shirts Gets the Same Privileges as an Ambulance": www.npr.org/blogs/money/2013/09/04/218890986/where-a-truck-full-of-t-shirts-gets-the-same-privileges-as-an-ambulance.

31. For a description of Sohel Rana's ties and influence, see Yardley, "The Most Hated Bangladeshi, Toppled from a Shady Empire."

32. The ILO reports a ratification rate of 86 percent for its core conventions, which relate to matters such as freedom of association, underage workers, and prohibitions on discrimination. See http://ilo.org/global/standards/introduction-to-international-labour-standards/conventions-and-recommendations/lang--en/index.htm.

33. Devnath, "Bangladesh Raises Minimum Wage for Garment Workers After Unrest."

34. Zain, "Bangladesh Passes New Labor Law: Workers Granted More Leeway to Form Trade Unions."

35. The text of the Accord, as well as signatories and factory inspection reports, may be viewed at www.bangladeshaccord.org/.

36. Kerman, "Universities to Require Vendors to Adopt Labor Standards."

37. Bhasin, "Walmart, Gap Lead Coalition to Create New Bangladesh Safety Pact." The text of the Alliance along with membership and action plans are at www.bangladeshworkersafety.org/action-plan.

38. Locke, *The Promise and Limits of Private Power.* For a treatment on the role of Western firms' corporate social responsibility programs in Bangladesh in particular, see Nasrullah and Rahim, *CSR in Private Enterprises in Developing Countries: Evidences from the Ready-Made Garments Industry in Bangladesh.*

39. For discussions of sourcing decisions, see Greenhouse, "Some Retailers Rethink Role in Bangladesh," and Banjo, "Inside Nike's Struggle to Balance Cost and Worker Safety in Bangladesh." See also "Asia Clothing Exports: China, Vietnam, Bangladesh, Indonesia, and Pakistan Statistical Report," Emerging Textiles, March 25, 2014.

40. Greenhouse and Manik, "Stalemate Over Safety in Bangladesh."

41. Brooks, "The Republic of Fear." Brooks's article was based on the arguments and evidence presented in Gary Haugen and Victor Boutros' 2014 book, *The Locust Effect* (Oxford: Oxford University Press).

42. Yardley, "The Most Hated Bangladeshi, Toppled from a Shady Empire."

43. U.S. apparel trade data are from OTEXA. Data are based on square meter equivalents.

44. Import penetration data for apparel are reported in American Apparel and Footwear Association, *ApparelStats 2012*, 7.

45. Ikenson, "Washington's Coddling of U.S. Textile Industry Is Hurting Shoppers." U.S. import tariffs are found in the Harmonized Tariff Schedule of the United States.

46. Information on trade agreements in effect worldwide is available from the WTO trade agreement database, accessible at http://rtais.wto.org/UI/PublicMaintainRTAHome .aspx. As of mid-2014, the United States had free-trade agreements with Australia, Bahrain, Chile, Colombia, Israel, Jordan, Korea, Morocco, Oman, Panama, Peru, and Singapore. Agreements were also in effect with Canada and Mexico under NAFTA, the Central American countries under CAFTA, and a group of African countries under AGOA. For details see www.ustr.gov/trade-agreements/free-trade-agreements.

47. The countries involved in the TTP negotiations are Australia, Brunei Darussalam, Canada, Chile, Japan, Malaysia, Mexico, New Zealand, Peru, Singapore, and Vietnam. Details regarding the content and negotiations are at http://ustr.gov/tpp.

48. Petri and Plummer, "The Trans-Pacific Partnership and Asia-Pacific Integration: Policy Implications," Peterson Institute for International Economics Policy Brief, June 2012; David Rosnick, "Gains from Trade: The Net Effect of the Trans-Pacific Partnership Agreement on U.S. Wages," Center for Economic and Policy Research, September 2013. For a brief review of the TPP debate, see Lydia DePillis, "Everything You Need to Know About the Trans Pacific Partnership," *Washington Post*, December 11, 2013.

49. Marc Davis, "Congress Urges Inclusion of 'Yarn Forward' Rule in TPP," Sourcingonlinejournal, July 16, 2013.

50. U.S. negotiating objectives for TPP are at www.ustr.gov/tpp/Summary-of-US-objectives.

51. American Apparel and Footwear Association, *ApparelStats 2014*.

52. Otexa data based on square meter equivalents.

53. Ito, "Chinese Investment Pours into Vietnamese Textile Industry on Free Trade Hopes."

54. Reichard, "Textiles 2013: The Turnaround Continues."

55. National Council of Textile Organizations. "Yarn-Forward Rule Spurs Investment in U.S. Textile Industry."

56. Trade data for used clothing is available on the OTEXA website.

57. Mfonobong Nsehe, "Ten African Multimillionaires You've Never Heard Of."

58. www.metl.net/about/company-profile.

BIBLIOGRAPHY

Aaronson, Susan A. *Trade and the American Dream: A Social History of Postwar Trade Policy.* Lexington, KY: University Press of Kentucky, 2004.

Aaronson, Susan A. *Taking Trade to the Streets: The Lost History of Public Efforts to Shape Globalization.* Ann Arbor, MI: University of Michigan Press, 2004.

Aaronson, Susan A., and Michele Rioux. "Striking a Proper Match? Strategies to Link Trade Agreement and Real Labor Rights Improvements." *Executive Summary: Labour Global Governance* (George Washington University).

Adamopoulos, Tasso, and Diego Restuccia. "The Size Distribution of Farms and International Productivity Differences." *American Economic Review* 104, 3 (June 2014):1667–1697.

Aggarwal, Vinod K. *Liberal Protectionism: The International Politics of Organized Textile Trade.* Berkeley: University of California Press, 1985.

Aiken, Charles S. *The Cotton Plantation South: Since the Civil War.* Baltimore: Johns Hopkins University Press, 1998.

Ali, Abdulsamad. "Clothes Worth Sh960m from China Set Ablaze." *The Nation* (Nairobi) (July 17, 2004).

Allwood, Julian, Cecilia de Rodriguez Soren, and Nancy Bocken. "Well Dressed?" University of Cambridge Institute for Manufacturing, 2006.

American Apparel & Footwear Association. "The U.S. Apparel and Footwear Industries: A Primer" (July 3, 2008).

———. "TRENDS: An Annual Statistical Analysis of the U.S. Apparel & Footwear Industries" (Annual 2007 Edition).

———. "ApparelStats 2012."

———. "ApparelStats 2014."

Amnesty International. "People's Republic of China: Internal Migrants: Discrimination and Abuse—The Human Cost of an Economic 'Miracle.'" Amnesty International, AI Index: ASA 17/008/2007 (March 1, 2007).

Anderson, Kym, ed. *New Silk Roads: East Asia and World Textile Markets.* Cambridge: Cambridge University Press, 1992.

Anderson, Kym, William Martin, and Dominique van der Mensbrugghe. "Doha Merchandise Trade Reform: What Is at Stake for Developing Countries?" *World Bank Economic Review* 20, 2 (2006): 169–195.

Anderson, Thomas M. "Monsanto's Dominance Continues." *Washington Post* (May 18, 2008): F3.

Andrews, Edmund L. "U.S. to Seek Curbs on Chinese Clothing Exports." *New York Times* (August 3, 2005): 13.

_____. "White House Makes Deals for Support of Trade Pact." *New York Times* (July 26, 2005): 3.

Anthony, W.S., and William D. Mayfield, eds. *Cotton Ginners Handbook*. Washington, DC: U.S. Department of Agriculture, 1994.

Baden, Sally, and Catherine Barber. *The Impact of the Second-Hand Clothing Trade on Developing Countries*. Oxfam (September 2005).

Baffes, John. "Cotton Subsidies, the WTO, and the 'Cotton Problem,'" Policy Research Working Paper 5663, The World Bank, May 2011.

Baghdadli, Ilhem, Hela Cheikhrouhou, and Gael Raballand. "Strategies for Cotton in West and Central Africa: Enhancing Competitiveness in the 'Cotton 4.'" World Bank Working Paper No. 108. Washington, DC: World Bank, 2007.

Bakken, Børge, ed. *Migration in China*. Copenhagen: NIAS, 1998.

Banjo, Shelly. "Inside Nike's Struggle to Balance Cost and Worker Safety in Bangladesh." *Wall Street Journal*, (April 21, 2014).

Baragona, Steve. "Brazil Says Farm Bill Violates Trade Rules." Voice of America, February 20, 2014.

Barasa, Lucas. "Cheap Imports Killing Kenya's Textile Industry." Nation (Nairobi) (November 24, 1998).

Barnett, Barry J. "Economic Challenges of Transgenic Crops: The Case of Bt Cotton." *Journal of Economic Issues* 33, 3 (September 1, 1999): 647.

Bassett, Thomas J. "Producing Poverty: Power Relations and Price Formation in the Cotton Commodity Chains of West Africa." In *Hanging by a Thread: Cotton, Globalization, and Poverty in Africa*, edited by William G. Moseley and Leslie C. Gray. Columbus: OH: Ohio University Press, 2008.

Batson, Andrew. "China Eco-Watchdog Gets Teeth." *Wall Street Journal* (December 18, 2007): A4.

Beazer, William F. *The Commercial Future of Hong Kong*. New York: Praeger, 1978.

Becker, Hank. "Insecticides Reduced in Runoff from Bt Cotton." USDA Agricultural Research Services (March 7, 2001).

Berger, Suzanne, and Richard K. Lester, eds. *Made by Hong Kong*. Hong Kong: Oxford University Press, 1997.

Bhagwati, Jagdish. *In Defense of Globalization*. New York: Oxford University Press, 2004.
_____. *Termites in the Trading System*. New York: Oxford University Press, 2008.

Bhasin, Kim. "Walmart, Gap Lead Coalition to Create New Bangladesh Safety Pact." *Huffington Post* (May 30, 2013).

Bingen, Jim. "Genetically Engineered Cotton: Politics, Science, and Power in West Africa." In *Hanging by a Thread: Cotton, Globalization, and Poverty in Africa*, edited by William G. Moseley and Leslie C. Gray. Columbus,OH: Ohio University Press, 2008.

Birnbaum, David. *Birnbaum's Global Guide to Winning the Great Garment War*. New York: Fashiondex, 2005.

Birns, Jack. *Assignment Shanghai: Photographs on the Eve of the Revolution*. Berkeley: University of California Press, 2003.

Bjork, Christopher. "Inditex Builds for the Future." *Wall Street Journal* (March 19, 2014).

Blackburn, Elliott, "Cotton Stripped from Texas Tech Seal." *Lubbock Avalanche-Journal* (May 5, 2005).

Blackshear, Jason, Phillip Johnson, and Heidi Gum. "Profitability and Cost of Production of Roundup Ready versus Conventional Cotton Varieties in the Southern High Plains of Texas." 2002 *Beltwide Cotton Conferences*, Atlanta, GA (January 8–12, 2002).

Blewett, M.H. *Surviving Hard Times: The Working People of Lowell*. Lowell, MA: Lowell Museum, 1982.

_____. *The Last Generation: Work and Life in the Textile Mills of Lowell, Massachusetts, 1910–1960*. Amherst: University of Massachusetts Press, 1990.

Blue, Gregory. "China and Western Social Thought in the Modern Period." In *China and Historical Capitalism: Genealogies of Sinological Knowledge*, edited by Timothy Brook and Gregory Blue. Cambridge: Cambridge University Press, 1999.

Blustein, Paul. "A Pakistani Setback." *Washington Post* (December 26, 2001): A01.

_____. "Textile Makers Fight for Limits; With Caps Expiring, U.S. Industry Fears Glut of Chinese Imports." *Washington Post* (October 13, 2004): E01.

Bolle, Mary Jane. *Bangladesh Apparel Factory Collapse: Background in Brief*. Washington: Congressional Research Service, June 2013.

Bonacich, Edna, and Richard P. Appelbaum. *Behind the Label: Inequality in the Los Angeles Apparel Industry*. Berkeley: University of California Press, 2000.

Bradsher, Keith, and Andrew Martin. "World's Poor Pay Price as Crop Research Is Cut." *New York Times* (May 18, 2008): 1.

Brandis, R. Buford. *The Making of Textile Trade Policy, 1935–1981*. Washington, DC: American Textile Manufacturers Institute, 1982.

Brandon, Hembree. "Exports, China Dominate Cotton Outlook." *Southeast Farm Press* (August 14, 2007).

Brattain, M. "Making Friends and Enemies: Textile Workers and Political Action in Post-World War II Georgia." *Journal of Southern History* 63, 1 (February 1997): 91–138.

Breeden, James O., ed. *Advice Among Masters: The Ideal in Slave Management in the Old South*. Westport, CT: Greenwood Press, 1980.

Brill, Bernard. "Textiles." *In The McGraw-Hill Recycling Handbook*, edited by Herbert F. Lund, 17.1–17.12. New York: McGraw Hill, 2001.

Brooks, David. "The Republic of Fear." *New York Times*, (March 25, 2014).

Brookes, Graham, and Peter Barfoot. *GM Crops: The First Ten Years—Global Socio-Economic and Environmental Impacts*. Dorchester, UK: PG Economics, October 2006.

Brown, Paul. "Monsanto Drops GM 'Terminator'; Worldwide Pressure Forces Drugs Company to Back Down on Attempt 'To Dominate Food Supplies.'" *The Guardian* (October 5, 1999): 2.

Bruchey, Stuart. *Cotton and the Growth of the American Economy: 1790–1860*. New York: Harcourt, Brace, 1967.

Buckley, J. Taylor. "Starting at the Bottom: Plucky Entrepreneurs Roll Out Cotton Toilet Tissue." *USA Today* (August 14, 1998): 2B.

Bussey, Jane. "China to Collar Textiles?" *Miami Herald* (July 22, 2004), C1.

Byerly, Victoria. *Hard Times Cotton Mill Girls: Personal Histories of Womanhood and Poverty in the South*. Ithaca, NY: ILR Press, 1986.

Callender, Guy S. "The Early Transportation and Banking Enterprises of the States in Relation to the Growth of Corporations." *Quarterly Journal of Economics* 17 (1903): 114–131.

Carr, Stephen J. "Improving Cash Crops in Africa: Factors Influencing the Productivity of Cotton, Coffee, and Tea Grown by Smallholders." World Bank Technical Paper No. 216. Washington, DC: World Bank, 1993.

Carter, Jimmy. "Subsidies' Harvest of Misery." *Washington Post* (December 10, 2007): A19.

CBC News. "Chronicle of the Major Events Since 2005: Deaths in the Bangladeshi Garment Industry Have Been Attributed to Fires, Stampedes, and Building Collapses; Many Fires Have Gone Unreported." Retrieved from www.cbc.ca/news2/interactives/timeline-bangladesh/.

Cha, Ariana Eunjung. "New Law Gives Chinese Workers Power, Gives Businesses Nightmares." *Washington Post* (April 14, 2008): A1.

Chan, Anita. *China's Workers Under Assault: The Exploitation of Labor in a Globalizing Economy (Asia and the Pacific)*. Armonk and London: M.E. Sharpe, 2001.

Chace, Zoe. "Interviews with the Korean and Bangladeshi Businessmen Who Designed the 1970s Collaboration." Retrieved from www.npr.org/blogs/money/2013/12/05/247360903/nixon-and-kimchee-how-the-garment-industry-came-to-bangladesh.

————. "Where a Truck Full of T-Shirts Gets the Same Privileges as an Ambulance." Retrieved from www.npr.org/blogs/money/2013/09/04/218890986/where-a-truck-full-of-t-shirts-gets-the-same-privileges-as-an-ambulance.

Chang, Leslie T. *Factory Girls: From Village to City in a Changing China*. New York: Random House, 2008.

Chao, Kang, and Jessica C.Y. Chao. *The Development of Cotton Textile Production in China*.Cambridge, MA: Harvard University, East Asian Research Center, 1977.

Chaudhry, Rafiq M. *Cost of Production in the USA and Other Countries*. Washington, DC: International Cotton Advisory Committee.

————. *Update on Costs of Producing Cotton in the World*. Washington, DC: International Cotton Advisory Committee.

Chen, Hsiou-Lien, and Leslie Davis Burns. "Environmental Analysis of Textile Products." *Clothing and Textiles Research Journal*, 24 (2006): 248–261.

Chesneaux, Jean. *The Chinese Labor Movement 1919–1927*. Stanford, CA: Stanford University Press, 1968.

China Daily. *Graduates Prefer Hukou over High Salary*. (Updated: April 22, 2008). Retrieved from www.chinadaily.com.cn/citylife/2008-04/22/content_6635797.htm.

China Daily. *Hit the Door*. (Updated: May 12, 2008). Retrieved from www.chinadaily.com.cn/bw/2008-05/12/content_6676238.htm.

Chokki, Toshiaki. "Labor Management in the Cotton Spinning Industry." In *Japanese Economic History 1600–1960: The Textile Industry and the Rise of the Japanese Economy*, edited by Michael Smitka. New York: Garland Publishing, 1998.

Christy, David. *Cotton Is King*. Reprinted in *Cotton Is King and Pro—Slavery Arguments*, edited by E.N. Elliott. Augusta, GA: Pritchard, Abbott & Zoomis, 1860.

Clay, Jason. *World Agriculture and the Environment: A Commodity-by-Commodity Guide to Impacts and Practices*. Washington, DC: Island Press, 2003.

Cline, Michael E., et al. "Socioeconomic Impacts of Manufacturing in Selected Arkansas and Texas Communities." Technical Document #2, Manufacturing Sector Dynamics (April 2008).

Cline, William R. *The Future of World Trade in Textiles and Apparel* (rev. ed.). Washington, DC: Institute for International Economics, 1990.

Cobb, Thomas R. *An Inquiry into the Law of Negro Slavery in the United States of America*. New York: Arno Press and the *New York Times*, 1858, reprinted 1968.

Coclanis, P.A. "Introduction: African Americans in Southern Agriculture, 1877–1945." *Agricultural History* 72, 2 (Spring 1998): 135–139.

Cohen-Lack, Nancy. "A Struggle for Sovereignty: National Consolidation, Emancipation, and Free Labor in Texas, 1865." *Journal of Southern History* 63, 1 (February 1992): 57–98.

Conkin, P.K. "Hot, Humid and Sad." *Journal of Southern History* 64, 1 (February 1998): 3–22.

Conti, Delia B. *Reconciling Free Trade, Fair Trade, and Interdependence: The Rhetoric of Presidential Economic Leadership*. Westport, CT: Praeger, 1998.

Cook, Sarah, and Margaret Maurer-Fazio, eds. *The Workers' State Meets the Market: Labour in China's Transition*. London: Frank Cass, 1999.

Copeland, Brian R., and Scott M. Taylor. *Trade and the Environment: Theory and Evidence*. Princeton, NJ: Princeton University Press, 2003.

Copeland, Melvin Thomas. *The Cotton Manufacturing Industry of the United States*. New York: Augustus M. Kelly, 1966.

Cotton Grower. "NCC Believes Brazil WTO Case Resolved." *Cotton Grower* (February 20, 2014).

Coulson, Andrew. *Tanzania: A Political Economy*. Oxford: Clarendon Press, 1982.

Council for Textile Recycling. *Don't Overlook Textiles!* (1997).

Dalzell, Robert F., Jr. *Enterprising Elites: The Boston Associates and the World They Made*. New York: W.W. Norton, 1987.

Daniel, Pete. *Breaking the Land: The Transformation of Cotton, Tobacco, and Rice Cultures Since 1880*. Urbana and Chicago: University of Illinois Press, 1985.

———. "Rhythm of the Land." *Agricultural History* 68, 4 (Fall 1994): 1–22.

———. "The Transformation of the Rural South: 1930 to the Present." *Agricultural History* 55, 3 (July 1981): 231–248.

Daniels, C. "Gresham's Laws: Labor Management on an Early-Eighteenth-Century Chesapeake Plantation." *Journal of Southern History* 62, 2 (May 1996): 205–238.

Danielson, Anders, and Gun Eriksson Skoog. "From Stagnation to Growth in Tanzania: Breaking the Vicious Circle of High Aid and Bad Governance?" In *From Crisis to Growth in Africa?*, edited by Mats Lundahl. London: Routledge, 2001.

Davis, Marc. "Congress Urges Inclusion of 'Yarn Forward' Rule in TPP." *Sourcingonline-journal* (July 16, 2013).

Day, Richard H. "The Economics of Technological Change and the Demise of the Sharecropper." *American Economic Review* 57, 3 (June 1967): 427–449.

Dean, Judith M. "The Effects of the U.S. MFA on Small Exporters." *Review of Economics and Statistics* 72, 1 (February 1990): 63–69.

————. "Market Disruption and the Incidence of VERs Under the MFA." *Review of Economics and Statistics* 77, 2 (May 1995): 383–388.

Deane, Phyllis. *The First Industrial Revolution*, 2nd ed. Cambridge: Cambridge University Press, 1979.

DeBow, J.D.B., ed. "A Mississippi Planter." In *Industrial Resources of the Southern and Western States* (3 volumes). Washington, DC: DeBow, 1852.

De Jonquiérés, Guy. "Clothes on the Line." *Financial Times* (July 19, 2004): 13.

De Jonquiérés, Guy, and Frances Williams. "Top WTO Nations Hail Deal on Doha." *Financial Times* (August 2, 2004): 1.

De Melo, Jaime, and David Tarr. "Welfare Costs of U.S. Quotas in Textiles, Steel and Autos." *Review of Economics and Statistics* (1990): 489–497.

Delmer, Deborah P. "Agriculture in the Developing World: Connecting Innovations in Plant Research to Downstream Applications." *Proceedings of the National Academy of Sciences of the United States of America*, Vol.102, No. 44, "Stretch Effect on Stress Fibers" (November 1, 2005): 15739–15746.

Dmurger, Sylvie, et al. "Geography, Economic Policy, and Regional Development in China." Working Paper 8897. Cambridge, MA: National Bureau of Economic Research, April 2002. Retrieved from www.nber.org/papers/w8897.

DePillis, Lydia. "Everything You Need to Know About the Trans Pacific Partnership." *Washington Post* (December 11, 2013).

Destler, I.M. *American Trade Politics*, 3rd ed. Washington, DC: Institute for International Economics, 1995.

————. *American Trade Politics*, 4th ed. Washington, DC: Institute for International Economics, 2005.

Destler, I.M., Haruhiro Fukui, and Hideo Sato. *Textile Wrangle: Conflict in Japanese–American Relations, 1969–1971*. Ithaca, NY: Cornell University Press, 1979.

Devnath, Arun. "Bangladesh Raises Minimum Wage for Garment Workers After Unrest." *Bloomberg News*, November 14, 2013.

Dewan, Shaila. "Black Farmers' Refrain: Where's All Our Money?" *New York Times* (August 1, 2004).

Dickerson, Kitty. *Textiles and Apparel in the Global Economy*, 3rd ed. Upper Saddle River, NJ: Merrill, Prentice-Hall, 1999.

Dickson, Marsha A. "Personal Values, Beliefs, Knowledge, and Attitudes Relating to Intentions to Purchase Apparel from Socially Responsible Businesses." *Clothing and Textiles Research Journal*, 18 (2000): 19–30.

Dickson, Marsha A., and Eckman, Molly. "Social Responsibility: The Concept as Defined by Apparel and Textile Scholars." *Clothing & Textiles Research Journal* 24, 3 (2006): 178–191.

Dickson, Marsha A., Suzanne Loker, and Molly Eckman. *Social Responsibility in the Global Apparel Industry*. New York: Fairchild Books, 2009.

Dodge, Bertha S. *Cotton: The Plant That Would Be King*. Austin, TX: University of Texas Press, 1984.

Dodson, Charles. "Financial and Structural Characteristics of U.S. Commercial Cotton Farms, 1991–1992." Economic Research Service, No. 715.

Dollar, David, and Benjamin Jones. "China: An Institutional View of an Unusual Macroeconomy," NBER Working Paper W19662, November 2013.

Donaldson, G.F., and J.P. McInerney. "Changing Machinery Technology and Agricultural Adjustment." *American Journal of Agricultural Economics 55*, 5 (December 1973): 829–839.

Doorey, David J. "Can Factory List Disclosure Improve Labor Practices in the Apparel Industry? A Case Study of Nike and Levi-Strauss." CLPE Research Paper 01/2008, Vol. 4, No. 1 (2008).

Dougherty, Carter. "Trade Theory vs. Used Clothes in Africa." *New York Times* (June 3, 2004): col. 3, p. 1.

Dougherty, Peter J. *Who's Afraid of Adam Smith?: How the Market Got Its Soul*. Hoboken, NJ: John Wiley & Sons, 2002.

Dowd, Brian M. "Organic Cotton in Sub-Saharan Africa: A New Development Paradigm?" In *Hanging by a Thread: Cotton, Globalization, and Poverty in Africa*, edited by William G. Moseley and Leslie C. Gray. Athens, OH: Ohio University Press, 2008.

Dowd-Uribe, B.,"Engineering Yields and Inequality? How Institutions and Agro-Ecology Shape Bt Cotton Outcomes in Burkina Faso." *Geoforum*, 2013.

Dublin, T. *Farm to Factory: Women's Letters, 1830–1860*, 2nd ed. New York: Columbia University Press, 1993.

————. *Transforming Women's Work: New England Lives in the Industrial Revolution*. Ithaca, NY: Cornell University Press, 1994.

————. *Women at Work: The Transformation of Work and Community in Lowell, Massachusetts, 1826–1860*. New York: Columbia University Press, 1979.

Dupre, Daniel. "Ambivalent Capitalists on the Cotton Frontier: Settlement and Development in the Tennessee Valley of Alabama." *Journal of Southern History 56*, 2 (May 1990): 215–240.

Earle, Carville. "The Price of Precocity: Technical Choice and Ecological Constraint in the Cotton South, 1840–1890." *Agricultural History 66*, 3 (Summer 1992): 25–60.

Eckes, Alfred E., Jr. *Opening America's Market: U.S. Foreign Trade Policy Since 1776*. Chapel Hill, NC: University of North Carolina Press, 1995.

Economic Research Service. "Briefing Room: Cotton Trade," July 19, 2002.

Economy, Elizabeth C. *The River Runs Black: The Environmental Challenge to China's Future*. Ithaca: NY, Cornell University Press, 2004.

Ederington, Josh, Arik Levinson, and Jenny Minier. "Trade Liberalization and Pollution Havens," *Advances in Economic Analysis and Policy, Berkeley Electronic Press 4*, 2 (2004).

Eisa, Hamdy M., et al. "Cotton Production Prospects for the Decade to 2005: A Global Overview." World Bank Technical Paper No. 231. Washington, DC: World Bank, 1994.

Eisler, B. *The Lowell Offering*. Philadelphia: J.B. Lippincott, 1977.

Elizondo, Gabriel. "U.S. Farmers Scramble to Buy Brazil's Farmland." *Aljazeera* (September 12, 2012).

Ellenberg, George B. *Mule South to Tractor South: Mules, Machines, and the Transformation of the Cotton South*. Tuscaloosa: University of Alabama Press, 2007.

Emerging Textiles. "Apparel Manufacturing Labor Costs in 2008." Statistical Report. (May 23, 2008). Retrieved from www.emergingtextiles.com.

————. Duty-Free Access for Bangladesh and Cambodia Offered by New U.S. Bill (October 19, 2007). Retrieved from www.emergingtextiles.com.

————. Slowdown in Sight as Chinese Quotas Are Being Lifted: Sri Lanka Fighting for Apparel Trade Advantages (Country Report)(December 11, 2007). Retrieved from www.emergingtextiles.com.

————. "China Textile & Clothing Production Costs Country Report" (March 18, 2014). Retrieved from emergingtextiles.com.

————. "Asia Clothing Exports" (March 25, 2014). Retrieved from emerging-textiles.com

Engels, Friedrich. *The Condition of the Working Class in England*. Translated and edited by W.O. Henderson and W.H. Chaloner. New York: Macmillan, 1958.

English, Beth. *A Common Thread: Labor, Politics and Capital Mobility in the Textile Industry*. Athens, GA: University of Georgia Press, 2006.

Environmental Protection Agency. *Municipal Solid Waste in The United States: 2005 Facts and Figures*.

Environmental Working Group. *All Over the Map*. Retrieved from www.ewg.org/farmeditorials.

Fafchamps, Marcel. *Market Institutions in Sub-Saharan Africa: Theory and Evidence*. Cambridge: MIT Press, 2004.

Farnie, D.A. *The English Cotton Industry and the World Market, 1815–1896*. Oxford: Clarendon Press, 1979.

Fears, Darryl. "USDA Is Called Lax on Bias: GAO Accuses Agency of Inaction on Racial Discrimination." *Washington Post* (May 18, 2008): A6.

Featherstone, Liza, and United Students Against Sweatshops. *Students Against Sweatshops*. London: Verso, 2002.

Feng, Wang, Xuejin Zuo, and Danching Ruan. "Rural Migrants in Shanghai: Living under the Shadow of Socialism." *International Migration Review* 36, 2 (Summer 2002): 520–545.

Ferleger, L. "Sharecropping Contracts in the Late Nineteenth-Century South." *Agricultural History* 67, 3 (Summer 1993): 31–46.

Finlay, Mark R. "The Industrial Utilization of Farm Products and By-Products: The USDA Regional Research Laboratories." *Agricultural History* 64, 2 (Spring 1990): 41–53.

Foley, Neil. "Mexicans, Mechanization, and the Growth of Corporate Cotton Culture in South Texas: The Taft Ranch, 1900–1930." *Journal of Southern History* 62, 2 (May 1996): 275–302.

_____. *The White Scourge: Mexicans, Blacks, and Poor Whites in Texas Cotton Culture.* Berkeley and Los Angeles: University of California Press, 1997.

Fong, Mei. "A Chinese Puzzle." *Wall Street Journal* (August 16, 2004): B1.

Fong, Mei, and Sky Canaves. "South China's Factories Lose Edge as Costs Climb." *Wall Street Journal* (Asia) (February 25, 2008): 1.

Frankel, Jeffrey A. "The Environment and Globalization." In *Globalization: What's New,* edited by Michael Weinsten. New York: Columbia University Press, 2005.

Frankel, Jeffrey A. and Andrew Rose. "Is Trade Good or Bad for the Environment?" *Review of Economics and Statistics* 87,1 (Winter 2005): 85–91.

Friedman, Thomas. *The Lexus and the Olive Tree: Understanding Globalization.* New York: Anchor, 2000.

Friman, H. Richard. "Rocks, Hard Places, and the New Protectionism: Textile Trade Policy Choices in the United States and Japan." *International Organization* 42, 4 (Autumn 1988): 689–723.

_____. *Patchwork Protectionism: Textile Trade Policy in the United States, Japan, and West Germany.* Ithaca: Cornell University Press, 1990.

Frisvold, George B., and Jeanne M. Reeves. "Economy-Wide Impacts of Bt Cotton." *Proceedings of the Beltwide Cotton Conferences,* January 2007.

Fulton, M. "The Future of Canadian Agricultural Cooperatives: A Property Rights Approach." *American Journal of Agricultural Economics* 77 (December 1995): 1144–1152.

Galenson, Walter, ed. *Economic Growth and Structural Change in Taiwan: The Postwar Experience of the Republic of China.* Ithaca: Cornell University Press, 1979.

Gardner, B.L. "The Federal Government in Farm Commodity Markets: Recent Reform Efforts in a Long-Term Context." *Agricultural History* 70, 2 (Spring 1996): 177–195.

"Garment Sector Will Survive After Quotas." just-style.com (June 22, 2004).

Garside, A.H. *Cotton Goes to Market: A Graphic Description of a Great Industry.* New York: Frederick A. Stokes, 1935.

Ghosh, Palash. "Despite Low Pay, Poor Work Conditions, Garment Factories Empowering Millions of Bangladeshi Women." *International Business Times* (March 25, 2014).

Giles, John. *China's Labor Market in the Wake of Economic Restructuring.* The World Bank: Development Research Group.

Gillham, Fred E.M., et al. *Cotton Production Prospects for the Next Decade.* World Bank Technical Paper No. 287. Washington, DC: World Bank, 1995.

Glade, Edward H., Jr., Mae Dean Johnson, and Leslie A. Meyer. "U.S. Cotton Distribution Patterns, 1993/94." Economic Research Service/USDA, No. 940.

Glade, Edward H., Jr., Leslie A. Meyer, and Stephen MacDonald. "Cotton: Background for 1995 Farm Legislation." *Agricultural Economic Report,* No. 706 (April 1995): 1–30.

Glade, Edward H., Jr., Leslie A. Meyer, and Harold Stults. "The Cotton Industry in the United States." Economic Research Service/USDA, No. 739.

Goodman, Peter S. "In China's Cities, a Turn from Factories; Labor Pool Shifts as Urban Workers Seek Better Lives." *Washington Post* (September 25, 2004), A1.

—————. "In NC, a Second Industrial Revolution: Biotech Surge Shows Manufacturing Still Key to U.S. Economy." *Washington Post* (September 3, 2007): A1.

Grassley, Senator Chuck. "Smearing Lipstick on a Pig" (December 19, 2007). Retrieved from www.theconservativevoice.com/article/29841.html.

Gray, Leslie C. "Cotton Production in Burkina Faso: International Rhetoric versus Local Realities." In *Hanging by a Thread: Cotton, Globalization, and Poverty in Africa*, edited by William G. Moseley and Leslie C. Gray. Athens, OH: Ohio University Press, 2008.

Greenhouse, Steven. "Some Retailers Rethink Role in Bangladesh." *New York Times* (May 1, 2013).

Greenhouse, Steven, and Julfikar Ali Manik. "Stalemate Over Safety in Bangladesh." *New York Times* (June 26, 2014).

Greider, William. *One World, Ready or Not: The Manic Logic of Global Capitalism*. New York: Simon & Schuster, 1997.

Gresser, Edward. "It's Expensive Being Poor." *Far Eastern Economic Review* (June 10, 2004).

—————. *Who Gets Hit?* (June 11, 2003). Progressive Policy Institute. Retrieved from www.ppionline.org/ppi_ci.cfm?knlgAreaID=108&subsecID=900010&contentID=251757.

Grim, V. "The Politics of Inclusion: Black Farmers and the Quest for Agribusiness Participation, 1945–1990s." *Agricultural History* 69, 2 (Spring 1995): 257–271.

Grove, Wayne A. "The Mexican Farm Labor Program, 1942–1964: Government-Administered Labor Market Insurance for Farmers." *Agricultural History* 70, 2 (Spring 1996): 302–320.

Gwin, Adrian. "Looking Back: No Cotton Picking for Me, Thanks." *Charleston Daily Mail* (January 9, 1999): 6A.

Halegua, Aaron. "Getting Paid: Processing the Labor Disputes of China's Migrant Workers." *Berkeley Journal of International Law* 26, 1 (2007).

Hale, Angela, and Jane Wills, eds. *Threads of Labour: Garment Industry Supply Chains from the Workers' Perspective*. Malden, MA: Blackwell, 2005.

Hall, Jacquelyn Dowd, et al. *Like a Family: The Making of a Southern Cotton Mill World*. New York: W.W. Norton & Company, 1987.

Hammond, James Henry. "On the Admission of Kansas," speech before the U.S. Senate, March 4, 1858. *Congressional Globe*: 959.

Hammond, Matthew B. "Correspondence of Eli Whitney Relative to the Invention of the Cotton Gin." *American Historical Review* 3, 1 (October 1897).

Hanlan, J.P. *The Working Population of Manchester, New Hampshire, 1840–1886*. Ann Arbor, MI: UMI Research Press, 1981.

Hansen, Karen Tranberg. *Salaula: The World of Secondhand Clothing and Zambia*. Chicago and London: University of Chicago Press, 2000.

Hareven, T.K. *Family Time and Industrial Time: The Relationship Between the Family and Work in a New England Industrial Community*. New York: Cambridge University Press, 1982.

Hareven, Tamara K., and Randolph Langenbach. *Amoskeag: Life and Work in an American Factory-City*. Hanover: University Press of New England, 1978.

Harrison, Ann, and Jason Scorse. *Moving Up or Moving Out? Anti-Sweatshop Activists and Labor Market Outcomes*. NBER Working Paper No. 10492 (May 2004; rev. June 2006).

Harney, Alexandra. *The China Price: The True Cost of Chinese Competitive Advantage*. New York: Penguin Press, 2008.

Hart, Chad E. "Agricultural Situation Spotlight: How the Brazil–U.S. Cotton Dispute Could Affect Iowa's Agriculture." *Iowa Agricultural Review* 10, 3 (Summer 2004).

Hartley, Matt. "Grain Farmer Claims Moral Victory in Seed Battle." *The Globe and Mail* (Canada) (March 20, 2008).

Hartman, Laura P., Dennis G. Arnold, and Richard E. Wokutch, eds. *Rising Above Sweatshops*. Westport, CT: Praeger, 2003.

Harrison, Ann, and Jason Scorse. "Improving the Conditions of Workers? Minimum Wage Legislation and Anti-Sweatshop Activism." *California Management Review* 48, 2 (2006): 144–160.

Hayes, Keri. "Aquaculture Gets Hooked on Oilmeals." *Bluebook Update Online Archive*.

Hayter, Delmar. "Expanding the Cotton Kingdom." *Agricultural History* 62, 2 (1988): 225–233.

Hearden, Patrick J. *Independence and Empire: The New South's Cotton Mill Campaign 1865–1901*. DeKalb, IL: Northern Illinois University Press, 1982.

Heath, Rachel, and Mushfiq Mobarak. "Supply and Demand Constraints on Educational Investment: Evidence from Garment Sector Jobs and the Female Stipend Program in Bangladesh." Yale University Working Paper (October 2011).

Helpman, Elhanan, Oleg Itskhoki, Marc-Andreas Muendler, and Stephen Redding. "Trade and Inequality: From Theory to Estimation." Harvard University Working Paper (March 2014).

Hertel, Thomas, and Fan Zhai. "Labor Market Distortions, Rural–Urban Inequality and the Opening of China's Economy." World Bank Policy Research Working Paper No. 3455 (November 2004).

Hessler, Peter. "Letter from China: Boomtown Girl, Finding a New Life in the Golden City." *New Yorker* (May 28, 2001): 108–119.

Hethorn, Janet, and Connie Ulasewicz. *Sustainable Fashion: Why Now? Exploring Issues, Practices and Possibilities*. New York: Fairchild Books, 2008.

Hirst, F.W. *From Adam Smith to Philip Snowden: A History of Free Trade in Great Britain*. New York: Adelphi, 1925.

Hitt, Greg. "Politics and Economics: Textile Makers Tap Political Opportunity; Industry Uses Voters' Economic Unease to Win Protections, Derail Free-Trade Plans." *Wall Street Journal* (Eastern Edition) (October 18, 2006): A4.

_____. "Textile Industry Wants Renewed Protections." *Wall Street Journal* (Eastern Edition) (August 6, 2008): A3.

Holleran, Philip M. "Child Labor and Exploitation in Turn-of-the-Century Cotton Mills." *Explorations in Economic History* 30 (1993): 485–500.

Honig, Emily. *Creating Chinese Ethnicity: Subei People in Shanghai 1850–1980.* New Haven: Yale University Press, 1992.

————. *Sisters and Strangers: Women in the Shanghai Cotton Mills 1919–1949.* Stanford, CA: Stanford University Press, 1986.

Huang, Jikun, Ruifa Hu, Cuihui Fan, Carl E. Pray, and Scott Rozelle. "Bt Cotton Benefits, Costs, and Impacts in China." *Journal of Agrobiotechnology Management and Economics* 5 (4), 2002.

Hufbauer, Gary Clyde, and Kimberly Ann Elliott. *Measuring the Costs of Protection in the United States.* Washington, DC: Institute for International Economics, 1994.

"Human Rights in China." *Institutionalized Exclusion: The Tenuous Legal Status of Internal Migrants in China's Major Cities.* Report by HRIC (November 6, 2002).

Hutchins, B.L., and A. Harrison. *A History of Factory Legislation.* New York: Burt Franklin, 1903.

ICAC. "Biotechnology Applications in Cotton, Concerns, and Challenges." Retrieved from www.icac.cotton info/speeches/chaudry/2007/Pakistan march 2007.pdf.

————. "Executive Summary of the Report of the Second Expert Panel on Biotechnology of Cotton." Retrieved from www.icac.org/cotton_info/tis/biotech/documents/expert_panel_2/english.html.

————. "Limitations on Organic Cotton Production." *The ICAC Recorder* (March 2003).

ICAC, and Gérald Estur. "Africa's Cotton in the World." *Seminar on Cotton in Africa,* Arusha, September 6–8, 2007.

IDEAS Centre Geneva. "Cotton Newsletter 101: Last But Not Least" (February 21, 2013).

Ikenson, Dan. *Threadbare Excuses: The Textile Industry's Campaign to Preserve Import Restraints.* Trade Policy Analysis No. 25. Washington, DC: CATO Institute, Center for Trade Policy Studies, 2003.

————. "Washington's Coddling of U.S. Textile Industry Is Hurting Shoppers." *Forbes* (July 23, 2013).

Inside U.S. Trade. "Bush Officials Win Hayes, Aderholt Votes with Assurances on Textiles" (July 29, 2005). Retrieved from www.insidetrade.com.

————. "NCTO CAFTA Endorsement Based on Three Promises to Help U.S. Industry" (May 13, 2005). Retrieved from www.insidetrade.com.

————. "Opponents, Supporters See Textile Republicans Supporting DR-CAFTA" (July 15, 2005). Retrieved from www.insidetrade.com.

Iredale, Robyn, Naran Bilik, and Fei Guo, eds. *China's Minorities on the Move: Selected Case Studies.* Armonk,NY: M.E. Sharpe, 2003.

Irwin, Douglas A. *Against the Tide: An Intellectual History of Free Trade.* Princeton, NJ: Princeton University Press, 1996.

————. *Free Trade Under Fire.* Princeton, NJ: Princeton University Press, 2002.

Islam, Syful. "LDCs Duty-Free Access: New Trade Bill Worries U.S. Textile Bosses." *The New Nation* (December 26, 2007).

———. "U.S. Textile Bosses Want Bangladesh to Work Together to Extend China Cap." *The New Nation* (Internet Edition) (December 27, 2007).

Israel, Debra, and Arik Levinson. "Willingness to Pay for Environmental Quality: Testable Implications of the Growth and Environment Literature," *Contributions to Economic Analysis & Policy* 3(1) 2004.

Ito, Manubo. "Chinese Investment Pours Into Vietnamese Textile Industry on Free Trade Hopes." *Nikkei Asian Review* (February 3, 2014).

Jacobson, Timothy Curtis, and George David Smith. *Cotton's Renaissance: A Study in Market Innovation*. Cambridge: Cambridge University Press, 2001.

James, Sallie. "Race to the Bottom?: The Presidential Candidates' Positions on Trade." Trade Briefing Paper No. 27. Washington, DC: CATO Institute, April 15, 2008.

James, Sallie, and Daniel Griswold. "Freeing the Farm: A Farm Bill for All Americans." Trade Policy Analysis No. 34. Washington, DC: CATO Institute, April 16, 2007.

Jeter, Jon. "The Dumping Ground: As Zambia Courts Western Markets, Used Goods Arrive at a Heavy Price." *Washington Post* (April 22, 2002): A1.

Johnson, Charles S., Edwin R. Embree, and W.W. Alexander. *The Collapse of Cotton Tenancy*. Chapel Hill, NC: University of North Carolina Press, 1935.

Johnson, G.L. "A Forward Look at Agricultural Policy Analysis (Based on 1945–1995 Experiences)." *Agricultural History* 70, 2 (Spring 1996): 153–176.

Jones, Charisse. "Eco-Friendly Homes Are Moving into the Mainstream." *USA Today* (November 1, 2007): 13A.

Josephson, H. *The Golden Threads: New England's Mill Girls and Magnates*. New York: Duell, Sloan and Pearce, 1949.

Josling, Timothy. *Agricultural Trade Policy: Completing the Reform*. Washington, DC: Institute for International Economics, 1998.

Jouanjean, Marie-Agnès. "Targeting Infrastructure Development to Foster Agricultural Trade and Market Integration in Developing Countries: An Analytical Review." *ODI report*, 2013.

Just-style.com. "Cambodia: Garment Sector Will Survive After Quotas" (June 22, 2004). Retrieved August 10, 2004, from www.just-style.com/news_detail.asp.

Kane, N.F. *Textiles in Transition: Technology, Wages, and Industry Relocation in the U.S. Textile Industry, 1880–1930*. Westport, CT: Greenwood Press, 1988.

Karp, Jonathan. "Deadly Crop: Difficult Times Drive India's Cotton Farmers to Desperate Action." *Wall Street Journal* (February 18, 1998): 1A.

Kerman, Hannah. "Universities to Require Vendors to Adopt Labor Standards." *Brown Daily Herald* (March 3, 2014).

Kiers, E. Toby, et al. "Agriculture at a Crossroads." *Science* 320 (April 18, 2008): 320–321.

Kim, Seung-Kyung. *Class Struggle or Family Struggle? The Lives of Women Factory Workers in South Korea*. New York: Cambridge University Press, 1997.

Kinnecom, Kimberly. *Independent Tribune* (June 7, 2008).

Knight, John, Lina Song, and Jia Huaibin. "Chinese Rural Migrants in Urban Enterprises: Three Perspectives." In *The Workers' State Meets the Market: Labour in China's Transition*, edited by Sarah Cook and Margaret Maurer Fazio. London: Frank Cass, 1999.

Köll, Elisabeth. *FromCotton Mill to Business Empire: The Emergence of Regional Enterprises in Modern China*. Cambridge: Harvard University Press, 2003.

Krishna, K.M., and L.H. Tan. *Rags and Riches: Implementing Apparel Quotas Under the Multi-Fibre Arrangement*. Ann Arbor: University of Michigan Press, 1998.

Kristof, Nicholas D., and Sheryl WuDunn. *Thunder from the East: Portrait of a Rising Asia*. New York: Alfred A. Knopf, 2000.

Kuhn, Anthony. "Migrants: A High Price to Pay for a Job." *Far Eastern Economic Review* (January 22, 2004): 30–32.

Kung, Lydia. *Factory Women in Taiwan*. New York: Columbia University Press, 1994.

Kunz, Grace L., and Myrna B. Garner. *Going Global: The Textile and Apparel Industry*. New York: Fairchild Publications, 2007.

Kurtzman, Joel, and Glenn Yago. *Opacity Index 2007–2008: Measuring Global Business Risks*. Milken Institute, April 2008.

Kutting, Gabriela. "Globalization, Poverty and the Environment in West Africa: Too Poor to Pollute?" *Global Environmental Politics* 3, 4 (2003): 42–60.

Lakhal, Salem Y., and Souad H'Mida. "The Economics of Organic and Conventional Cotton Cultivation in Mali: Country and Farmers Analysis." 2007 Oxford Business & Economics Conference, Oxford University, UK (June 24–26, 2007).

Landes, D.S. *The Wealth and Poverty of Nations: Why Some Are So Rich and Some So Poor*. New York: W.W. Norton, 1998.

Lang, Mahlon G. "The Future of Agricultural Cooperatives in Canada and the United States: Discussion." *American Journal of Agricultural Economics* 77, 5 (December 1995): 1162–1165.

Lapierre-Fortin, Émanuéle. "Constructing Fair Trade from the Bottom-Up: An Examination of Notions of Fairness in the Conventional Cotton Trade of Burkina Faso." Undergraduate Honours Thesis, University of Toronto at Scarborough, April 14, 2008.

Laws, Forrest. "China Cotton Consumption Trends Up." *Western Farm Press* (February 18, 2006).

———. "Growers Say: Flex May Revolutionize Weed Control." *Southwest Farm Press* (November 3, 2005).

Layton, Lyndsey. "Chemical Law Has Global Impact: E.U.'s New Rules Forcing Changes by U.S. Firms." *Washington Post* (June 12, 2008): A1.

Lee, Ching Kwan. *Against the Law: Labor Protests in China's Rustbelt and Sunbelt*. Berkeley: University of California Press, 2007.

———. *Gender and the South China Miracle: Two Worlds of Factory Women*. Berkeley: University of California Press, 1998.

Lemire, Beverly. *Fashion's Favourite: The Cotton Trade and the Consumer in Britain, 1660–1800*. New York: Oxford University Press, 1991.

Levinson, Arik. "Technology, International Trade, and Pollution from U.S. Manufacturing," *American Economic Review*, forthcoming.

Liang, Zai, and Zhongdong Ma. "China's Floating Population: New Evidence from the 2000 Census." *Population and Development Review* 30, 3 (September 2004): 467–488.

Lichtenstein, J. *Field to Fabric: The Story of American Cotton Growers*. Lubbock, TX: Texas Tech University Press, 1990.

Limão, Nuno. "Are Preferential Trade Agreements with Non-Trade Objectives a Stumbling Block for Multilateral Liberalization?" *Review of Economic Studies* 74, 3 (July 2007): 821–855.

Ling, Pan. *In Search of Old Shanghai*. Hong Kong: Joint Publishing,1982.

Locke, Richard. *The Promise and Limits of Private Power*. Cambridge: Cambridge University Press, 2013.

Losciale, Alessandra. "Rules May Ease Aches of Workers: Employers Protest Ergonomic Standard." *Denver Post* (January 2, 2001): Business Sec., p. C-01.

Lovely, Mary, and David Popp. "Trade, Technology, and the Environment: Why Have Poor Countries Regulated Sooner?" NBER Working Paper No. 14286, August 2008.

Lynch, John. *Toward an Orderly Market: An Intensive Study of Japan's Voluntary Quota in Cotton Textile Exports*. Tokyo: Sophia University, 1968.

MacBride, Samantha. *Recycling Reconsidered: The Present Failure and Future Promise of Environmental Action in the United States*. Cambridge: MIT Press, 2011.

Mackenzie, Peter W. "Strangers in the City: The Hukou and Urban Citizenship in China." *Journal of International Affairs* 56, 1 (September 22, 2002): 305.

Macnaughtan, Helen. *Women, Work and the Japanese Economic Miracle: The Case of the Cotton Textile Industry, 1945–1975. (Routledge Curzon Studies in the Modern History of Asia)*. London and New York: RoutledgeCurzon, 2005.

Magnusson, Paul, et al. "Where Free Trade Hurts: Thirty Million Jobs Could Disappear with the End of Apparel Quotas." *Business Week Online* (December 15, 2003).

Malone, Scott. "Low-Wage Nations Import Share to Surge." *Women's Wear Daily* (June 3, 2004): 1.

Marcus, A.I. "The Wisdom of the Body Politic: The Changing Nature of Publicly Sponsored American Agricultural Research Since the 1830s." *Agricultural History* 62, 2 (1988): 4–26.

McCracken, Elizabeth. "The Lives They Lived: Rose Freedman, B. 1893: Out of the Fire." *New York Times* (December 30, 2001): Sec. 6, col. 1, p. 19.

McGrane, Sally/Pavia. "Smarter Clothes." *Time* (July 3, 2008).

McNamara, Dennis L. *Textiles and Industrial Transition in Japan*. Ithaca: Cornell University Press, 1995.

Metcalfe, Mark R., and Barry K. Goodwin. "An Empirical Analysis of the Determinants of Trade Policy Protection in the U.S. Manufacturing Sector." *Journal of Policy Modeling* 21, 2 (March 1999): 153–165.

Meyer, Leslie, Stephen MacDonald, and Linda Foreman. "Cotton Backgrounder." U.S. Department of Agriculture, Economic Research Services, CWS-07B-01 (March 2007).

Micklethwait, John, and Adrian Wooldridge. *A Future Perfect: The Challenge and Promise of Globalization*. New York: Random House, 2003.

"Millions Go Up in Smoke as Fire Guts Huge Market." *Panafrican News Agency (PANA) Daily Newswire* (September 6, 2000).

Minchin, Timothy J. *What Do We Need a Union For?* Chapel Hill: University of North Carolina Press, 1977.

"The Misery of Manufacturing." *The Economist* (September 27, 2003): 61–62.

Mitchell, R.B. *International Historical Statistics: The Americas, 1750–1993*. London: Macmillan Reference, 1998.

Mkandawire, Thandika, and Adebayo Olukoshi, eds. *Between Liberalisation and Oppression: The Politics of Structural Adjustment in Africa*. Dakar, Senegal: CODESRIA, 1995.

Mkandawire, Thandika, and Charles C. Soludo, eds. *African Voices on Structural Adjustment: A Companion to Our Continent, Our Future*. Trenton, NJ: Africa World Press, 2003.

"Mobility in China: Off to the City." *The Economist* (September 1, 2001): 36.

Moore, John H. *The Emergence of the Cotton Kingdom in the Old Southwest: Mississippi, 1770–1860*. Baton Rouge: Louisiana State University Press, 1988.

————. "Two Cotton Kingdoms." *Agricultural History* 60, 4 (Fall 1986): 1–16.

Moran, Theodore H. *Beyond Sweatshops: Foreign Direct Investment and Globalization in Developing Countries*. Washington, DC: Brookings Institution Press, 2002.

Morrissey, James A. "Customs Finds Illegal Chinese Apparel Shipments." *Textile World* (July 15, 2008).

————. "Textile Manufacturers Have Stake in Farm Bill." *Textile World* (May 13, 2008).

Morse, Stephen, and Richard Bennett. "Impact of Bt Cotton on Farmer Livelihoods in South Africa." *International Journal of Biotechnology* 10, 2/3 (2008): 224–239.

Morse, Stephen, Richard Bennett, and Yousouf Ismael. "Comparing the Performance of Official and Unofficial Genetically Modified Cotton in India." *AgBioForum* 8, 1 (2005): 1–6.

Morse, Stephen, Richard Bennett, and Yousouf Ismael. "Environmental Impact of Genetically Modified Cotton in South Africa." *Agriculture, Ecosystems & Environment* 117, 4 (December 2006): 277–289.

Moser, Charles K. *The Cotton Textile Industry of Far Eastern Countries*. Boston: Pepperell Manufacturing Company, 1930.

Moseley, William G., and Leslie C. Gray, eds. *Hanging by a Thread: Cotton, Globalization, and Poverty in Africa*. Athens, OH: Ohio University Press, 2008.

Mui, Ylan Q. "Ikea Helps a Town Put It Together: Manufacturing Jobs Come Back to Southern VA." *Washington Post* (May 31, 2008): A1.

Nasrullah, Nakib Muhammad, and Mia Mahmudur Rahim. *CSR in Private Enterprises in Developing Countries: Evidences from the Ready-Made Garments Industry in Bangladesh.* Cham, Switzerland: Springer, 2014.

Nathan Associates. "Changes in Global Trade Rules for Textiles and Apparel: Implications for Developing Countries" (November 20, 2002).

National Council of Textile Organizations. "Government of China Industry Subsidies" (May 19, 2008).

———. "International Textile Groups Urge U.S. Government Monitoring of Chinese Apparel Exports," September 15, 2008.

———. "Obama Backs Key Textile Provisions," October 29, 2008.

———. "Yarn-Forward Rule Spurs Investment in U.S. Textile Industry," April 7, 2014.

National Labor Committee. "Behind the Label 'Made in China.'" *Executive Summary* 1 (1998).

New York Times editorial board. "The Farm Bill Could Have Been Worse." *New York Times* (January 29, 2014).

Newman, Cathy. "Dreamweavers." *National Geographic* (January 2003).

Ngai, Pun. "Women Workers and Precarious Employment in Shenzhen Special Economic Zone, China." *Gender and Development* 12, 2, Trade (July 2004): 29–36.

Nike, *Innovate for a Better World.* Retrieved from http://nike_responsibility.com.

Nixon, Richard M. "Special Message to the Congress on United States Trade Policy" (November 18, 1969). Accessed at www.presidency/ucsb.edu/publicpapers.

Nixon, Ron. "Farm Bill Compromise Will Change Programs and Reduce Spending." *New York Times* (January 27, 2014).

Nordas, H.K. "The Global Textile and Clothing Industry Post the Agreement on Textiles and Clothing." WTO Working Paper ERSD. Geneva, Switzerland: World Trade Organization, 2004.

Nordhaus, Ted, and Michael Shellenberger. *Break Through: From the Death of Environmentalism to the Politics of Possibility.* New York: Houghton Mifflin, 2007.

Norris, Lucy. "Cloth That Lies: The Secrets of Recycling in India." In *Clothing as Material Culture,* edited by S. Kchler and D. Miller. Oxford: Berg, 2004.

———. "Creative Entrepreneurs: The Recycling of Second-Hand Indian Clothing." In *Old Clothes, New Looks: Second Hand Fashion,* edited by A. Palmer and H. Clark. Oxford: Berg, 2004.

"No Sweat, Sportswear." *The Economist* (August 21, 2004).

Novak, James L., Greg Traxler, Max Runge, and Charles Mitchell, Jr. "The Effect of Mechanical Harvesting Technology on Southern Piedmont Cotton Production, 1896–1991." *Agricultural History* 69, 2 (Spring 1995): 349–367.

Nsehe, Mfonobong. "Ten African Multimillionaires You've Never Heard Of." *Forbes,* April 25, 2013.

"Off to the City." *The Economist* (September 1, 2001): 36.

Olmstead, Alan L., Bruce F. Johnston, and Brian G. Sims. "Forward to the Past: The Diffusion of Animal-Powered Tillage Equipment on Small Farms in Mexico." *Agricultural History* 60, 1 (Winter 1986): 62–72.

"One of the World's Oldest Recycling Industries." *The Massrecycler* 8, 4 (September/ October): 1.

Oxfam. "Cultivating Poverty: The Impact of U.S. Cotton Subsidies on Africa." Oxfam Briefing Paper No. 30. Oxfam International, 2002.

_____. "Fairness in the Fields: A Vision for the 2007 Farm Bill." Oxfam America, 2006.

_____. "'White Gold' Turns to Dust: Which Way Forward for Cotton in West Africa?" Oxfam Briefing Paper No. 58. Oxfam International, March 2004.

Paarlberg, Robert, with foreword by Norman E. Borlaug and Jimmy Carter. *Starved for Science: How Biotechnology Is Being Kept Out of Africa*. Cambridge: Harvard University Press, 2008.

Pan, Suwen, et al. *The Impact of U.S. Cotton Programs on the World Market: An Analysis of Brazilian and West and Central African WTO Petitions*. Lubbock, TX: Texas Tech University, 2004.

Park, Young-Il, and Kym Anderson. "The Rise and Demise of Textiles and Clothing in Economic Development: The Case of Japan." *Economic Development and Cultural Change* 39, 3 (April 1991): 531–548.

Pereira, Joseph. "Protests Spur Stores to Seek Substitute for Vinyl in Toys." *Wall Street Journal* (February 12, 2008): B1.

Petri, Peter A. and Michael G. Plummer."The Trans-Pacific Partnership and Asia-Pacific Integration: Policy Implications." *Peterson Institute for International Economics Policy Brief*, June 2012.

Pew Research Center. Pew Global Attitudes Project, June 12, 2008.

_____. "Beyond Red vs. Blue: The Political Typology," June 26, 2014.

Pinchbeck, Ivy. *Women Workers and the Industrial Revolution, 1750–1850*. London: Virago, 1969.

Platt, Brenda. *Weaving Textile Reuse into Waste Reduction*. Washington, DC: Institute for Local Self-Reliance, 1997.

Polanyi, Karl, with foreword by Robert M. MacIver. *The Great Transformation*. Boston: Beacon Press, 1944.

Pollack, Andrew. "Widely Used Crop Herbicide Is Losing Weed Resistance." *New York Times Business* (January 14, 2003).

Pollin, Robert, Justine Burns, and James Heintz. "Global Apparel Production and Sweatshop Labor: Can Raising Retail Prices Finance Living Wages?" PERI Working Paper Series No. 19. Amherst: University of Massachusetts Amherst, Political Economy Research Institute, rev. April 2002.

Pomeranz, Kenneth. *The Great Divergence: China, Europe and the Making of the Modern World Economy*. Princeton, NJ: Princeton University Press, 2000.

Poonyth, Daneswar, et al. "The Impact of Domestic and Trade Policies on the World Cotton Market." FAO Commodities and Trade Policy Research Working Paper No. 8. FAO, Commodities and Trade Division, April 2004.

Porter, Michael E. *The Competitive Advantage of Nations*. New York: The Free Press, 1990.

Porto, Guido, Nicolas Depetris Chauvin, and Marcelo Olarreaga. *Supply Chains in Export Agriculture, Competition, and Poverty in Sub-Saharan Africa*. Washington: World Bank, 2011, p. 177.

Pramanik, Al Amin. "Poverty and Ready-Made Garment (RMG) Workers in Bangladesh." Macquarie University Working Paper (November 2012).

Prentice, Chris. "Plains Cotton Sells U.S. Mills as Textile Boom Continues." *Reuters,* June 11, 2014.

Pressley, Sue Anne. "The South's New-Car Smell: As Auto Plants Replace Region's Textile Mills, an Economy and a Way of Life Undergo Changes." *Washington Post* (May 11, 2001): A22.

Progressive Policy Institute. "Who Gets Hit? A Summary of Tariff Policy in 2002" (June 11, 2003).

Quinn, John James. *The Road Oft Traveled: Development Policies and Majority State Ownership of Industry in Africa*. Westport, CT: Praeger, 2002.

Reed, David. *Economic Change, Governance and Natural Resource Wealth: The Political Economy of Change in Southern Africa*. London: Earthscan, 2001.

Reichard, Robert. "Textiles 2013: The Turnaround Continues," *Textile World* (January/ February 2013).

Reidl, Brian. "Seven Reasons to Veto the Farm Bill." The Heritage Foundation, May 12, 2008.

Reidy, Joseph P. *From Slavery to Agrarian Capitalism in the Cotton Plantation South: Central Georgia, 1800–1880*. Chapel Hill: University of North Carolina Press, 1992.

Reuters. "California OKs Phthalates Ban on Children's Products" (October 15, 2007). Retrieved from www.reuters.com/article/healthNews.

Richards, H.I. *Cotton and the AAA*. Menasha, WI: George Banta, 1936.

Richardson, Karen. "Food Shortage Recasts Image of 'Organic.'" *Wall Street Journal* (June 25, 2008): C1.

Roberson, Roy. "Herbicide-Resistant Weeds Plague Cotton, Peanut Growers." *Delta Farm Press* (September 28, 2007).

Roberts, Kenneth, et al. "Patterns of Temporary Labor Migration of Rural Women from Anhui and Sichuan." *China Journal*, 52 (July 2004): 49–70.

Robson, R. *The Cotton Industry in Britain*. London: Macmillan, 1957.

Rose, Mary B. *Firms, Networks and Business Values: The British and American Cotton Industries Since 1750*. Cambridge: Cambridge University Press, 2000.

Rosen, Ellen Israel. *Bitter Choices: Blue-Collar Women in and out of Work*. Chicago: University of Chicago Press, 1987.

————. *Making Sweatshops: The Globalization of the U.S. Apparel Industry*. Berkeley: University of California Press, 2002.

Rosengarten, T. *All God's Dangers: The Life of Nate Shaw*. New York: Alfred A. Knopf, 1974.

Rosnick, David. "Gains from Trade? The Net Effect of the Trans-Pacific Partnership Agreement on U.S. Wages," Center for Economic and Policy Research, September 2013.

Rosoff, Robert J. "Beyond Codes of Conduct: Addressing Labor Rights Problems in China." *China Business Review Online* (March/April 2004).

Rostow, W.W. *The Process of Economic Growth*, 2nd ed. New York: Norton Library, 1962.
————. *How It All Began: Origins of the Modern Economy*. New York: McGraw-Hill, 1975.

Rothgeb, John M., Jr. *U.S. Trade Policy: Balancing Economic Dreams and Political Realities*. Washington, DC: CQ Press, 2001.

Rothstein, Morton. "The New South and the International Economy." *Agricultural History* 57, 4 (October 1983): 385–402.

Rozelle, Scott, J., Edward Taylor, and Alan DeBrauw. "Migration, Remittances, and Agricultural Productivity in China." *American Economic Review* 89, 2 (May 1999): 287–291.

Saidazimova, Gulnoza. "Central Asia: Child Labor Alive and Thriving" (June 12, 2008). Retrieved from www.laborrights.org/stop-child-labor/cotton-campaign/1464.

Sakeleris, Nicholas. "Wizard of Wind Power: Entrepreneur Bets He Can Make Alt Energy Pay." *Dallas Business Journal* (March 2, 2014).

Sansom, Allison. "From Trash to Treasure." *Commentator*. Plains Cotton Cooperative Association (Winter 2007): 9.

Saxonhouse, Gary, and Gavin Wright. "Two Forms of Cheap Labor in Textile History." In *Japanese Economic History 1600–1960: The Textile Industry and the Rise of the Japanese Economy*, edited by Michael Smitka. New York: Garland, 1998.

Sayre, Charles R. "Cotton Mechanization Since World War II." *Agricultural History* 53, 1 (January 1979): 105–124.

Schapiro, Mark. *Exposed: The Toxic Chemistry of Everyday Products and What's at Stake for American Power*. Vermont: Chelsea Green Publishing, 2007.

Schiller, Wendy J. "Trade Politics in the American Congress: A Study of the Interaction of Political Geography and Interest Group Behavior." *Political Geography* 18, 7 (September 1999): 769–789.

Schlosser, Eric. "Urban Life: Saturday Night at the Hacienda." *Atlantic Monthly* 282, 4 (October 1998): 22.

Schmidt, James D. *Free to Work: Labor Law, Emancipation, and Reconstruction, 1815–1880*. Athens, GA: University of Georgia Press, 1998.

Schnepf, Randy. "Status of the WTO Brazil–US Cotton Case," Congressional Research Service, December 12, 2013.

Schott, Jeffrey J., and Johanna W. Buurman. *The Uruguay Round: An Assessment*. Washington, DC: Institute for International Economics, 1994.

Schrank, Andrew. "Ready-to-Wear Development? Foreign Investment, Technology Transfer, and Learning by Watching in the Apparel Trade." *Social Forces* 83, 1 (September 2004): 123–156.

Scott, Maurice. "Foreign Trade." In *Economic Growth and Structural Change in Taiwan: The Postwar Experience of the Republic of China*. Ithaca: Cornell University Press, 1979.

Sengupta, Somini. "On India's Farms, a Plague of Suicide." *New York Times* (September 19, 2006).

Shui, S., John C. Beghin, and Michael Wohlgenant. "The Impact of Technical Change, Scale Effects, and Forward Ordering on U.S. Fiber Demands." *American Journal of Agricultural Economics* 75, 3 (August 1993): 632–641.

Simon, Bernard. "Monsanto Wins Patent Case on Plant Genes." *New York Times* (May 22, 2004).

Sinderbrand, Rebecca. "From the Start, Sit-In Was a Concerted Effort." *The Hoya* 80, 31 (February 9, 1999): 1.

Slater, Keith. *Environmental Impact of Textiles: Production, Processes and Protection.* Cambridge, England: Woodhead Publishing, 2003.

Smale, Melinda, Patricia Zambrano, and Mlodie Cartel. "Bales and Balance: A Review of the Methods Used to Assess the Economic Impact of Bt Cotton on Farmers in Developing Economies." *AgBioForum* 9, 3 (2006): 195–212.

Smedes, Susan D. *Memorials of a Southern Planter.* Baltimore: Cushing and Bailey, 1887.

Smitka, Michael, ed. *Japanese Economic History 1600–1960: The Textile Industry and the Rise of the Japanese Economy.* New York: Garland, 1998.

Snyder, R.E. *Cotton Crisis.* Chapel Hill: University of North Carolina Press, 1984.

Solinger, Dorothy J. *Contesting Citizenship in Urban China: Peasant Migrants, the State, and the Logic of the Market.* Berkeley: University of California Press, 1999.

Song, Byung-Nak. *The Rise of the Korean Economy*, 2nd ed. Hong Kong: Oxford University Press, 1997.

Spar, Debora, and Jennifer Burns. "Hitting the Wall: Nike and International Labor Practices." *Harvard Business School Press*, Case 9-700–047, 2000; rev. 2002.

Sparshott, Jeffrey. "U.S. Eyes Textile Pact with China." *Washington Times* (August 2, 2005): C7.

Spencer, Jane. "Ravaged Rivers: China Pays Steep Price as Textile Exports Boom; Suppliers to U.S. Stores Accused of Dumping Dyes to Slash Their Costs." *Wall Street Journal* (Eastern Edition) (August 22, 2007): A1.

Speth, James Gustave. *The Bridge at the Edge of the World: Capitalism, The Environment, and Crossing From Crisis to Sustainability.* New Haven: Yale University Press, 2008.

Spiegelman, Matthew, and Robert H. McGuckin III. "China's Experience with Productivity and Jobs." Report No. R-1352-04-RR, June 2004.

Stein, Leon, ed. *Out of the Sweatshop: The Struggle for Industrial Democracy.* New York: Quadrangle/New York Times Books, 1977.

Steinberg, Theodore. *Nature Incorporated: Industrialization and the Waters of New England.* Cambridge: Cambridge University Press, 1991.

Stiglitz, Joseph. *Globalization and Its Discontents.* New York: Norton, 2003.

———. "Inequality Is Not Inevitable." *New York Times* (June 26, 2014).

———. *Making Globalization Work.* New York: Norton, 2007.

Street, James H. *The New Revolution in the Cotton Economy: Mechanization and Its Consequences.* Chapel Hill: University of North Carolina Press, 1957.

STRtradenews. "As Quotas End, Textile and Apparel Imports from China Face More Hurdles" (July 17, 2008).

_____. "When Customs Knocks" (June 27, 2008).

Sumner, Daniel A. *A Quantitative Simulation Analysis of the Impacts of U.S. Cotton Subsidies on Cotton Prices and Quantities.* (Prepared for WTO Dispute Panel.) Davis, CA: University of California Agricultural Issues Center.

_____. "Reducing Cotton Subsidies: The DDA Cotton Initiative." In *Agricultural Trade Reform and the Doha Development Agenda.* New York: Palgrave Macmillan, 2006.

Swan, Shanna H., et al. "Decrease in Anogenital Distance Among Male Infants with Prenatal Phthalate Exposure." *Environmental Health Perspective* 113, 8 (August 2005).

Tanzer, Andrew. "The Great Quota Hustle." *Forbes* (March 6, 2000): 119–125.

Temu, Andrew E., and Jean M. Due. "The Business Environment in Tanzania after Socialism: Challenges of Reforming Banks, Parastatals, Taxation and the Civil Service." *Journal of Modern African Studies* 38, 4 (December 2000): 683–712.

Tervil, "Millions Go Up in Smoke as Fire Guts Huge Market," *Panafrican News Agency*, September 6, 2000.

The Economist. "A Survey of Sub-Saharan Africa" (January 17, 2004).

_____. "Get Your Green Pants Here" (May 31, 2008): 71.

_____. "How to Make Africa Smile: A Survey of Sub-Saharan Africa" (January 17, 2004): 3–16.

Thomas, H. *The Slave Trade: The Story of the Atlantic Slave Trade, 1440–1870.* New York: Simon & Schuster, 1997.

Thomas, Parakunnel Joseph. *Mercantilism and the East India Trade.* New York: A.M. Kelley, 1965.

Tokarick, Stephen. *Measuring the Impact of Distortions in Agricultural Trade in Partial and General Equilibrium.* Washington, DC: IMF, 2003.

Tonelson, Alan. *The Race to the Bottom: Why a Worldwide Worker Surplus and Uncontrolled Free Trade Are Sinking American Living Standards.* Boulder, Colorado. Westview Press, 2000.

Townsend, Terry. "Subsidies Beyond 2006." Paper Presented to the Liverpool Cotton Association, Liverpool, October 2, 2003.

Tracy, David. "Out with the New: Where the Japanese Shop for Old Clothes." *International Herald Tribune* (May 12, 1995).

Traxler, Greg, and Jose Falck-Zepeda. "The Distribution of Benefits from the Introduction of Transgenic Cotton Varieties." *AgBioForum* 2, 2 (1999): 94–98.

Trela, Irene, and John Whalley. "Global Effects of Developed Country Trade Restrictions on Textiles and Apparel." *Economic Journal* 100 (December 1990): 1190–1205.

Tsurumi, E. Patricia. *Factory Girls: Women in the Thread Mills of Meiji Japan.* Princeton NJ: Princeton University Press, 1990.

Tucker, B.M. *Samuel Slater and the Origins of the American Textile Industry, 1790–1860.* Ithaca, NY: Cornell University Press, 1984.

Underhill, Geoffrey R.D. *Industrial Crisis and the Open Economy: Politics, Global Trade and the Textile Industry in the Advanced Economies.* New York: St. Martin's Press, 1998.

U.S. Department of Agriculture. "Adoption of Genetically Engineered Crops in the U.S.: Cotton Varieties," August 2008.

————. *The Classification of Cotton.* Agricultural Handbook 566. Washington, DC: USDA, 2001.

————. "The Cotton Industry in the United States." Agricultural Economic Report No. 739. Washington, DC: USDA, July 1996.

————. "New Technologies for Cotton Gins Combine for Big Savings."Agricultural Research Service, May 2006.

U.S. Department of Agriculture Foreign Agricultural Service, "Cotton Losing Share to Man-Made Fiber," April, 2012.

U.S. Department of Labor. *Wages, Benefits, Poverty Line, and Meeting Workers' Needs in the Apparel and Footwear Industries of Selected Countries.* Washington, DC: U.S. Department of Labor, ILAB, 2000.

U.S. International Trade Commission. www.dataweb.usitc.gov.

————. "Textiles and Apparel: Assessment of the Competitiveness of Certain Foreign Suppliers to the U.S. Market (Vol. 1)." Investigation No. 332-448, Publication No. 3671. Washington, DC: USITC, 2004.

————. "The Economic Effects of Significant U.S. Import Restraints." Investigation No. 332-325, Publication No. 3201. Washington, DC: USITC, 1999; 2nd update, 1999.

————. "The Economic Effects of Significant U.S. Import Restraints." Investigation No. 332-325, Publication 3701. Washington, DC: USITC, June 2004; 4th update, 2004.

Varley, Pamela, ed. *The Sweatshop Quandary: Corporate Responsibility on the Global Frontier.* Washington, DC: IRRS, 1998.

Vitale, Jeffrey, et al. "The Economic Impacts of Second Generation Bt Cotton in West Africa: Empirical Evidence from Burkina Faso." *International Journal of Biotechnology* 10, 2/3 (2008): 167–183.

Wakeman, Carolyn, and Ken Light, eds. *Assignment Shanghai: Photographs on the Eve of Revolution.* Berkeley: University of California Press, 2003.

Wang, Fei-Ling. *Organizing Through Division and Exclusion: China's Hukou System.* Stanford: Stanford University Press, 2005.

Wang, Feng, and Xuejin Zuo. "Inside China's Cities: Institutional Barriers and Opportunities for Urban Migrants." *American Economic Review* 89, 2 (May 1999): 276–280.

Wang, Shenghui, David R. Just, and Per Pinstrup-Andersen. "Bt-Cotton and Secondary Pests." *International Journal of Biotechnology* 10, 2/3 (2008): 113–121.

————. "Tarnishing Silver Bullets: Bt Technology Adoption, Bounded Rationality and the Outbreak of Secondary Pest Infestations in China." Selected Paper Prepared for Presentation at the American Agricultural Economics Association Annual Meeting. Long Beach, CA: July 22–26, 2006.

Ware, C.F. *The Early New England Cotton Manufacture: A Study in Industrial Beginnings.* Boston: Houghton Mifflin, 1931.

Waters, Tony. "Beyond Structural Adjustment: State and Market in a Rural Tanzania Village." *African Studies Review* 40, 2 (September 1997): 59–89.

Weiss, Rick. "Firms Seek Patents on 'Climate Ready' Altered Crops." *Washington Post* (May 13, 2008): A4.

Weisskopf, "Targeting the Olympic Sweatshop," *Time* (June 14, 2007).

Westcott, Paul C., C. Edwin Young, and J. Michael Price. *The 2002 Farm Act: Provisions and Implications for Commodity Markets*. (Electronic rep. from the ERS). Agricultural Information Bulletin No. 778, USDA, Economic Research Service, November 2002.

Wexler, Alexandra. "Cotton's Crown Threatened by Manmade Fibers." *Wall Street Journal* (April 25, 2014).

Whalley, John, and Shunming Zhang. "A Numerical Simulation Analysis of (Hukou) Labour Mobility Restrictions in China." *Journal of Development Economics* 83, 2 (July 2007): 392–410.

Whayne, J. M. "Black Farmers and the Agricultural Cooperative Extension Service: The Alabama Experience, 1945–1965." *Agricultural History* 72, 3 (Summer 1998): 523–551.

Whigham, T. "Paraguay and the World Cotton Market: The 'Crisis' of the 1860s." *Agricultural History* 68, 3 (Summer 1994): 1–15.

Wicks, Rick, and Arne Bigsten. "Used Clothes as Development Aid: The Political Economy of Rags." (Report of a Study for Sida-The Swedish International Development Cooperation Agency). Gteborg, Sweden: Gteborg University, Department of Economics, 1996.

Williams, Frances. "Talks Unravel over Cotton." *Financial Times* (September 16, 2003): 21.

Willoughby, Lynn. *Fair to Middlin': The Antebellum Cotton Trade of the Apalachicola/Chattahoochee River Valley*. Tuscaloosa, AL: University of Alabama Press, 1993.

Woeste, Victoria Saker. *The Farmer's Benevolent Trust: Law and Agricultural Cooperation in Industrial America, 1865–1945*. Chapel Hill: University of North Carolina Press, 1998.

Wolf, Martin. *Why Globalization Works*. New Haven: Yale University Press, 2004.

Woodman, H.D. *King Cotton and His Retainers: Financing and Marketing the Cotton Crop of the South, 1800–1925*. Lexington, KY: University of Kentucky Press, 1968.

Woodman, Sophia. "China's Dirty Clean Up." *New York Review* (May 11, 2000): 50–52.

Woodruff, N.E. "Mississippi Delta Planters and Debates over Mechanization, Labor and Civil Rights in the 1940s." *Journal of Southern History* 60, 2 (May 1994): 263–284.

Workers Rights Consortium. "Global Wage Trends for Apparel Workers, 2001–2011." Washington, DC, 2013.

World Bank. *A World Bank Country Study: Tanzania at the Turn of the Century-Background Papers and Statistics*. Washington, DC: Government of Tanzania and the World Bank, 2002.

————. *World Development Report*. Washington, DC: World Bank, 2003.

————. *World Development Report* 2008: *Agriculture for Development*. Washington, DC: World Bank, 2007.

World Trade Organization. "Sub-Committee Set Up on "Cotton." *WTO News*, November 19, 2004.

Wrenn, L.B. *Cinderella of the New South: A History of the Cottonseed Industry, 1855–1955*. Knoxville, TN: University of Tennessee Press, 1995.

Wright, Gavin. *The Political Economy of the Cotton South: Households, Markets, and Wealth in the Nineteenth Century*. New York: W.W. Norton, 1978.

————. "Cheap Labor and Southern Textiles, 1880–1930." *Quarterly Journal of Economics* (November 1981): 605–629.

Wu, Xiaogang, and Donald J. Treiman. "The Household Registration System and Social Stratification in China: 1955–1996." *Demography* 41, 2 (May 2004): 363–384.

Yardley, Jim. "The Most Hated Bangladeshi, Toppled From a Shady Empire," *New York Times* (April 30, 2013).

"Young Migrant Workers Shun Hard Labor in Cities" (October 21, 2006). Retrieved from www.china.org.cn/english/2006/Oct/185485.htm.

Zain Al-Mahmood, Syed. "Bangladesh Passes New Labor Law: Workers Granted More Leeway to Form Trade Unions." *Wall Street Journal* (July 15, 2013).

Zhao, Yaohui. "Leaving the Countryside: Rural-to-Urban Migration Decisions in China." *American Economic Review* 89, 2 (May 1999): 281–286.

Zhu, Yu. "China's Floating Population and Their Settlement Intention in the Cities: Beyond the *Hukou* Reform." *Habitat International* 31, 1 (March 2007): 65–76.

Zinman, Greg. "Vintage T-Shirts: Could Yours Be Worth Big Bucks?" *Washington Post* (October 17, 2004): M06.

INDEX